*THE CITY
AND SOCIAL
THEORY*

THE CITY AND SOCIAL THEORY

Michael Peter Smith

Basil Blackwell · Oxford

First published in the United Kingdom 1980
by Basil Blackwell, Publisher, Ltd
5 Alfred Street, Oxford OX1 4HB

Copyright© St Martin's Press, Inc.

ISBN   hbk   0 631 12151 X
            pbk   0 631 12351 2

Text printed in the United States of America

TO PAT, WITH LOVE

Preface

In both social science and popular literature *urbanism* has become a catchword. It is often looked upon as the root cause of much of the misery that afflicts society. Yet research in urban culture and social structure yields divergent answers to the question of whether such central features of urban life as density, crowding, the complex division of labor, formal social controls, anonymity, heterogeneity, and the rapid pace of change are alienating or liberating to human development. A basic theme of *The City and Social Theory* is that we often mistakenly label as "urban problems" what are in fact a variety of society-wide ills produced by economic and social inequality. To a considerable extent, the erroneous designation of society-wide defects as urban problems stems from the ideas of the social theorists treated in this book.

This book analyzes the diagnostic and prescriptive writings of five major theorists of urban culture and personality—Louis Wirth, Sigmund Freud, Georg Simmel, Theodore Roszak, and Richard Sennett. Each presents a model of basic human needs and examines the ways in which these needs are either frustrated or fulfilled by urban civilization. Each offers, finally, a plan for overcoming those conditions deemed harmful to human well-being. The theorists were chosen, in part, because they depict the modern city as a repressive social institution. In Wirth's view, for example, the dense and heterogeneous city creates conditions that weaken our capacity to act rationally, to determine consensual values, and to make those values the basis of planned moral and political order. In contrast, Richard Sennett contends that density and heterogeneity are no longer hallmarks of urban life—that cities have become too orderly and that the attempt to impose harmony is bound to stifle the diversity, conflict, and disorder that people need in order to grow. The three remaining theorists also view urban life as repressive. Freud considers sexuality and aggressiveness, Simmel affection and creativity, and Roszak communal solidarity and transcendent vision as the faculties suppressed by urban civilization.

The five theorists were also chosen because each offers a set of measures for overcoming urban alienation. Each presents a different answer to the question: "What can be done to render the urban environment nonalienating?" In my view, this is an important and intriguing question. Yet it is also, in part, misleading, because it focuses our attention upon "the city" as the cause of a host of social ills that can more properly be attributed to changing patterns of capitalist economic development since the Industrial Revolution.

The first three chapters, which are primarily expository, examine the substantial body of original theoretical works of Wirth, Freud, and Simmel. Chapter 1 explores the image of urban life set forth by Wirth, whose diverse writings are a culmination of the thinking of the Chicago School of urban sociology. They also have influenced many of the basic assumptions underlying the theory and practice of rational-comprehensive urban planning. It is for these reasons that I have chosen to discuss Wirth's theories in the opening chapter of the book. The Wirthian urban planner is cast in a struggle against "ecological" conditions deemed to presage urban disorganization. To counteract such conditions Wirth advocated the recreation of a supposedly lost normative and political order through the application of scientific method and technical expertise to policy making.

Chapter 2 takes up Sigmund Freud's model of human personality and the types of discontent that he considered to be inherent in any highly developed urban setting. Freud's dialectical model of personality contradicts the Wirthian view that planning can reorder the external environment [can be reordered by planning] to eliminate psychological disorder. Nevertheless, Freud did offer a "politics of rehabilitation" that might render the institutions of urban civilization less anxiety-producing: he favored a combination of individual therapy and piecemeal readjustment of social and economic institutions that would make these institutions less repressive and social conflict less likely.

The social theory of the German conflict sociologist Georg Simmel is explored in Chapter 3. Simmel viewed the "metropolis" as offering the promise of heightened personality development and at the same time posing the risk of creating personalities so benumbed by overstimulation and the tyranny of material objects as to be incapable of responding humanely to their environment. Because Simmel believed social conflict to be an inevitable and potentially creative force, he regarded central planning by technical experts as unlikely, impermanent, and potentially detrimental to his basic normative goal—the pursuit of individual creativity.

Chapter 4 moves from classical to modern images of urban life and human fulfillment. In this chapter I explore the characterizations of city life, human consciousness, and technocratic planning found in the writings of two quite different contemporary American social theorists, Theodore Roszak and Richard Sennett. Roszak views the human personality as essentially both communal and spiritual at its core; Sennett considers humans to be basically alone and empty at their core. Both of these theorists disdain "technocracy," dislike bureaucratic social controls, and favor a radically decentralized political system. Yet, because of their divergent underlying assumptions, they advance markedly contradictory diagnoses of the "urban condition" and plans for overcoming urban alienation.

My own position on the concerns raised by the five social theorists is presented in Chapters 5 and 6. Chapter 5 is intended to reveal the mythological dimensions of the five theories of urban life. Starting from a social-structural intellectual perspective, I also attempt to show that many social pathologies thought to be rooted in ecological, biological, or technological necessity are in fact attributable to the social structure and economic organization of particular societies. I illustrate the ways in which social theories presented as general theories of the "urban condition" very often are time- and culture-bound.

The remainder of *The City and Social Theory* is reconstructive as well as critical. Chapter 6 describes the contemporary American urban milieu as the byproduct of the development of corporate capitalism and presents a critique of the role that urban planners have played in legitimizing the unequal distribution of the social costs and benefits of that development. I close the book by addressing the following issue of social reconstruction: "What is to be done to create a more democratic, humane, and egalitarian society to replace the socially structured inequalities that characterize contemporary American metropolitan life?"

In writing this book, I have received support from many quarters. David Lewis, Robert Binstock, and Barry Rossinoff offered encouragement at the time of the book's conception. Robert Beauregard and Louis Friedlander provided searching and insightful reviews of the original manuscript that were very helpful to me. Don Strickland, Steve Nock, and Jane Weiss commented thoughtfully on various ideas discussed in the book. Hermann Borghorst's collaborative research with me helped sharpen my critique of ritual political conflict. George Ruberg contributed useful research assistance. I also wish to thank all the people at St. Martin's Press who nurtured this book along, especially, Edward Cone, Diana Ward, William Cannon, and, most of all, Bert Lummus, an excellent editor whose timely encouragement was invaluable. Finally, my gratitude to my wife Pat goes beyond normal boundaries. Without her love, sacrifice, and inspiration, this book would not have been written.

September 1978   M. P. S.

CONTENTS

THE CITY
AND SOCIAL
THEORY

Chapter 1
Louis Wirth
And Urban Social
Order

The American sociologist Louis Wirth (1897–1952) is best known for his deductive theoretical essay "Urbanism as a Way of Life." This essay, first published in 1938, was a work of grand synthesis. It codified the prevailing thought of European social theorists and of earlier members of the Chicago School of Sociology on the postulated psychological and behavioral consequences of living in cities. Yet Wirth's interests were more extensive, encompassing the sociology of knowledge, social deviance, communications theory, and urban planning, as well as urban social theory. The theme of this chapter asserts that Wirth's abiding concern for establishing a consensual moral order in the face of urban social diversity provides the basic connective tissue uniting all these diverse interests.

Chapter one is divided into three parts, as are the next two chapters of this book. The first part examines the key concepts and assumptions underlying the theoretical structure of Wirth's social thought. Central to the foundations of his theoretical framework are his particular adaptation of the classical community-society distinction; his analysis of the relationship between individual role conflict and "social disorganization"; and his assumptions about how certain conditions of city life relate to both role conflict and social disorganization.

Once the underlying theoretical structure of Wirth's social thought is made explicit, I then turn in the second part of chapter one to his specific analysis and critique of the urban condition. In Wirth's view, the ecological and demographic structure of city life, particularly the large size, high population density, and heterogeneous population mix resulting from urbanization, produced numerous social and social-psychological consequences. Wirth held that these consequences, taken together, constituted a new pattern of culture, a "way of life," that he termed *urbanism*. This part of chapter one examines in detail the culture of urbanism and its postulated antecedents. Wirth's "urban

1

way of life" amounts to a catalogue of personal, social, and political problems in maintaining normative order, which he viewed as likely, but possibly avoidable, concomitants of urbanization.

Like the other theorists treated in this book, Louis Wirth chose not to stop with a diagnosis of what he believed to be the causes of an undesirable value dissensus in the urban world. He also offered a major prescription for his particular diagnosis of urban social malaise in the form of rational-comprehensive urban planning. The third part of chapter one considers this prescriptive aspect of Wirth's social theory. For Wirth, the basic planning question may be framed as follows: *"What is to be done to establish consensual value priorities, and hence policy priorities, in the face of urban subcultural diversity and political conflict among special interest groups?"*

Wirth answers this question by calling for extensive use of social science research in policy planning, and by calling upon planners to become actively involved in "reorganizing" a presumably disorganized polity and society along more rational lines. Wirth's views on the proper "guidance" function of social scientists, other intellectuals, and planners were a natural outgrowth of his theoretical diagnosis of the barriers to consensual order in urban society. Yet, as we shall see, his intense commitment to rational-comprehensive urban planning also blinded him to some of the insights contained in his more purely sociological thought, as well as to some of the positive functions of social conflict in inducing needed social change. In this part I also consider Wirth's assessment of who ought to reshape urban social forms, where urban planning can best be introduced, how it should be practiced, and how it can be reconciled with tenets of political democracy. Wirth's oversights in translating social theory into social action are also considered in the final sections of chapter one.

THE ECOLOGICAL AND THE MORAL ORDER

Some social theorists have defined "community" in organic terms, stressing the spontaneous competition and mutual interdependencies that emerge from living together.[1] Others regard "community" as a psychic phenomenon, stressing the shared sentiments underlying social consensus and collective action.[2] On this question Louis Wirth stands squarely with the former. Wirth held that common experiences, goals, and understandings, to which he gave the term "consensus," powerfully induce social cohesion. Nonetheless, he chose to differentiate these *cultural* variables from the basic *organic* variables that make up "community." For Wirth, a "community" emerged as natural, unplanned symbiotic ties developed. People initially lived together on the basis of close spatial proximity, kinship ties, and both competitive and common interaction. Out of these sprang a division of labor and an organic or "ecological" interdependence. Wirth used the concept "community" to designate this "natural" interdependence. In contrast, Wirth uses the term "society" to refer to the "willed and contractual [consensual] relationships between men which . . . are less directly affected than their organic relationships by their distribution in space."[3]

Wirth, as did sociologist Robert Park, posited a threefold hierarchical typology of social order. Higher forms of social cohesion sprang up from and rested upon lower ones. First is the symbiotic or ecological order, a system of competition, conflict, and temporary equilibrium based on sheer spatial interdependencies. Next is the cultural order, a set of commonly accepted understandings growing out of human interaction and communication. Finally is the moral and political order, resting upon a shared cultural system overlayed upon a competitive-symbiotic system. The moral and political order emerges when common norms are articulated, common goals are set, and rules are worked out to enforce norms and achieve goals.[4]

As a "human ecologist,"[5] Wirth conceived of the symbiotic community as an aggregation of living forms bound together in a web of interdependence. From the ecological perspective, the struggle for survival in a particular milieu creates a spatial pecking order and a place for each member and species of organism in the overall division of labor. This provides to each part a function in the whole and to the whole an evolving equilibrium. As each part competitively struggles to achieve its own ends, it unintentionally serves some functions for other organisms. These inadvertent by-products create bonds of mutual interdependence. However, in a symbiotic community, even in a mutually beneficial rather than a parasitic one, "the order and cohesion that prevail are based not upon communication, mutual awareness, and the acceptance of social norms, but rather upon the morphology and elementary reflexes or instincts which are built into organisms and which operate automatically."[6]

The human community rests upon, but is more than, such an ecological base. Upon the ecological substructure are superimposed higher levels of interdependence engendered by economic, cultural, political, and moral ties. Each of these higher levels of cohesion is explicitly based on mutual awareness, communication, and some degree of conscious coordination and control.

Wirth held that the process of development from community to society represents a shift from spontaneous to deliberate bases of social cohesion and social order. Initially, "the competitive cooperation which the occupancy of a common habitat demands creates a common ecological base upon which social relationships may develop."[7] Upon this base is built a complex division of labor, technological interdependence, and gradually, economic interdependence. These evolving relationships eventually call forth a political order—a set of norms and institutions that formally regulate and control behavior. Law, the state, and enforcement mechanisms are created to insure the cooperation which heretofore rested on the unstable natural equilibrium of the symbiotic community.

Wirth viewed community and society as continuous rather than discrete variables. Each concept may be located at an opposite pole on a continuum. Every existing social group may be plotted on the continuum somewhere between these poles, depending upon the extent to which that group tends toward either pole. In "Human Ecology," Wirth criticized those early writers who mistook the ideal-typical community-society distinction for concrete reality. For Wirth, "all communities are also societies and all human societies bear at least some of the characteristics of communities."[8] Every social group exists because of ecological as well as social-psychological ties. "Community" and "society" are not two distinct kinds of groups, but rather two facets of life in all human groups. These two facets are linked by the phenomenon of communication.

Unlike plant and other animal life, the human community is always more than a symbiotic "living together." Through communication, human beings become conscious of common interests and participate in common endeavors. They develop common hopes and ideals "which are not built into the organisms but which exist in language, collective symbols, laws and customs, in short, in a social heritage."[9] Symbiotic community involves acting alike because of being alike. Consensual society involves acting alike because common goals have been identified, even when people are existentially different. Through communication, common ideas, ideals, and sentiments develop. A cultural and political order is born.

In Wirth's view, formal authority need not entail coercion. Human communication has the power to convert the rules which constitute the political order into the shared values and understandings that make up the moral order. The moral order represents the end point in a long process of historical development from "community" to "society." When communication is successful, common values, ideals, symbols, and understandings come to be "taken for granted." These common underlying assumptions form the basis of any society's moral order. Once a moral order develops, the problem of social tyranny is resolved. Within the moral order, group conduct is regulated and controlled not by external coercion but by "uncoerced consensus."[10]

The Paradox of Consensus

Along with classical European social theorists such as Ferdinand Tonnies and Emile Durkheim, Wirth believed that the overwhelming trend in the modern world consisted in a worldwide evolution from community to societylike social relationships; from status-based to contractual relations; from homogeneous aggregates tied together by "mechanical solidarity" to heterogeneous units based on a complex division of labor; from primary to secondary group affiliations; and from folk to urban culture.[11] However, unlike many of these early social theorists, Wirth did not believe that cultural integration was inherently impeded by increased heterogeneity and the decline of folk cultures. The integration of larger social wholes was possible provided that heterogeneity was accompanied by growing self-consciousness of societywide common interests.

Although possible, the process of building societywide consensus has been extremely difficult in modern urban societies. For one thing, heterogeneity among diverse subcultures and segmental interest groups sets the stage for heightened group conflict. Increased contact among groups increased the possibilities for friction. Wirth believed that the increased frequency and closeness of contact among groups was encouraged by the high population density of the urban environment. Thus the combination of urban density and heterogeneity powerfully threatened social harmony and consensual integration. Not only would heightened intimacy and familiarity increase the range of areas over which conflict might develop; the increased frequency of such relationships would also increase opportunities for friction, disagreement, and conflict. As Wirth succinctly put it: "To know one another better is often to hate one another more violently."[12]

This statement clarifies Wirth's perception of the paradoxical modern urban condition. Here Wirth suggests that when diverse subcultures do interpenetrate, social conflict is the most likely by-product. When people's lives touch each other more intensively and extensively in the dense and heterogeneous urban milieu, hate is more likely to result than love. Conversely, Wirth elsewhere suggests that when people fail to experience such intense human contacts, when their relationships are indifferent and superficial, social cohesion also is threatened. Wirth believed that such indifference to others made people more cynical, sophisticated, secular, and normless. All these changes served to undermine the ability of elites to build mass commitment to societywide shared values, beliefs, and ideals.

The Wirthian paradox may be stated as follows: In a heterogeneous society, public opinion can be led toward a growing awareness of societywide common interests. But the task of developing a consensual sense of the "common good" is made increasingly problematic by subcultural and interest-group heterogeneity. When accompanied by high population density, heterogeneity may force social contacts which lead to increased friction and heighten the chances of disorder. To protect themselves against impending disorder at both the psychic and social levels, city dwellers tend to retreat into their private pursuits, their particularistic interest group, or their parochial subculture. Under these circumstances, idealism diminishes, and with it the possibility for discovering common values and interests. In a large, dense, and heterogeneous environment, both popular engagement in and popular withdrawal from public life undermine the possibility for achieving social consensus.

Urbanization and modernization make increasingly more difficult the task of discovering communitywide interests and generating a sense of community for the "city-as-a-whole." In particular, the mechanization of life, cultural provincialism, the ever-increasing segmentation of life, and the refined division of labor form the structural basis for social conflict and undermine the sense of human belonging together. As kinship, status, and the crude division of labor are replaced by technological change, social mobility, a minute division of labor, and the corresponding rise of special interest groups, the community takes on new meaning and new problems.[13]

Primary group folk life gives way to technological civilization. This necessitates new bases for social integration as old ties are torn asunder. The issue of collective action for the "community-as-a-whole" becomes increasingly problematic as the division of labor produces increasingly divergent interests. Economic changes from local self-sufficient markets to a world of international trade, finance, and politics result in a world bound together in a "delicately and unstably equilibriated international interdependence."[14]

The growing functional irrelevance of geographic proximity as a social bond also creates problems of social cohesion. Although increasingly interdependent technologically, contemporary human communities have little other than this linkage and the mass media to foster the communication essential for the emergence of consensual values and interests. Important interests within communities are affected by repercussions from without. The growing number of corporate groups, the wide territorial dispersion of their memberships, and the growth in the number of corporate group identifications and affiliations "often obscure the fact that every society is also in some degree community."[15]

Wirth contends that common values and interests can be discovered and acted upon even in the face of modernization, urbanization, and global interdependence. Yet the structural conditions created by these forces make the job of discovering common ties (objective community) and generating a sense of belonging together (subjective community) immeasurably more difficult than when people lived together in tribes, primary groups, and folk societies.

The City, Role Conflict, and "Disorganization"

True to the assumptions of both classical social theorists and the Chicago School,[16] Wirth argues that in primitive societies normative consensus rests upon authority, custom, and sanctions which reinforce traditional understandings. Modern social systems, no matter how refined their formal laws and sanctions, cannot achieve what Wirth perceived to be the nearly perfect consensus of "folk societies." As kinship declines, urban societies increasingly come to rely on formal and rational bases for achieving unity, solidarity, and social control. In urban "society," spontaneously generated conventions become unreliable and infrequently utilized. Ideologies are developed to sanctify formal actions and institutions of social control. They become surrogates for custom and tradition.[17]

The consensual values of any "society," whether organization, city, or nation, are revealed in collective action. What people actually do is a better clue to what a collectivity values than are the symbols and verbal utterances which legitimize action. In modern urban societies actual participants in national consensus are few. Instead, the population distribution into relatively homogeneous interest groups insures greater intragroup than intergroup cooperation, greater *segmental* than *integral* consensus.

Because consensus is a product of human interaction and common experiences, "the limits of consensus are marked by the range of effective communication."[18] For Wirth, interest groups interfered with the development of societywide consensual values because they segmented human experience. Interest groups narrowed the range of effective communication to the boundaries of the faction. In urban society they fostered the development of diverse and sometimes mutually incompatible ways of viewing the world. The multiplicity of ideologies that developed to support these world views "may be taken as a symptom of impending or actual disorganization of the ethos of a society."[19]

Wirth held that ideologies engender disorganization because they are fraught with ambiguity. They may be used to mask as well as to reveal the real common interests and objectives of groups. Ideologies are means for justifying group purposes and actions to members and to outside audiences. Since they are means as well as statements of ends, ideologies "must be ambiguous enough to enlist widespread support and yet definitive enough to attract attention."[20]

But this very ambiguity breeds suspicion, cynicism, and mistrust. To protect themselves from manipulation by ideologues, modern urbanites wear armors of detachment, suspicion, and distrust. The very idea of moral commitment to ideals becomes subject to careful scrutiny. In modern urban society:

> Every faith is suspect, no prophet is regarded as infallible, no leader sincere, no mission inspired, and no conviction unshakable. We cultivate a lack of confidence towards those who are our partners and our leaders, and we privatize our existence.[21]

This cynicism and excessive privatization of life is a precursor of what Durkheim has termed "anomie." By *anomie* is meant a sense of normlessness and emptiness which fosters individual pathology, communal disorganization, and social disorder.

Ironically, then, Wirth believed that ideologies deliberately contrived to engineer within-group conformity in the face of the breakdown of customary norms actually engender between-group mistrust, social isolation, and anomic behavior. Like the social and planning theorist Karl Mannheim, Wirth held that this situation might be reversed if intellectuals were to play an independent and objective role in society.[22] Instead, many intellectuals have chosen to become advocates of the ideologies of various contending pressure groups. They have developed a proprietary interest in maintaining the world view of the groups whose causes they espouse. Thus, they are unlikely to readily relinquish their role as symbol manipulators. When confronted by mass aloofness, they are likely to redouble their efforts. However, because this is likely to trigger even more rigid defenses on the part of the public, their increased effort is bound to be self-defeating in the long run.

For Wirth, human personality is a social product that is strongly influenced by changing social roles. Therefore, he believed that the personality was threatened with fragmentation as well as cynicism because of the changed nature of group affiliations in the heterogeneous urban milieu. Wirth agreed with Georg Simmel that the proper subject matter of sociology was the process of interpersonal relations and social interaction. According to this perspective, personalities play roles in the groups in which they participate. Roles are defined by the reciprocal claims and expectations that role players within a system develop regarding each other's behavior. Viewed collectively, the social structure is the pattern or system which develops out of the regular interaction of role players. Out of these regularized interrelationships emerges a "society" which is the bearer of the collective culture. Both culture and personality are products of the process of social interaction.

In modern urban society, social roles are highly variable. They depend upon varying conditions of group structure and particular situations which stimulate social participation. Because role expectations are so variable within the wide variety of social circles to which an individual belongs, they are a major source of strain. The urban setting in particular provides individuals with a great number and diversity of only partially overlapping social circles. This situation presents the individual with "successively varying and simultaneously divergent or conflicting conceptions of himself."[23] The stress provided by such "role conflicts" can lead to various forms of personal maladjustment. Modern urban culture thus produces highly differentiated personality types, many of whom suffer "adjustment" problems as a result of conflicting role expectations. Such persons experience difficulty satisfactorily integrating the various fragments of their personalities.

For Wirth, then, their urban personality takes on a schizoid quality stemming from the sense of fragmentation experienced by segmented role playing. The transitory, superficial, and *secondary* nature of most human interaction replaces the *primary* social ties of family, kinship, and neighborhood that once securely anchored the personality in a structure of stable socioemotional controls. Moreover, to defend against the severely stressful role conflicts that might arise if people played all their contradictory secondary roles intensely and authentically, Wirth's urban personality type assumes a posture of reserve similar to what Georg Simmel termed the blasé attitude.[24] Yet this does not free the urban personality from experiencing the cross-pressures of Robert Park's "marginal man."[25] To wit:

> Whereas, in an earlier society it was unusual to meet a stranger, under the conditions of life in great cities, it is an equal rarity to meet someone who is familiar. . . . Today all of us are men on the move and on the make, and all of us by transcending the bounds of our narrower society become to some extent marginal men.[26]

City life frees the individual from socioemotional controls. But the price of this increased mobility is lost intimacy, anonymity, and ultimately anomie.

As spontaneous informal social controls break down, society comes to be held together by formal social controls such as professional specialization, interdependence, and corporatist self-control, supplemented by bureaucracy. Functional interdependence exacerbates social as well as individual disorganization by segmentalizing and thereby further differentiating and separating individuals and groups from common experiences out of which common values, mores, customs, and societywide collective action might spring.

Urban density also contributes to the increased impersonality of social structures and to stereotyped mental images. People begin to use short-hand signals to differentiate meanings amidst all this complexity. Uniforms and other visual symbols come to denote the role of bureaucratic functionaries. Role relationships based on a single function replace extensive human relationships where whole personalities relate to each other. Lost in the process is the intensity, extent, and subtlety of interaction possible in relations of kinship or friendship.[27]

Wirth's theory of personality formation sharply contrasts with the psychoanalytic theory of Sigmund Freud and his instinctualist followers. Wirth agreed with such post-Freudian thinkers as Karen Horney and Harry Stack Sullivan that the root of psychic conflict and personal disorganization resided in the prevalent cultural and role conflicts operative in society, rather than in the personality's inner-psychic dynamics.[28] He believed that these external conflicts were most frequent and most pronounced in societies which demanded the performance of mutually incompatible social roles. In this view, insecurity, frustration, and personality problems are not distributed evenly among or within contemporary urban societies as they might be if sheer technical complexity or harsh social controls inherently frustrated universal instincts.[29] Rather, people participate in a highly differentiated set of social roles. In many cases the "constellation of social situations" in which people are placed form a social matrix of more or less mutually compatible roles. For persons so situated, personality is more durably integrated because the roles which the individual must perform coalesce to some degree. However, many members of modern urban societies no longer live in relatively restricted social worlds, having stable values, norms, and expectations. When the diverse roles an individual must perform are incompatible with each other maladjustment, insecurity, and frustration are the likely by-products.[30]

Personal and Social Disorganization

What is the relationship between personal disorganization and social disorganization? Wirth held that social disorganization could be measured by the extent to which the members of any given social system lose their common understandings. For Wirth, a society is disorganized if it lacks shared values, meanings, and the reciprocally acknowledged claims and expectations which underlie the capacity for collective action. As a close student of culture, Wirth argued that the best indicator of whether any aggregate of people is a consensual social order capable of collective action is the commonality of "what they take for granted."[31] Both consensus and collective action, for Wirth, rest upon common, unstated understandings and reciprocally shared expectations and claims. Without such reciprocal interpenetration there can be no common goals, and thus no stable social order.

However, in Wirth's view, mere deviation from settled norms and understandings does not constitute disorganization. Only if such deviations symbolize or form the basis of *normative conflict* does disorganization occur.[32] In primitive societies people often deviated from prevailing social norms while still acknowledging their validity. But in the modern urban milieu, disorganization is more common than deviance. Sudden changes brought about by migration, technological innovation, contact with alien groups, and the like, create value cleavages. Disorganization may result from the tensions experienced by those who are influenced by conflicting value expectations which call for mutually incompatible responses to given situations. It may also result when two or more independent normative systems claim the loyalty of a segment of society which at the ecological level is interdependent with the rest of society. Finally, it may result because the multiplicity of value systems become so broad in their appeals to the individual as to create ambiguity. This very ambiguity may provoke tension and social conflict.

An unorganized society is different from a disorganized society. Wirth believed that in large modern cities individuals frequently experienced minimal primary-group relations, and their secondary relations tended to be both amoral and segmental. For him, such functional interdependencies which transpired below the level of either value consensus (organization) or value conflict (disorganization) were states of unorganized social relations. This state of affairs created the conditions for disorganization, but did not in and of itself guarantee it. The multiplication of norms, and the segmentalization of life did, however, increase the likelihood that those norms that did impinge upon unorganized individuals and social relations would provoke role conflicts and tensions. In turn, such stresses would impede the development of common understanding and societywide collective action.

Wirth felt that social *organization* could best be understood when viewed in contrast to the conditions of *un*organization, *dis*organization, and *re*organization. All four are manifest forms of human activity. Crowds, mobs, and social movements are, in his view, disorganized social processes. They lack order, continuity, regularity, and consensual purpose. Mere deviation from cultural norms is not necessarily an indicator of social disorganization; such deviation might be a form of reorganization if it were deliberately undertaken in an attempt to redefine the prevailing consensus. Disorganization is characterized by anomic loss of common understanding. Deliberately deviant attempts to introduce new understandings require organization, and hence consensus.

In the final analysis, Wirth viewed the complex role differentiation of the urban milieu has having mixed consequences for individual personality development and for social cohesion. All social sytems set some limits on the potential for personal development; yet within those limits, each system offers a range of options in the form of diverse social roles and attendant patterns of personality development. The city is a social matrix which offers the widest arena for personality formation. Wirth concurred with Adam Smith's contention that some unique personality types can only be found in cities. Not only are cities more tolerant of diversity in personality development; they also create a hospitable culture for the development of persons of competence, talent, and genius. Certain areas of cities become supportive abodes for the cultivation of distinctive personality types. This is what gives the city its distinctive color and verve. Yet these very benefits produce unintended consequences. On the individual level, they threaten stable personality development. On the social level, the social problems of urban community actually rise out of the conflicts of attitudes, values, personalities, and social insitutions which both support and shape the diverse subcultures found in any city. These conflicts, in turn, engender further conflict and are thus good indices of social change, growth, and resulting disorganization.[33]

This then, is the underlying set of beliefs and assumptions that give coherence to Wirth's social theory. Ecological and demographic changes in the scale and complexity of human settlements pose problems of social order. The increased social and cultural diversity resulting from urbanization make it more difficult for common ideas, ideals, and sentiments to develop. The multiplicity of competing subcultural and ideological demands upon individual personality also create the possibility of heightened cynicism, role conflict, and personal disorganization. This, in turn, further frustrates efforts to socially or politically organize the "community-as-a-whole." Each of these themes is reechoed in Wirth's most explicitly urban social theory and social criticism.

URBANISM AS A WAY OF LIFE

"Urbanism as a Way of Life" is Louis Wirth's most explicit and comprehensive statement of the influences that city life exerts upon personality and social life. For Wirth, "urbanism," like the community-society distinction, is an ideal-typical construct. Urbanism is one polar point on a continuum of structural, psychological, and behavioral characteristics upon which all actual human settlements tend to arrange themselves. The opposite pole is occupied by the rural-folk society. In "Urbanism as a Way of Life," Wirth attempts to define the city in purely sociological and ecological terms. He defines it as a permanent settlement characterized by three key structural features: large *size*, high *density*, and social *heterogeneity*. Each of these structural characteristics is treated as a distinct, independent ecological variable. Wirth recognized, of course, that the three tended to be interconnected in the real world. For instance, large numbers living in a restricted area produce high density of settlement. Nonetheless, he believed that it was fruitful to treat each variable separately, "since each may be connected with significantly different social consequences."[34]

Having posited size, density, and heterogeneity as the three irreducible components of a city, the remainder of Wirth's classical article attempts to derive a set of hypotheses about the relationships between urban social organization, personality, and behavior from his basic definition of the city. From each independent variable Wirth derives a slightly different, but mutually reinforcing, cluster of interrelated conditions of city life. Before examining each of these clusters in detail, it is useful to consider Wirth's own summary of the basic propositions advanced in his deductive theory. According to Wirth:

> Large numbers account for individual variability, the relative absence of intimate personal acquaintanceship, the segmentalization of human relations which are largely anonymous, superficial, and transitory, and associated characteristics. Density involves diversification and specialization, the coincidence of close physical contact and distant social relations, glaring contrasts, a complex pattern of segregation, the predominance of formal social control, and accentuated friction, among other phenomena. Heterogeneity tends to break down rigid social structures and to produce increased mobility, instability, and insecurity, and the affiliation of the individuals with a variety of intersecting and tangential social groups with a high rate of membership turnover. The pecuniary nexus tends to displace personal relations, and institutions tend to cater to mass rather than individual requirements. The individual thus becomes effective only as he acts through organized groups.[35]

Wirth's theory is an extraordinarily complex interweaving of hypothesized causal relationships linking ecological variables to social and political consequences.

The Consequences of Size

In Wirth's view, both social and personality differentiation increase along with increases in population size. Large numbers entail a wide range of individual variation. Because differentiated individuals participate in a process of both competitive and cooperative interaction with others, individual differentiation gives rise to diverse occupational structures, subcultures, and ideological subgroups. In turn, such social differentiation leads to increased voluntary spatial segregation among a wide variety of racial, ethnic, social status, occupational, and interest-based groupings. With time, increased personal and social differentiation weakens the traditional bonds of kinship, neighborhood, and family structure. Competition and formal social controls function as imperfect substitutes for the traditional social bonds that once held folk societies together.

One of the most pronounced features of the urban "way of life," according to Wirth, is an increased significance of formal social controls.[36] Size, density, and heterogeneity contribute to the replacement of spontaneously generated custom by formal controls. Particular controls such as law, bureaucracy, segregation of land uses, professional norms, organized interest groups, courts and police services, the clock and the traffic signal, formal representation, mass media, and the corporate structure are viewed by Wirth as inevitable concomitants of urbanism because they serve essential functions.

In the face of increased specialization, formal controls serve to coordinate activities in various ways. First, complex tasks that call for cooperation, such as mass production and distribution, thereby can be accomplished. Secondly, in a world where the complex structure of social roles can lead to role conflict and personal disorganization, formal controls serve to integrate roles, simplify and clarify norms, and punish or "cure" social deviance stemming from role conflict. Thirdly, formal controls provide predictable routines in the face of the glaring contrasts and overstimulation caused by the density and diversity of the urban setting. Fourthly, formal controls diminish the social friction accompanying such urban phenomena as the breakdown of informal controls, competitiveness, overstimulation, the rise of special interest groups, and the intermittent physical contacts experienced by spatially and occupationally segregated individuals. Finally, some formal controls serve to reduce exploitation before it occurs (e.g., professional codes) or to punish exploiters (e.g., laws against unfair business practices).

Accompanying this movement toward increased formalism is a second set of relationships stemming directly from increased population size. Any community which extends beyond a few hundred members limits the possibility that each member of the collective can know all others personally. Thus increased size is directly related to the increased impersonality and superficiality of interpersonal relationships. Primary relationships are displaced by secondary ones. People no longer touch each other as whole personalities. This has a number of psychological and social consequences. Relationships tend to become more reserved and utilitarian. Much more communication takes place indirectly through intermediaries, rather than face to face. Special interest groups emerge as one of the key intermediary social structures standing between the individual and others and between the individual and government.[37] Heterogeneity also contributes to the rise of special interest groups by making simple class structures more complex and less rigid, thereby increasing individual social mobility. With increased mobility, the number and variety of tangential, transitory, interest-based group affiliations increases.

As the "personal mutual acquaintanceship" characteristic of the cohesive neighborhood declines, the possibility that personalities will become atomized increases.[38] Urban dwellers have contact with many more people than do rural dwellers; but their knowledge of those with whom they come into contact is less intensive. They have more acquaintances, but fewer friends. Acquaintanceships tend to be segmental, that is, based on the single specialized functional roles which others perform. Viewed collectively, individual segmentation leads to the proliferation of secondary over primary human contacts. In the urban milieu, people are increasingly interdependent technologically, but distinct sociologically. Their dependence upon others rests upon "a highly fractionalized aspect of the other's round of activity."[39]

Such segmental and secondary contacts alter the quality of social interaction. Urban social contacts, even when face to face, tend to be impersonal, superficial, segmental, and transitory. This development is partially a function of increased size of one's milieu and partially a function of a blasé attitude assumed by those confronted with the "psychic overload" produced by increased size. This blasé attitude is reinforced by the desire of urban dwellers to protect themselves from the personal expectations and claims of a myriad of strangers.

Once engendered, the heightened superficiality, anonymity, and transitoriness of interpersonal relationships have additional consequences. Wirth held that they contribute to the increased spirit of rationality and sophistication that characterizes urban dwellers. When interpersonal relationships are role-based rather then holistic, people come to be regarded in instrumental and utilitarian terms. Rationality and sophistication undermine traditional, personal, and emotional controls over individual behavior and personality development. Without such controls people become mere means to the realization of individual or institutional ends. The heightened freedom from spontaneous, informal controls is accompanied by a loss of the spontaneous self-expression found in primary group affiliations. Lost, as well, are the morale and sense of direct participation and involvement in common concerns that derive from living in an integrated society. Eventually, a state of "anomie" is reached. The various forms of "social disorganization" discussed elsewhere in Wirth's writings follow from this disintegration of the moral order.

Utilitarian and segmental relationships tend to become institutionalized in a variety of formal social controls, most notably professional codes of conduct and corporate bureaucracy. Segmental and utilitarian relationships increase the specialization of tasks, particularly professional occupational tasks. If diverse tasks are pursued without coordination and control, social disorder might result. Furthermore, the pure operation of the "pecuniary nexus" contributes to predatory and exploitative relationships which, if left unchecked, also might lead to social disorder. Thus, formalized "professional codes" and "occupational etiquette" are required to check competition and help insure "the efficient functioning of the social order."[40] Similar functions are performed by the corporate bureaucratic form. Corporate bureaucracy subordinates the competitiveness of the entrepreneur to the utility, efficiency, limited liability, and increased coordination of the corporation.

The Consequences of Density

Density reinforces the effect of numbers by further differentiating human activity and adding to the complexity of social structure. Scarce space can only support large numbers if differentiation and specialization occur. As Georg Simmel has indicated, the close physical contact engendered by high density "produces a shift in the mediums through which we orient ourselves to the urban milieu," and to our fellow citizens.[41] We become insensitive to personal inner eccentricities while elements of purely external visual identity become increasingly important in establishing social expectations. Those with whom we interact are stereotyped beforehand by uniforms, artifacts, and other visual symbols of status or role, causing us to lose our sensitivity to the concrete world of nature and to human uniqueness and intimacy. Frequent physical contact, unaccompanied by close social intimacy, accentuates the Simmelian spirit of urban reserve and may give rise to loneliness.[42]

Added to this, the "close living together" of people devoid of emotional and sentimental ties fosters a pervasive spirit of competition, self-aggrandizement, and mutual exploitation. Crowding and congestion among socially distant people give rise to social friction, irritation, and frustration. The attendant nervous tension is accentuated by the rapid pace and complicated technology under which life in a dense urban milieu must be lived. This tempo and technology are necessitated to impose predictable routines on a large, compact, unattached mass, which otherwise would become dominated by a spirit of random aggrandizement and exploitation. To wit: "The clock and the traffic signal are symbolic of the basis of our social order in the urban world."[43] Formal social controls, thus, impose order on an otherwise chaotic situation.

Following Simmel, Wirth further suggests that nervous stimulation is accentuated by the glaring contrasts to which the urban dweller is exposed. But unlike Simmel, who focused on sharp contrasts of individual personality and excessive commodities (see chapter three) as forces producing nervous stimulation, Wirth focuses on contrasts of social conditions and social worlds: 1. Spatial differentiation and segregation in the urban milieu are fostered by economic forces, social forces that attract people and groups to certain residential areas, social forces that cause them to avoid other areas, and inertia. Consider these forces in turn: (a) *Economic forces:* The competition for scarce space in densely populated urban areas impels an economic drive for land-use patterns which maximize the highest economic yield. It is more efficient, hence more economical, to functionally divide land areas to create distinctive industrial, commercial, and residential urban zones. As place of work becomes divorced from place of residence, areas proximate to commercial and industrially concentrated areas become both socially and economically undesirable for residential uses. "Higher land uses" eventually displace the residential uses to which such areas are put. The remaining residential areas become highly differentiated. (b) *Social attraction:* Such pull factors as prestige, healthfulness, aesthetic values, ethnic identification, shared tastes, shared class culture, accessibility to amenities, and the like, account for the establishment of a wide variety of self-selected residential communities. (c) *Social avoidance:* Such push factors as prejudice, avoidance of glaring differences in life style, noise, smoke, dirt, and other disamenities, and forced migration further distribute the population into more or less distinct "social worlds." (d) *Inertia:* Still other social worlds emerge as a function of custom, habit, and social drift.

For all these reasons the different parts of a city take on specialized functions. As a result of these demographic and economic trends, the city as a whole is a world of glaring visual contrasts. The city "tends to resemble *a mosaic of social worlds* in which the transition from one to the other is abrupt."[44] 2. The abrupt juxtaposition of divergent personalities, social areas, and ways of life exposes the individual to glaring contrasts "between splendor and squalor, between riches and poverty, intelligence and ignorance, order and chaos."[45] 3. The juxtaposition of the diverse but "functional" social worlds to which the urban populace is exposed also increases its sense of relativism and tolerance. Toleration of differences and divergent modes of life become essential prerequisites of both rationality and secularization. By implication, increased tolerance serves as a buffer against the social friction and potential social confict which increased frequency of contact among relatively segregated subcultures encourages.

Curiously, Wirth never makes clear why it is reasonable to expect that urban residents will be exposed to abrupt juxtapositions of divergent personalities, areas, and ways of life if they spend most of their time living in relatively homogeneous social worlds. Nor does he attempt to reconcile the contradiction between his picture of the urban dweller as a normless social isolate with his picture of social life as consisting of a mosaic of cohesive "social worlds." These oversights paper over crucial contradictions in his theory. Only an outside social analyst or perhaps an automobile passenger "passing through" the city can be expected to be overstimulated by abrupt transitions among specialized urban zones. Furthermore, when urban contacts are made outside the social worlds in which people are anchored, they are likely to take place when people engage in commercial or bureaucratic activity. By Wirth's own reasoning, in such situations individuals tend to immunize themselves from stimuli by the blasé attitude, superficiality, and the like. But if such secondary relationships have truly become matters of indifference, it is unreasonable to expect either harmful overstimulation or increased tolerance to result. Mental life is simply unmoved by indifferent relationships, one way or the other.

The Consequences of Heterogeneity

The chief social consequence of urban heterogeneity is its impact on the class structure. Wirth argued that increased heterogeneity leads to increased social interaction among the rich variety of personality types engendered by large size and high density. Heterogeneous social interaction breaks down rigid class distinctions and greatly complicates the class structure and social stratification system. In the urban milieu the individual becomes highly mobile. Traditional allegiances break down. At the social level these two developments result in a qualitatively different pattern of group affiliations than is characteristic of traditional societies.

In traditional social orders group memberships were concentric. Participation in one group entailed participation in a series of other groups that could be hierarchically arranged in a series of concentric circles. Narrow social circles fell within the circumference of more inclusive ones. These memberships encompassed all of the roles which the individual was likely to play throughout the course of life. They were fixed, mutually compatible, and provided the individual with a stable place in the social order and, presumably, a stable personality stemming from the absence of severe role conflict.

In contrast, the Wirthian urban milieu is characterized by a segmental and transitory pattern of group affiliations. Group allegiances are determined as a result of the unique interest of each individual. Interests arise out of the different aspects of each person's social life. When group affiliations are extensions of individual interests, "the individual acquires membership in widely divergent groups, each of which functions only with reference to a single segment of personality."[46] For this reason, individual participation in the group life of a mobile and fluid society does not securely anchor the personality in a fixed sense of meaning and identity. Turnover in group membership tends to be high. People continue to define and redefine their "self" through a highly variable pattern of intersecting group memberships. In the geographically and socially mobile urban world, place of work, place of residence, and interests fluctuate. Organizational participation no longer promotes "intimate and lasting acquaintanceship" as it once did in a more stable folk society.

As a result of all this fluctuation and mobility, urban personality structure becomes fluid, anomic, detached, and disintegrated. Anomic personalities make up the fluid urban mass which Wirth believed made collective behavior in urban society so unpredictable and problematic. In the urban milieu:

> There is little opportunity for the individual to obtain a conception of the city as a whole or to survey his place in the total scheme. Consequently he finds it difficult to determine what is to his own "best interests" and to decide between the issues and leaders presented to him by the agencies of mass suggestion.[47]

Mass media is not the only formal institution operating on the disintegrated urban personality. Mass production and the impersonal market also structure the modern urban development process. An already highly depersonalized environment is further depersonalized by the standardization of work process and products and by the heightened importance of the "pecuniary nexus"—all of which go hand in hand with the capitalist system of production. The cash nexus implies that personal relations have been displaced as the basis of human association by "the purchasability of services and things."[48] Under the conditions of mass production, mass markets, mass advertising, and the pecuniary nexus, urban institutions and facilities become adjusted to the needs of "the average person." The needs of particular individuals thereby are given short shrift. Urban public services in particular become adjusted to mass requirements.

Although a leveling tendency clearly accompanies all of these developments, Wirth is skeptical about the implications of this development. For Wirth, leveling was at best a mixed blessing. It entailed commercialism, depersonalization, uprootedness, the decline of binding traditions and sentiments, the subordination of particular to mass needs, personal disintegration, and potentially disruptive mass behavior. Leveling means that if the members of "mass society" wished to be politically effective, they must subordinate some of their individuality to the demands of mass movements. But the collective behavior of mass movements was highly unpredictable and hence highly problematic for the prospects of social order.

No less of a problem from Wirth's perspective was the divisive influence of special interest groups. To participate effectively in the socioeconomic and political life of the city, "urban individuals" either joined organized groups or immersed themselves in mass movements. However, through either choice the individuals were unlikely to realize the common good of the city as a whole. As part of the mass, they were subject to mass persuasion and manipulation by opinion-forming elites. As dedicated interest-group members they were likely to behave in a rampantly particularistic fashion, thereby undermining the basis for normative consensus and social order.

Interest Groups and Political Disorganization

Wirth's mistrust of interest groups is rooted in part in his belief that their presence makes it more difficult for political systems to organize political demands in such a way that public policy can satisfy basic human needs. He also believed that the "overchoice" made available by the presence of highly differentiated interest groups impedes people's abilities to know which actions and policies of government and other centers of power actually serve their own "best interests" (i.e., satisfy basic needs for economic security, social participation, and political power).

As the urban class structure becomes highly differentiated, Wirth envisages the number of organized interest groups multiplying to meet "as great a variety of objectives as there are human needs and interests."[49] This proliferation of groups serves to confuse people concerning which public policies are in their own best interests because the multiplication of groups *changes the basis upon which interests are organized into politics.* In less complicated social systems, people's economic status and a few other basic determinants of everyday existence are closely linked to the groups to which they belong. But, in urban society, often "there is only the most tenuous relationship between the economic position or other basic factors that determine the individual's existence in the urban world and the voluntary groups with which he is affiliated."[50] This incongruity makes the polity much more difficult to organize. In simpler social systems, the groups to which an individual belongs can articulate a small set of basic human needs which the political system can absorb, adapt to, and still maintain stability. In a more complicated urban society, all sorts of exotic felt needs find expression through group activities. It becomes more difficult to discover commonalities and to fulfill basic needs amidst all of this complexity and group differentiation. Self-government is reduced to whatever emerges as a result of the unstable equilibrium of contending pressure groups.

Furthermore, the individual acquires status and expresses his personality largely through the activities of this panoply of voluntary groups. Intersecting, contradictory groups separate the individual personality into a myriad of mutually incompatible facets. The way politics and social life are organized in urban society contributes to the development of disorganized personalities. In the face of highly differentiated organizational structures, the consistency and integrity of the personality is left to the inner strength of the individual will. But since the structural environment itself fosters further social differentiation and fragmentation of personality, this is a rather slender reed upon which to rest the hope for inner consistency and integrated personality structure. Hence Wirth concludes: "Personal disorganization, mental breakdown, suicide, delinquency, crime, corruption, and disorder might be expected under these circumstances to be more prevalent in the urban than in the rural community."[51] And politics offers little hope for alleviating these problems so long as the ecological, social, and political structure impede the ability of the political order to become organized. Without organization supported by consensus, political systems can neither absorb demands nor fulfill basic human needs.

Cultural Disorganization, Crime, and Delinquency

Just as the multiplicity of conflicting interest groups impedes the *political* organization of the "community-as-a-whole," so the multiplicity of conflicting subcultures found in the urban mosaic impedes the development of common cultural understandings that might regulate behavior informally. This absence was viewed by Wirth as a basic cause of crime and delinquency. In an early essay he argued that the values, traditions, and modes of living of diverse cultures and subcultures may be so different that what is deemed criminal in one culture is regarded as heroic in another.

Wirth argued from anthropological evidence that in homogeneous cultures, with little class differentiation, informal social controls were a spontaneous product of shared sentiments, customs, and institutions which the small, isolated, and relatively undifferentiated group quite easily transmits from one generation to the next. As Wirth put it:

> The community secures the allegiance, participation, and conformity of the members not through police, courts, and jails, but through the overwhelming force of community opinion, through the immediate, voluntary, and habitual approval of the social code by all.[52]

Wirth believed that although no social system could be entirely free of personal friction, rivalry, and impulsive behavior, primitive systems were relatively free from the sharp cultural schisms that characterize urban society. Hence they fostered more integrated personality structures and more stable social organization. Personal and social disorganization were functions of the "mutation of cultural values" caused by urbanization, war, social upheaval, migration, social contact among divergent subcultures, or even by generational conflict as one generation routinely attempted to socialize the next.

Wirth assumed that in urban civilization most people are exposed to experiences which conflict with the values and attitudes of their original cultural matrix. Indeed, Wirth hypothesized that urban unrest, or in his words "physical and psychic tension," is a direct result of underlying culture conflicts. For example, if immigrants are viewed as living in a dual cutural milieu, Wirth argued that much of their behavior which is labeled strange, delinquent, or even criminal becomes perfectly explicable as a by-product of cultural conflict—the loosening of the informal social controls of the Old World culture without their adequate replacement by a firmly rooted alternative value system. Cultural conflicts per se do not make people delinquent; delinquency may be regarded as a function of the inability of an individual to deal with the stress produced by cultural conflict in a socially approved way. In this case, delinquency is a form of heightened but unresolved self-consciousness, akin to other socially disvalued coping mechanisms such as fantasy, brooding, or suicide.[53]

In the modern metropolis such cultural conflicts are not confined to immigrant families. They occur most markedly, in Wirth's view, among urban families and communities: "especially where, as in the case of city life, contacts are extended, heterogeneous groups mingle, neighborhoods disappear, and people deprived of local and family ties are forced to live under the loose, transient, and impersonal relations that are characteristic of cities."[54]

For Wirth, culture and personality are indivisible. Each is unthinkable without the other. Group culture is based on customs, manifests itself in individual habits, and is broken down by the interaction of individuals practicing divergent habits and customs. Human conduct is the by-product of the social roles which individuals assume as they are acculturated into various social groups. These roles may be integrated with each other or they may be contradictory. The more contradictory the roles which impinge on the individual members of a social system, the greater the likelihood of unresolved role conflict and its social consequences.

According to Wirth, role and culture conflict are most likely to lead to crime and delinquency in specifiable situations, most of which are found in city life. Among these are situations (a) where social life is highly mobile and culture is in a state of flux, "as in those areas of cities where there is no organized family or community life and where the social framework, which ordinarily supports the individual in his conduct, disintegrates or fails to function"[55]; (b) where formal law varies from traditional norms; (c) where conduct within a social group has a different meaning than that which obtains for the same behavior in the dominant society, or where sanctioned conduct in one group violates the laws or customs of another group to whose code one also may be subject; (d) where the basic group to which the individual belongs is itself "a result of the incomplete blending" of different cultures. Thus the multi-group nature of city life is viewed as conducive to the creation of incompatible social roles which, in turn, can lead to delinquent and criminal behavior.

Cultural Reorganization through Scientific Rationality

Although Louis Wirth viewed all the psychological, political, and social problems just described as consequences of *ecological* changes in urban spatial structure, he believed that such problems could be alleviated by *cultural* means. In his view, the secularized culture of "urbanism" undermined traditional value systems that had formed the basis of social order. Yet the emergent secular culture also offered the possibility that a new consensual value system, rooted in deference to "objective science," might replace the traditional understandings that had held smaller-scale societies together. Wirth hoped that a growing deference to the "objective" knowledge of social scientists, other intellectuals, and planners would form the basis of a new normative order. This would make possible a scientifically rooted value hierarchy that could establish clear priorities for solving urban social problems.

Wirth believed that knowledge and ideas were instrumental in both the maintenance and the change of cultural systems. A major frustration in dealing with Wirth is that just as one is about to pin him down as an ecological determinist on the basis of extensive analysis or advocacy of the importance of ecological variables for understanding human personality and social life, one encounters a statement such as the following, which absolves him of charges of environmental determinism, but illustrates the confusion of his theory of personality and social development.

> In the ecological studies of delinquency, insanity, family disorganization, religious life, political behavior, and social institutions, it has sometimes been naively assumed that, once the spatial distribution of people, institutions, functions, and problems has been traced and their concentration and dispersion noted, there remains nothing for the ecologist to do but relate these phenomena to other ecological data to arrive at valid explanations. This view overlooks the fact that social life is a complex interdependent

whole. Material conditions of existence are, of course, important factors in the determination of social structure and personal characteristics and behavior. . . . But they are not the whole of social life. On the contrary . . . attitudes, personalities, cultural forms, and social organizations and institutions may have as significant an effect in shaping ecological patterns and processes as the latter have in conditioning social and socio-psychological phenomena.[56]

Consider, as a case in point, the formative impact of the *culture* of urbanism, which urbanization and ecological change initially created. This emergent secular culture has undermined common understandings; contributed to the diffusion of social problems; and affected the spatial distribution of people seeking to flee from social conflict and social problems. As Wirth has noted:

A society is possible in the last analysis because the individuals in it carry around in their heads some sort of picture of that society. Our society, however, in this period of minute division of laborur, of extreme heterogeneity and profound conflict of interests, has come to pass where these pictures are blurred and incongruous.[57]

Paradoxically, Wirth held that urban culture engenders substantively irrational behavior at the same time it fosters a pervasive spirit of functional rationality. Without common language, symbols, and meanings mutual understanding is much more difficult. In conflict situations appeal no longer can be made to common criteria of relevance and truth. The intellectual and social worlds are held together by words. When these words fail to convey the same meanings to those who use them, social disintegration is likely.

In his preface to Karl Mannheim's *Ideology and Utopia,* Wirth contends that we have reached a point of cultural crisis. The failure to reach "common understandings" has led to widespread mass disillusionment. High expectations for scientific progress, accompanied by dissensus among scientists, particularly social scientists, has encouraged a nostalgic yearning for a past age characterized by certainty in firmly founded knowledge. But such an age is permanently lost.

In the face of the growing secularization of knowledge, many have sought escape in fantasy, cynicism, anti-intellectualism, or gross oversimplification of complex social reality. Wirth believed that all of these trends indicated a growing depreciation of the value of thought. This impending "twilight of modern culture" might be forestalled, but only if careful, resolutely planned steps were taken. The urban predicament of "chaos and unsettlement" could be mastered if the conditions which brought about the social and intellectual upheaval were fully comprehended. The changing pattern of knowledge and thinking must be understood as a dynamic social process. Social and political judgments must be traced to their "specific interest-bound roots in society, through which the particularity, and hence the limitations, of each view will become apparent."[58]

Once this awareness of the subjectivity of current social knowledge was understood, Wirth felt the burden of ambiguity, anomie, and social fragmentation would become more bearable. When people know that there is no single truth in the social world, they will be less distressed by their inability to find it. As individuals become aware of the limitations of their own views, they are likely to hold those views more skeptically and tentatively. This, in turn, is likely to lead to a slackening of intense ideological conflict. "Working agreements" can then evolve concerning the facts and inferences that each party can accept as minimally relevant to intellectual discourse. This is the essential first step in establishing a secularized culture rooted in deference to a scientific mode of thought.

Wirth believed it important to distinguish the content of ideas and ideals from the symbolic forms in which they are expressed and from the ways they are used. In "Ideas and Ideals and Sources of Power in the Modern World" (1947), he questions the meaning of the aphorism "Knowledge is power." He asks, "Are ideals the determiners of men's destinies whether or not specific groups of human beings become organized around these ideals? . . . Is it the ideas and ideals, or is it education, propaganda, preaching, persuasion, coercion, deception, advertising, and control over instruments of communication that constitute power?"[59] Do people do battle over ideals and ideas or over symbols, stereotypes, and slogans?

His answers to these questions stress the dual role of social structure and culture in processing ideas and ideals. Most people are socialized into the ideas and ideals they hold. These are usually the well-established social beliefs that are reinforced by social sanctions. They are part of the culture, and as such, they are given the credibility to mold personality and conduct. Conventional beliefs form part of the uncoerced consensus which, along with common language and understandings, forms the basis of all collective action.

Ideas and ideals are transmitted within a culture by various socialization agencies. The most important of these agencies beyond the family include (a) the education system and religious institutions; (b) diverse interest groups, both political and nonpolitical; and (c) the mass media and the persons who select the ideas and ideals they transmit. Mass media in particular have served to shrink the moral and intellectual universe. An emerging world secular culture, in Wirth's view, is experienced by many as a "tower of Babel," but it is nonetheless real. Yet ideas and ideals operating at this level lack the nonrational sources of legitimacy enjoyed by the tribe, folk culture, or localized community. Indeed, the legitimization of these ideas is impeded by national, religious, racial, and economic barriers. Before a world secular culture can become institutionalized, its ideas and ideals "must establish linkages with accepted cultural elements and undergo a process of assimilation."[60] This has been largely accomplished in the realm of science, but politics, ethics, philosophy, and religion lag far behind.

The spread of alien ideas and ideals has a "transitionally" disruptive influence on existing cultures. This can be seen in the "disorganizing" influence of colonization, migration, and technological change. Yet Wirth held that it is in this transitional stage that social scientists, other intellectuals, and planners can play a crucial role. New modes of social organization, new attitudes, and particular personalities can shape new material conditions of existence and create new social structures and cultural forms. For example, by transmitting ideas and ideals rationally, intellectuals can create new "common understandings" based on the emerging world culture of objective science. By using the mass media effectively, they can convert them from instruments for symbolic manipulation to tools for rational persuasion and public education. By establishing "working arrangements" by which rational intellectual discourse can proceed, they can make the burden of ambiguity and rapid social change more bearable. It is to this phase of Wirth's thought—his answer to the question "What is to be done to establish rational policy planning as a basis for social consensus?"—that we now turn.

WHAT IS TO BE DONE?—THE POLITICS OF PLANNING AND CONSENSUS

The lack of mechanisms for creating consensus based on informed consent has implications for effective urban policy planning. In a nutshell, Wirth believed that there was a widening gap between our need to politically organize the "community-as-a-whole" and our ability to do so. Or as Wirth congently put it:

> While our problems of community life have become increasingly complicated and technical, our social life has become highly mobile and tenuous, and its sphere of concerted thought and action as ambiguous and as fleeting as the headlines on the front page of our metropolitan press . . . [w]e lack a universe of discourse based upon common meanings and have failed to develop an adequate technique for integrating the diverse and often conflicting motives of special interest groups. It is this growing disparity between our interdependence and our capacity to act as a unit . . . that has driven the friends of democracy to despair. . . . [61]

In order to enable the "community-as-a-whole" to act as a unit, Wirth advocated increased reliance upon rational-comprehensive urban planning. He felt that such an approach, grounded in objective science, held the promise of rational intellectual discourse about social ills and policy problems that might transcend the limited and particularistic perspectives of special interest groups. He hoped that careful empirical research would become a basic planning tool, providing the vital link between theoretical analysis and public policy.

Although somewhat eclectic in his own research, Wirth favored "human ecology" as the approach best suited to provide urban planning with a well-grounded theoretical basis. The ecological perspective was a valid starting point for urban planners and policy makers, in Wirth's view, because ecological analysts were especially adept at identifying the ever shifting "natural areas" in which social problems existed and distinguishing these from arbitrary administrative or political boundaries. Moreover, he perceived the science of human ecology as the approach most capable of developing clear indicators of the dynamic demographic and ecological processes that underlie unplanned social change. He reasoned that to plan sensibly for the future, the present and the processes that created and transform the present must be clearly understood.

Wirth claimed that since human ecologists best understand the shifting realities of demographic and ecological change, their views should be given greater weight in economic, social, and physical planning. In particular, he felt that human ecologists were best able to grasp the nature and impact of the social, technological, and demographic interrelationships obtaining between the center and periphery of metropolitan areas. For him the metropolitan region was a living economic and social "entity," a phenomenon with a real existence, rather than an artificial political unit.

As an "entity," the metropolitan region had major implications for social control, community organization, and social planning. For example, if the distribution of crime and disease, transportation patterns, economic interdependence, and sociocultural phenomena all transcend political boundaries, yet police, health officials, politicians, and planners are hemmed in by artificially narrow jurisdictions, "community" level relationships cannot be organized, planned, or controlled: a consensual "society" cannot develop.

For Wirth, contemporary political and administrative boundaries were not products of rational reflection. They were drawn before the socioeconomic forces triggered by the industrial revolution "had begun to reshape the pattern of social existence and of social intercourse."[62] Since they were a throwback, in Wirth's view, to a primitive and parochial age, they should be abandoned. Human ecologists could contribute to urban planning by drawing more realistic pictures of social reality for policy makers and the general public.

Wirth advocated a metropolitanwide domain for urban planners. He argued that traditional administrative and political boundaries originally had been drawn to meet particular historical contingencies which were no longer operative. Nonetheless, these initial boundaries had become entrenched in law and custom. Despite this formal institutionalization, an underlying natural or "symbiotic" evolution had created new migration patterns, new spatial relationships, and a more elaborate division of labor. These trends, in turn, created new symbiotic interdependencies or "communities." "Society" could not consciously order and control these underlying forces unless economic, social, and land use planning districts were redrawn along metropolitan lines.

This is not to say that Wirth was committed to comprehensive metropolitan planning as an end in itself. Wirth valued metropolitanwide planning primarily as a tool for achieving rational control of the pace and direction of socioeconomic change. He thought that rational-comprehensive planning could solve those social and policy problems (e.g., housing, transportation, taxation) whose scope transcended traditional small-scale local jurisdictions. To realize other cherished values, Wirth was quite willing to criticize administrative boundaries for being too large to achieve given purposes. For instance, in "Human Ecology," Wirth argues that the goal of adequate scientific investigation of the social life of cities requires the development of "the smallest possible units" for gathering data. He praises the United States Census Bureau for recognizing this need by dividing cities into small census tracts and gathering aggregate data on the population living within these tracts.[63]

This suggests that Wirth was neither a pure centralist nor decentralist; rather, he was opposed to the kind of administrative *arbitrariness* which defined geographic jurisdictions that were either too large or too small to take into account the socioeconomic realities of "natural areas" or to achieve particular purposes. In his words: "Administrative areas only rarely coincide with . . . ecological or natural areas. In the study of urban life . . . the types of land use and . . . residential areas . . . do not conform to the neat lines of precincts, wards, and other political and administrative boundaries. Neither do crime, disease, family disorganization, and . . . political alignments fit these static patterns. . . . They have patterns of their own, and they shift in accordance with the total conditions of life."[64] Because he believed that many pressing social and policy problems were metropolitanwide, or even national in scope, he tended to favor centralized control of the planning process.

Centralization, Decentralization, and Need Fulfillment: The Optimal Planning Unit

For Wirth, human fulfillment is in large part a matter of enhancing individual freedom against the "encroachments" of the collectivities of which people are always a part. In earlier historical periods, freedom was defined not in personal but in geographic terms. People's status and the scope of their freedom were determined by such "anchorages" as a house, the manor, the village, the principality, or the city. The concept of "sovereignty" is best understood in such areal terms. Historical conflicts between localism, regionalism, or centralism as the appropriate unit within which "sovereignty" ought to reside are in fact struggles over which domain will have the power to define people's status, socialize them into loyalty, and set the legitimate scope of their freedom.

This choice also involves the persistent philosophical question of the proper balance to be drawn between "freedom from outside interference, on the one hand, and security and enrichment of life that can come only from participating in a larger world, on the other."[65] Given his definition of self-actualization and his focus upon the limiting aspects of parochial loyalties, Wirth tended to opt for an activist federal government and participation in the larger social world. His choice is apparent in the logic of his 1937 article "Localism, Regionalism, and Centralization."

In this essay Wirth addressed himself to arguments developed by such philosophical "localists" as Thomas Jefferson and G. D. H. Cole who had attacked political centralization as a threat to both individual freedom and popular control over common affairs.[66] Wirth responded to this commonly held belief by offering a carefully reasoned defense of centralized national governmental responsibilities. His argument remains today one of the most trenchant apologies yet advanced for centralized political control over decentralized administrative planning units. Wirth's argument proceeds along several major lines.

The autonomy of small, local, self-sufficient units has already been undermined by developments in transportation and communication technology which have enlarged the market, increased economic interdependence, and further refined the complex division of labor. By and large, this increased mobility of persons, goods, and enterprises can be viewed as a healthy development: "This new freedom has liberated the forces that make for greater efficiency and productivity. By emancipating individuals and communities from absolute dependence upon purely local circumstances, their potential stability and security have been increased, *provided the instruments of control could be ex-*

tended to coincide with the enlarged sphere of interdependence that has emerged in recent decades."[67] In small groups, collective goals develop spontaneously through nonrational processes in which rumors, gossip, and even mere physical gestures play an important part. Social interaction has a personal, emotional tone. In the modern metropolitan environment, logic replaces tradition as the chief basis for creating consensual understandings and agreements. This, in turn, limits the scope of both consensus and collective action to purely secular activities. Symbolic mass-media appeals are the modern functional equivalents of the nonrational processes that both arouse and bind together more primitive social groups. Although powerful in particular instances, the scope of the impact of such advertising and propaganda in large-scale secular societies tends to be restricted to purely secular concerns. Symbol manipulation is therefore less shrouded in mystery, and hence easier to control. Centralized organizations can yield widespread social benefits under democratic controls, provided that the governing elites of urban societies can learn to use advanced techniques of communication to create both popular understandings and popular participation in the formation of public policy.

Centralized federal policy direction also is necessary because the powers and jurisdiction of the federal government correspond to the actual scope of corporate economic enterprise. Both commercial and manufacturing firms have become increasingly bureaucratized and national or even international in scope. They have acquired the private planning resources to make vital location and relocation decisions based on comprehensive knowledge of labor supply, markets, taxation considerations, and whether local legislation is favorable or unfavorable to a "dynamic business climate." Given these economic developments, traditional state and local regulatory activities are inadequate to the task of regulating the economy in the public interest.

There are, of course, some risks entailed in increased political centralization. Wirth recognized that centralized government was usually assumed to entail an arrogant, insensitive, and parasitic bureaucracy which dominates society. He acknowledged that even beneficent centralized regimes might be wasteful and unresponsive because their distance from sources of revenue might lead to bureaucratic boondoggling and their distance from local conditions might lead to ignorance, excessive formalism, and delay. He also recognized that the size and diversity of the electorate in a large-scale centralized jurisdiction might make it difficult for the majoritarian popular will to emerge. This, in turn, might leave the realm of public policy making open only to negotiated settlements among the strongest and best organized pressure groups.

For Wirth, however, this picture of political centralization was overly pessimistic. Wirth raises four arguments in particular in defense of political centralization. First, the benefits of the division of labor, the attraction of outstanding talent, and economies of scale can only be achieved in large units which have eliminated duplication of functions and avoided the pettiness of "localism." Second, the larger heterogeneous unit offers its residents greater freedom of movement, more opportunity for self-development, enhanced economic productivity, and "greater possibility of orderly, balanced, or planned development" than is possible in any small-scale, localized unit.[68] Third, and in Wirth's view, most important, some vital functions can only be undertaken by centralized government. These can be subsumed under the category of assuming the risks of technological and economic development through such policies as unemployment insurance, investment in educational needs and rural development, and subsidized development of highways, public works, and housing production.

Finally, Wirth indicates that greater political centralization of responsibility and revenue-raising capacity need not entail greater administrative centralization. Through grant-in-aid programs to states and through states to local communities, the benefits of national resources and a consideration of national needs can be balanced against local needs and conditions, thereby facilitating administrative flexibility and sensitivity to legitimate local differences.

Through such imaginative jurisdictional mixes it may be possible to achieve collective security and social order without unduly sacrificing personal initiative or individual freedom. Having attempted to weigh rationally the costs and benefits of localism and centralization, Wirth concludes that they may not be real alternatives at all, or at least not necessarily mutually exclusive modes of social organization. Judgments about the advisability of certain political structures depend on the purposes we seek to fulfill and the extent to which the chosen mode is compatible with other goals to which society is committed. Such goals as physical security, risk assumption, heavy capital investment, and the like, may be best achieved by centralized political authority; other (unspecified) purposes may best be achieved with a maximum of local automony. For some problem areas (e.g., crime, recreation, and family disorganization) regional units may be the most rational.

For Wirth, many governmental functions could benefit from an imaginative admixture of interstate compacts, "home rule" agreements, or even city-states, if these served to match resources with problems. He felt that whatever served to match the scope of a jurisdiction to the scope of actual social problems was desirable and should not be overlooked, even though some such arrangements (e.g., city-states) were probably utopian "for the present."[69]

Metropolitan Planning as a Vocation

What then was Wirth willing to support "for the present" as a non-utopian planning ideal? In an essay first published in 1942, Wirth spelled out in considerable detail his views on metropolitan-regional planning as a desirable vocation for social scientists and other policy-oriented intellectuals.[70]

Following his theoretical and normative penchant for "society"-like social arrangements—a deliberate, rational, consensual ordering of human relationships—Wirth "the planner" felt that social problems cried out for rational treatment. Rational urban planning entails treating the metropolitan region rather than the city as the appropriate planning unit. In his view, the key problems that call for planning expertise are systemic or regionwide. The supercity is the emergent form of urban community: industry, housing markets, and labor markets are all metropolitan in scope.

Even in 1942, the suburbanization of people and of industrial and commercial development in America were sufficiently pronounced for Wirth to comment upon the significance of this developing metropolitanization of economy and society. Wirth was one of the earliest commentators to take note of the "flight from the central cities."[71] He proposed concrete steps to deal with that flight, including changes in governmental form to keep pace with changed economic and social realities.

In "The Metropolitan Region as a Planning Unit," Wirth assessed the impact of suburbanization upon the physical structure of cities, local government structure, the urban tax base, and evolving ways of life. He pointed out that suburban residential trends, coupled with the then outward movement of both residential and business districts within city boundaries, threatened the inner urban core with blight, depopulation, and decay.

The consequences of the depopulation of the core city noted by Wirth include the following:

- The declining central-city tax base, due to
  1. a decline in the value of real property stemming from blight and decay,
  2. increased tax delinquency,
  3. the relocation of industry and people;
- The rising costs of basic urban public services—education, sanitation, fire and police protection—in the face of this decline in tax revenues;
- The small scale of urban public-housing policy and the incompatibility between even this meagre effort and the lending policies of

the Federal Housing Administration which favored suburban development and treated older central-city areas as poor risks;

- The development of high-speed through traffic to the city outskirts and suburbs, resulting in congestion at the center and an additional urban disamenity, a "residential vacuum" at the central-city core.

To cope with these developments Wirth felt that the urban planner's activities must extend to the widest possible planning region. Metropolitanwide planning could encompass all of the forces and factors that the planner must analyze and control.

Wirth recognized that there were several different ways to conceptualize a metropolitan region. A region may be viewed as consisting of a dominant central city, whose influence is greatest over those areas most proximate to it and diminishes indefinitely with greater geographic distance. Alternatively, a metropolitan area may be viewed as this same sphere of influence, but with clearly delineated outer boundaries once another competing metropolitan region's outer boundaries are reached. Thirdly, the planners may view metropolitan areas merely as arbitrarily drawn zones which divide the country as a whole for purely administrative purposes, rather than to designate functional spheres of influence.

Unhappily for planners, in Wirth's view, all three of these views have been used to define relevant planning units, although the concepts are neither internally consistent nor consistent with one another. All three are static views of social reality. Cities are fluid, not static; they are products of spontaneous growth rather than rigid design. This makes the planner's job more difficult. He must map out a fixed area to analyze and control even though the social reality he is seeking to shape is constantly shifting and dynamic.

From Wirth's perspective, the planner must not accept this "chaos" as an inevitable condition. To wit: "The rationale of planning is that even if we must accept the past as given, and read its lessons, the future is ours to influence if not to make. . . . The way in which we conceive of the planning area may in itself become an important factor in the shaping of the cities, the regions and the nation of the future."[72]

Because of political constraints, the ability of planners to shape the future is limited. They lack the power to define the optimal planning area. Compromises, reluctantly, may be necessary; yet, if too many political concessions are made, the perfectionist ideal of rational-comprehensive planning will be unduly diluted. Thus, in Wirth's view, compromises of rationality are to be avoided. If planners must err, let it be on the side of more rather than less comprehensive planning areas. Wirth advises metropolitan planners to strive to incorporate as much of the periphery as possible into their planning domain. Only in this way can areawide problems be addressed. Wide domain is also necessary if planners are to select an area in conformity with the region as an economic unit.

And who is the political enemy of Wirth's metropolitan planning ideal? With whom must his planners compromise? To wit: "We live in an era which dissolves boundaries, but the inertia of antiquarian lawyers and lawmakers, the predatory interests of local politicals, real estate men, and industrialists, the parochialism of suburbanites, and the myopic vision of planners have prevented us from a full recognition of the inescapable need for a new planning unit in the metropolitan region."[73]

Wirth's Critique of Neighborhood Planning

Ironically, although Wirth obviously recognized that the city was first and foremost a human settlement and treated it as such in his more purely academic writings, his writings on urban planning placed major emphasis on the city's economic function. As a planning theorist, Wirth viewed the city less as a human community than as a "workshop and . . . center of interchange of goods and services."[74] Wirth advised planners to consider basic economic questions when drawing the boundaries of the urban planning region. He asks rhetorically: Are the city's wholesale and retail trade markets regional, national, or worldwide? Does it draw its raw materials regionally, nationally, or internationally? What is the scope of its banking and credit structure? What is the newspaper circulation area and the mass-media listening area? Where does the area draw its labor supply?

Even when he does treat the social functions of cities as a planner, Wirth's focus is regional rather than local or neighborhood based. For instance, he counsels other planners to investigate the "area over which such urban institutions as hospitals, schools, churches, theaters, and clubs are patronized by the people of the hinterland."[75] Likewise, he selects as significant planning data such "facts" as the areas over which suburbanites maintain ties with people in cities and areas over which professional service and recreation networks are maintained.

This way of framing questions is really a way of begging the question: "What is the optimal planning unit for enhancing popular control over public policy?" Many contemporary commentators have argued that the best way to enhance the political power of small-scale, neighborhood-based, urban social networks is to create neighborhood planning units. But despite his awareness of the "fact" and the social functions of urban neighborhoods,[76] Wirth never asked questions designed to highlight their sociological or political significance. Given his mistrust of "localism" and his belief that small-scale social networks chiefly functioned to set restrictions on individual mobility and choice, Wirth was disinclined to ask such questions. Rather, each of the questions which he does ask calls attention to those social phenomena (e.g., housing and labor markets) that lend support to his preferred goal—a metropolitanwide geographic scale for urban planning. Other ways of viewing the city are ignored.

Nor is this merely a matter of oversight. Wirth could hardly be expected to institutionalize the "urban mosaic" by factoring neighborhoods into the planning process because he believed that the mosaic itself was a major source of the conditions of life he sought to cure by planning—personal and social disorganization, role conflict, and the lack of societywide consensual values.

This may seem surprising in view of the romanticization of the small town and rural life that forms the basis of Wirth's theory of folk-urban social change. However, Wirth believed that history was a linear and progressive unfolding of the liberating power of reason and science. He viewed the neighborhood as a traditional form of social organization that was bound to decrease in significance as society became more secular, impersonal, and urban. Thus, even if Wirth had not personally favored individual social mobility, he would have been unlikely to assign decision-making authority to institutions such as neighborhood social networks. He hoped and expected that such networks eventually would wither away.

Indeed, in an essay devoted to "The Scope and Problems of the Community," Wirth explicitly attacks the efforts of "community organizers" who labor in the vineyards of urban neighborhoods. He criticizes the attempts by community organizers to create new neighborhood institutions, to mobilize collective action, and to pass legislation on behalf of local community needs. In his words:

> Some believe that the hope of our social order lies in the return to the local ties of neighborhood. The trend of our civilization, however, has generally been sensed to lead in the opposite direction. There can be no return to the local self-contained neighborly community except by giving up the technological and cultural advantages of this shifting, insecure, and interdependent, though intensely interesting and far-flung, community life, which few would be willing to do.[77]

Partly because of his "cosmopolitan" bias apparent in this statement, and because of his penchant for rational planning on behalf of the "community-as-a-whole," and his belief that community organization efforts were "sporadic" and merely "common sensical," Wirth felt that community organization work should be replaced by more "rigorous" social policy planning. For Wirth, the institution

building, legislative, and mobilization activities of community organizers were viewed as parochial, unscientific, and potentially disruptive of rationally guided social consensus. In place of these locally
based political activities, Wirth preferred to institute a "type of community organization which takes on the character of social planning."[78] In effect, Wirth would wish away the political conflict engendered by or on behalf of the least mobile segments of the social
class structure. He would displace this by "scientific" activities such
as the collection and analysis of "facts," and the rational selection and
implementation of policies based on these "facts."

"Wirth the planner's" lack of perspective on the limits of comprehensive urban planning and on the continuing vitality of urban neighborhoods is especially ironic in view of "Wirth the social theorist's"
sensitive and subtle academic treatment of the limitations of thinking
in regional terms. In a little essay on "The Limitations of Regionalism," Wirth explores the analytical and psychological uses of the concept "region."[79] He observes that in different social disciplines the
concept has been assigned a wide variety of meanings. Among these
are the prevalence of certain cultural characteristics of the population
(e.g., language, dialect, forms of social organization); the interdependence of component parts regardless of whether or not cultural homogeneity and cohesion are present (e.g., a trade area); the existence of
common problems such as crime or disease.

In Wirthian theory, regions are facts, but they are also states of mind
which often form the basis of social plans and movements. Humans
are located in space. Natural space sets limits and offers possibilities
for human development. But humans are active, creative beings. They
can mold as well as be shaped by their environment. There are physical facts of nature as well as facts of culture which can influence the
way we identify regions. The former include climate, topography, and
natural resources; the latter include the spatial distribution of peoples,
institutions, social forms, languages, customs, and ways of life. Although physical facts are relatively fixed in space, cultural facts undergo movement from place to place and time to time which complicates the task of collecting data needed to comprehend and control
social life.

Modernization has progressively altered our dependence upon nature and upon particular geographic habitats. Technological developments, particulary in transportation and communications, have the
power to undo even the most traditionally reinforced correlations between regional habitat and regional culture.

However, Wirth the social theorist thought it well to remember that
when regional cultures do persist, they do so because of the momentum of established customs and institutions, not because of the physi-

cal conditions of existence. By and large, the power of the physical environment has been overcome by advanced civilizations. Wirth agreed with Sigmund Freud that mature civilizations would progressively "emancipate themselves from the soil and from the natural context out of which and in which they developed." Unlike nature, however, culture was a far more resilient phenomenon. Indeed, Wirth the social theorist goes so far as to say that the force of "established institutions and habits is so great that often it requires a cataclysm to uproot them."[80]

Such inherited regional loyalties may undergo gradual change over a period of time. For instance, the demarcation lines between states and regions and between different cultures are undermined by nationalizing trends. Such developments as nationwide collective bargaining contracts tend to standardize regional wage differentials. National taxation and revenue distribution and redistribution patterns, and standardized minimum wages, postal rates, mail order houses, and the like, gradually weave together a national way of life. In the process, regional forms of expression and ways of life are gradually transformed. On a normative level, Wirth was not terribly sorry to see these patterns, which he tended to view as excessively parochial, undermined by changes in the national political economy.

Yet Wirth the social theorist recognized why regionalism continued to persist as a mode of collective consciousness, despite great technological and economic changes and nationalizing trends in public policy and corporate expansion. Such forces as shared customs, common interests, historical conflict or rivalry with other regions (e.g., North vs. South), regional art forms and schools, and the perceived threat of centralized control—all reinforce regionalism as a state of mind. In short, once a culture is created, its maintenance is self-reinforcing.

Carried to an extreme, Wirth feared that regional loyalties might become the stuff of demagogues who exploit them for their own purposes. What might have been a healthy check against giantism, standardization, and uniformity could become instead a pattern of isolation, parochialism, jingoism, and separatism. States of mind might harden into dogma and ultimately degenerate into cults which might erupt as reactionary social movements. Yet, in the last analysis, Wirth concludes that sensitivity to genuine regional differences can avoid the kind of arbitrary and stereotyped treatment of people which fosters seething resentment and converts colorful social differences into self-defensively rigid cults.

Ironically then, the mind of Wirth the social theorist does not always overlap with the mind of Wirth the urban planner. The mind of the former is keenly sensitive to subtle social differences based initially on regional proximity, but maintained by culture. The mind of the latter is unable to focus upon equally poignant social differences based on the persistence of ethnicity and/or urban neighborhood cohesion, and also maintained by cultural forces. While able to discern the independent power of established customs and institutions in maintaining southern regionalism as a state of mind, even in the face of technological change, he is unable to apply this same logic to account for the persistence of friendship, kinship, and urban neighborhood solidarity in the city.

"Citizen Participation" in Metropolitan Planning

Louis Wirth was radically unwilling to support the devolution of public authority to actual urban neighborhoods or to support the efforts of community organizers to politicize urban subcultures. Yet he was keenly interested in finding ways to factor the will of abstract "citizens" into metropolitan planning and policy making. Wirth believed the basic goal of metropolitan planning is the integration of the various aspects of community life "through rational direction of all the available resources to the *socially-to-be-defined* end of a more satisfying existence."[81] The basic function of "citizens" is to contribute to the social definition of the goals that planning ought to pursue.

Wirth believed that it was both possible and desirable to reconcile rational-comprehensive planning with principles of political democracy. Establishing "socially-to-be-defined ends" entails acquiring the informed consent of "citizens" before public policies are chosen and plans are implemented. He felt that planners could perform a vital function in this respect by "informing the citizenry." Planners are envisioned as "helpers," aiding citizens "to choose more wisely" by reducing the costs of acquiring information and by calling attention to the social costs and value implications entailed in pursuing particular goals. Thus Wirth's concept of "democratic planning" becomes essentially Rousseauistic. The people, *as individuals,* express the general will by defining collective ends and articulating consensual values; but consensus can only emerge if people become aware of their "enlightened social interests."

The job of enlightenment, similar to the "guidance" function of Jean Jacques Rousseau's legislator, is assumed in Wirth's theory by social planners. This vital role is best illustrated in the following statement:

> The planners may be able to help citizens to choose more wisely by informing them of the implications and the mutual compatibility of the various goals that are being considered, of the alternative means of reaching them, and of the probable costs involved in resources, *as well as in personal and cultural values.*[82]

Here it becomes apparent that Wirth assumes that planners are not only the best analysts of empirical reality and logical consistency but also the best judges of the factors affecting personal and cultural values. The scope of their guidance function is broadly defined: planners are envisaged as crucial mediating interpreters of the facts, the logic, and the values of human existence for the uninformed citizen.

Despite this potentially elitist tendency, Wirth views this educative function of social scientists and planners as fully compatible with democracy. The chief check on planners as "public educators" remains their critical self-consciousness and sensitivity to the fact that other key elements of their environment besides physical resources—particularly the attitudes, capacities, and interests of human beings—are ends as well as means.[83] Aside from this internal ethical check, planners also can expect to be judged by the public in terms of their effectiveness, that is, by whether or not their plans actually lead to the ends they foresee. These checks will be sufficient, in Wirth's view, to protect the citizenry from manipulation by planning elites. Most importantly, if social planners fail to become public educators, public opinion will be shaped by those elites who already currently dominate the mass media. Without informed, rational planners as guides, Wirth feared that the public might become misled by mass-media propaganda and advertising into pursuing purely private rather than consensual social ends.

Because of his abiding fear of social conflict and his concern for peaceful consensus, Wirth argued that while increased popular participation in decision making was desirable, the citizen generally ought to be deferential to group spokespersons and elected political representatives except under extreme conditions. He felt that consensus did not always depend upon direct mass participation in politics. Rather, its achievement sometimes rested upon our "willingness to allow our representatives to speak for us even though they do not always faithfully represent our views . . . and upon our disposition to fit ourselves into a program that our group has adopted and to acquiesce in group decisions unless the matter is fundamentally incompatible with our interests and integrity."[84]

Despite this statement Wirth was no simple neoelitist arguing that mass ignorance was a healthy "slack," necessary for modern democracies to avoid becoming overloaded by excessive demands. Rather, because he mistrusted political movements and related forms of direct collective action, he asked people to tolerate some imperfections in representative institutions and processes while the media of mass communication were being reformed. This is made clear by Wirth's concern about the quality of information about public affairs possessed by mass publics. This concern led him to call for "unrelenting effort for popular education and for access to reliable sources of information."[85] Wirth felt that issue-oriented public education by social scientists and planners would enable citizens to participate more effectively in public discussions of controversial issues. Yet he also felt that to be effective at reaching mass audiences public affairs programming was insufficient. In any social system, key ideas and ideals could best be vivified by art, literature, and even entertainment forms. Planning-oriented intellectuals must become sensitized to the educational potential of these forms.

For Wirth, the central problem of organizing and expressing democratic consensus in mass society was made more difficult by the mass nature of pubic opinion. He reasoned that effective collective action in a mass democratic society must swiftly and accurately ascertain the ever-shifting interests and attitudes of great popular masses before policy is determined. Since the motives and interests of members of modern mass societies are unstable, the spokespeople for social groups have an increasingly complicated task. They find it difficult simply to know for whom they are speaking, let alone how intense and enduring are the interests which they purport to represent. In Wirth's view, these facts, coupled with the frequent need for prompt decisions, challenge formal decision makers to use all available relevant knowledge about public opinion and to perfect advanced techniques for opinion formation and measurement. An ability to communicate mutually under conditions of "mass society" must be perfected if consensual policies are to emerge.

But this presents a paradox: "In order to communicate effectively with one another we must have common knowledge, but in a mass society it is through communication that we must obtain this common body of knowledge."[86] Thus we must hope that through increased contact and common experiences we can haltingly and gropingly deepen effective communication. This long-run optimism is based on Wirth's assumption that the basic nature and life experiences of human beings are sufficiently similar that, regardless of different initial values and interests, putting oneself in the other person's shoes will have a beneficial cumulative effect.

Modern "mass society" consists of both organized groups and detached masses. The latter are bound together to some degree by the mass media. To overcome inertia, mobilize action, and obtain uncoerced consent, some degree of consensus is needed at both the group and the mass level.

However, in modern urban societies, secularization has undermined traditional loyalties. The force of religion, parochial loyalties, and all dogmas and ideologies resting solely on tradition unsustained by reason has been weakened. For Wirth, increased secularization entailed increased skepticism and less naivete. But ironically, secularization also entailed a great blending of old beliefs into new loyalties. Mass followings were attracted by perverting and diluting formerly incongruous ideas and ideals into "new syncretisms" designed to have the broadest mass appeal. Such growing ambiguity in symbol manipulation by molders of public opinion was no accident. It was a logical outgrowth of growing skepticism and decreased naivete. Wirth argued that opinion-forming elites had responded to this new situation by inventing new ways to make the irrational appear rational. In the modern "urban" world, market research into actual prejudices, interests, and predilections is matched by the growing subtlety of appeals designed to get people to become interested in goods and ideas they were not previously concerned about.

Public opinion is shaped in large part by organized groups, particularly those groups with the power, prestige, skill, resources, and organization to have their group interests count. But people's group interests and affiliations represent only a segment of their interests as human beings. These other interests often never get organized into politics. The same is true of the interests of the unorganized masses and the sentiments, attitudes, and opinions of those at the bottom of the social structure. As Wirth puts it: "In the course of the flow of communication the interests and grievances, the sentiments, attitudes, and opinions of the people at the bottom may become grossly distorted, and the people at the top may find themselves so remote from their constituents that they may either be ignorant of their actual feelings or may seriously misinterpret the fragmentary knowledge that they do have."[87]

This concern had the virtue of causing Wirth to focus upon the numerous ways that the "general public" had been excluded from effective participation in public decision making. His own basic normative concerns explain why he chose to concentrate on the mass communication media as a major research focus. His studies of the way communication channels are organized in mass societies call attention to the "one way" nature of mass communications, to elite ownership of the media and control over their content, as well as to the prospects for using the media to stimulate mass participation in political decision making.[88] We now consider the implications of these concerns for rational planning.

Mass Communication and Rational Planning

In his 1947 Presidential Address to the American Sociological Society, Wirth raised the issue of "Consensus and Mass Communication." In this address Wirth focused on the social power of social science. Wirth believed that social scientists lacked the knowledge needed to "unlock the power requisite to put our existing knowledge usefully to work."[89] He thus directed his remarks to the way in which consensus as formed in mass societies differed from the conditions under which consensus functioned in more primitive and primary social groups.

Wirth defined the *mass* as an aggregate of large numbers, of widely dispersed, heterogeneous, highly differentiated people who, *as a mass*, are anonymous to each other. The mass is unorganized; it has no common customs, institutions, or rules governing individual action. When people exhibit mass behavior, they do so as unattached individuals who have temporarily suspended their affiliations to particular groups, role configurations, or organizations. When their social and political interests are not defined for them through these affiliations, people find themselves with "no appreciable reciprocal interaction between themselves and others similarly situated."[90] They lack concrete experience and thus are subject to manipulation by opinion-forming elites. Elites seek to lead members of the mass to support goals which the latter are in no way involved in formulating.

Perhaps more importantly, the organizations in which people do participate have grown enormously in size in modern urban societies. Large-scale business, labor, government, religious, and professional organizations appear to dominate existence and characterize civilization. Such organizations themselves have come to approximate masses. The price of growing technological development and interdependence has been a lost sense of belonging and of concrete participation in organizational life. Wirth believed that the very future of democracy rested on the inventive ability of social scientists and planners to develop ways by which "effective contact" and "two-way communication" could be maintained between members and leaders of these giant structures.[91]

This task is especially problematic because of emerging trends in an increasingly urbanized world. In an essay dealing with the role of ideas and ideals in urban society, Wirth noted that the spread of literacy, formal political participation, and secularization generally had widened the audience for the marketplace of ideas. But, because the audience of politics has become a mass: "What decides which ideas will triumph is not their truth value, but the effectiveness with which they are presented."[92] Furthermore, the marketplace of ideas is increasingly under the risk of monopolistic domination by those in control of mass society's normative and intellectual production and distribution system. These may be state or private monopolists.

Nor did Wirth underestimate the extent to which irrational factors have the potential to shape mass tastes, mass movements, and even mass hysteria. He believed that, even in secular societies, factual evidence often takes a back seat to loyalty to one's group and to the need to manipulate ideas to fuel the actual tensions, rivalries, and conflicts that exist in the world. In this context, intellectuals and social planners can play an important role. For Wirth, their essential task is to call public attention to the hidden values and unstated assumptions articulated by "the creators, molders, and disseminators of ideas and ideals."[93] This task is easier in the realm of ideas, where scientific methods can be used to determine the correlation between advocated ideas and reality. Ideals, on the other hand, are more difficult to refute. What social scientists and planners can do is to determine the extent to which articulated ideals are compatible with the cultural values of the groups exposed to them. Additionally, they can discover and call attention to the interrelationships among various competing ideals and point out their contradictions and inconsistencies.

To perform this task well, planners, social scientists, and other intellectuals must become self-aware and self-critical. Once this is accomplished they will be well equipped to clarify their own and other elite messages, thereby rendering them more reliable, coherent, and internally consistent to the mass public.

For Wirth, the diffuse ideas and ideals that abound in the modern world will be more readily received if they have consequences which satisfy human needs. Particularly crucial human needs are the needs for "security, freedom, creativeness, self-realization, and social participation."[94] Harnessing ideas and ideals in the pursuit of human needs will be more likely if "knowledge elites" can avoid becoming the pawns of those power groups who merely seek to use symbols to manipulate public opinion and popular action in their own interests.

Despite these skeptical concerns about the domination of communication channels by commercial and vested-interest group elites, Louis Wirth believed that America was "on balance" a democratic society whose political elites seriously attempted to rule by persuasion and rational consensus building rather than by fraud or force. For Wirth, America in the 1940s had worked out pragmatic arrangements, including the Bill of Rights, contractual forms, bargaining, persuasion, and compromise, which placed limits on conflict and the struggle for domination or agreement. It was this very consensual renunciation of force that Wirth felt placed such a premium on the art of engineering public consent. This was also why he sought to preserve the integrity of the mass media from capture by demagogues and hucksters. He believed that in mass societies, the mass media comprised the only adequate vehicle to counteract social fragmentation and to build support for consensual public policy. He thus hoped to convert the mass media into the basic planning tool for communicating the information, "common understandings," and "citizen feedback" needed to plan rationally but democratically for the "community-as-a-whole."

CONCLUSION

Louis Wirth posited a theory of unplanned or evolutionary change. This theory held that the growing size, density, and heterogeneity of the urban environment would lead directly to a variety of changes in social life and human consciousness. He anticipated an emerging metropolitan "way of life" characterized by a decline in the social significance of family and kinship ties; the replacement of territorially based loyalties by interest group affiliations, and of primary by secondary forms of association; the gradual assimilation of ethnic groups; and the decline of the neighborhood as a significant social unit. As these informal social controls weakened, Wirth wished to see them replaced by a consensual political order based upon principles of rationality and scientific planning. To achieve this objective he was willing to assign important political functions to urban planners. His persistent fear of societal "disorganization" and his mistrust of political interest groups prompted him to advocate the replacement of politics by planning.

In the process, he revealed a lack of perspective concerning both the limitations of rational-comprehensive urban planning and the continuing vitality of urban neighborhoods. He also failed to recognize that community organization and political conflict are often the only means available to organize the interests of the lower strata of society into politics. Because planning is inherently a political process, this was no slight oversight.

Notes

1. Herbert Spencer, *The Evolution of Society* (Chicago: U. of Chicago Press, 1967); see also Jay Rumney, *Herbert Spencer's Sociology: A Study in the History of Social Theory* (New York: Atherton, 1966); Ferdinand Tonnies, *Fundamental Concepts of Sociology*, trans. C. P. Loomis (New York: American Book Co., 1940); and the early studies in the field of "human ecology." These early studies are summarized and reviewed in James A. Quinn, "Topical Summary of Current Literature on Human Ecology," *American Journal of Sociology*, 46 (September 1940), 191–226. See also Amos Hawley's classic formalization of ecological theory, *Human Ecology: A Theory of Community Structure* (New York: Ronald Press, 1950).
2. See Auguste Comte, *Auguste Comte and Positivism: The Essential Writings*, ed. Gertrud Lenzer (New York: Harper and Row, 1975); Robert M. MacIver, *On Community, Society and Power: Selected Writings*, ed. Leon Bramson (Chicago: U. of Chicago Press, 1977).

3. Louis Wirth, "The Scope and Problems of the Community" (1933), Louis Wirth, *On Cities and Social Life*, ed. Albert J. Reiss (Chicago: U. of Chicago Press, 1964), p. 166.

4. See Albert J. Reiss, "Introduction," Wirth, *On Cities and Social Life*, p. xix; see also Robert Park, "The Urban Community as a Spatial Pattern and a Moral Order," Ernest W. Burgess, ed., *The Urban Comunity* (Chicago: U. of Chicago Press, 1926).

5. The discipline of "human ecology" is concerned with the way in which people's social relationships are affected by their habitat, particularly by differences in their physical aggregation and spatial distribution, and with the ways in which human beings seek to cope with and/or reconstruct their physical environment. See Robert Park, "The City: Suggestions for the Investigation of Human Behavior in the City Environment," Park, *Human Communities* (New York: Free Press, 1915); and Louis Wirth, "Human Ecology," *American Journal of Sociology*, 50 (May 1945), 483–488, for elaboration of the perspective and methods of human ecology; see also the works by Hawley and Quinn cited above in n. 1.

6. Wirth, "World Community, World Society, and World Government," (1948), Wirth, *On Cities and Social Life*, p. 323.

7. Ibid., p. 328.

8. Wirth, "Human Ecology," p. 484.

9. Wirth, "The Scope and Problems of the Community," p. 168.

10. Wirth, "World Community, World Society, and World Government," p. 328.

11. Wirth derived these ideas from Ferdinand Tonnies, *Community and Society*, trans. C. P. Loomis (East Lansing, Mich.: Michigan State U. Press, 1956); Henry Sumner Maine, *Ancient Law* (London: John Murray, 1870); Emile Durkheim, *The Division of Labor in Society* (Glencoe, Ill.: Free Press, 1947); Charles Cooley, *Social Organization* (New York: Scribner's, 1902); and Robert Redfield, "The Folk Society," *American Journal of Sociology*, 3 (January 1947), 293–308.

12. Wirth, "World Community, World Society, and World Government," p. 329.

13. See Wirth, "The Scope and Problems of the Community," p. 169.

14. Ibid.

15. Ibid., p. 170.

16. The Chicago School of Sociology included such previously cited seminal theorists as Park and Burgess, as well as R. D. McKenzie. It also included a host of empirical researchers too numerous to mention. Representative works include Park, Burgess, and McKenzie, *The City* (Chicago: U. of Chicago Press, 1925); and Burgess, ed., *The Urban Community* (Chicago: U. of Chicago Press, 1926); for a discussion of the scope and impact of this school see Robert E. L. Faris, *Chicago Sociology: 1920–1932* (Chicago: U. of Chicago Press, 1970).

17. See Wirth, "Ideological Aspects of Social Disorganization," *American Sociological Review*, 5 (August 1940), 476.

18. Ibid., p. 479.

19. Ibid.

20. Ibid., p. 480.
21. Ibid., p. 482.
22. See Karl Mannheim, *Ideology and Utopia*, trans. Louis Wirth and Edward Shils (New York: Harcourt, Brace and World, 1936).
23. Wirth, "Social Interaction: The Problem of the Individual and the Group," *American Journal of Sociology*, 44 (May 1939), 968.
24. See my discussion of Simmel's concepts of urban reserve and the blasé attitude in chap. 3 below. See also Georg Simmel, "The Metropolis and Mental Life," Richard Sennett, ed., *Classic Essays on the Culture of Cities* (New York: Appleton-Century-Crofts, 1969), pp. 47–60.
25. See Robert Park, "Human Migration and the Marginal Man," Sennett, ed., *Classic Essays on the Culture of Cities*, pp. 131–142.
26. Wirth, "Consensus and Mass Communication," *American Sociological Review*, 13 (February 1958), 13.
27. See Don Martindale, "Prefatory Remarks: The Theory of the City," Max Weber, *The City*, trans. and ed. Don Martindale and Gertrud Neuwirth (New York: Free Press, 1958), pp. 38–42.
28. See Karen Horney, *Our Inner Conflicts: A Constructive Theory of Neurosis* (New York: Norton, 1945); Harry Stack Sullivan, *The Interpersonal Theory of Psychiatry* (New York: Norton, 1953); Sullivan, *The Fusion of Psychiatry and Social Science* (New York: Norton, 1964).
29. On the view that sheer technical complexity frustrates the basic instinct toward communal cooperation, see my discussion of Theodore Roszak's social thought in chap. 4 below. For the Freudian view that social life inherently frustrates universal instincts, regardless of differences in culture and social structure, see chap. 2 below.
30. See Wirth, "Social Interaction: The Problem of the Individual and the Group," p. 977.
31. Quoted in Reiss, "Introduction," Wirth, *On Cities and Social Life*, p. xvii.
32. The following discussion of organization, disorganization, and reorganization is based upon Wirth, "Ideological Aspects of Social Disorganization," pp. 474–476, and upon Reiss, "Introduction," Wirth, *On Cities and Social Life*, p. xxiii.
33. See especially Wirth, "The Scope and Problems of the Community," p. 175.
34. Wirth, "Urbanism as a Way of Life," *American Journal of Sociology*, 44 (July 1938), 9.
35. Ibid., p. 1.
36. See ibid., pp. 13–14, 16 for Wirth's discussion of these various formal controls.
37. Ibid., p. 14.
38. Ibid., p. 12.
39. Ibid.
40. Ibid., p. 13.
41. Ibid., p. 14; see also Simmel's discussion of the psychic responses to overstimulation and mental overload in chap. 3 below.
42. Ibid. p. 16.
43. Ibid.

44. Ibid., p. 15.
45. Ibid., p. 14.
46. Ibid., p. 16.
47. Ibid., p. 17.
48. Ibid.
49. Ibid., p. 22.
50. Ibid.
51. Ibid., p. 23.
52. Wirth, "Culture Conflict and Misconduct," *Social Forces,* 9 (June 1931), 485.
53. Ibid., p. 491.
54. Ibid., p. 488.
55. Ibid., p. 491.
56. Wirth, "Human Ecology," p. 487.
57. Wirth, "Preface," Mannheim, *Ideology and Utopia,* p. xxiii.
58. Ibid., p. xxvi.
59. Wirth, "Ideas and Ideals as Sources of Power in the Modern World" (1947), Wirth, *On Cities and Social Life,* p. 148.
60. Ibid., pp. 151–152.
61. Wirth, "The Scope and Problems of the Community," p. 170.
62. Wirth, "Localism, Regionalism, and Centralization," *American Journal of Sociology,* 44 (May 1939), 494. For a full discussion of Wirth's views on the planning role of human ecologists, see also Wirth, "Human Ecology," pp. 485–488.
63. Wirth, "Human Ecology," p. 485.
64. Ibid.
65. Wirth, "Localism, Regionalism, and Centralization," p. 495. The exegesis which follows in this section is based upon pp. 494–507 of this article.
66. See Adrienne Koch, *The Philosophy of Thomas Jefferson* (Gloucester, Mass.: Peter Smith, 1957); G. D. H. Cole, *Guild Socialism Restated* (London: Leonard Parsons, 1921); and Cole, *Social Theory* (London: Methuen, 1920).
67. Wirth, "Localism, Regionalism, and Centralization," p. 497, emphasis added.
68. Ibid., p. 503.
69. Ibid., 507.
70. The following section is based upon Wirth's "The Metropolitan Region as a Planning Unit" (1942), Wirth, *On Cities and Social Life,* pp. 304–318.
71. Ibid., p. 306.
72. Ibid., p. 311.
73. Ibid., p. 317.
74. Ibid., p. 313.
75. Ibid., p. 314.
76. See Wirth's classic book on Jewish neighborhood social organization, *The Ghetto* (Chicago: U. of Chicago Press, 1928).
77. Wirth, "The Scope and Problems of the Community," p. 176.
78. Ibid.
79. The remainder of this section is based upon Wirth's "The Limitations of Regionalism" (1951), Wirth, *On Cities and Social Life,* pp. 207–220.

80. Both of the above quotations are drawn from ibid., p. 215.
81. Wirth, "Localism, Regionalism, and Centralization," p. 508, emphasis added.
82. Ibid., p. 509, emphasis added.
83. Ibid.
84. Wirth, "Consensus and Mass Communication," p. 10.
85. Ibid., p. 11.
86. Ibid., pp. 4–5.
87. Ibid., p. 8.
88. See Reiss, "Introduction," Wirth, *On Cities and Social Life*, p. xxi.
89. Wirth, "Consensus and Mass Communication," p. 1.
90. Ibid., p. 3.
91. Ibid., p. 4.
92. Wirth, "Ideas and Ideals as Sources of Power in the Modern World," p. 152.
93. Ibid., p. 154.
94. Ibid., p. 155.

Chapter 2
Sigmund Freud
And the Dialectics
Of Nature and Culture

Henrik Ibsen and Fyodor Dostoevsky offer two markedly contrasting views on the effects of civilization on "natural man." Where Ibsen was a rationalist, but not a democrat, Dostoevsky was a populist democrat, but not a rationalist. In Ibsen's play *An Enemy of the People* the protagonist, Dr. Stockmann, defends his elitist preferences by attacking the theory that modern culture demoralizes. Seeking to demonstrate that those who have acquired advanced scientific knowledge are better equipped to rule than the common man, Stockmann declares: "[T]he theory that culture demoralizes is only an old falsehood that our forefathers believed in and we have inherited."[1] Stockmann hopes that "scientific progress" may some day rid society of the theory that assigns moral worth to primitive "natural man."

Fyodor Dostoevsky was perhaps the most forceful nineteenth-century critic of Ibsen's point of view. His characters often reflected his basic confidence in the simple virtues of the rural peasant, whose moral standards and basic goodness had become corrupted by urban life and detached scientific rationality. For example, in one of his moments of near despair, Dostoevsky's "underground man" has this to say about his garretlike urban existence: "What is it that civilization softens in us? Civilization only produces a greater variety of sensations in man . . . and through [this] development, man may even come to find enjoyment in bloodshed. Have you ever noticed that the subtlest slaughterers have always been the most civilized gentlemen?"[2]

Sigmund Freud shared Ibsen's confidence in scientific rationality and his elitist tendencies. Yet he also shared Dostoevsky's conviction that the principle function of advanced urban civilization was to rechannel natural instincts in subtly insidious ways. Freud's combination of elitism and mistrust of civilization produced a novel theory of modernization and consciousness. The radical individualism of Freud's ego psychology often has obscured an implicit model of "social health" and an incrementally reformist bent that can be gleaned from his social theoretic writings. Except for Herbert Marcuse,[3] who overinterprets this side of Freud's thought, few social theorists have chosen to mine either Freud's depth psychology or his more directly sociopolitical writings for insights into the contemporary urban condition.

Why then have I chosen to devote attention to Freud in a book that deals with urban social and planning theory? Because Freud generally is not treated as an "urban" social theorist, or as a "planning" theorist, it is necessary to state my rationale for including him in this work at the outset.

First, although not usually viewed as an "urban" social theorist, it is both appropriate and useful to consider him one. When Freud spoke of "civilization," he had in mind the process of "modernization" and the characteristics of urban life in the industrial capitalist cities of his own time. When he wrote his major works in social theory (1910–1930), modernization, technological development, and industrial capitalism were still largely urban phenomena. Throughout his works, Freud treats as indicators of "civilization" a variety of different early twentieth-century socioeconomic developments that originated or occurred almost exclusively in cities. These include advances in science and technology; increased human control over space, time, and nature; developments in mass transportation; the breakup of small town life and of kinship networks by geographic mobility; and the development of social communities into ever larger social wholes. Furthermore, the central hallmarks of "civilization" that Freud treats extensively—intellectual and scientific activity, cultural institutions, technological change, and large-scale formal social controls—were most fully developed in the large, industrial, capitalist urban settlements of Freud's time. It was from this early twentieth-century city life that Freud drew his most vivid examples of the ways he believed "civilization" alienated the "natural personality" from basic instinctual needs and drives.

Secondly, Freud used the concepts "civilization" and "culture" interchangeably to designate a cultural system that he contrasted to both primitive social life and the nature of presocial people. This is the same way that Louis Wirth used the concept "urbanism" to designate the cultural system that he assumed to be the by-product of dense and heterogeneous existence in large cities. It is also consistent with the contrast between the "natural" personality and the "urban" life style found in the works of Georg Simmel and Theodore Roszak.[4] Freud's usage is consistent as well with the interchangeable usage of "civilization" and "urban life" found in the writings of other contemporary social theorists.[5] Conceptually then, Freud's "civilization" is a condensation symbol, a metaphoric way of communicating. Instead of referring to a specific set of referents, it condenses a whole host of symbolic meanings. It thus serves the purpose in Freud's thought that "urbanism" does for Wirth, "metropolitan life" for Simmel, "urban technocracy" for Roszak, and the "suburban fortress" for Richard Sennett.[6]

This similarity suggests a third reason why I discuss Freud. The form of grand theoretical speculation that he employs offers a useful contrast model, at several different levels of analysis, with the other theorists treated herein. At the analytical level, all five theorists posit an underlying theory of human nature and basic needs (a state of nature) that is disrupted by modern (urban, or in Sennett's case, city-suburban) conditions of life. These conditions produce alienation from an essential human nature. The alienation must be addressed by some combination of individual coping mechanisms (a therapeutic program) and environmental reconstruction (politics and planning). At the epistemological level, Freud offers other useful contrasts. His theory is dialectical rather than linear. Dialectical logic thrives on the exposition of phenomenal contradictions rather than upon the comprehension of historical regularities and continuities. It treats "contradictions" as normal and compatibilities as the deviations from normality to be explained. At this level, Freud's epistemology is similar to that of Georg Simmel (or, for that matter, of Karl Marx), but quite distinct from the linear, deductive theory of Louis Wirth. Finally, at the normative level, Freud's basic attitudes and values toward modern urban life, work, science and technology, social groups, political and social conflict and cooperation, political action, and planned environmental reconstruction provide numerous opportunities for instructive contrast with more purely social and planning theory.

These three reasons for analyzing Freud are supplemented by the fact that Freudian thought has had a highly significant, if not always immediately perceived, influence on the way in which "urban social problems" are defined and addressed. Most obviously, Freudian thought has directly influenced the activities that are considered "planning" and "social policy analysis" in the fields of social work, mental health, and family planning. In these fields, Freud's emphasis on "adjustment therapy" is still highly influential. In my view, many social service professionals who labor in these vineyards (as well as many of their clients) have been too quick to treat systemic defects by individual therapy. Starting from the inner psychodynamics of Freudian theory, they have held the individual responsible for symptoms engendered by structural stress and have counseled resignation and adjustment to social conditions that are neither inevitable nor universal, but are historically specific developments, subject to human manipulation and control. Such practitioners and their clients may be more aware of Freud's psychoanalytic formulations than of his often quite ambivalent attitude toward "adjustment," as reflected in his more social theoretic works. It is to this audience that my review of Freud's critique of "civilization" in this chapter and my critique of Freud in chapter five are addressed.

Perhaps less obviously, Freud's skeptical tone, his emphasis on caution, prudence, and calculation, his call for gradual "mutual adjustment" of social and political differences, and his fears concerning the potentially destabilizing effects of comprehensive social change have provided ammunition for "incrementalist" critics of rational-comprehensive planning.[7] Like the incrementalists, Freud cautions those who would alter existing institutions to proceed prudentially, in a piecemeal fashion, and never to expect too much. It is to incrementalist thinkers that I direct my critique of the Freudian model of "problem solving" in chapter five and argue that Freud's purportedly universal theory of human nature is both time and culture bound. It fails to transcend the fictional model of "homo economicus" that proved so useful to nineteenth-century liberal-capitalist doctrine.

Finally, I have chosen Freud, because, despite the inadequacies of his overall theoretical prespective and often pernicious influence of his theory on social planning and policy analysis, he did offer some insightful observations often overlooked by those who, like myself, reject his basic assumptions about the origins of human misery. Those who dismiss Freud in toto because of his psychobiological determinism, his penchant for elitist political forms, or his reactionary attitudes toward women fail to benefit from his insights about such matters as the pervasiveness of repressive social forms, the possibilities for developing critical self-consciousness, and the centrality of both work and play to human development. It is for the skeptical and the critical spirit that I highlight these features of Freud's critique of contemporary "civilization."

Before turning to this critique, I first examine the theoretical structure of Freud's depth psychology by briefly presenting the components of a simplified Freudian model of human personality to elucidate his diagnosis of the human condition in modern urban civilization. Freud's prescriptions for the problematic conditions he diagnosed form the basis of the third part of this chapter. In Freud's case this basic question may be framed as follows: *"What is to be done to increase the individual ego's capacity to calculatively extract pleasure from the environment, while still maintaining society's ability to curb aggressive behavior?"*

THE FREUDIAN MODEL OF PERSONALITY

In Freudian psychology the mind comprises three levels of consciousness: the unconscious, the preconscious, and the conscious. The *ego,* or "self," resides at the level of consciousness, where it functions as "the *point of contact* between the individual and his environment."[8] At both the conscious and the preconscious levels, the ego also serves as the mediator between the demands of reality and the deep-seated instinctual drives buried in that part of the unconscious which Freud termed the *id*.[9] The ego is the calculative faculty of the psyche. It considers information from the environment and calculates the probable risks and satisfactions of various lines of conduct in light of past experiences, socially derived and internalized norms, and basic instinctual drives. In performing this function the ego is a bridge between environment and psychic demands.

The level of preconsciousness stands between consciousness and unconsciousness.[10] The preconscious contains latent psychic contents. These can penetrate into consciousness once they have passed through a mechanism that Freud termed the "censor," a repressive psychic mechanism[11] between the unconscious and the preconscious. It protects the ego from overstimulation by unrealistic, infantile, erotic wishes, which Freud termed the "oceanic feeling." Freud believed that the feeling of being at one with the environment was tantamount to a "regressive" pattern of ego development.

Freud's treatment of "mature" ego functioning is at the heart of the radical individualism of his social thought. The mature ego maintains a sharp line between the "self" and external reality, including social reality. During the state of being in love, as well as during many states deemed "pathological," Freud held that the boundary between the ego and the external world becomes blurred and uncertain. In the latter instances, a person's own body or thoughts, perceptions, and feelings may appear alien; the pathological individual also sometimes attributes to the external world characteristics that emanate from the thoughts and feelings of the ego.

As in the case of love and pathology, the mentality of the infant also does not clearly distinguish the ego from the external world. However, the infant gradually learns to distinguish those feelings which are internally derived, and thus are constantly available to him, from those sources of stimulation outside the ego. In the latter case, a tendency arises to avoid those objects which cause displeasure. For Freud these "avoidance reactions" constitute the first steps toward the introduction into the psyche of the *reality principle,* whose operation is essential to future personality development. But in some individuals the primordial ego-feeling, which appears as a sense of limitlessness and communion with the external world, continues to exist side by side with the mature differentiating ego. This residue of childhood experience is the source of the "oceanic feeling" which "regression" can bring to the forefront of consciousness.[12]

By "protecting" consciousness from unrealistic wishes for perfect pleasure and complete happiness, the censor enables the ego to calculate probable risks and satisfactions to be derived from the external world more realistically, thereby protecting the organism from abandonment to the unregulated pursuit of pleasure. The pleasure principle is never satiated. Without the censor it may "burn out" the organism. Being blind to threats arising from the environment, it may lead to self-destruction if left unregulated.[13]

The deepest level of mental life in Freudian thought is the unconscious. The unconscious is the seat of the two basic instinctual drives, the erotic or libidinal instinct, which Freud termed *eros,* and the aggressive or death instinct, which he termed *thanatos.* These drives reside in the id part of the unconscious. In addition to the id, the unconscious also includes the internalized mores and taboos of civilization. These moral standards and prohibitions reside in a part of the unconscious Freud called the *superego.* Fear of punishment and guilt are the two basic driving forces of the superego. The psychic materials of the id and superego are repressed from consciousness but remain active at the unconscious level. They are the source of an inner dialectical struggle which can lead to neuroses.[14]

Freud held that this unconscious struggle between nature and culture is a struggle between id drives and superego commands. The primordial instincts are locked in a dialectical struggle with the internalized regulations of advanced civilization. In addition to this source of inner turmoil, Freud held that the two basic classes of instincts— love and death—themselves existed in a dialectical tension within the id. The erotic of sexual instinct was at heart a drive for unity and communion with others. In contrast, the death instinct expressed the individual's desire to dissolve such connections and return to an anxiety-free, inorganic state of rest.

Eros includes the uninhibited sexual instinct per se, as well as "sublimated" instinctual impulses toward other "objects" of erotic attraction. In Freudian theory, a "sublimation" is a displacement of sexual energy onto higher objects. The concept *libido* is used by Freud to denote the amount of psychic energy absorbed by these erotic instincts. Libido is defined as a variable force that can serve as a measure of the processes and transformations taking place in the realm of sexual excitation. It is a quantity of the energy of all those instincts subsumed under the concept eros.[15]

The death instinct is expressed in sadism, hate, and aggression. It is partially directed toward the external world in the form of aggressiveness and destructiveness, partially directed inward, where it furnishes the superego with much of the psychic energy needed to discipline the id. The strength and intensity of the death instinct derive from its ability to provide the individual with a high degree of narcissistic pleasure, "owing to its presenting the ego with a fulfillment of the latter's old wishes for omnipotence."[16] When moderated or "aim-inhibited," this instinct can be directed outward to satisfy people's vital needs and insure their control over nature. Yet because it is a primordial, self-subsisting, instinctual disposition to destructiveness, it represents the chief threat to civilized existence within Freud's model of personality. Turning aggression outward runs the risk of unleashing destructive behavior, violence, and disorder.

For Freud, "civilization is a process in the service of eros, whose purpose is to combine single human individuals and after that families, then races, peoples, and nations, into one great unity, the unity of mankind."[17] But to recruit libidinal energy for these purposes, civilization requires that erotic libido be transformed by sublimation into "aim-inhibited," ego-directed libido. Since in Freud's view psychic energy is a fixed sum, energy transformed in this way is denied sexual expression. For Freud, this "abandonment of sexual aims" or "desexualization" is one of the chief prices the individual must pay to live in modern urban civilization.[18] The price is painful because sexual love is infinitely more intense and complete than aim-inhibited love.

To insure that sufficient libidinal energy is desexualized so that it may be devoted to building the institutions of urban civilization, the superego must function as the conscience of the Freudian personality. It must recruit the ego to direct and control the pleasure principle, as well as the death instinct, which threatens the dissolution of civilized existence. The superego's moral imperatives are derived from the values, expectations, and demands of the family and other sources of authority in the larger community. Initially, the superego functions externally as the child imitates the actions of external authority figures out of fear of punishment or loss of love. Eventually, external norms are internalized at the unconscious level as personal moral standards. The internalized superego is a harsh taskmaster because the deeply repressed unconscious wishes and instincts cannot be hidden from its view. It demands renunciation of wishes and instincts as well as actions. Its actions are necessary to the development of modern civilization, but they also impose a heavy burden of guilt and inner turmoil on the individual psyche.

In the context of this struggle among ego, id, and superego, the mentally healthy prototype of the Freudian model of personality is the calculating egoist who has developed a sufficiently strong ego to (a) objectively perceive reality, (b) efficiently steer a life course which will enable the extraction of as much pleasure as possible from the external world, (c) constructively channel aggressiveness into taming the environment without destroying it, (d) avoid unnecessary risks to the preservation of the organism and the species, and (e) avoid the pitfalls created by an overharsh superego. At best, the Freudian personality is a rational economizer of psychic energy that chooses when, where, and how to best channel its instincts. At worst, it is driven to self-destruction by inner turmoil or the tyranny of the instincts.

Freudian theory thus posits a model of the personality as a never fully socialized individual organism, whose inner drives always do battle with the socially defined expectations thrust upon it by the institutions of urban civilization. As Dennis Wrong has noted, Freud's view of the superego inappropriately has become a model for the social science concept of internalized social norms. According to the concept of internalization, individuals gradually learn to accept as their own norms which initially are externally imposed by various social structures. However, through usage the very thrust of Freudian theory—the dialectical tension between powerful inner impulses and superego controls—has been lost. In modern socialization theory, the individual is a conformist who acquires habits of compliance to social norms. Incompatible norms produce role conflict and ambiguity; compatible norms produce joy in conformity. This conceptualization, although compatible with Wirthian notions of normative conflict and consensus, ignores the heart of Freud's view of the individual's dynamic inner urge to deviate from social norms. For Wirth, deviance is a result of conflict among divergent subcultures. Freud suggests a far more radically individualistic picture of the human condition and a far less socialized view of human nature. For Freud, inner impulses, buried beneath the level of conscious thought, await the conditions for their release and fulfillment. To stabilize and pacify these drives, society imposes regulatory mechanisms that shape the superego, or conscience. When social norms become internalized, they join inner drives that already inhere in human nature, there to do continuous battle to shape the conscious behavior of the individual.[19]

THE DISCONTENTS OF URBAN CIVILIZATION

What are the basic features of the civilization that people have come both to rely on and to doubt in growing numbers? In Freudian social theory, civilization includes all the achievements and regulations that people have established to set themselves apart from other animals, protect themselves against nature, adjust their mutual relations, and regulate the distribution of material wealth.[20]

The achievements of civilized existence include all those endeavors that foster higher mental activities: intellectual and scientific development, artistic expression, and those cultural activities that elevate the role of ideas in human life. The contributions of religious systems, philosophy, and the ideals of individual perfection, communal achievement, and humanitarianism are among the hallmarks of civilization. The demands imposed by these endeavors lead to further achievements and to further demands that psychic energy be appropriated for civilized purposes. But to obtain this allocation of psychic energy, as well as to insure material security, civilized forms of social existence impose compelling regulations upon the individual. These regulations restrict sexual expression, contain the primordial aggressive instinct, and regulate the distribution of social goods.

Dimensions of Urban Civilization

Freud considers the nature and consequences of the various features of modern urban civilization as they are exhibited in human communities. These features include advanced technology, the displacement of spontaneity by order, instinctual sublimation, formal political and social regulations upon individual freedom of action, the repression of sexuality, and the control of aggressive behavior. Let us consider these features in turn.

Technological development. The use of tools represents a perfecting by humanity of sensory and motor organs, and thereby enhances the power of human will over time, space, and nature. Motor power, transportation innovations, eye glasses, the telescope and microscope, the camera, the telephone, and the like all serve these purposes. They are part of the contemporary urban individual's cultural acquisition. Through them the urban citizen becomes a kind of prosthetic god, yet does not feel happy with this newly acquired omnipotence. As though seeking to repudiate these utilitarian achievements, "we welcome it as a sign of civilization . . . if we see people directing their care to what has no practical value whatever, to what is useless . . . to reverence [of] beauty."[21]

Compulsive cleanliness and order. Dirt comes to be defined as the antithesis of civilization. Members of modern urban civilization are appalled to think that in Shakespeare's time a big dung heap graced the lawn of his father's house. We use soap to remove all natural body odors and with them the sexual satisfaction that animals still derive from the sense of smell.

We are even more compulsive in demanding order than in our desire for cleanliness. Yet Freud held that order is no more than the opposite of spontaneity: "Order is a kind of compulsion to repeat which, when a regulation has been laid down once and for all, decides when, where, and how a thing shall be done, so that in every similar circumstance one is spared [the unpleasantness of] hesitation and indecision."[22] Order may be useful for efficiently conserving psychic forces, but it robs life of spontaneous drive fulfillment. Order is part of the tragedy of modern urban culture; it brings frustration, but it cannot be done without.

Civilization eventually brings about major changes in our instinctual dispositions, the fulfillment of which is "the economic task of our lives."[23] Some of our instincts are "used up" in a manner which appears in the individual as a character trait. Initial anal eroticism, for example, is changed in the course of civilized socialization into a penchant for parsimony, order, and cleanliness.

Sublimation of the instincts. Art, science, and intellectual development—the hallmarks of modern urban life—are in Freud's view mere by-products of sublimated instinctual energy. Advanced civilization is built upon the renunciation of instincts. Since psychic energy, like financial savings, is a fixed sum, he held that energy "spent" on intellectual and social development is of necessity unavailable for instinctual gratification.

Regulation of social and political relationships. Social and political relationships include all those relations which impose role expectations on the individual, such as neighbor, friend, sexual "object," family member, and citizen. If role expectations and constraints were not imposed, in Freud's view, social and political relationships would be subject to the individual's arbitrary will; stronger psychological beings would define them in terms of their own instinctual impulses and material interests. Thus, "[t]he replacement of the power of the individual by the power of community constitutes the decisive step in civilization."[24] Because Freud was such a radical individualist, he held that the community's "power" consists of a restriction of each member's power to "extract satisfactions" from interpersonal relationships, rather than an extension of all members' power to live cooperatively.

Freud held that through cultural development, the next step in the regulation of social and political life consists in making law the expression of ever more numerous collectivities of people. Like the classical German urban social theorists, Freud envisaged informal rules among castes, classes, and racial and status groups being replaced by formal regulations applying to all. The purpose of this universalistic inclusiveness is to leave no one to the whim of brute force.

Hence, in the Freudian view, no civilization can provide full individual liberty. Individual autonomy was greatest in the "state of nature," where it had little value since it could be defended only by the strongest. Civilization develops by progressively imposing restrictions on individual freedom of action. But as civilization develops, the relationship between eros and civilization becomes contradictory. This contradiction expresses itself first as a tension between family role claims and larger community role claims upon the individual. Close-knit families tend to cut themselves off from contact and communication with others. The young adult is torn between family expectations and larger social demands. Puberty and initiation rites become necessary to enable the individual to detach from the family. Similar tensions are experienced as a result of cross-pressures engendered by trying simultaneously to fulfill the roles that worker, mate, and parent impose upon individuals. Acting out any social role entails the withdrawal of psychic energy from other pursuits.

Repression of sexuality. Freud conceded that the economic structure of a society might influence the amount of personal freedom allowed, but he believed that all socioeconomic systems required some measure of instinctual renunciation. This is because any developed civilization must expropriate large amounts of psychic energy for its own purposes. In his view, such energy must be withdrawn from sexuality. Freud's basic argument proceeds along the following lines: Civilization expropriates sexuality and then, fearing revolt by the suppressed elements, engages in additional precautionary measures. Conventional mores define certain objects of sexual expression as taboo, certain modes of sexuality as perversions, thereby disregarding individually acquired and innate dissimilarities in sexual tastes. Many are thus denied satisfying sexual enjoyment which those of more conventional tastes are allowed to experience. Yet even heterosexual genital love is restricted by the institution of monogamous marriage. To these prohibitions only the weak have fully submitted; those of stronger will have either violated the social norms or complied only because of the compensating measure of security obtained thereby.

Civilization demands other sacrifices. Even monogamous marriages threaten civilization when truly erotically based. It is possible to conceive of a "community" consisting of erotically linked dyads, each self-sufficient. "When a love relationship is at its height there is no room left for any interest in the environment."[25] If this state of affairs were allowed to persist, the only ties linking people to their environment would be common work and common interests (e.g., survival, mastery over nature). But these bonds of "necessity" are insufficiently intense to motivate regular participation in community life. Hence it becomes necessary to obtain the "withdrawal" of psychic energy from even this now quite restricted form of sexual expression.

The ideals of friendship, neighborliness, and love of humanity are introduced by the institutional elites of civilization. Freud treats these values as purely instrumental rather than intrinsic. Their aim is to inhibit the dyadic erotic relationship by "binding the members of the community together in a libidinal way."[26] Friendship, neighborliness, and love of humanity have in common the building of psychic identifications. In Freudian theory, such identifications withdraw psychic energy from sexuality. What others, like Theodore Roszak, might term spiritual ties, Freud, the radical individualist, dismisses as useful fictions. For instance, in his view, the social norm "Love thy neighbor as thyself" engenders friendship and other ties which are valuable not in and of themselves, but only because they serve to repress aggressive instincts.

Control of aggression.   The political implications of Freud's theoretical formulation of the individual as at heart a "savage beast" are numerous. In Freudian social theory, because aggression is instinctual rather than environmentally determined, all contemporary social systems are incessantly threatened with disintegration. Because instincts are stronger than rational interests, methods are employed by the elites of society to "incite people into identifications and aim-inhibited relations of love."[27] But these symbolic appeals are unable to check the more subtle expressions of exploitative human aggression. In Freud's view, the growing awareness with age of these more subtle transgressions is likely to extinguish any individual's youthful idealism.

The Marxian perception of human nature is that people are basically good and well disposed toward each other, but are corrupted by capitalist institutions into ill will, hostility, and competitiveness.[28] This view holds that if private property were abolished, and through income redistribution all basic material needs could be satisfied, none would have reason to regard anyone else as an enemy, and human aggression would disappear.

Surprisingly, Freud does not quarrel with this view on economic or ethical grounds. He concedes that inequalities of wealth do lead to misery and exploitation. Indeed, in a footnote in *Civilization and Its Discontents* he goes so far as to say: "Anyone who has tasted the miseries of poverty in his own youth and has experienced the indifference and arrogance of the well to do, should be safe from the suspicion of having no understanding or good will towards endeavors to fight against the inequality of wealth among men and all that it leads to."[29] However, on psychological grounds, Freud argues that even if the abolition of private property were to deprive some individuals of their increased power to exploit others, this would deny the human love of aggression only one of its major instruments.

In Freud's analysis, aggressiveness existed prior to the creation of private property relations, reigning very nearly supreme in primitive times when property itself was very limited. Thus he held that if denied an outlet in property relations, the aggressive instinct would still emerge in sexual relationships, relations among groups, peoples, and nations, and in scapegoating of all varieties. Because of these beliefs, he held that contemporary civilization must impose severe restrictions on the aggressive instinct, even if the price were unhappiness.

The Origin and Development of Unhappiness in Civilization

According to Freud, communal existence has a twofold origin. The compulsion to work is forced upon us by external necessity—the need to survive. The erotic urge also has encouraged communal existence. It has led to coupling, thence to the development of the primitive family, the power of whose head originally was unrestricted. The desire of bands of brothers to overcome this absolute power of the patriarch led to the slaying of the primal father as the first collective act of civilization. But this act was an act of violent aggression. It opened up the possibility of a war of each against all. For Freud, the next step in the development of civilization was an imposition of social controls upon the basic instincts. "The foundation of social institutions was based on the realization that a desperate act of self-denial was required if humanity was not to perish utterly in a strife of brother against brother."[30] This awareness, in the form of the incest taboo, was the primordial act of self-discipline and self-denial upon which the further development of civilization rested.

Thus from eros and anake—love and necessity—civilization was born. Its subsequent development rested on the power of self-denial. The cooperation of these powers—love, necessity, and self-denial—has made it possible for people to live together in increasingly larger social communities. But Freud held that this very combination of forces in civilized life has produced widespread unhappiness.

The unhappiness of civilized urban existence is a function of four conditions of life: (1) the finiteness of psychic energy, meaning that human energy can be expropriated for the demands of civilization only at the price of instinctual frustration; (2) the unpleasant work required to build contemporary civilization; (3) the diminished intensity and completeness of the pleasures that remain available in diluted form within civilization; and (4) the melancholic longing for a more primitive mode of existence, which is based on illusions about the nature of the past.

Freud held that within contemporary civilization we can never obtain all we desire. We are confronted by the finiteness of our own psychic energy and by the power of the reality principle. The pursuit of happiness in civilization becomes a problem of "the economics" of the libido. Because psychic energy is finite, it can be appropriated for the labors of civilization "only by deflecting the instincts from their material goal of perfect pleasure."[31] In searching for satisfactions that maximize pleasure while minimizing risk and pain, each person must find his or her own best route to reconciliation with the inevitable frustration of civilized urban existence. The predominantly erotic personality will seek to gain as much satisfaction as possible from emotional relationships with other people in the world as it is; the narcissist will make the self as independent from the external world as possible, obtaining compensatory satisfactions in the self-sufficient realm of inner mental processes; the "person of action," who feels capable of altering the world, "will never give up the external world on which he can try out his strength."[32]

Yet Freud believed that to rely exclusively on one technique of living as an adequate pattern of adaptation to contemporary civilization exposes the individual to danger. Any choice pushed to the extreme may prove disappointing. Since the success of any coping mechanism is never certain, it is radically imprudent to expect too much from any single channel. Or as Freud put it in an analogy that suggests the nineteenth-century capitalist origins of his purportedly general theory: "Just as a cautious businessman avoids tying up all his capital in one concern, so perhaps, worldly wisdom will advise us not to look for the whole of our satisfaction from a single aspiration."[33] Freud tells us to follow our basic personality predispositions, but to proceed cautiously, and never to expect too much.

Work, in particular, plays a key role in the Freudian quest for a satisfactory "economics of the libido." Freud held that work is the most effective technique for attaching the individual firmly to the reality principle. Work provides a secure anchor in a portion of reality and a well-defined role in the social community. It offers the possibility of displacing a large measure of libidinal energy. Aggressive, narcissistic, and even erotic impulses are displaced onto work itself and onto the relationships which the social structure of work life provides. This function lends work a value as important as its role in preserving and justifying one's existence in society.

Work, however, varies in its ability to perform this crucial function. Its effectiveness depends on whether it is creative, challenging, and voluntarily chosen, or intellectually and emotionally undemanding and merely undertaken in order to survive. To wit:

> Professional activity is a source of special satisfaction if it is a freely chosen one—if . . . by means of sublimation, it makes possible the use of existing

inclinations, or persisting or constitutionally reinforced instinctual impulses. And yet . . . the *great majority of people work only under the stress of necessity,* and this natural human aversion to work raises most difficult social problems.[34]

But even the higher order of satisfactions derived from professional work, art, science, and the like can be pursued only if psychic energy is rechanneled or "sublimated" from the pursuit of pure instinctual fulfillment to the pursuit of civilized aims. Sublimation of the instincts enables people to refocus instinctual aims onto nonsexual or nonaggressive objects. This prevents the instincts from encountering frustrations from the external world. Psychic energy is shifted to objects and purposes which are socially legitimate.

Happiness is defined by Freud as the sudden satisfaction of dammed up basic needs. As such it can be experienced only episodically. Prolonged pleasurable situations produce only mild contentment. "We are so made that we can derive intense enjoyment only from a contrast and very little from a state of things."[35] Thus our own internal makeup requires sharp contrasts in order to experience intense pleasure. Even before we encounter the frustrations of civilized life, our own nature restricts our capacity to experience pleasure by limiting its frequency. But civilized life more profoundly insures unhappiness by limiting the intensity and completeness of pleasurable satisfactions.

The three basic sources of unhappiness in Freudian thought are (1) our own body, which is doomed to degeneration, and thus produces anxiety; (2) the external, natural world, which introduces the reality principle as a source of frustration; and (3) the inadequacy of our social relations in the family, state, and society, which may be the most painful of all sources of suffering. To cope with the intensity of these sufferings, people tend to moderate their claims. They lower their expectations for happiness within contemporary civilization. In this way the pleasure principle, when confronted with obstacles, becomes tempered by the more moderate reality principle. Merely escaping unhappiness, through *deflection, substitution,* or *intoxication,* becomes a chief goal of civilized existence.

For instance, voluntary social isolation protects against the suffering engendered by human relationships. In Freud's view, a more common and more satisfactory alternative is to "become a member of the human community," constructively using the power of science to tame nature and render it subservient to human will. Yet too many find this route too burdensome and turn instead to attempts to desensitize themselves to suffering. Intoxication, yoga, and mysticism are prime examples. These may temporarily or permanently kill the instincts. Intoxicants make us incapable of receiving unpleasurable impulses.

Yoga and mysticism allow us to achieve only the mild happiness of quietude.

Such taming of the instincts, as well as all instinctual renunciations achieved by the mature superego, profoundly dilute human happiness:

> The feeling of happiness derived from the satisfaction of a wild instinctual impulse untamed by the ego [through its agent the superego] is incomparably more intense than that derived from sating an instinct that has been tamed.[36]

Art, science, work, and the mastery of nature thus absorb large quantities of displaced psychic energy which otherwise might be externalized in frustrating ways or turned in against the self. However, the satisfaction afforded by these civilized displacement channels is tame and incomplete when compared to the gratification of purely instinctual impulses.

Civilization breeds further unhappiness by frustrating our sublimated aspiration for human fellowship. The reality of day to day civilized existence only serves to underline the "inadequacy of the relations which adjust the mutual relationships of human beings in the family, the state, and society."[37] Social life engenders even more unhappiness than the natural world and the limitations of the human body. Physical nature and human decay appear inevitable. People find it possible to reconcile themselves to renunciations necessitated by nature. In contrast, the social sources of suffering appear to be something well within the realm of human control. Despite our very limited success in this respect, "we cannot see why the regulations made by ourselves should not . . . be a protection and benefit for every one of us."[38]

In view of our lack of success in building stable communal order, we eventually entertain the possibility that our civilized institutions are in large measure responsible for our miserable state. Modern urban civilization appears as such a shackle that even a return to primitive conditions becomes an appealing alternative.

How has this hostility to modern urban civilization developed? In Freud's view, historical events lend fuel to this longing for a return to the primitive. First, voyages of discovery lead to contact with simple, apparently anxiety free cultures of primitive peoples. This, in turn, leads to a nostalgia for a return to "nature." Secondly, the public increasingly is aware that people's emotional problems largely derive from their inability to tolerate the extensive instinctual frustration which modern urban society imposes in order to achieve its cultural ideals. From the latter proposition many infer that a reduction or abolition of such demands would expand the possibilities for happiness. Freud held that this nostalgic rejection of civilized existence is based on a mistaken assumption that the carefree life of primitive peoples was due to relatively simple cultural demands. In Freud's view, it was due to the relative ease with which their basic wants were satisfied by bounteous natural conditions.[39]

In addition to these two proximate causes, Freud believed that the romantic rejection of contemporary urban civilization stems from an understandable disappointment and disillusionment with natural science and technology in the twentieth century. Increased control over space, time, and nature—indeed the virtual subjugation of the latter after many centuries of domination—has not been followed by a noticeable increase in the amount of pleasurable satisfactions that people experience in life.

Disappointment is inevitable since control over nature is not the sole precondition of human happiness. Yet the fact that scientific progress has not helped people to experience happiness adds a nostalgia for the past to the repertoire of human dissatisfactions. The limited satisfactions that science and technology do provide come to be viewed as "cheap enjoyments." Nostalgic social critics bemoan the unintended consequences of modern urban civilization:

> If there had been no railway to conquer distances, my child would never have left his native town and I should need no telephone to hear his voice. If travelling across the ocean by ship had not been introduced, my friend would not have embarked on his sea-voyage and I should not need a cable to relieve my anxiety about him; what is the use of reducing infant mortality when it is precisely that reduction which imposes the greatest restraint on us in the begetting of children . . . And finally what good to us is a long life if it is difficult and barren of joys, and if it is so full of misery that we can only welcome death as a deliverer?[40]

Because Freud defines happiness in terms of the calculating ego's subjectively extracting pleasure from the environment, he argues that such nostalgia is poorly grounded. In his view, it is impossible for people to entirely "put themselves in anyone else's shoes," particularly persons from earlier or more primitive cultures. From this individualistic assumption, it follows that we can never with certainty know to what extent people of earlier periods felt happiness. Nor can we know the role that their relatively more simple cultural conditions played in their feelings. To place ourselves, at our present level of cultural development, with our uniquely developed patterns of adaptation, into earlier peoples' joys and troubles is to ignore wide variations in subjective sensibility. Nostalgia for the past is bound to rest on a foundation of illusions.

What then, in a nutshell, is Freud's view of the human consequences of urban civilization? On the one hand, the customary inhibitions and externally imposed social controls characterizing modern urban life dilute the intensity of individual pleasure derived from the gratification of deep-seated instinctual impulses. Tamed instincts may protect the individual from vulnerability to external aggression or from emotional abandonment by one to whom he or she is fully committed in an act of love; but in the process they also render life experiences flat and stand in the way of necessary instinctual release.

To compensate for this loss of instinctual fulfillment, psychic energy can be displaced onto a variety of nonsexual objects or channeled into contributions to the development of modern society through "sublimation." In this way instinctual energy is released that otherwise would be stored as residual frustration. Yet the satisfactions derived from "sublimation" (e.g., work, artistic creativity, scientific efforts) are still far less intense than would be the full gratification of our primary impulses.

For Freud, "presocial people" knew no such restrictions on the possibilities of spontaneous instinctual satisfaction, nor did they have need of sublimations. To achieve the benefits of mutual self-protection and to reap the plenitudes derived from taming the power of nature, people entered into social community. The essence of social community for Freud was the voluntary renunciation by each community member of some of the possibilities for instinctual satisfaction in order to master nature, protect against aggression, and prosper economically.

Thus through the twin mechanisms of voluntary self-restriction and sublimation, people take their first steps as civilized beings. Metaphorically, they renounce their sense of smell, assume an upright carriage, and go forth able to see a more distant horizon. But in so doing they impoverish their instinctual life.

Unlike conventional social contract theorists, Freud acknowledged the full price to be paid for becoming civilized. Slightly less pessimistic than Thomas Hobbes,[41] Freud nonetheless shares the Hobbesian perception of civilized life as fraught with necessary restrictions on the basic impulses of the presocial individual. Unlike Hobbes, Freud was aware that without compensatory substitutive satisfactions, life under such a repressive Leviathan state would become unbearable and revolution inevitable.

Yet because of his basic fear of the consequences of the fully liberated id, which is said to contain aggressive as well as erotic drives, Freud is radically unwilling to relinquish social controls on individual behavior. Since aggression can be channeled easily into social life, "when the mental counter-forces which ordinarily inhibit it are out of action, it . . . manifests itself spontaneously and reveals man as a savage beast. . . ."[42] In consequence of this perpetual danger, social cohesion must be maintained by social institutions that provide externally imposed social controls. These controls are eventually internalized as norms of the mature superego.

The Civilizing Role of Guilt

The original personality in Freud's view remains untamed by civilization. It manifests itself in a hostility to the forms and demands of urban civilization and occasionally even to civilization per se. The task of reconciling the claims of the individual to happiness with the cultural claims of the group falls upon humanity as perhaps its most imposing struggle. An individual's ultimate fate hinges upon "whether such an accommodation can be reached by means of some particular form of civilization or whether this conflict is irreconcilable."[43]

Such an accommodation is made more difficult because civilization in general employs the superego to inhibit aggressiveness. Through the superego, aggression is internalized and directed back upon the self. The superego puts into action against the ego the same harsh aggressiveness that the ego seeks to satisfy on other external objects. The tension between superego and ego expresses itself first as a need for punishment brought on by a sense of guilt. Through guilt, the death instinct is weakened and disarmed.

But why should a person submit to the influence of social norms? Why should we feel guilty engaging in thoughts and acts which may well be beneficial and enjoyable to the ego? Initially it is because of the need for love rooted in our helplessness and dependence on others. This need can best be described as a fear of the loss of love. Lost love may lead to a number of painful consequences—withdrawal of protection, punishment, the social anxiety brought on by loss of approbation from significant others. When such motives for obedience to authority remain in the forefront, external social controls are only as effective as the detection mechanisms that society has at its disposal. That is, people constrained by fear of loss of love will refrain only from acts which please the ego so long as there is a high probability of being found out and punished in some way. "Social anxiety" becomes the driving force of the external superego.

But with time, external social controls become internalized. The fear of lost love and of "being found out" are replaced by an inner sense of values and judgment. This internalized superego is far more effective than external authority because nothing, not even thoughts and wishes, can be hidden from it. "The superego torments the sinful ego with the same feeling of anxiety and is on the watch for opportunities for getting it punished by the external world."[44]

Paradoxically, at this stage of psychic development the superego, or conscience, punishes most severely those whose behavior is most beyond reproach. This occurs because the frustrated and unfulfilled instinctual satisfactions of those who have successfully repressed their actions must be channeled somewhere; they thus turn in against the ego. They provide the psychic energy which drives the superego to help the ego dominate the instincts. The more repressed the personality, the more instincts are turned inward, and the harsher is the superego.

Beyond internal frustration, new external frustrations reinforce the strength of the superego. For example, in the face of misfortune, a person engages in self-examination. Instead of blaming the environment, people tend to blame themselves for their plight. This heightens the expectations of the internalized superego, which, in turn, imposes new prohibitions and punishment on the self. Threatened by loss of support from the external environment, the individual responds by guilt, heightened inner resolve, and behavioral adaptation.

But how does external authority become internalized as superego? Aggressive resentment against external authority emerges as the result of initial instinctual renunciations. This resentment must itself be renounced to avoid punishment and loss of love. To cope with this added burden, the individual actually begins to identify with and to internalize external authority. In Freud's terms: "he takes the unattackable authority into himself. The authority now turns into his superego and enters into possession of all the aggressiveness which the child would have liked to exercise against it."[45] The severity of the superego represents aggressiveness toward external authority now turned inward aganst the self.

In Freudian social theory, this sense of internalized guilt is absolutely crucial to the development of contemporary civilization. Guilt keeps the death instinct and its tendency to dissolve the larger community in check, thereby enabling the erotic impulse toward communal growth, development, and solidarity to prevail. Yet even though this sense of ever increasing guilt is the cement that holds human communities together, guilt may well "reach heights that the individual finds hard to tolerate."[46]

For this reason, civilized life is inherently incapable of fulfilling individual wants. Civilized unhappiness is the hallmark of contemporary social life. To cope with guilt, contemporary urbanites give up a large measure of freedom of action. But in so doing, they experience permanent internal struggle, frustration, and unhappiness. To overcome fear and insecurity, they accept radical unhappiness.

In *Civilization and Its Discontents* Freud makes clear that modern civilization, rather than inducing joy in conformity, instead relies on a continuous sense of guilt to maintain the social bond. Herein lies the double bind. People experience the unhappiness of guilt both when they conform and when they deviate from social controls. Without an overriding sense of guilt to repress inner drives, no social order would be possible. Guilt is so powerful that it binds conformists and recaptures deviants.[47] Guilt becomes powerful precisely because society's norms have become internalized and have come to be viewed as one's own. They have implicated the ego in the struggle against the id.

The internalized superego is at the heart of the common distinction between primitive shame cultures, which rely exclusively on external controls, and contemporary guilt cultures, which create inner controls and institutionalize inner sanctions in the form of self-doubt, self-hate, and self-alienation. Self-alienation for Freud is the rejection and repression of an important dimension of the personality. The person who always conforms, thereby frustrating the strongest instinctual and spontaneous motives, may feel less conscious guilt than the deviant. Having repressed guilt feelings by conformity, the conformist is less likely than the deviant consciously to seek purgation and expiation, and hence is more likely to develop severe neuroses stemming from pent-up impulses and repressed guilt.

The more people in any culture have internalized the basic norms of the culture and thereby strengthened their superego—in short, the more people have become "adult"—the more secure the culture becomes and the less need it has for external coercion. Yet, except for the universally internalized prohibitions against murder, incest, and cannibalism, the other instinctual claims vary widely in the degree and extent to which they have been internalized.[48] This is because of the dialectical tension between individual and social development in Freudian thought.

Individual development is a product of the egoistic urge toward happiness and the "altruistic" urge toward communion with others. As the individual personality develops, the latter urge usually functions to impose restrictions on the former. However, a different dialectic affects the course of the development of civilization. At the level of social development, the most important aim is creating social unity; the pursuit of happiness either egoistically or altruistically takes a back seat to this primary aim. Paralleling the inner struggle of egoistic and altruistic urges is the outer struggle between the conflicting priorities of individual and cultural development. The inner struggle takes place within the erotic libido. In Freud's view, this inner dialectic offers the hope of eventual accommodation between individual and social urges as the erotic drive toward community is compatible with increased social unity. This is true even though today the egoistic and altruistic urges warring within "the economics of libido" often "oppress" the individual. The dialectic of libido is unlike the larger struggle between the erotic and aggressive instincts—eros and death. In Freud's view, the larger dialectic is probably irreconcilable.[49]

At the social development level, Freud holds that civilization develops its own superego which guides cultural growth. The superego of any epoch is a manifestation of the residual impressions created by the charismatic personalities of great leaders. Such people are often ridiculed because they are so far ahead of their time as to appear social deviants. The visibility of such symbolic superego figures, as well as the visibility of group socialization practices, makes it easier to detect the properties and operations of the superego in the cultural community than within the individual. The communal superego sets up demands, subsumed under the term ethics. Ethics, for Freud, is an attempt by society to shape the norms of the superego in order to curb the aggressive instinct internally, when external cultural regulations fail to tame it. The chief command of social ethics is the previously discussed one to love thy neighbor as thyself. But such an imperative troubles itself too little with the requirements of the ego. It also underestimates the strength of the id.

Hence Freud believed that it was sometimes good therapy to resist the demands of an overharsh superego as well as the ethical demands of the larger community. Both of these are insufficiently sensitive to the great difficulty the ego experiences trying to control the powerful id. To expect perfection via complete instinctual renunciation is to invite either revolution or permanent neurosis. Freud believed that external commands which are impossible to fulfill produce harmful, unanticipated consequences. Repression can cause as much unhappiness as aggressiveness.[50]

At this point Freud implicitly suggests a preference for politics over ethics as a way to lessen the degree of unhappiness accompanying both unbridled aggression and ethically based repression:

> I too think it quite certain that a real change in the relations of human beings to possessions would be of more help . . . than any ethical commands; but the recognition of this fact among socialists has been obscured and made useless for practical purposes by a fresh idealistic misconception of human nature.[51]

Despite this comment, however, Freud is not willing to counsel major structural change. He is hesitant about environmental restructuring, even though he concludes that both the ends and the means of civilization may not be worth the price. He views the numerous restrictions on instinctual life, tragically, as developmental trends in the evolution of civilization "which cannot be averted or turned aside and to which it is best for us to yield as though they were necessities of nature."[52]

Freud rejects the role of consoling prophet. His fateful question remains, whether civilization will be able to tame the aggressive disturbances of communal life in a world whose technology has made possible widespread human destruction. Initially Freud concluded that the very knowledge of this destructive potential is itself a major source of unrest and anxiety which calls forth erotic social impulses to guard against the death instinct. But a final sentence of *Civilization and Its Discontents,* added after the rise of Hitler, leaves us with this melancholy uncertainty: "But who can forsee with what success and with what result?"[53]

WHAT IS TO BE DONE?—THE POLITICS OF THERAPY

Although not a prophet, Freud did have a "plan" which primarily was the familiar call for individual "adjustment" to environmental "realities." Yet it also called for some particular environmental readjustments that were liberal, incremental, and reformist. Freud was torn between his perceptions of the consequences of civilization's restrictions and his belief that without a considerable degree of instinctual renunciation civilized life would not be possible. *The Future of an Illusion* (1927) is perhaps the least pessimistic of Freud's philosophical writings. The tension between his liberal reformist inclinations, reflected in some passages of this work, and his conservative expectations for the human condition is less evident in the later *Civilization and Its Discontents* (1929). The later work resolves the tension by proclaiming the inevitability of instinctual renunciation and the need to cultivate compensatory substitutive satisfactions.

Yet in a final uncompleted work Freud reiterated the view that the demands of civilization were basically repressive. We must, he felt, "include the influence of civilization among the determinants of neurosis. It is easy . . . for a barbarian to be healthy; for a civilized man the task is hard."[54] This tension in Freud's social theory is reflected in his answers to the question, "What is to be done?"

Individual Therapy: Liberating the Calculative Ego

Freud's view of history was geared toward the recovery of the ego from neurotic tendencies through a process of self-discovery, self-discipline, and liberation from religious and cultural myths and superstitions. Freud wanted to restore a weakened "ego-strength." He believed that through strengthening the individual ego and displacement of religion by science, *rational-purposive* activity could increasingly come to displace automatic activity driven by unconscious impulses. Calculative activity could be substituted for reflexive activity.

Through psychoanalysis Freud believed it possible for an individual to make available to his ego "those energies which, owing to repression, are inaccessibly confined in his unconscious, as well as those which his ego is obligated to squander in the fruitless task of maintaining these repressions."[55] In the Freudian perspective psychoanalysis frees those who undergo it from pent-up guilt feelings, thereby rendering them capable of satisfying society's demands with the least possible self-sacrifice. In essence, Freudian therapy is geared to the ideal of nineteenth-century laissez-faire economic theory—the maximization of individual productivity and thereby the satisfaction of social objectives at least cost to the individual, in this case in terms of painful instinctual renunciation.

The enhanced "ego-strength" also serves to moderate the harshness of the superego. If left unchecked, Freud felt that an overharsh superego would trap the individual in an endless cycle of guilt-transgression-suffering-expiation. As Paul Roazen has said: "A harsh superego . . . can all too easily be bribed by suffering into permitting the gratification of forbidden wishes. The increased self-mastery gained through [psychoanalytic] treatment involves greater awareness of instinctual needs, less dependence on earlier emotional positions, and a less harsh superego."[56]

But mental health from the psychoanalytic perspective entails not only increased calculative-instrumental rationality, greater realism, and enhanced ego-strength; it also entails a recognition of and accessibility to intense individual satisfactions without allowing sentimentality, emotionalism, or primordial drives to dominate the personality. In Freudian social theory the conditions engendered by the complexities and constraints of civilized urban life can best be dealt with by accepting the environment as given and "extracting" as much pleasure from it as possible. By recognizing the necessity of partial and intermittent need fulfillment, of substitutions and sublimations, people can find life in civilized society bearable, if unfulfilling.

Short of psychotherapy or open resistance, Freud observed that people have worked out numerous therapeutically useful substitutions and deflections for instinctual gratification. Among these are work, whose functions we have already discussed above, as well as play, jokes and humor, and various forms of nonsexual love such as membership in human groups, identification with such groups, and love of humanity.

In his 1907 work *Creative Writers and Day Dreaming*,[57] Freud drew close parallels between the imaginative fiction writer and the child at play. Each creates a fantasy world for the self, which is taken very seriously. Play is the opposite of reality, not of seriousness. Most people give up this important source of imagination as they mature; they cease to play, and in so doing they relinquish the yield of pleasure once derived from play. In adult life, childhood play-acting is replaced by fantasizing, which, out of shame, the adult hides from others. Adult fantasies are motivated by broken-down and unfulfilled wishes. The function of fantasy for Freud is wish fulfillment, a key mechanism by which people deal with unsatisfying reality, but one which can have dangerous repercussions if channeled outward onto social objects rather than diverted into play.

Humor, like play, deflects basic drives into socially acceptable channels. In another early work, *Jokes and Their Relation to the Unconscious*,[58] Freud argued that the majority of cynical jokes are aimed at social institutions, most particularly the institution of marriage. Freud suggested that this was so because the marriage institution constituted one of the most regulative and suppressive institutions of civilization in the sphere of sexual expression. In similar fashion, jokes serve as outlets for attacks on the great, the dignified, and the institutions in which one has a collective share (e.g., the nation) but which are protected from direct disparagement by inhibitions and external restraints. Through jokes, instincts find expression which cannot otherwise be satisfied because they have been repressed. Social restrictions against hostility or sexual expression, for example, are overcome by tendentious humor, which allows the individual to exploit something ridiculous in a perceived enemy or an object of sexual attraction.

Jokes are important substitutive satisfactions as well as useful deflections. They help people to cope with the unhappiness of modern civilization by opening up sources of pleasure which have been rendered inaccessible by repression. Jokes provide pleasure in themselves as a result of play with words. They also trigger new pleasure by releasing repressions and suppressions. Laughter discharges pent-up psychic energy and thereby lightens the burden of civilized unhappiness.

And what about love as an answer? Freud's radical individualism and his nineteenth-century image of personality as a prudential calculator of pleasures and pains is nowhere more apparent than in his analysis of love. "Love" is defined by Freud as a patently utilitarian effort to obtain individual pleasure by creating satisfying emotional relationships with "objects" in the external world, particularly its "social objects." In loving and being loved people seek "comfort." Instead of merely "avoiding unpleasure" the lover seeks the direct fulfillment of erotic instincts. Freud believes that this option has the advantage of providing "intensely satisfying" (individual) experience, when expressed in its sexual form. But for Freud's "prudential calculator" its chief disadvantage is clear: love provides immediate and intense pleasure but runs a high risk of causing intense pain and suffering. The person in love is defenseless against the suffering entailed in losing a cherished "love object."[59]

To avoid such pain, people have attempted to express love in forms other than sexual. Freud contends that a small minority can find happiness through nonsexual love, but only if a crucial mental step is taken. A minority can make themselves "independent of" their love "objects," and thereby avoid the threat of painful loss, by displacing what they desire out of being loved onto the act of loving itself.

Some direct their love not to specific people but to humanity in general. Genital love is turned away from its sexual aim; the erotic instinct becomes an "aim-inhibited" impulse. The stormy agitations of genital love are replaced by a more mellow, steadfast, affectionate feeling. Freud expresses two main objections to this alternative:

> A love that does not discriminate seems to me to forfeit a part of its own value by doing an injustice to its object; and secondly not all men are worthy of love.[60]

In Freud's discussions of group psychology aim-inhibited love is treated as one of the basic ties that bind individuals in groups.[61] Here, too, his radically atomistic view of social life is apparent. Groups are viewed as by-products of the individual's search for pleasurable substitutive satisfactions. For Freud, individuals give up a large measure of their distinctiveness in groups and subject themselves to group suggestions in order to experience a sense of harmony akin to but much milder than the erotic instinct. From the standpoint of obtaining self-mastery, Freud sees five counterproductive consequences following from individual participation in groups. The consequences of group psychology include (1) the collective inhibition of each individual member's intellectual functioning; (2) a tendency for unconscious mental forces to dominate consciousness, as a diminished individual sense of responsibility weakens inhibitions; (3) a heightened susceptibility to suggestion; (4) intensification of the affective side of the mind and corresponding intensification of emotions; and (5) a heightened passion for authority. Lost in this view is any sense that participation in group life can provide needed economic support, political strength, or heightened social consciousness.

Aside from actually participating in group activities, Freud held that an individual may seek satisfaction for frustrated libidinal energy by identifying with particular reference groups. Identification, for Freud, entails suspension of the ability to objectively criticize the object identified with. Such identifications may blind individuals to real threats and adversary interests that exist in the external environment.

However inadequate from the standpoints of simple justice or inner self-mastery, aim-inhibited affection does function to bind people together into human communities. For Freud, this function is an indispensable aid to shared interest in work as a social bond. It binds people together more intensively than does work alone. Aim-inhibited love makes friends of strangers. Friendship is valued by civilization because it provides a less exclusive social tie than does genital love. But for Freud, friendship, like love of humanity and other higher order pleasures, is less basic, and hence less complete and intense, than instinctual pleasure. People remain unhappy in civilization because the benefits and pleasures which civilized existence offers never fully compensate for instinctual renunciation.

Incremental Reforms as Aids to Rational Calculation

In addition to the individual-level actions discussed above, Freud's later writings contain the elements of a moderately reformist public policy program. Little attention has been devoted to this side of Freud's thought, perhaps because it appears incompatible with his pessimistic view of human nature. Yet Freud considered himself a therapist and social critic as well as a social theorist. When acting in these roles he implicitly offers a limited program for environmental reform which includes educational and political components. The first component is designed to liberate calculative intelligence from superstition, so that inner self-regulation might become possible. The political component calls for enlightened leadership, moderate economic redistribution to eliminate "surplus privation," and a liberalization of the range of satisfactions available in society.

The secularization of education and social controls.   Freud's ideal for society was the same as his ideal for the individual—the ascendancy of secular reason and the ability to calculate prudently in order to control both the irrational drives of the id and the excessive guilt engendered by an overharsh superego. Religion is described as mere "wish fulfillment" in *The Future of an Illusion.* Rebutting Marx, Freud argued that if religion had truly been the opiate of the masses, if it had "succeeded in making happy the greater part of mankind, then no one would dream of striving to alter existing conditions."[62] Instead, discontent with civilization is widespread and religion has achieved very little, despite its prominent role in society.

Freud saw a danger to contemporary civilization in the unleashed rebelliousness of the "great mass of the uneducated and suppressed, *who have every reason to be* enemies of culture."[63] Because Freud believed that for the lower classes religion was the principal inhibitor of aggressive instincts and that through science, ultimately, they would be persuaded that there was no God, he argued that the relation between culture and religion must be revised. Culture must come to rest on secular supports. Freud held that the only ways to prevent violent uprising by those "who have every reason" to destroy civilization were reeducation and secularization, systematic supression, or deliberate exclusion of the lower and working classes from all channels of intellectual enlightenment. The Freud of *The Future of an Illusion* rejected the latter two forms of institutionalized repression. Instead he favored "reeducation" of the masses by enlightened leaders and a secularization of cultural supports. Yet he assumed that this would not be an easy task.

In response to their plight, Freud assumed that the masses would develop hostility toward the institutions of contemporary civilization. Forced to choose between acting upon this hostility and the sense of helplessness that abandonment of civilized protections would bring, the masses often turned for comfort to religion. Religion provided comfort by creating the illusion that the inexorable powers of nature could be tamed, cajoled, or even bribed into appeasement. By thus robbing nature of part of its power, people would no longer feel defenseless.

Yet, as religion became less naturalistic, human expectations concentrated upon religion's social task: "to adjust the defects and evils of culture, to attend to the sufferings that men inflict on each other in the communal life, and to see that the laws of culture, which men obey so ill, are carried out."[64] In short, religion became the keeper of civilized morality by rooting obedience to social norms in the mythical promise of an afterlife. Gods became transcendent, supernatural forces. Their hegemony over nature was justified by a rich store of ideas "born of the need to make tolerable the helplessness of man."[65]

Religious ideas posit a future state of human perfectibility which provides a transcendent purpose for accepting human suffering, unhappiness, and injustice in everyday life. Death is made to foreshadow a new mode of existence rather than representing, as it did for Freud, a peaceful return to a state of inorganic lifelessness, whose only benefit is that it puts to rest the inevitable anxiety, frustration, and tension that characterize human existence.

Freud asks why people continue to cling to religious beliefs despite their obvious nonconfirmability. For Freud, dogmas of religion stem neither from experience nor from rational reflection. Instead they constitute deep-seated and intense "wish fulfillments." They are illusions whose strength is the strength of the oldest, strongest, and most unyielding wishes of humanity—desires for protection through love, for the establishment of a moral order that guarantees justice, and for escape from the finality of death.[66]

Freud rejects the arguments of those who claim that religious doctrines ought not to be questioned because they provide the fear and inhibition which prevent a chaotic war of each against all. In his view, so long as religion prevails, resting as it does on wish fulfillment and hope in transcendent salvation, pleas for his desideratum, a life guided by wish renunciation and "acquiescence in fate," would fall on deaf ears. Freud believed it was precisely wish renunciation which could lead to the creative reinvestment of psychic energy upon which a "realistically" rooted social order could maintain itself. With time Freud hoped and expected that the religious justification for instinctual renunciation gradually would be replaced by secular-rational intellectual justifications of self-denial. Among the justifications which he himself believed to be most compelling were community survival, social peace, mutual adjustment, mastery over nature, the extraction of wealth to satisfy human needs, and the regulation of the distribution of wealth.

Freud held that in place of prohibitions emanating from God, the rational basis for particular social controls must be made apparent. Freud's argument for secularized social controls included four basic steps.[67] First, the prohibition against aggression is the product of rational necessity, not divine command. It rests upon the equal danger that all members of the community would face if there were no such prohibition. Second, if it were recognized widely that all cultural laws and institutions were the products of human creation rather than divinely ordained, "The rigid and immutable nature of these laws and regulations would . . . cease,"[68] along with their claims to sanctity. People would then come to recognize that the human purpose of laws was not to rule them but to serve their interests. They would become less hostile to laws and regulations per se. Third, they would then seek to improve rather than to abolish the legal order. "One may prophesy but hardly regret that this process of *remodeling* will not stop at dispelling the solemn air of sanctity surrounding the cultural laws, but that a general revision of these must involve the *abolition* of many of them."[69] To do so will help to reconcile people to civilization, because its burdens will become less harsh. Finally, people will be less likely to rebel because they will be less likely to feel themselves deceived by the "symbolic disguisings of the truth" supplied by religion. Instead of deluding the public with religious myths, it is better to expose people to reality. This step is necessary, in any case, for mature intellectual development.

Having thus dismissed religion as a support for social controls, Freud attempts to elucidate his paradoxical position that although people tend to be ruled by their passions and instincts, it is necessary to replace the affective basis of allegiance to culture by a set of rational criteria of obligation. Freud concedes that some believers are bound to religion and culture by affective ties; but a vast number of others obey the laws of religion and civilization only out of fear of punishment. He predicts that these will break free from religion, and from civilized regulations which are justified on purely religious grounds, as soon as they are persuaded of the unreality of religious dogma. If civilization remains tied to religion, people will lose confidence in other civilized authority figures when they abandon religion. The specter of rebellion and revolution, which he feared, will threaten civilization.

Freud further held that religious dogmas retard individual intellectual development. They socialize people to accept without criticism absurd and contradictory wish fulfillments which form the content of religious beliefs. They handicap, through prohibitions, people's one real weapon for controlling their instincts: their intelligence. Religion represses the development of the "radiant intelligence of the healthy child."[70] It replaces curiosity with dogma and healthy sexual development with prohibition.

In *The Future of an Illusion*, Freud advocates steps to improve the human condition by reforming society's educational institutions. He recommends education's conversion from a religious-repressive basis to a rational-liberating basis. In Freud's view, the gradual de-mystification of education offers hope for a future in which "perhaps we may dig up a treasure which can enrich culture, and it is worthwhile to make the experiment of a non-religious education." Yet ever skeptical, Freud concludes that, should this route prove unsatisfactory: "I am ready to give up the reform and to return to the earlier, purely descriptive judgment: man is a creature of weak intelligence who is governed by his instinctual wishes."[71]

Until proven wrong, however, the Freud of *Illusion* is much more of a liberal-rationalist than might be expected. He argues that if brought up soberly, if given the opportunity to develop their intellect fully, people may need neither religion nor other intoxicants to support their existence. "Secular" individuals will have "come to terms with" their utter helplessness and insignificance in the universe. Having given up comforting illusions, people can venture into the real world unfettered by unrealistic wishes. Thrown upon their own resources, they will be forced to learn to use them well. Or as Freud himself succinctly puts it:

> Thus by withdrawing his expectations from the other world and concentrating all his liberated energies on this earthly life [man] will probably attain to a state of things in which life will be tolerable for all and no one will be oppressed by culture any more.[72]

There is a final reason why Freud advocates education as a reliable route to gradual social change. He feels that, unlike religious illusions, scientific beliefs are capable of self-correction through observation of reality and testing of the assumptions on which scientific theories are based. Unlike religion, reason and science do not have a delusional character. Sounding almost like John Stuart Mill, Freud asserts, "The voice of the intellect is a soft one, but it does not rest until it has gained a hearing. Ultimately, after endlessly repeated rebuffs, it succeeds."[73]

In *The Future of an Illusion* Freud expresses confidence that scientific work can discover many of the currently inexplicable realities of the external world. Through this increased understanding, people may increase their power over the external universe and more rationally regulate their own lives. In Freud's view, science is no illusion. Science still leaves many questions unanswered, but "it would be an illusion to suppose that we could get anywhere else what it cannot give us."[74]

Politics: resignation, reform, or revolution? We have seen that Freud's view of the impact of culture on personality was a tragic one. Culture is a dialectical phenomenon which both frustrates and fulfills human needs. Despite its capacity to thwart human development, Freud saw little to be gained and much to be risked by undertaking major changes in the social structure of urban civilization. Since he viewed neurosis as basically derived from inner mental conflict rather than from environmental factors, he feared that comprehensively changing the environment might only serve to loosen social controls necessary to any social system. He believed that, despite all their repressive tendencies, controls of the many by the few at least serve to channel and pacify aggressive drives and the death instinct. Hence Freud's elitist tendencies derive from his pessimism concerning the ability of large masses to curb their instinctual drives and render them subservient to either a strong ego or an internally directed superego.

To control the aggressive instinct Freud believed that all societies must, to some degree, repress the individual. Since for Freud aggressive drives were not created by property relationships, he explicitly rejects the Marxian hope that a radical restructuring of property relationships might end human exploitation. Even in *The Future of an Illusion*, Freud argued that culture was imposed on the rest of society by a minority that understood how to use the resources of power and coercion. He saw such elitism as an unavoidable component of any political order. Unlike Wirth, he offered little hope that human relations might somehow be fundamentally reorganized to end the suppression of the instincts by cultural elites. To do so might bring a golden age, but it seemed more probable to Freud that every culture must be built on instinctual renunciation and social coercion.[75] However, he did believe that some incremental steps might be taken to loosen overharsh internal and external controls, in order to avoid the harmful social consequences of the "frustration-aggression syndrome."

Accordingly, Freud set three limited objectives for those who would use politics and planning to restructure modern institutions. He sanctioned measures by policy makers to diminish the weight of the instinctual sacrifices which society imposes; to reconcile the individual to these sacrifices that must remain; and to create compensatory activities for accepting these latter social controls.

Implicit in Freud's elitist view is that mass "citizen participation" in policy making is virtually inconceivable. Far more skeptical than Louis Wirth, Freud described the masses as a "lazy and unintelligent" aggregate that constantly fought against instinctual renunciation and was only partially susceptible to rational persuasion. Hence Freud felt that charismatic elites were essential to "set an example" of superego control. The function of leadership in this view is to induce the masses to submit to the discipline of pleasurable instincts upon which the continued existence of culture depends.[76]

Ever skeptical about the prospects of a just society, Freud reluctantly concluded that repression was a necessary ingredient of modern civilization, at least in the foreseeable future. Over the long run, he did hold out the previously discussed hope for change. Through elitist educational reforms, he believed it might be possible to train the instincts in order to realize less repressive modes of existence. But this could be accomplished only if future generations were successfully socialized into "self-discipline" by a "throng of superior, dependable, and disinterested leaders."[77]

Freud held that if disinterested and charismatic political elites could be found who had superior insight into the necessities of life (human needs), they would be more likely to control their own instinctual wishes (human wants) and to serve as a role model for others to follow. But to maintain influence, policy-making elites may yield to popular demands that wants be fulfilled rather than needs. To avoid this possibility, Freud goes so far as to suggest that it may be necessary that elites "should be independent of the masses by having at their disposal means of enforcing their authority."[78]

Nor did Freud hold out much hope that technological developments might generally improve the human lot by overcoming economic scarcity. In Marxian social thought, exploitation by the few of the many is less likely once the problem of material scarcity has been solved by automation, increased productivity, and advanced technological development. Social theorists like Herbert Marcuse, for example, attribute repression to economic scarcity and foresee an end to repression following upon the development of technologically advanced postscarcity economies. Freud, in contrast, sees little chance for an end to repression in this way, precisely because repression is rooted in the would-be tyranny of the instincts. For Freud, modern technology makes possible ever more sophisticated instruments of death and destruction.[79] Since both the erotic and the aggressive instincts are timelessly enmeshed in human nature, the only sure way to tame the death instinct is through repressive sublimation. Historical variations in socioeconomic structure may alleviate, but they can never fully erase, the anxiety, frustration, and unhappiness that stem from rechanneling the primal instincts.

This does not mean Freud was unalterably opposed to any change in the prevailing pattern of economic distribution in capitalist society. He believed that patterns of extreme economic maldistribution might unleash a dangerous potential for violent revolution. Steps undertaken to redress such maldistribution would at least address one of the basic causes of aggression. That he at least implicitly sanctioned such steps is clear from his discussion of the socioeconomic condition he termed "surplus privation."[80]

Freud defines "frustration" as the feeling experienced when a person realizes an instinct cannot be satisfied. "Prohibitions" are the means that cause frustrations. The condition produced by a prohibition is a "privation." In Freudian theory, some prohibitions affect everyone and others deprive only particular groups or classes. For instance, the prohibitions against incest, cannibalism, and murder apply to everyone and hence are "universal privations." In contrast, in any society the neglected lower classes experience a "surplus of privation" owing to their inferior power, means, and opportunity for instinctual gratification. Like Marx in at least one respect, Freud held that the neglected classes were a continuous source of political instability because they resent the privileges of the favored classes, suffer discontent, and wish to rid themselves of surplus privation. Recognizing the reality of exploitation, they fail to internalize the prohibitions of the culture that exploits them.

It might be expected that Freud would have little sympathy for these underprivileged strata because of his fear of the aggressive potential and lack of self-discipline of the masses. But this is not really the case. Freud appears to distinguish between political actions and policies undertaken to alleviate *surplus* privations, which may be both justifiable and effective, and those undertaken to alter *universal* privations, which are for him a foolhardy denial of essential human nature. In *The Future of an Illusion* Freud has the following to say about surplus privation:

> But if a culture has not got beyond the stage in which the satisfaction of one group of its members necessarily involves the suppression of another, per- haps the majority—it is intelligible that these suppressed classes should develop an intense hostility to the culture; a culture, whose existence they make possible by their labor, but in whose resources they have too small a share. . . . [A] culture which leaves unsatisfied and drives to rebelliousness so large a number of its members neither has a prospect of continued exis- tence, nor deserves it.[81]

The implication of these statements is that unless political steps are taken to alleviate surplus privation by planned redistribution of resources, rebellion is inevitable. And since, in Freud's view, rebellion unleashes the destructive potential of the death instinct, it is preferable to use society's distributive and redistributive mechanisms to insure that all social classes have sufficient means to pursue the sublimations and other substitutive satisfactions necessitated by universal instinctual repression. If this is not done, "dangerous outbreaks" threaten to unleash the war of each against all, which Freud wished to avoid.

Yet consistency with Freud's basic themes suggests that he believed even steps to eliminate surplus privation should be undertaken with the utmost prudence. To the extent that Freud countenanced any political action or socially planned changes in reality, it can be inferred that such activities must be firmly rooted in (a) clear understanding of present reality; (b) prudential calculation of costs as well as benefits of proposed action; and (c) psychoanalytic insight into human nature, the role of the instincts, and the dangers of unrealistic wish fulfillment for both individual and civilization.[82]

Because social planners are also human, and the human intellect often is a tool of our impulses, comprehensive social planning may be viewed from the Freudian perspective as a dangerous invitation to repression by planning elites. If social engineers let their wishes and impulses get the best of their awareness of reality, their prudential reason, and their sense of the limitations of human resources, they will seek to impose their own impulses on society. Their superior reason then becomes a mere tool to rationalize their own repressive acts.[83]

This antiutopian view of comprehensive social planning is strongly implied in one of the more direct passages from *Civilization and Its Discontents*:

> One can try to recreate the world, to build up in its stead another world in which its most unbearable features are eliminated and replaced by others . . . in conformity with one's own wishes. But whoever, in desperate defiance, sets out upon this path to happiness will as a rule attain nothing. Reality is too strong for him. He becomes a madman, who for the most part finds no one to help him in carrying through his delusion.[84]

Although Freud rejected radical environmental restructuring, he did believe that there was an area within which planned human efforts to alleviate human misery and suffering was worthwhile. Without such a margin, psychotherapy itself would make little sense. These efforts were especially sensible when undertaken to reduce surplus privation. But surplus privation was not the only historical contingency that might justify planned action to reduce the weight of instinctual sacrifices. Some historical periods—for example, Victorian Europe—allowed too little erotic satisfaction to the population. By producing too many neurotic individuals, such periods denied psychic energy from being effectively channeled to creative activities.[85] Forced inward upon the self, an overharsh superego engenders excessively self-absorbed individuals.

Moreover, when repression becomes unbearable for large masses of people, the specter of revolution once again haunts civilization. Hence both to rechannel frustrations constructively outward and to avoid revolutionary upheaval, some degree of carefully planned environmental change may be necessary. Such restructuring would be geared toward providing people with the opportunity to find substitutive channels for the release of pent-up instinctual frustrations. While Freud nowhere fully specified what these might be (save for renouncing religious superstitions, reforming educational institutions, marginally redistributing economic resources, and liberating the individual from an overdeveloped superego through psychotherapy), such incremental reformist planning is consistent with the thrust of his analysis.

Despite the overall pessimism of Freud's political reflections, the implications of his faith in the therapeutic value of rationalism and science and carefully calculated social reforms were not lost sight of by future generations of psychotherapists and social planners.[86] Freud himself recognized the potential political implications of his efforts to demythologize authority, but shied away from them. Having demythologized religion in *The Future of an Illusion,* Freud asks rhetorically whether our other "cultural possessions," including political institutions, which are highly valued and which regulate human behavior, are not also built on a foundation of assumptions that are mere illusions. He surmised that such an inquiry might well justify such suspicions but that to deal with these questions was beyond the scope of his current inquiry.[87] His reticence is hardly surprising. To do so might have lowered the credibility of political authority and led to destructive consequences which Freud feared.

CONCLUSION

In the final analysis the Freudian personality stands as a tragic figure—victimized by the privations which modern civilization imposes, subject to occasional human cruelties which no system of social control can fully regulate by law; confronting an unvanquished nature that episodically lashes out to confirm its boundless energy—yet unable to do without the protection, security, and mastery over nature which civilized institutions do provide, however imperfectly. Yet, in the face of this tragedy, people are not entirely helpless. They can "cope" with civilized repression through psychotherapy or their own self-disciplined pursuit of pleasure. They can marginally change the environment through enlightened leadership, legislative reform, and incremental planning once both mass education and social controls have become secularized. They can use politics and planning, prudentially and in moderation, to reduce "surplus privation" and liberalize external social controls. Beyond this, Freud is unwilling to go.

Notes

1. Henrik Ibsen, *An Enemy of the People* (New York: Holt, Rinehart and Winston, 1961), p. 170.
2. Fyodor Dostoevsky, *Notes from Underground* (New York: Dutton, 1960), p. 21.
3. See Herbert Marcuse, *Eros and Civilization* (London: Routledge and Kegan Paul, 1956).
4. See chaps. 3 and 4 below.
5. See, for example, Gino Germani, "Urbanization, Social Change and the Great Transformation," Germani, ed., *Modernization, Urbanization & the Urban Crisis* (Boston: Little, Brown, 1973), 3–58; Kenneth Boulding, "The Death of the City: A Frightened Look at Postcivilization," Oscar Handlin and John Burchard, eds., *The Historian and the City* (Cambridge: M.I.T. & Harvard U. Press, 1963), pp. 133–145.
6. See Richard Sennett, *The Uses of Disorder: Personal Identity and City Life* (New York: Vintage, 1970), and chap. 4 below.
7. For a classical statement of the incrementalist critique of rational-comprehensive planning, see Charles Lindblom, "The Science of 'Muddling Through'," *Public Administration Review*, 9 (Spring 1959), 79–88.
8.. Paul Roazen, *Sigmund Freud: Political and Social Thought* (New York: Knopf, 1968), p. 259.
9. In addition to the specific citations, the most useful works for understanding Freudian depth psychology are Freud's *Papers on Metapsychology*, vol. 14, and *The Ego and the Id*, vol. 19, *The Complete Psychological Works of Sigmund Freud*, ed. James Strachey (London: Hogarth, 1953).
10. On the dynamic relationship among consciousness, the preconscious, and the unconscious, see Freud, *Papers on Metapsychology*, "The Unconscious," chaps. 4–7, 180–204.
11. In *Papers on Metapsychology*, pp. 141–146, Freud defines "repression" as an early stage of condemnation of an instinct, lying between "flight" and "condemnation." In a repressed state, instinctual drives are "turned away" and kept at a distance from consciousness, to avoid punishment or a sense of guilt.

12. See Freud, *Civilization and Its Discontents* (New York: Norton, 1961), pp. 11–14.

13. For a good example of the self-destructive potential of the unregulated desire to consume, see Martin G. Kalin, *The Utopian Flight from Unhappiness: Freud Against Marx on Social Progress* (Chicago: Nelson Hall, 1974), p. 128.

14. David Elkind, "Freud, Jung and the Collective Unconscious," *New York Times Magazine*, October 4, 1970, p. 94.

15. Freud, *Three Essays on the Theory of Sexuality*, vol. 7, *The Complete Psychological Works of Sigmund Freud*, pp. 217–218, 244.

16. Freud, *Civilization and Its Discontents*, p. 68; see also Freud, *The Ego and the Id*, p. 40.

17. Freud, *Civilization and Its Discontents*, p. 69.

18. Freud, *The Ego and the Id*, p. 40.

19. See Dennis Wrong's stimulating essay, "The Oversocialized Conception of Man in Modern Sociology," *American Sociological Review*, 26 (April 1961), 183–193.

20. Freud, *Civilization and Its Discontents*, p. 36; Freud, *The Future of an Illusion* (Edinburgh: Horace Liveright & The Institute of Psychoanalysis, 1928), p. 9.

21. Freud, *Civilization and Its Distontents*, p. 39.

22. Ibid., p. 40.

23. Ibid., p. 43.

24. Ibid., p. 42.

25. Ibid., p. 55.

26. Ibid.

27. Ibid., p. 59.

28. See Karl Marx, *Capital: A Critique of Political Economy* (New York: International Publishers, 1947); Marx, *Grundrisse*, ed. David McLellan (London: Macmillan, 1971); Marx, *Essential Writings of Karl Marx*, comp. David Caute (New York: Macmillan, 1967); and Marx, *Writings of the Young Marx on Philosophy and Society*, ed. and trans. Lloyd Easton and Kurt Guddat (Garden City, N.Y.: Doubleday Anchor, 1967).

29. Freud, *Civilization and Its Discontents*, p. 60 fn.

30. H. Stuart Hughes, *Consciousness and Society* (New York: Vintage, 1961), p. 146.

31. Kalin, *The Utopian Flight from Unhappiness*, pp. 158–159.

32. Freud, *Civilization and Its Discontents*, pp. 30–31.

33. Ibid., p. 31.

34. Ibid., p. 27 fn.

35. Ibid., p. 23.

36. Ibid., p. 26. Freud expressed this theme as early as 1908. See his *Civilized Sexual Morality and Modern Nervous Illness*, vol. 9, *The Complete Psychological Works of Sigmund Freud*, pp. 177–204.

37. Freud, *Civilization and Its Discontents*, p. 33.

38. Ibid.

39. Ibid., p. 34.

40. Ibid., p. 35.
41. See Thomas Hobbes, *Leviathan*, ed. C. B. MacPherson (Baltimore: Penguin, 1968).
42. Paul Roazen, *Sigmund Freud: Political and Social Thought*, p. 271; see also pp. 269–270, where Roazen explores Freud's views on the "functions" of social coercion and his differences from the social contract theorists John Locke and Thomas Hobbes regarding the state of nature and the costs and benefits of social and political community.
43. Freud, *Civilization and Its Discontents*, p. 43.
44. Ibid., p. 72. The discussion which follows is based upon ibid., pp. 73–80.
45. Ibid., p. 76.
46. Ibid., p. 80.
47. Dennis Wrong, "The Oversocialized Conception of Man in Modern Sociology," pp. 183–193.
48. Freud, *The Future of an Illusion*, p. 19.
49. Freud, *Civilization and Its Discontents*, p. 88.
50. Ibid., pp. 90–91.
51. Ibid., p. 90.
52. Ibid., p. 92.
53. Ibid.
54. Paul Roazen, *Sigmund Freud: Political and Social Thought*, p. 253.
55. Freud, quoted in ibid., p. 277.
56. Paul Roazen, *Sigmund Freud: Political and Social Thought*, p. 282.
57. Freud, *Creative Writers and Day Dreaming*, vol. 9, *The Complete Psychological Works of Sigmund Freud*, 102–140.
58. Freud, *Jokes and Their Relation to the Unconscious*, vol. 8, *The Complete Psychological Works of Sigmund Freud*, 102–140.
59. Freud, *Civilization and Its Discontents*, p. 29.
60. Ibid., p. 49; see also pp. 48–51.
61. See Freud, *Group Psychology and the Analysis of the Ego*, vol. 18, *The Complete Psychological Works of Sigmund Freud*, 88–122.
62. H. Stuart Hughes, *Consciousness and Society*, p. 140. See also Freud, *Civilization and Its Discontents*, p. 60.
63. Freud, *The Future of an Illusion*, p. 68.
64. Ibid., p. 31.
65. Ibid., p. 32.
66. Ibid., pp. 45–53.
67. For Freud's extensive discussion of these arguments see ibid., pp. 68–78.
68. Ibid., p. 73.
69. Ibid., p. 77, emphasis added.
70. Ibid., p. 82.
71. Both of the quotations in this paragraph are found in ibid., p. 84.
72. Ibid., pp. 86–87.
73. Ibid., p. 93. For a similar defense of rational discourse in the "free marketplace of ideas" see John Stuart Mill, *On Liberty* (New York: Liberal Arts Press, 1956).
74. Ibid., p. 98.

75. See Hughes, *Consciousness and Society*, p. 136; Roazen, *Sigmund Freud: Political and Social Thought*, passim; and Freud, *The Future of an Illusion*, pp. 11–14.

76. Freud, *The Future of an Illusion*, p. 12.

77. Ibid., p. 14; see also Hughes, *Consciousness and Society*, p. 137. Freud's belief in attempts to expose people to a fully secularized and scientifically based education at an early age is rooted in his basic psychological assumption that a person's ultimate course of psychic development is determined by early childhood experiences.

78. Freud, *The Future of an Illusion*, p. 13.

79. See Kalin, *The Utopian Flight from Unhappiness*, for a good contrast between Marx, Marcuse, and Freud on the consequences of technology.

80. See Freud, *The Future of an Illusion*, chap. 2, for his discussion of this concept and for the discussion presented in the following paragraphs.

81. Ibid., p. 20.

82. See Kalin's discussion of the role of "pessimism and progress" in psychoanalysis, which supports the thrust of the inferences made here. Kalin, *Utopian Flight from Unhappiness*, pp. 190–192. Freud clearly believes that the steps taken to eliminate surplus privation should fall far short of the abolition of private property. In his view the communist system is based on an untenable psychological illusion, for in abolishing private property "we have in no way altered the differences in power and influence which are misused by aggressiveness, nor have we altered anything in its nature." See Freud, *Civilization and Its Discontents*, p. 60.

83. Hughes, *Consciousness and Society*, p. 143.

84. Freud, *Civilization and Its Discontents*, p. 28.

85. Kalin, *Utopian Flight from Unhappiness*, p. 194.

86. See Roazen, *Sigmund Freud: Political and Social Thought*, pp. 283–285. Roazen compares Freud's faith in rationalism and science to the confidence of later generations of psychoanalysts that new scientific knowledge would place improved "preventative measures" in the hands of families, social institutions, and planners, thereby improving the functioning of society.

87. Freud, *The Future of an Illusion*, pp. 59–60.

Chapter 3
Georg Simmel: Individuality and Metropolitan Life

Georg Simmel (1858–1918) brought to the study of city life a brilliant mind, a penetrating perception, and an intuitive methodology which combined to produce a seminal body of insights on social life and the urban condition. Although he was not a systematic social theorist, Simmel's intellectual influence has been more widely felt than many more disciplined but less inspired thinkers. His writings on the urban capitalist money economy, inspired by Marx, but differing from him in several key respects, still represent one of the most profound analyses of the unsettling role of money for humankind's sense of time, scale, group formation, and human relatedness. His thoughts on the overstimulating aspects of metropolitan life were a source of inspiration for Louis Wirth as well as for contemporary psychological theorists. Likewise, his theory of urban interest groups powerfully influenced group theory in political science; his conflict theory formed the basis of much of the important work of conflict sociologists; and his concern for the underlying meaning of social forms was the precursor of contemporary work on symbolic communication.[1]

As Pitirim Sorokin[2] long ago observed, Simmel's work cannot really be termed scientific. His writings are a series of speculative generalizations, using facts as examples, to illustrate intuitively derived insights into the nature of the individual in society. Thus it is in light of the profundity of his philosophical sociology, rather than his scientific accuracy, that Simmel's writings must be interpreted and judged.

Georg Simmel's work is the work of an artist seeking to create for his audience, through paradox, "the experienced relations and activities of ourselves and of the varieties of confrontations through which we live."[3] To accomplish this he juxtaposes opposites to recall the irony of life. By stating contradictions he seeks to provide his audience with a sense of the polar potentialities inherent in human existence.

Simmel's is a dynamic model of human society and a dialectical view of historical development. His basic dialectical dualism is the tension between form and content. He posits a fundamental tension between the essential flux of our inner-subjective life and the limitations of the objective forms it can assume.[4] The dynamics of human existence stem from mankind's ceaseless struggle to reconcile this and other paired, interacting polarities that characterize the human condition. Psychic contents and social forms, stability and flexibility, conformity and individuation, harmony and conflict, compliance and resistance are among the most compelling polarities. Simmel believed people must reconcile these tensions within their own personalities and in their social existence, through creative synthesis.[5]

For Simmel, no particular social or political system but the very nature of human existence consists of a dialectical tension between individual creativity—which produces new social roles, social organizations, and forms of human interaction—and the power of these latter forms to become objectified, break loose from their original human purposes, take on a life of their own, and constrain future creativity and innovation. Once institutionalized, social forms, in his view, force life into generalized schemata, thereby robbing the individual personality of its uniqueness. The struggle between life and form becomes, for Simmel, a struggle between individuality and generalization.[6]

The following brief passages nicely capture both the intensity of Simmel's intuitive style and his implicit normative commitment to the forces of life, creativity, and individuality in the face of ceaseless struggle:

> Left to itself . . . life streams on without interruption; its restless rhythm opposes the fixed duration of any particular form. Each cultural form, once it is created, is gnawed at varying rates by the forces of life. As soon as one is fully developed, the next begins to form; after a struggle that may be long or short, it will inevitably succeed its predecessor.[7]

> The solid organizational forms which seem to constitute or create society, must constantly be disturbed, disbalanced, gnawed at by individualistic irregular forces, in order to gain their vital reaction and development through submission and resistance.[8]

Because of this commitment to individuality and creative life, Simmel's central question becomes: *"What can be done to insure that individual creativity will be able to overcome the growing objective cultural forms of urban capitalism?"*

SIMMEL'S MODEL OF MIND, SELF, AND SOCIETY

Georg Simmel wrote during a period of rapid technological development and major social and political change. Old institutional structures were continually faced with the need to adapt or die. Additionally, improved communication facilitated the diffusion of new ideas and engendered new forms of social life.[9] Simmel's central concern was the meanings and uses of these new social forms.

As the founder of the school known as "sociological formalism," Simmel believed that the only real social phenomenon was the individual human being. Society, for Simmel, is nothing more than an abstract term denoting the interactions between real individuals. Form and content rather than groups or institutions are the basic units of his sociological analysis. Diverse individual personalities and their inner creative drives constitute the content of social reality. The various relationships and interdependencies that develop between and among individuals comprise the forms of social interaction.

The proper function of sociology, in Simmel's view, is to grasp the deeper meanings and uses of recurring forms of social interaction. Forms, for Simmel, are like geometric abstractions. Their meaning can be separated analytically from the concrete reality through which they are expressed. The best method for discerning the meaning of such recurrent forms as rituals, customs, artistic conventions, and the like is intuitive insight, a "method" at which Simmel was uniquely adept.[10]

To convey his intuitive insights to others, Simmel chose a new mode of exposition. As described by Don Martindale, this mode consisted of "the isolation and comparison of particular relations manifested in widely different social contexts."[11] By means of this approach Simmel was able to isolate and detect the subtle implications of such distinctive but recurring forms of sociation as sociability, competition, and power relationships entailing super-subordination. In Simmel's view, these basic forms remain constant above and beyond historical contingency.

The potentialities inherent in all forms of interaction are polar dualisms. Simmel's belief in the inherent dialectical tension between form and content, solidarity and antagonism, conformity and individuation, submission and resistance stems in large measure from his psychological assumptions. Like Freud's, Simmel's view of human nature stresses the ambivalence of the basic instincts. Inner contradiction is seen as basic. For Simmel, "the conflict between society and individual is continued in the individual himself as the conflict among his component parts."[12]

The component parts of Simmel's psychological model of the individual exist in three concentric layers. The mind or intellect resides at the level of conscious thought. The mind is a differentiating organism that sorts out and seeks to make comprehensible distinctions out of the vast and highly diverse contents of the external world. The next layer, between the conscious mind and the psychic core of the personality, contains a whirling stream of images and impulses which periodically threaten to overpower both the intellect and the core, which carries "the real sense and substance of our life."[13]

This inner core of personality contains a bedrock of intimate psychic contents which form the basis of the individual's spiritual existence; Simmel held that it was the urbanite's essential task to discover and to cultivate this core. The twin dangers that threaten to frustrate the urban individual's creative search for spiritual refinement are the growing spirit of objectivity and rationalization on the one hand; the growing overexposure of the senses to external stimuli on the other. Simmel traces both of these developments to an emergent metropolitan "way of life."

The spirit of rationalization creates an urban social structure that rewards intellectual over emotional development. This threatens to dry up the wellsprings of the individual's emotional and spiritual being. The bombardment of the psyche by excessive sensory stimuli stirs up the intermediate layer of personality. This threatens to create a personality dominated by the "momentary impulses and isolated irritabilities" that reside at this level.[14] The components of the psyche, then, are permanently at war with one another.

Yet unlike many social theorists who have sought to harmonize the external world through either physical or socioeconomic planning, as a way to help people overcome these inner tensions, Simmel held that environmental contradictions are essential to human personality development. They cannot be planned away.

First, conflict is necessary for people to know the world. As a differentiating organism, the mind needs discordant stimuli in order to function. Only through the alternation of contrasts can the personality experience the environment. For Simmel, a perfectly harmonious, planned society is a denial of the nature of the mind.[15]

Second, and more paradoxically, the personality must experience coercion by various forces in the external environment if it is ever to discover the essential self buried deep in its inner core. Coercion is an irreplaceable triggering mechanism. It triggers the dialectics of resistance. In Simmelian thought, coercion gives the deeper, more meaningful, and more intimate undercurrent of the personality room to surface and be experienced as an irreplaceable entity which cannot be coerced or inhibited by any external social forces. Normally this undercurrent is concealed from consciousness by the rapidly moving stream of "momentary impulses" at the intermediate level of personality and by the routines of everyday life. Both of these barriers to deeper consciousness are altered when the personality experiences coercion.

Coercion "dams up" the torrent of rapidly alternating impulses swirling at the second layer. The deeper but more persistent undercurrent of personality thereby is given room to come to the surface. Coercion also interrupts the rhythm of everyday life. Both toleration of and opposition to this disruption make "conscious and effective the deeper currents of the most intimate and substantial life, which [we become aware] cannot be inhibited by any external means."[16]

Finally, external conflict and contradiction, particularly the tension between life and form, are the driving forces behind new modes of human existence. Simmel held that when forms of sociation become cultural forms they take on a causal power of their own. They become fixed formal constraints. They stand in permanent opposition to the creative life processes found deep within the personality. But this very tension lies behind the creative impulse to modify old forms and replace them with more vital modes of existence. The tension is the engine of all social change.[17]

Old forms are experienced by new creative forces as oppressive bonds in the realms of economics, politics, social life, art, science, and culture in general. Yet, once the new forces emerge, they too demand for themselves a permanence and universal validity which transcends the moment of their creation. Thus eventually the dynamic personality forces of any era begin to rebel against "form as such," even as they are contributing unwittingly to the creation of new forms. In Simmel's view, this creative antagonism between dynamic, creative life and "form as such" is especially characteristic of what he termed the modern age (1910–1918).

In place of the overriding grand ideals of earlier eras (e.g., the Enlightenment's commitment to reason), Simmel's "modern urban dwellers" give narrow and partial answers derived from their specialized occupational roles to cosmic questions concerning the meaning of existence. The modern age is too conceptual, too specialized, and too heterogeneous to permit the development of a simplifying conceptual ideal purporting to capture the essential meaning of life.

Nonetheless, in Simmelian thought, the modern repulsion against closed systems of all kinds represents a grand idea, the idea of formless life itself as the basic metaphysical reality, the purest expression of the creative essence of all being. Hence the modern urban desire for originality in cultural, social, and artistic expression functions to reassure people "that life is pure, that it has not diluted itself by absorbing extrinsic, objectified, rigid forms into its flow."[18] From this powerful subliminal motive springs the ideal of modern existential individualism and its attendant rebellion against the external role constraints of modern life.

METROPOLITAN LIFE AND ITS ROLE CONSTRAINTS

For Georg Simmel, social relationships always arise initially to serve basic human drives or purposes. The individual personality is the immediate, irreducible datum of historical reality. The individual's drives, interests, and psychic states make up the contents of all forms of sociation. In Simmel's view, the basic drives underlying social existence include survival, acquisitiveness, power seeking, and protection of cherished goods. Other ends that prompt individuals to enter into social relationships include erotic, religious, and play instincts, the felt need for assistance and education, and countless other more specific subjective incentives to collective action.

These inner motivations are the driving forces of human nature. They give purpose and direction to life. They are inner psychic rather than social phenomena. For Simmel, these inner drives and goals are either generally human or uniquely subjective in nature. They may, however, become "factors in sociation." This occurs, and the person becomes a social being, when actions undertaken to fulfill inner motivations serve to transform mere aggregates of isolated individuals "into specific forms of being with and for one another—forms that are subsumed under the general concept interaction."[19]

Yet once created, Simmel held that *social* forms tend to become fixed *cultural* predispositions. Such social forms as social roles, art forms, and organizational routines take on a life of their own. Originally created so that individuals can cope with the concrete demands of practical existence, social forms become separated from their initial entanglement with practical life. Culture is the medium through which this transformation occurs.

In the contemporary urban world, social forms and role constraints increasingly tend to determine human drives and purposes, rather than reflecting them. Inexorably, they begin to restrict rather than to reflect individual creativity.

Form and Content in Social Life

In Simmel's view, "the 'fetishism' which Marx assigned to economic commodities represents only a special case of [the] . . . general fate of the contents of culture."[20] All objective social forms are paradoxical. Originally created by and for individual human beings, they take on a developmental logic of their own. As forms are freed from their subjective origins, they outstrip their original purposes. In this way, for instance, modern technology produces products whose very development generates a series of closely related but unnecessary by-products.

The real tragedy of modern urban culture, in Simmel's view, lies in this emancipation of means and their conversion into ends in themselves. By an immanent logic of cultural development, social forms become bound by their own laws. Social organization becomes emancipated from human purposes. In the process, emergent properties of social organization "turn away from the direction by which they could join the personal development of human souls."[21] They exist to perpetuate themselves. This basic theme recurs in several different ways in Simmel's writings. The following five variations are illustrative of Simmel's underlying commitment to individual creativity as the basic value of human existence in an increasingly urbanized world.

The functions of role playing and ritual sociability. For Simmel, the increasing autonomy of social forms impoverishes human potential. It gradually leads to the dominance of form over content (e.g., the power of formal vs. empirical justice, bureaucratic formalism, ritualistic play, prescribed art forms). When forms become dominant, they take from the concrete realities of life "only what they can adapt to their own nature, only what they can absorb in their autonomous existence."[22] Consider, for example, Simmel's analysis of the character of *sociability*. The autonomous form of this particularly urban mode of association demands such traits as tact, amiability, and cordiality. These formal requirements preclude the spontaneous expression of individual personality in all of its "personal poignancy and autonomy."[23] Tact in particular is a socially useful but individually repressive form of interaction. Its essential social function is to establish limits, resulting from the claims of others, on the impulses and desires of the individual. To display the deeply personal intimacies of one's life, one's ups and downs of mood, feeling, and taste, as if one were in the presence of a close friend or a loved one, is regarded as tactless in most contemporary urban social contexts.

The requirements of sociability in urban society, then, constrain human beings. Social existence forces people to mask the dynamic complex of forces, ideas, and potentialities that is their nature. To avoid the breakdown of sociability which would result from fully exposing others to the fluctuating totality of psychic contents, urban dwellers assume distinctive social roles in particular social contexts. They are parents, professionals, sports enthusiasts, or social activists, depending on the context.

Assuming these roles serve to simplify other people's perceptions, they thereby facilitate interaction. But social roles are social forms. Like other purely formal properties, they tend to take on an autonomous existence. Originally assumed to enable the individual personality to "make of himself a differentiated and clearly defined [and hence communicable] phenomenon,"[24] these roles eventually come to determine the metropolitan personality's material existence and the range of other forms in which that life can be cast.

To act out ritual sociability, human beings learn not only to act discretely toward others, but also to act discretely toward the inner self. Metropolitan dwellers in particular, censor the purely personal, subjective contents of their lives from public view. Even such objective attributes as talent, resources, and fame, which might jeopardize ritual sociability, often are concealed from public view.

Yet ever the dialectician, Simmel viewed ritual sociability as stemming from positive as well as negative motives. He believed that human beings would be radically unwilling to repress their self-expression for purely negative reasons. Like Freud, Simmel believed that people enter into sociable relationships and accept the self-repression this entails not only to avoid the self-destruction of psychic overload, but also to fulfill the basically democratic goal of mutual pleasure. For Simmel, sociability entails such positive social values as reciprocal joy, liveliness, and relief. This is society's compensation for individual repression.

In Simmelian theory, such shared emotional experiences are possible only among formal equals. Formal equals stand in a social relationship unimpeded by purely personal expressions of the self. Such personal revelations can introduce ambiguity and strain into a relationship. Sociability, for Simmel, is a ritual game played to avoid the projection into a relationship of the unequal objective conditions which underlie all social systems. Ritual egalitarianism also masks the unique subjectivity of individual personality. To avoid conflict or friction, the sociable person creates an artificial world, a *semblance* of equally situated and similarly "natural" individuals. This fiction is willingly embraced because of the functions it serves.

Paradoxically, in the urban setting, Simmel's sociable person is self-deluded into believing that highly ritualized social gatherings such as parties actually allow a return to a state of people "as people," unencumbered by the complexity, conflict, and responsibilities of workaday urban existence. In Simmel's words:

> And forgetting these daily encumbrances at a social gathering, we fancy ourselves to return to our natural-personal existence. But under this impression we also forget that sociable man is constituted by this personal aspect, not in its specific character and in its naturalistic completeness, but only in a certain reservedness and stylization.[25]

Many social theorists have viewed the relatively greater equality of circumstances thought to characterize earlier human communities as giving free rein to natural, spontaneous human impulses. In contrast, Simmel held that in any society the sociability values of interaction can be gained only if the others with whom a person interacts also gain them. They are indivisible, collective benefits. Accordingly, even in earlier periods of history, people needed to act "as if" all were equal in nature and condition in order to experience conflict-free sociability. Human beings periodically become *sociable* equals, albeit in reality remaining unequal in talent, social status, power, subjective feeling, and other contents of life.

Thus, ironically, Simmel held that when people are totally unencumbered by the social roles which, taken together, seek to determine their existence, they become less open, spontaneous, and uniquely individual. By abandoning all the roles that distinguish them from others in a pure act of sociability, sociable individuals become irreducible common denominators—colorless, diluted, deindividuated beings. This is the fate of primitives as well as urbanites who seek escape from social complexity in ritual sociability.

Role conflict and the dialectics of resistance. City life poses a second major problem for individual creativity and self-expression. It makes too many role demands on the individual. These, in turn, engender role conflict, which may trigger the dialectics of resistance. The role expectations of the modern urban world are dialectically linked to the human need for autonomy. On the one hand, the competing claims and expectations of the various primary and secondary groups to which the individual belongs are major sources of role strain. They generate cross-pressures which sometimes produce inner turmoil, thereby reducing the ability of the individual to exercise autonomous choice. On the other hand, when taken collectively, the very weight of the total claims upon the individual's time and loyalty, when combined with the incompatibility of such claims (e.g., job vs. family requirements), produce a compelling urge for autonomy. This, in turn, prompts the modern urbanite to withhold some portion of his innerself from commitment to any of the various competing claims thrust upon him by others.

Simmel perceives contemporary urban "society" as a set of institutional imperatives which place heavy claims on the individual to function well as a member of an organic unit. In this struggle to achieve unity, completeness, and self-fulfillment, the human being has the capacity to act out many roles. At any given time, any one of these parts of the whole personality may be experienced as the individual's proper self. Yet, just as the individual confronts the many role requirements of urban institutions "as by an alien party,"[26] so, too, the personality may experience inner conflict engendered by its very capacity to assume multiple roles, many of which are partially incompatible when pursued simultaneously.

Sometimes the urban personality seeks temporary relief from pressing role expectations by retreating to the privacy of study, thoughts, or dreams. Simmel held that freedom is a continuous process of temporary liberation from all the social forces that make claims on the time, energy, and commitment of the individual. Each of these relations, which implicate the individual in complex urban society, seeks to extend its claims to the entire personality. Each competing claimant is profoundly indifferent to all other competing claims and interests. Thus the individual is limited both by the larger number of claims on his commitment and interest, and also by the relentlessly egoistic, "one-tracked and monopolistic pressure" of each claim for the whole of his presence. Confronting these often incompatible pressures, "the individual must *mark off* some *reserve* of forces, devotions, and interests that he has taken away from these relations."[27]

This one may do by fighting not for total independence, but for the right to choose which particular interdependent relationships will be entered into, and to what extent, and in what manner. Because the pressures for commitment are continuous, the fight for autonomy must be renewed following each victory. The absence of relations, whether achieved through voluntary isolation or by establishing priority among claims, is never fully secure. Rather, it represents "an incessant release from ties which actually limit the autonomy of the individual or which strive to do so."[28]

Yet in no case can any individual personality be totally absorbed within a single relationship. Some core within the personality invariably is withheld. Some facet of that which is not withheld is always developed in another direction. As Simmel puts it: "Even in the best case, one is married only with part of one's personality, however great that part be—even as one is never wholly a citizen of a city, wholly an economic man, wholly a church member."[29]

Despite Simmel's deep commitment to richly differentiated personality development, he recognized that the struggle for unbridled individual autonomy was a double-edged sword. In Simmelian social theory, freedom derives its meaning, value, and consciousness only as a reaction against a compelling social bond. Paradoxically, however, the individual may seek freedom in order to use it for the purpose of "making the self count" in given relationships. Freedom thus becomes a power relationship. The individual inevitably both ties and is tied to others. When freed temporarily from the social bond, the individual may use that freedom for "the domination and exploitation of other men."[30] It follows that those with the power resources to rise above most social bonds, including elites who more often exert than become subject to claims for individual loyalty, are likely to dominate exploitatively. Thus Simmel feared that the freedom necessary for creative contemplation and inner self-mastery might also be turned outward against the weak by the strong. The dialectics of resistance, triggered by excessive role strain, might lead to creative release or to new forms of repression, depending on circumstances.

Simmel knew that social and political groups vary in terms of the proportion of the members' total personality they absorb. He also recognized that too little commitment to group life might be as great a threat to autonomous personality development as was too much. The smaller the portion of the total personality a group absorbs, the more easily that group can become dominated by a single individual or a small elite. Intragroup elitism arises from indifferent, segmental memberships; such memberships are the sine qua non of modern urban life. In contrast, when a considerable portion of members' personalities was involved in group life, as in the Greek city states, or the burghers of medieval cities, Simmel held that elite domination was impracticable, if not contradictory.[31] This is because members devoted time and energy to collective decision making in direct proportion to the amount of their total personality that the collectivity absorbed.

The uses of impersonality and formal controls. Despite this danger of elitism, Simmel was inclined to examine all facets of a complex question. He felt that the formal and impersonal laws and organizations of urban society might enhance in some respects the very individual power and freedom that they threatened in other ways. For example, although they were less flexible and more impersonal than were the customary norms of small groups, laws and formal organizational requirements also were less arbitrary, ambiguous, and extensive. The consequences of this distinction are made clear by Simmel's analysis of the positive functions of urban impersonality and formal social controls.

For Simmel, group size, impersonality, and individual power are closely interrelated. In his view, "[I]t is hard to reconcile personal relations, which are the very life principle of small groups, with the distance and coolness of objective and abstract norms without which the large group cannot exist."[32] The unity and cohesion of large collectivities, such as cities and bureaucracies, are possible only through a refined division of labor; formal, abstract rules of law; and various complex organizational structures which serve as linking mechanisms. "The large group gains its unity, which finds its expression in the group organs and in political notions and ideals, only at the price of great distance between all of these structures and the individual."[33]

But this greater distance between formal structures and the individual and among persons does not necessarily entail less freedom or greater powerlessness. Simmel distinguishes the formality and impersonality of law from its scope and extensiveness. Custom, unlike formal law, regulates a wide variety of aspects of life. When the power of social customs to regulate behavior breaks down in large groups, it is replaced by law. Law is a rigorous and objective embodiment of collective norms. Formalized norms are clearly enunciated and require severe "surveillance of socially necessary inhibitions."[34] Nonetheless they are more bearable to the individual than is the cohesive power of custom, since the urbanite's sphere of freedom, mobility, and individualization is greater outside the realm where formal rules are rigorously enacted. Indeed, the spread of social mobility and individuation of values and life style is what prompts the need for clearer determination and greater formality and explicitness of normative prohibitions in the first place. Hence, outside the realm of formal law, Simmel argued that informal social controls necessarily would be weaker in the large-scale metropolitan setting than in smaller, more traditional social communities.

An additional source of increased freedom in the metropolis stems from the different organizational needs of the larger collectivities as against small, organized groups. Large-scale collectivities, with greater resources and a more refined division of labor, do not continuously claim the total personality of every member. They can afford not to exploit some human energies which need only be drawn upon during times of emergency.[35] In modern parlance, this relatively greater "organizational slack" of the metropolis and its large-scale organizations facilitates the city's survival potential in the face of rapid migration and other sources of rapid change and organizational stress.

Personal vs. social integration. Yet the complex division of labor which is highly functional at the social level also has negative consequences at the level of individual personality. In Simmel's view, the most severe source of role conflict in the modern urban milieu emerges from the heavy pressure which society exerts on the individual to develop the functional, occupational specialization which most fully contributes to a well-integrated social whole. A large social group, such as a city, requires a complex division of labor to function as a unity. Only a complex specialization of functions and division of labor can produce the interdependence which cohesively links each to all. In Simmel's view, the requirements of work specialization demand the virtual exclusion of other human roles the individual might wish to play.

Mirroring this effort by society to integrate the individual's behavior into the social fabric is the individual's own drive toward wholeness, causing a rebellion against any personal definition solely in terms of a single occupational role. "The individual strives to be rounded out in himself, not merely to help to round out society."[36] For Simmel, this struggle between the one-sided demands of the whole and the individual quest for wholeness and self-perfection is inevitable and insoluble.

Rejecting the conventional philosophical dichotomy between individual egoism and societal altruism, Simmel held that the individual's urge toward self-fulfillment may be an ideal whose aim is neither egoistic subjective happiness nor narrow self-interest, but rather *self-perfection*. Simmel defines self-perfection as an objective, "super-personal value realized in the personality."[37] The pursuit of excellence and integrity (wholeness) is often mistaken for egoism, which is held to be incompatible with social development. In Simmel's view, self-perfection, far from being incompatible with social development, is a primary source of social innovation and creative social change. The world is enriched by the presence of human beings who stimulate our aspirations by personifying perfection itself.

Additionally, Simmel argues that the very effort of modern urban society to integrate the individual part to the whole is itself a kind of egoism. The egoism of the organizational demand for social integration "does violence to the individual for the benefit and utility of the many." It often leads to an "extremely one-sided individual specialization, and even atrophy."[38] The metropolitan, industrialist capitalist economy seeks to incorporate the individual in fixed form into its own structure. Its claims are especially pronounced if the individual wishes to achieve self-realization in an unorthodox, economically superfluous, or socially unappreciated manner. Specialization tends to be incompatible with personality development, both because it ignores or destroys a person's harmonious wholeness and because it "foists contents on the individual that are wholly inimical to the qualities usually called general-human."[39]

Human vs. social development. As with Nietzsche, human fulfillment for Simmel is an act of transcendence. The development of *humankind,* as against the development of any particular individual or society, is based on "the elevation and objective enrichment of the type 'man' himself."[40] Contributions to the development of humanity—religious, scientific, and aesthetic achievement, and objective productions that are not aimed at any utilitarian goals—are difficult to create. They require the pursuit of excellence, whereas the norms of society promote a leveling of its members. For Simmel, social conventions and specialized, socially valued roles regulate human behavior in urban society by creating an average standard of performance. Society employs social sanctions in ways that make it difficult for potentially innovative members to transcend this average.

As we have seen, society also requires that expression of the individual's purely personal qualities—strength, depth of thought, greatness of conviction, commitment to beauty, nobility, courage, and the like—be tempered by the twin requirements of sociability and specialization. Thus in Simmel's words:

> Society requires the individual to differentiate himself from the *humanly general* but forbids him to stand out from the *socially general*. The individual is thus doubly oppressed by the standards of society: He may not transcend them either in a more general or in a more individual direction.[41]

Role playing, specialization, role conflict, impersonality, and formal social controls all shape the metropolitan life style. These forces, in turn, are vitally affected by the pervasive impact of the urban capitalist money economy.

The Uses of Money

Georg Simmel's analysis of the social and psychological consequences of the money economy is extraordinarily complex and subtle. Several major consequences of capitalist development are discernible in Simmel's thought. A highly developed money economy creates conditions which foster changes in the way people relate to each other, their associational life, their work, and their culture.

Money and detachment. Simmel held that the conditions of an advanced economy facilitate a heretofore unattainable personal anonymity. This is because of three central characteristics of the monetary form. Money is *compressible*. Unlike concrete forms of wealth, such as land, money "permits one to make somebody rich by slipping a check into his hand without anybody noticing it."[42] Money is also *abstract* and *qualityless*. These features keep financial transactions hidden from perception and render them socially unrecognizable. Money likewise can have an effect at a distance. This enables it to be invested in remote locations or transactions and thereby withdrawn from the purview of the immediate environment.

In part for these reasons, in part because of growing work specialization and loosened, informal social controls, modern urban life is characterized by increased individual privacy. As Simmel puts it: "In less developed stages [of society] . . . the individual and his conditions cannot, to the same extent, protect themselves against being looked into and meddled with as under the modern style of life, which has produced an entirely new measure of reserve and discretion, especially in large cities."[43]

Additionally, the extensive exchange of money contributes to the rise of "noncommital" relationships based on the cash nexus. In a capitalist exchange economy, the totality of personality remains outside the economic relationship. Simmel held that, under these conditions, a person can increasingly come to depend upon an ever wider circle of other people without losing personal autonomy, without becoming extensively dependent on any one of these relationships. Those upon whom the individual becomes dependent are significant only in their economic function. This postfeudal form of interpersonal relationship greatly enhances individual autonomy. The modern urban dweller who has been absorbed into the industrial money economy

> depends on more people, but much less on a specific individual. Because he is dependent on the function and not on the bearer of the function, he can change and select the latter according to his own choice. This gives him an inner independence, a feeling of individual self-sufficiency. His freedom consists in his ability to change the individuals on whom he shall depend.[44]

In this way, the money economy fosters not only an increased potential for self-sufficiency, but also an increased emotional detachment from others. Relationships become less personal and more functional. Urban life becomes more and more rationalized. Because the modern metropolis is the seat of a highly developed money economy, Simmel viewed this growing tendency toward the rationalization of urban life as unavoidable. The dominance of the intellect over emotional life is intrinsically connected to the development of the money economy. For Simmel, the major social consequence of this is the transformation of personal relationships into exchange relationships. Exchange objectifies human interaction. By robbing relations of their purely spontaneous character, exchange converts the relations among people into relations among objects. As the exchange of self-contained objects of equivalent value comes to dominate human relationships, material goods take on a life of their own. In a fully developed money economy, "men act only as the executors of the tendencies toward shifts and equilibrium that are inherent in the goods themselves."[45] The subjective self becomes irrelevant to human relationships. These come to be defined solely in terms of exchange of objective value for objective value. Calculation and computation come to dominate other human traits as more and more time is spent in relations entailing the precise measure of value for value.

Simmel argued that the extensive use of money greatly facilitates exact exchange. Money expresses a general measure of value contained in all exchangeable objects. But by assigning all objects a precise exchange value, money becomes incapable of expressing any individual or personal meaning and value inherent in them. Thus objects, like relationships, become degraded: "the individual in them is leveled down to the general which is shared by everything salable, particularly by money itself."[46]

The poverty of human relationships is further accentuated because reciprocal monetary exchanges increasingly involve appreciation of only the benefits of the exchange, rather than the kind of subtle and grateful "being-for-one-another" involved in more intimate relations. People become instruments in each others' hands, rather than ends in themselves.

Not all exchange relationships entail precision and exactness. Exchanges of intellectual for affective values, or aesthetic values for encouragement and support, for instance, cannot be precisely measured. There is a certain incommensurability, consisting of each party's awareness that the relationship "can neither be exhausted nor realized by any finite return gift or other activity."[47] Here it is the relationship itself which is valued by each party, rather than any calculable benefits of the exchange. Each person gives of himself in full spontaneity, neither incurring nor expecting any precise duty or obligation in return.

Simmel held that, in urban environments, both the money economy and the dominance of the intellect share a matter-of-fact attitude toward the world. This robs human relationships of warmth, sensitivity, spontaneity, and charisma. Matter-of-factness excludes a great deal of reality which cannot be reduced neatly to logical or calculable operations.

Individuality and qualitative uniqueness in people and in things is reduced to the question "How much?" Since this question comes to dominate consciousness, matter-of-factness slips over into the normative realm. It becomes a way of evaluating life.

In a developed urban capitalist economy, Simmel held that utilitarian standards of judgment come to dominate the evaluative faculty. A rigidly formal justice replaces empirical justice; the former excludes purely personal factors from decision making. In human relationships only measurable achievements are valued. The warmth which often accompanies an awareness of another's unique individuality is replaced by an "inconsiderate hardness." Human contacts and relationships are cemented instead by an "objective balancing of service and return."[48] This calculability and increased formality leads directly to a loss of appreciation for "genuine individuality." Such appreciation entails an emotional openness to personal subjectivity which cannot be exhausted by logic. Market exchange relationships destroy intimacy; personalism is replaced by impersonality.

In Simmel's view, "industrial" capitalism's market production dominates the metropolitan economy. Market production almost entirely supplies the goods consumed in the modern metropolis. Remote producers are seldom if ever visible to consumers. The interests of producer and consumer are entirely unaffected by personal eccentricities.

They meet as "intellectually calculating economic egoisms."[49] Calculative exactness transforms the surface world into an arithmetic problem. Qualitative values are reduced to quantitative ones. The increased precision which this measure of value entails reduces the mystery and ambiguity of interpersonal ties.

The increasingly complex interdependence of these calculative-instrumental relationships necessitates a major change in the tempo and rhythm of life. Metropolitan dwellers must order their schedules and interactions with each other according to the "strictest punctuality in promises and services."[50] Without the external discipline of the clock, the entire structure of mutual interdependencies might break down. Punctuality is a key regulative and integrating mechanism of metropolitan life.

As in the case of calculability and exactness, punctuality begins as a "banal externality of life," but ultimately takes on a life of its own. It forces people to adhere to a fixed schedule of appointed rounds that reduces the possibilities of spontaneous human interaction. Each of these formal social controls is forced upon life by the money economy and the complex division of labor. In David Reisman's terminology, they become "other directed" role constraints.[51] They ultimately become connected with and strive to determine "the ultimate decisions concerning the meaning and style of life."[52] One of their major consequences is to devalue subjective, emotional, sentimental, irrational, and instinctive dispositions, which in Simmel's view are mankind's "sovereign traits."

In Simmel's model of human nature, these sovereign traits incessantly seek spontaneous expression. They "aim at determining the mode of life *from within*, instead of receiving the general and precisely schematicized form of life from without."[53]

But functional specialization and external role constraints conspire to create a highly schematized mode of existence. The coalescence of punctuality, specialization, calculability, and the brevity, scarcity, and exactness of interpersonal contacts creates a socioeconomic structure that rewards impersonality and abstract thinking. Roles within this structure foster the development of excessively specialized, highly rationalistic personality types. In the process of becoming socialized into metropolitan life, inner instincts and sentiments, the driving forces in the individual struggle for fellowship, self-mastery, and self-perfection are frustrated.

Money and group life. According to Simmel, money has associative as well as dissociative consequences. Money makes possible the rise of new forms of urban organization based upon shared economic interests. By complicating the social structure, through fostering a more refined division of labor, the metropolitan money economy contributes to the rise of special-interest groups. Persons radically different from each other in many respects may nonetheless share a common, impersonal interest in economic interaction.

On the other hand, money also fosters geographic and social mobility. This threatens to undermine traditional forms of association based on local and extended family ties. The growth of monetary exchange encourages the development of "rootless personalities" that do not know how to use their newly acquired freedom to achieve spiritual refinement. Such personality types become wholly attached to acquisitive values. They tend to experience freedom only as freedom from external control. They have no sense of transcendent purpose or direction in their lives.

Simmel believed that, in the modern urban setting, individuation developed to its fullest extent. No individual's overall pattern of group affiliations was exactly like that of any other individual. As the development of modern industrial society progresses, associations based on external coexistence or the accident of birth are more and more superceded by those based on shared interests, talents, and activities. Interest-group-based affiliations—trade, occupation, common rational purpose—create new interpersonal contacts. These "penetrate every nook and cranny of the contacts that are earlier, relatively more natural and that are held together by relationships of a more sensual kind."[54] Rationally shared interests become relatively more important in defining the identity of the mature individual than our earlier ties based on family, nationality, or geographic locale.

Through these developments the realm of freedom is extended. Dependence on group life has not ceased. Yet the newer forms of association are based on choice rather than tradition. In Simmel's view, contemporary metropolitan individuals can actualize their full potential as social beings by choosing with whom to associate, upon whom to become dependent, and how to make desires and beliefs felt.[55] As a rule, inherited and localized relationships offer fewer such choices. Custom, limited contacts, and well-defined family roles stand in the way.

Unlike group participation in the medieval era, where particular group affiliations had a deeper and more meaningful significance for the individual personality, but were more limited in number, modern urban group formation makes it possible for the individual to join a large number of widely diverse groups.

This pattern of group participation has several consequences for the individual personality. First, each individual loses similarities with every other individual. Each is no longer predominantly tied to a single primary group, but stands at a unique point of intersection of many groups. The more groups to which an individual belongs, the less likely are others to manifest exactly the same pattern of group affiliations. Each individual's pattern of group participation is unique; so also are the personalities which are the by-product of innumerable social influences.

This uniquely socialized individual personality faces new problems. Uncertainty and ambiguity replace the security and clarity of previously comprehensive and unambiguous social roles. The multiplicity of group affiliations gives rise to both inner tensions and external role conflict. At its most extreme, such inner turmoil can lead to schizophrenic breakdown.

At the same time, however, it is possible for multiple group affiliations to strengthen the integration of personality. They can enhance self-consciousness: "Conflicting tendencies can arise just because the individual has a core of inner unity. The ego can become more clearly conscious of this unity, the more he is confronted with the task of reconciling within himself a diversity of group-interests."[56] The need to resolve role conflicts deriving from the diversity of group interests in the urban milieu can give people a better grasp of themselves as personalities. Simmel's belief in this dual potentiality of membership in contemporary urban interest groups is nicely summed up in the following statement:

> An advanced culture broadens more and more the social groups to which we belong . . . ; but at the same time the individual is made to rely on his own resources to a greater extent and he is deprived of many supports and advantages associated with the tightly-knit, primary group. Thus, the creation of groups . . . in which any number of people can come together on the basis of their interest in a common purpose, compensates for that isolation of the personality which develops out of breaking away from the narrow confines of earlier circumstances.[57]

Money and work alienation: an unorthodox view. The detachment of self from others that accompanies increased individual autonomy is mirrored by detachment of urban dwellers from their work. Prior to the introduction of money as the central measure of worth and medium of exchange, human worth tended to be closely associated with the tasks which a worker performed. Without money, a person's talent for creating nonsubstitutable material objects (e.g., food, clothing, or shelter) was closely tied to survival. This made it difficult, if not impossible, to withdraw very much personality from one's productive role.

With the rise of a developed money economy and the spread of mass production, single productive objects become increasingly interchangeable. More types of functional roles can lead to the acquisition of money. Since money rather than concrete productive talent can insure survival, new occupational roles emerge. Occupational differentiation increases, and so too does the abstract nature of many occupations. Fewer people are directly engaged in directly productive roles. Money makes possible the enjoyment of the fruits of productive activity without concrete participation in its actual production. Because of the mass nature of the productive process, those roles which are directly productive become progressively less demanding upon consciousness.

Unlike Marx, who was deeply troubled by these developments, Simmel tended to stress the positive functions of work alienation. For Simmel, as personality becomes estranged from the products of work, it is liberated for development in other directions. In "The Web of Group Affiliations" Simmel discusses the relationship between work life and contemporary urban consciousness.[58] He argues that urban occupational life no longer requires the use of ideas derived from nonvocational life. When work thus becomes more narrow and specialized, the amount of consciousness "used up" by work is limited. An unspecialized occupation demands the appropriation of a great deal of imaginative psychic energy. This energy is denied to the individual for use in cultivating other interests. As a result, Simmel believed that the interests which persons in nonspecialized occupations can cultivate become dependent upon the all encompassing world of work. He describes these work-related interests as "enfeebled interests" which stand in the way of richly individuated personality development.

Simmel's model of personality development here begins to resemble the self-protective strategies of the aim-inhibited Freudian personality. Simmel characteristically calls for the withholding of deeply held emotional attachments to people, things, and particular pursuits, lest such identifications become so compelling as to preclude psychic energy from being "invested" in other facets of life. He warns that the person genuinely committed to work as a central goal develops an emotional life akin to the person absorbed by a great passion. Foreshadowing Herbert Marcuse, Simmel argued that such persons tend to lack richness, subtlety, grace, and refinement. They tend to be unidimensional.

Money and the tragedy of urban culture. At the cultural level, the money economy rewards calculability. It favors intellectualism over the cultivation of the emotive self. It contributes to a cultural predilection toward "scientistic" thinking. The scientistic thinker assumes that only that which can be quantitatively measured is real. This amounts to a discounting of qualitative values and an impoverishment of life. Finally, and perhaps most importantly, the economy of industrial capitalist cities grossly increases the amount of objects which confront the individual. Objects threaten to outstrip and overwhelm the human being's personal-subjective and creative life. This, for Simmel, is the real tragedy of capitalist culture. It fosters the growth of "objective spirit" in interpersonal relationships, overproduces overbearing cultural artifacts, and thereby deadens the creative spirit.

Simmel was critical of "objective culture" not only because it forced people into stylized and overly rationalistic modes of existence, but also because both of these consequences diverted and diluted the spirit of creativity. Simmel held that the growing supply of objectified spirit to be found in cities cluttered the mind and deadened the will to creativity.

In Simmelian psychology the absorptive capacity of the mind is limited. Hence the self normally selects from among the objects arrayed before it a limited number to become means to individual development. But in the industrial capitalist city, the infinitely growing supply of objective forms "places demands before the subject, creates desires in him, hits him with feelings of individual inadequacy and helplessness."[59] The individual cannot withdraw from the impact of this vast supply of material objects. Yet their sheer mass depresses the personality, causing an inability to assimilate and master their particular contents. In the urban environment, people are richer but more overloaded. City life confronts modern urbanites with the prospect of having everything but truly possessing nothing.

For Simmel, the tragedy of urban culture is the impoverishment of the creative spirit, its frustration in feelings of powerlessness and overstimulation. Simmel's sardonic conclusion to his essay "On the Concept and the Tragedy of Culture" poignantly captures this tragic flaw of urban capitalist development:

> The adornment and overloading of our lives with a thousand superfluous items, from which, however, we cannot liberate ourselves; the continuous "stimulation" of civilized man, who in spite of all this is not stimulated to expressions of individual creativity; the mere acquaintance with or enjoyment of a thousand things which stay in it only as ballast—all these long-lamented cultural ills are nothing more than reflections of the emancipation of the objectified spirit.[60]

Overstimulation and Psychic Overload

Simmel believed that this overloading combined with the density, heterogeneity, and space conquering technology of modern city life thrust a plethora of unexpected, discontinuous, rapidly changing images upon human consciousness. As a consequence, the finite psyche becomes overloaded with mental images. The metropolitan environment intensifies nervous stimulation. The predictable rhythms of rural life extract little consciousness from the individual. A highly developed metropolis makes greater demands.

The Simmelian person, it will be recalled, is a differentiating creature whose mind is stimulated by and responds to sequences of "momentary impressions" given off by the contents of the external environment. If the environment is dominated by relatively stable, permanent, and undifferentiated forces, as in the case of the simple social structure of small town life, little consciousness is required to comprehend the environment. In contrast, the rapid tempo, complex social roles, and overbearing artifacts of the modern metropolis create rapidly changing images. These place heavy demands upon consciousness.[61]

In order to cope with random and excessive stimulation, the intellect, the most adaptable of the inner psychic forces, develops its sophistication to a high point. In part this is because the intellect is less sensitive than the more unconscious psyche. In part, heightened intellectual sophistication also preserves the deeper inner subjective life from disturbance and disorientation by the potentially overwhelming external forces of metropolitan life.

Ironically, in Simmel's view, the individual copes with the heightened objectivity, impersonality, and overstimulation of the metropolitan environment by cultivating a highly personal subjectivity in one of two ways—by assuming a blasé attitude toward the world which protects the deeper subjective self from the environment, or by projecting the inner self upon the environment through exaggerated self-display. The former choice is reinforced by the individual's desire to avoid overstimulation and psychic overload. The latter is reinforced by the blasé attitude itself. The two choices are dialectically interrelated and mutually self-defeating. It is to these choices that we now turn.

The blasé attitude, antipathy, and urban reserve. For Simmel, the excessive nervous stimulation engendered by city life leads directly to a "blunting of discrimination" termed the blasé attitude. Simmel defines this attitude as "an incapacity . . . to react to new sensations with the appropriate energy."[62] The blasé posture is a product of three forces: physiological overstimulation, the cultural devaluation of genuine subjective differences flowing from industrial capitalism, and the desire to preserve the deep inner core of the personality in the face of both these developments.

Ever paradoxical, Simmel suggests that this deep-seated desire for self-preservation contains within itself the seeds of self-alienation. To protect the inner core from becoming overwhelmed, the metropolitan personality devalues the whole objective world. But since the human being is inherently in the world, since the knower existentially is part of the reality known, the devaluation of the "external" world unavoidably drags the personality down into the same feeling of worthlessness one has projected onto the world.[63]

Yet, in Simmel's view, metropolitan life would be unimaginable without the particular form of devaluation of others known as antipathy. For Simmel, "the whole inner organization of urban interaction is based on an extremely complex hierarchy of sympathies, indifferences, and aversions," both short-lived and enduring.[64] But the Simmelian zone of indifference is relatively limited in scope. This is because, as feeling beings, people tend to react to others with some determinate feeling.

Both pure indifference and the ambiguity engendered by innumerable contradictory stimuli are unnatural and unbearable to the personality. Thus antipathy, a kind of mild aversion, is the basic defense mechanism that protects the personality from the dangers of city life. Without this initially antagonistic posture toward others, urban life would be impossible. Thus, in Simmelian social theory, various forms, rhythms, and combinations of antipathy inhere in all metropolitan social relationships.

Far from being a form of alienation, antipathy, for Simmel, is the elemental form of urban sociation. Within the metropolis, this mild aversion makes possible an unprecedented amount of personal freedom and invididual mobility. More importantly, however, a general aversion to others also is a necessary prerequisite to particular shared sympathies. In Simmel's view, modern urban friendships are based on shared segmental interests and mutual personal choice. General aversion necessarily precedes the particular selection of one's friends.

Heightened display. The Simmelian urban dweller encounters difficulty expressing the subjective personality within the role constraints of metropolitan life because of the defenses which others assume to protect themselves from overstimulation. To cope with this situation, Simmel observed that many persons adopt and display the most exaggerated differences from others. In Simmel's view, a person who seeks to gain recognition in this way is usually attempting to cope with an inner sense of "negligibility" fostered by the large-scale, impersonal, highly regulated urban cultural environment subsumed under the term "objective spirit." Extravagances of manner, dress, life style, and personal idiosyncracy are assumed and projected as a way to "attract the attention of the social circle by playing up its sensitivity for differences."[65]

In an urban world where most people are indifferent if not mildly repulsed in the presence of others, "being different" takes on new meaning and significance. It is a way to stand out from others, to attract attention, and to gain a modicum of self-esteem. The metropolitan personality yearns to be recognized as somehow unique in a world of objective processes and things grown to such proportions as to dwarf the individual's unsatisfied yearning for personal "significance." Feeling trivial and impotent in the face of "objective culture" (i.e., the institutions, knowledge, social forms, artifacts, and mass mode of production of the metropolis), the individual rebels by flamboyantly displaying the subjective self. Or as Simmel succinctly puts it, the oppressive weight of objective culture

. . .results in the individual's summoning the utmost uniqueness and particularization, in order to preserve his most personal core. He has to exaggerate this personal element in order to remain audible even to himself.[66]

Although Simmel does not draw the obvious conclusion, heightened subjective display clearly is a self-defeating mechanism for coping with self-estrangement and social alienation. This is because the greater the number of people who choose to exaggerate their subjectivity in this way, the greater is the degree of differentiation in the external environment; the greater the differentiation, the more striking the contrasts, the more intensified the stimuli, and the greater the burden of psychic overload. Since detachment, aversion, and the blasé attitude are direct consequences of overstimulation and psychic overload in the first place, heightened display of subjectivity is bound to strengthen the very defense mechanisms which it is intended to penetrate. Nor does Simmel make the more subtle point that some forms of display such as flamboyant dress actually conceal more than they reveal of a person's inner subjectivity.

In a note devoted to the social functions of adornment in his larger work on "Secrecy,"[67] Simmel does advance the argument that personal adornment impresses others only when it symbolizes purely general human characteristics that conceal the will to power at the heart of all forms of exaggerated display. The intended function of adornment, according to Simmel, is to single out the personality, to stress it as in some sense outstanding—by filling others with pleasure. Yet for Simmel, pleasing another is essentially a means of expressing the will to power. By pleasing the other through adornment, the individual seeks to become an object of attention not received by others; he seeks to distinguish the self from others. This is only a short step from "wanting to be envied," a relationship within which one's sense of satisfaction is entirely dependent on the awareness of others that they are in some sense subordinate to the wearer of adornment. The self-image of the wearer is built not upon inner motivations, but upon the reactions of the envious person. The responses of the envier to the accentuated display of the personality concretized in physical adornment "prove" to the wearer that he or she is an individual worthy of recognition and admiration. Through adornment what a person has becomes "a visible quality of its *being*."[68]

Adornment likewise symbolizes personal freedom from social restraints. Its superfluousness, brilliance, and flamboyance convey the deceptive message that "no extant structure, such as is laid down by necessity, imposes any limiting norm upon it."[69] Ironically, the very accentuation of the personality in this way in the metropolitan environment projects neither personal qualities nor characteristics, but a purely impersonal trait—worldly fashion.

Since most new adornments can be worn by anyone who can afford them, their effect is general rather than individual. Like "style," adornments structure the contents of personal life and activities into a general form shared by and accessible to many. On the one hand, both adornment and style enlarge the individual "by adding something superindividual which goes out to all and is noted and appreciated by all";[70] on the other hand, they diminish the individual because they fail to express the uniqueness of a subjective life. As in the expressive aspects of a work of art, these latter values and attributes penetrate to the spectator's personal core. The superficial and the purely general may be appreciated by all, but they fail to penetrate to any person's inner core.

Paradoxically then, adornment creates distance rather than closeness among people. At the same time that it seems to exist only as a kind of favor to the observer, adornment, like jewelery, symbolically communicates to others: "I have something which you do not have. I have both money and a unique sense of style." But, since adornment is enmeshed in the superficial, the symbolically general quest for freedom, and the masked will to power, it triggers resistance by those it seeks to please.

Urban Privacy

If neither the blasé attitude nor heightened display provide a fully satisfactory answer to the urban personality's predicament, where does one turn for solace? For Simmel the answer lies in turning inward. In Simmelian social psychology, city life can enhance personality development by allowing the individual a good deal of room for privacy, contemplation, and inner reflection. The city crowd makes one feel lonely, but urban privacy sets one free. As we shall see in chapter four, this view is almost exactly the opposite of the thesis of Richard Sennett's book *The Uses of Disorder*. In Simmel's view, "the feeling of isolation is rarely as . . . intense when one actually finds oneself physically alone, as when one is a stranger, without relations, among many physically close persons at a party, on a train, or in the traffic of a large city. Close and intimate communities often allow no such intercellular vacuums."[71]

Because folk societies allow no room for privacy, for that periodic intentional turning away from society, they frustrate the human need for inner self-reflection, which is a primary driving force behind inner self-mastery and creative social change.

Simmel held that isolation, like freedom, is much more than the mere negation of association. Contemplative isolation might entail nostalgic reverie, the "lingering on of past relationships," or the anticipation of future relationships. Such activities of memory and imagination might take place in the mind of the "isolate" and in the mind of his "significant others." In this way, contemplative isolation actually becomes a type of interaction between two parties, "one of which leaves after exerting certain influences."[72] Understood in this way, the isolate continues to act and to live on in the memory of the departed party, and vice versa.

Thus, unlike later social theorists who tended to view urban social isolation as a likely cause of normlessness and alienation, Simmel held that at least some forms of isolation are functional components of social cohesion. Voluntary isolation, or privacy, can provide room for inner reflection and contemplation of the meaning and nuances of social relations. City life may make one feel lonely in a crowd; but it also provides the comforting assurance of a private realm of existence. Privacy, in turn, fosters personal individuation, social innovation, and more bearable and meaningful social relationships.

Role Playing and Urban Friendship

Simmel believed that no personal relationship could develop any intensity or nuance unless each party, through words and actions, revealed the self to the other. Reciprocal knowledge is acquired by each party forming a personal unity out of the fragments and facets of the self which each makes accessible to the other. This perceived unity is based upon only that portion of the total personality which the knower's perspective permits him to see. It depends on the forms which the knower's mind brings to the situation and the contents and forms received from the person known. Each relationship between two people creates a picture of each in the other's consciousness. Interaction subsequent to the first encounter likewise is based on mutually acquired pictures. Both are interwoven into a mysterious unity of being and conceiving which is analytically difficult to express but empirically clearly felt.[73]

Unlike other known objects, another person has the unique capacity to conceal or reveal the truth about parts of the self. Yet no person can fully reveal the whole of the inner personality to another because in large measure that inner reality is an utterly chaotic stream of consciousness, a "whirling of images and ideas" whose accurate and faithful presentation in terms of sequence and content would overwhelm consciousness and, in Simmel's view, "drive everybody into the insane asylum."[74] To avoid this chaotic psychic overload, we impose logic, order, and purpose upon our communications with others. We transform, reduce, and recompose the flux of our inner reality. In this sense all actions and communications are selective, stylized presentations of the self. Far from being deceptive, however, selective projection of fragments of our inner life is the only way that people in a highly differentiated world can intersubjectively communicate with one another.

Simmel held that the metropolis was the locus of particular social structural conditions—a highly differentiated and increasingly complex and fluid class structure—which fostered an entirely new form of social intimacy: the segmental friendship. In Simmelian social theory, friendship requires less personal abandon than the act of love. Because friendship entails less complete vulnerability than does love, it tends to melt reserves more readily. Yet, with growing personal and social differentiation in urban society, the shared intimacy of a comprehensive friendship becomes more difficult to achieve. In Simmel's words:

> Modern man, possibly, has too much to hide, i.e., too many secrets and idiosyncrasies to sustain a friendship in the ancient sense. Besides, except for their earliest years, personalities are perhaps too individualized to allow full receptivity, which always . . . requires much creative imagination and much divination which is oriented only toward the other.[75]

As a consequence of these obstacles, Simmel thought that modern urban friendships tended to become segmental, involving only one or a few selected aspects of personality, without involving most other dimensions. For instance, some modern friendships function solely on the affective level, others in terms of shared intellectual interests, common experiences, tastes, and the like. All of these types of specialized friendships, in Simmel's view, require a tacit mutual agreement by parties not to reveal aspects of themselves to each other which could painfully underline the limits of their mutual sharing.

Yet Simmel did not hold that specialized friendships destroyed all possibility for intimacy in the modern urban milieu. Although restricted in scope and bounded by discretion, differentiated friendships nonetheless could stem from and be reached by each party's ultimate inner core. Although only part of each person's periphery was reached, this part could feed upon "the sap of the ultimate roots of personality."[76]

Implicit in Simmel's view of specialized friendships is the notion that such friendships actually function to ward off the compulsion toward complete revelation, which is a driving force of both love and more comprehensive friendship in the ancient sense. Segmental friendships cut through and simplify the whirling stream of consciousness which can more freely enter into friendships that are less bounded by implicit restrictions.

Since complete revelation is a major factor accounting for the dissolution of interpersonal relationships, segmental friendships, while initially more difficult to cement, may actually be more enduring than either love or ancient friendship. Yet, ever the dialectician, Simmel recognized that, in the modern metropolis, people's interests often assume new directions. The opportunities for such shifts in interest or emphasis abound because of urban social heterogeneity. Accordingly, segmental friendships are bound to be only as stable as the interests of their participants are enduring. Held together by the thread of only one or a few common interests, segmental friendships contain within themselves the potential for either disintegration or reciprocal interpenetration and endurance.

Simmel believed the quality of such segmental relationships was closely related to the size of the group or social setting within which social interaction transpired. In Simmel's view, it is impossible in principle for a large, physically proximate group (e.g., a party, an urban crowd) to facilitate the sharing of "spiritual refinement." For Simmel, the reciprocal adaptations necessary when each party to a social relationship reveals either a comprehensively human or a refined personal aspect of their personalities to others are only possible in small, intimate gatherings. Such gatherings enable adaptation and convergence of the more refined, intimate, and, in Simmel's view, more valuable sides of people's personalities. As more persons come together, it is less likely that a convergence of higher impulses and interests can be found; the greater variety and divergence of initial impulses and interests means that a sense of sharing characteristics in common will be limited to the lowest common denominator of shared tastes. Thus, for instance, people enjoy large parties, despite their inability to experience shared refinement there, only because they share with other party goers the impulse to consume things which are enjoyable to the senses.[77] In Simmel's view, shared consumption of things is experienced at one of the lowest levels of personality development. Shared spiritual refinement operates at the highest level.

Friendship with particular people is possible in the Simmelian urban milieu despite the alienation from people in general that results from urban reserve. But general alienation and large size are not the only threats to urban friendship. Urban social structure also increases the ease with which people can engage in lying, secrecy, and deception. The social conditions of urban life make it easier for people to hide or distort true beliefs or facets of the self from others.

In the modern urban world, deception is easier to engage in, harder to detect, and more devastating in effect than was the case in more primitive settings. Deception is easier to engage in because the narrow world of primitive people was surrounded by only a few circumstances, facts, and social roles. These factors were easy enough for primitive people to verify by means of direct observation and concrete experience. In contrast, in the complex, modern urban social structure, everyday existence "rests on a thousand premises which the single individual cannot trace and verify to their roots at all, but must take on faith."[78] For this reason, deception under modern urban conditions of life becomes more devastating in effect. Simmel argued that all of modern science, the credit economy, and numerous other decisions of everyday life are based solely on peoples' assumptions of faith in the honesty of each other. Under such conditions of complex, impersonal interdependence, the lie becomes terribly dangerous. It questions the basis of the socioeconomic and political organization of modern urban life.

WHAT IS TO BE DONE?—THE POLITICS OF CREATIVE INDIVIDUALISM

In his own life, Georg Simmel identified with none of the political or social reformist groups of his age. He believed that none allowed sufficient room for individual autonomy.[79] There is a strong undercurrent of resistance to rational-comprehensive planning throughout Simmel's work. He also expressed skepticism regarding the centralized state socialist alternative to the urban capitalist money economy. He was somewhat more optimistic about the prospects of worker self-managed organizational democracy[80] as a response to the changes in human relatedness wrought by mass production and the spread of large-scale, hierarchically structured bureaucratic forms. At heart, however, Simmel was the quintessential individualist. His preferred response to the negative polarities inherent in the emergent metropolitan way of life was ceaseless individual struggle.

For Simmel, the city is a cultural object that comes into existence and achieves whatever unity it has from the partial contributions of uncomprehending individuals. The individual is the only social reality. Simmel maintained that the developed city may appear to be the result of conscious planning. Yet, in an apparent reference to classical economic theory, Simmel believed that the urban form arises "out of the accidental needs and desires of individuals," and that its unity stems from partial contributions of "cooperating but uncomprehending individuals."[81] At the normative level, this is the pattern of urban development that Simmel prefers. The needs and desires of individuals are the vital life forces. The blueprints of a preconceived planned ordering of life offered by some of Simmel's contemporaries were viewed by Simmel as fixed cultural forms that threatened to channel, pacify, and dry up the vital life forces.

As Simmel expresses the matter in "The Secret Society": "All system building, whether of science, conduct, or society, involves the assertion of power; it subjects the material outside of thought to a form which thought has cast. . . . [M]aking plans [and] . . . the constructive impulse both . . . are expressions of the will to power."[82] Simmel objected to planning because, by definition, planned social forms do not grow organically. They do not respond to life's vital forces. Indeed, the parts of a social plan, individual human beings, must be made to fit together in predetermined forms so that the whole edifice can be built. As a vitalist, who, like the philosopher Henri Bergson, saw life as a dynamic process, constantly reproducing and pushing beyond itself,[83] Simmel was bound to view planning not only as undesirable, but also as inherently self-defeating in the long run.

Given Simmel's dialectical view of the flow of history, there is no reason to assume that he believed the metropolitan way of life he described was a final resting place. More probably, he assumed city life to be in flux, despite its central tendencies. Indeed, considering his views on the dynamics of resistance, it is reasonable to suppose that he felt the experience of coercion by repressive social forms, by the industrial capitalist money economy, and by the overloading of our lives with external stimuli and the alien objects of mass production would trigger the dialectics of resistance. If so, to try to impose a planned structure on this dialectical ebb and flow might be foolhardy. It might only delay the inevitable resistance struggle and the emergence of countertendencies.

Additionally, at the individual level, Simmel does not assume the need for harmony within the individual. Hence he does not view external conflicts that generate inner tensions as a problem to be dealt with by planning. Both inner and outer conflicts are basic to his view of the process of development and growth.

Simmel's theme of the inherent conflict between life and form suggests that human beings are destined to be estranged in the world in which they live. The modern urban world, in Simmel's view, intensifies the perennial struggle between life and form into a rebellion against form-as-such. Life drives the creative personality toward formlessness. This drive is propelled by the modern urban dweller's fear that his individuality is threatened by oppressive formal constraints. Simmel had faith that individual struggle and human achievement could overthrow the heavy weight of outmoded forms. As a dialectician, he saw this life-form tension "as the indispensable basis for the birth of new forms, better adapted to the emerging forces of life."[84]

The achievement of selfhood, for Simmel, not only includes but rather requires discordant sentiments toward other individuals, social groups, and the larger social structure. In oppressive environments, resistance gives meaning and vitality to existence. Resistance is functional for the individual personality. It provides a sense of "inner satisfaction, distraction, relief." Without resistance the individual might find oppressive environments unbearable. He might be driven to "take desperate steps," or to leave society altogether. When oppression becomes open, resistance is absolutely vital. "It allows us to prove our strength consciously and only thus gives vitality and reciprocity to conditions from which, without such corrective, we would withdraw at any cost."[85]

In Simmelian thought, resistance can also prove functional for urban society. This is a lesson that urban planners would do well to learn. Resistance forces upon elites and on the rest of society a recognition of sources of dissatisfaction to which society must at least partially adapt if it is to survive. This is because both alternatives to resistance, "desperate steps" or total withdrawal, threaten the continued existence of the social fabric. Participation in social institutions and resistance to the repressive aspects of those institutions are thus dialectically intertwined.

Despite Simmel's inclination to avoid political prescription, one of his chief virtues lies in the crucial political questions that his theoretical perspective brings into focus. In addition to shedding important light on the perennial question of political obligation and resistance, Simmel's conflict perspective calls attention to the plight of subordinated classes in hierarchically structured social orders. In Simmel's view, socioeconomic and political elites serve their own segmental interests more often than they serve the interests of society at large or the city as a whole:

In every hierarchy . . . whoever is lowest in . . . [the] social order . . . not only has to suffer from the deprivations, efforts, and discriminations which, taken together, characterize his position [the social form of subordination]; in addition every new pressure on any point whatever in the superordinate layers is, if technically possible . . . , transmitted downward and stops only at him.[86]

In short, Simmel recognized that the lowest segments of the urban social order end up paying the price of any losses initially extracted from the interests of higher social strata. To cite an example, the reprimand from superior to employee in a hierarchical work situation is transmitted downward by the employee shouting unnecessarily at his subordinate. The latter, in turn, lacking a channel for expressing annoyance upward, tends to take out the frustration on his or her children, in the only domain where the lowly subordinate feels powerful.

Reflecting this recognition, Simmel, as already noted, fully considered the negative potentialities of the increased freedom accompanying city life. In Simmel's view, complete freedom can only truly liberate the individual creative spirit in a world in which each person is more or less equal in strength and privilege. Since such equality of condition exists nowhere, Simmel argues, "complete freedom necessarily leads to the exploitation of . . . inequality by the more privileged, to the exploitation of the stupid by the clever, of the weak by the strong, of the timid by the grasping."[87] Furthermore, in the metropolitan industrial capitalist economy, the advantages gained by the freedom of the privileged are cumulative. In Simmelian theory, this problem is even more serious than Marx assumed; capital accumulation by those who have surplus capital is only a specific example of the more general Simmelian proposition that "in all power relations an advantage, once gained, facilitiates the gaining of additional advantages."[88]

Because of this dictum, although he was skeptical of the practicability of centralized state socialism, Simmel entertained the proposition that the only effective way to create the necessary precondition for free competition would be to socialize the means of production. This, he argued, might entail not the suspension of freedom, but rather the suspension of the major instrument—private property—which inevitably suppresses some people's freedom for the benefit of others.

Simmel held that, in theory, the historical contradiction between freedom and equality could be resolved in one of two ways, both of which were bound to be temporary palliatives, since each ignored what he believed to be the realities of human nature. The first method of resolution was coercion of the advantaged by the rest of society. By the suspension of private ownership, the freedom of the powerful, talented, and privileged to accumulate even greater advantages might be suppressed. Relative economic equality might then be possible. At this stage, the full freedom of each member of the social order could once again be exercised. The alternative method would be to elevate the norm of fraternity to a position of preeminence over both freedom and equality. The full exercise of fraternity would require "the ethical renunciation to utilize natural gifts."[89] This too might restore the equality that had been destroyed by unfettered freedom. Fraternity would elevate the "humanly general" to a position of priority over the individually unique.

Why were these political prescriptions deemed fruitless by Simmel? Recall that the Simmelian individual is a differentiating creature. Human sensitivity, consciousness, and motivation all rest on the basic need for differences in external stimuli. Accordingly, Simmel believed that after a brief period of adjustment to the leveling effects of either state socialism or fraternal voluntarism, man's "utterly inevitable" passion for domination and his sense of envy, greed, and oppression would once again reappear. These feelings would base themselves on whatever differences, however slight, remained in the socialist state or the fraternal community.[90] The very psychological structure of the mind remains sensitive to differences. This is how a person becomes aware of the world and shapes his reactions to it.

Simmel's doubts about state socialism and fraternity also stem from his belief that human nature requires outlets for competition as well as socialization.[91] Both are paired, interacting, instinctive needs. In Simmel's theory of human nature, one needs to act *against* as well as with others.

Finally, Simmel concluded that no purely general organizational form could permanently either coordinate diverse social relationships or eliminate relationships of command and subjection. As we have seen, Simmel placed little confidence in deliberately planned blueprints, however compelling the compulsion to build a better social order. He held that both life and human nature were inherently too fluctuating and contradictory to fit into the fixed-role requirements of any preconceived social structure. All schematized social orders confronted an irreconcilable obstacle: "the intrinsically variable nature of man, which never precisely fits conceptually fixed forms."[92]

Despite this skepticism concerning large-scale social reconstruction, Simmel did believe that democratic socialism was technically possible in small-scale social organizations, such as the workplace. He thought that worker self-managed organizational democracy might provide the technical benefits of super-subordination without degrading subordinates. In small-scale organizations, it might be possible to approximate the ideal of each member having a turn at playing the superordinate role. Super-subordinate relationships within the organization would thus be based on reciprocity.

For worker self-managed socialism to work, Simmel believed that the contributions as well as the rewards of each individual to the whole must be visible. Small organizations might prevent socialist distributive mechanisms from breaking down because of individual resentment. The fairness of each member's contribution/reward ratio could be seen and acknowledged by all in a small group. This was not possible in society at large.[93]

Simmel's model of successful worker-controlled socialism was the Familistère de Guise, a French cast-iron factory founded by a disciple of the French "utopian" socialist, Fourier. Participants in this factory were guaranteed a minimum existence. Free education and child care were provided for workers' children.[94] In discussing the governmental form best suited to perpetuate the mutual benefits of this system, Simmel describes what can only be called an organizational democracy. Viz.:

> We would then have an ideal organization, in which A is superordinate to B in one respect or at one time, but in which, in another respect or at another time, B is superordinate to A. . . . A small scale example might be the production association of workers for an enterprise for which they elect a master and foremen. While they are subordinate to him in regard to the technique of the enterprise, they yet are his superordinates with respect to its general direction and results. . . . Simultaneous superordination and subordination is one of the most powerful forms of interaction. In its correct distribution over numerous fields, it can constitute a very strong bond between individuals, merely by the close interaction entailed by it.[95]

The above passage is as close as Simmel comes to endorsing any particular form of planned social reconstruction. Despite this endorsement of organizational democracy, Simmel's more basic answer to the unsettling, oppressive, and potentially degrading conditions of industrial urban capitalism is psychological rather than structural. Recall that Simmel views work alienation as potentially liberating. He relegates the world of work to a peripheral role in self-actualization. In his view, work life is only one among a great many affiliations which shape the personality of the urbanite. The more diverse the group memberships of the individual, the richer the personality. Absorption in the world of work threatens to make the metropolitan personality one-dimensional. Accordingly, Simmel's views on organizational democracy, while important, do not cut to the heart of his answer to the question "What is to be done to overcome alienation?" On balance, Simmel prefers the individual act of self-transcendence to the collective act of worker self-control.

In the final analysis, the goal of enhancing the personality's sense of dignity, worth, and self-mastery may be achieved by increasing the level of detachment of the self from the external world of roles, activities, and alien objects that often dominate the personality. Thus, ironically, the very depersonalization of the producer-consumer relation and the alienation of the worker from his previously all-consuming work role in the modern city actually allow the personality "to withdraw from work and to become based upon itself."[96]

As with work, so also with all other external activities and social roles. True self-awareness and inner self-mastery may be realized only "if the individual feeling of life grows more psychologically independent of external activity in general and, in particular, of the position which the individual occupies within the sphere of this external activity."[97]

The self-actualized Simmelian personality experiences spiritual transcendence. At a minimum, given the realities of power and domination, this detachment of the subjective self from the external objective world renders life in an inherently unjust world more bearable. At best, this autonomization of inner feelings can become a deep commitment to spiritual refinement, a devotion to the values of beauty, knowledge, and significance that transcend all connections with the external world.

CONCLUSION

For Georg Simmel, the highest form of human development is inner-directed self-perfection. The fulfilled personality follows the laws of its own nature in working out a way of life that reflects each person's unique particularity and incomparability. The metropolis is essential to this mode of fulfillment, because, unlike earlier social forms, the metropolis cultivates a rich variety of social circles and a wide social orbit which give the personality room to grow in many diverse directions. The metropolitan milieu provides the individual with the opportunity to integrate highly diverse contents of life into a unique, richly individuated pattern of personality development.

At the same time, metropolitan existence exerts countertendencies. Role specialization and personality traits functional for the money economy are rewarded; other, more emotional and spiritual inclinations are discounted or frustrated. Psychic overload is engendered by excessive nervous stimulation and urban industrial capitalism's overbearing artifacts. This reinforces the same "matter-of-factness" that the division of labor and the advanced money economy encourage. Moreover, many of the mechanisms, including planned social changes, intended to cope with frustration, overstimulation, powerlessness, and the pervasive "objective spirit," actually compound the problem of self-mastery rather than solving it. Still, one promising social change would be the introduction of worker-controlled organizational democracy in small-scale work settings. This could overcome the degredation of hierarchically structured conditions of modern work life.

Ironically, in view of Simmel's antitechnocratic posture, Simmelian social theory also contains "one best way" to actualize the personality in face of the contradictions of social existence. By rising above the barriers thrown up by objective culture, the truly refined individual can devote the self to a life of delicacy, spirituality, and idealism. By refusing to allow specialization to overshadow other interests and relationships, the refined individual can pursue the quest for a uniquely subjective self. By rejecting the seductions of the objects and stimuli that clutter up existence, another step is taken toward self-fulfillment. By cultivating true segmental friendships, by leaving room for privacy, contemplation, and inner reflection, the subjective spirit is reached. The metropolis provides both barriers and opportunities for realizing the generally human and the personally unique and irreplaceable. Simmel leaves it up to the individual to realize both of these values—humanism and subjective life—by transcending the heavy weight of objective spirit in the modern urban world.

Notes

1. Among the insightful works in these fields that have been directly or indirectly influenced by Simmelian thought see Stanley Milgram, "The Experience of Living in Cities," *Science*, 167 (March 13, 1970), 1461–1468; David Truman, *The Governmental Process* (New York: Knopf, 1971); Lewis Coser, *The Functions of Social Conflict* (New York: Free Press, 1964); and Irving Goffman, *Interaction Ritual* (New York: Doubleday Anchor, 1967).
2. See Pitirim Sorokin, *Contemporary Sociological Theories* (New York: Harper, 1928), pp. 489–507; see also Kurt H. Wolff, "Introduction," *The Sociology of Georg Simmel* (New York: Free Press, 1969), p. xlvi.
3. Kaspar Naegele, "Attachment and Alienation: Complementary Aspects of the Work of Durkheim and Simmel," *American Journal of Sociology*, 63 (May 1958), 583.
4. See Simmel, "Faithfulness and Gratitude," *The Sociology of Georg Simmel*, p. 386.
5. Theodore Abel, "The Contribution of Georg Simmel: A Reappraisal," *American Sociological Review*, 24 (August 1959), 478; see also Simmel, "Individual and Society in 18th and 19th Century Views of Life," *The Sociology of Georg Simmel*, p. 59.
6. Georg Simmel, "The Conflict in Modern Culture," *Georg Simmel: The Conflict in Modern Culture and Other Essays*, trans., with introduction by, K. Peter Etzkorn (New York: Teachers College Press, 1968), p. 22.
7. Ibid., p. 11.
8. Simmel, "Knowledge, Truth, and Falsehood in Human Relations," *The Sociology of Georg Simmel*, p. 315.
9. K. Peter Etzkorn, "Introduction," *Georg Simmel: The Conflict in Modern Culture and Other Essays*, p. 1.
10. Don Martindale, *Institutions, Organizations, and Mass Society* (Boston: Houghton Mifflin, 1966), pp. 16–19.
11. Ibid., p. 17.
12. Simmel, "Individual and Society in 18th and 19th Century Views of Life," p. 59.

13. Simmel, "Superordination and Subordination and Degrees of Domination and Freedom," *The Sociology of Georg Simmel*, pp. 300–301.
14. Ibid.
15. Georg Simmel, "Conflict," Simmel, *Conflict and the Web of Group Affiliations*, trans. Kurt H. Wolff and Reinhard Bendix (New York: Free Press, 1955), pp. 13–16; see also Donald N. Levine, Ellwood Carter, and Eleanor Gorman, "Simmel's Influence on American Sociology," pt. 1, *American Journal of Sociology*, 81 (January 1976), 824.
16. Simmel, "Superordination and Subordination," p. 300.
17. See Levine, Carter, and Gorman, "Simmel's Influence on American Sociology," p. 824. The paragraphs which follow are based upon Simmel, "The Conflict in Modern Culture," pp. 14–21.
18. Simmel, 'The Conflict in Modern Culture," p. 19.
19. Simmel, "Sociability," *The Sociology of Georg Simmel*, p. 41; see also "The Social and the Individual Level," ibid., p. 27.
20. Simmel, "The Conflict in Modern Culture," p. 42.
21. Ibid.
22. Simmel, "Sociability," *The Sociology of Georg Simmel*, p. 43.
23. Ibid., p. 45.
24. Ibid., p. 46.
25. Ibid., p. 48.
26. Simmel, "Individual and Society in 18th and 19th Century Views of Life," pp. 58–59.
27. Simmel, "The Isolated Individual and the Dyad," *The Sociology of Georg Simmel*, p. 121.
28. Ibid.
29. Simmel, "Superordination and Subordination," p. 202.
30. Simmel, "The Isolated Individual and the Dyad," p. 122.
31. See Simmel, "Superordination and Subordination," p. 203.
32. Simmel, "On the Significance of Numbers for Social Life," *The Sociology of Georg Simmel*, p. 97.
33. Ibid., p. 96.
34. Ibid., p. 102.
35. Ibid., p. 92.
36. Simmel, "Individual and Society in 18th and 19th Century Views of Life," p. 59.
37. Ibid.
38. Ibid.
39. Ibid., p. 61.
40. Ibid., p. 63.
41. Ibid., pp. 63–64.
42. Simmel, "Secrecy," *The Sociology of Georg Simmel*, p. 335.
43. Ibid.
44. Nicholas Spykman, *The Social Theory of Georg Simmel* (Chicago: U. of Chicago Press, 1925), p. 221.
45. Simmel, "Faithfulness and Gratitude," p. 388.

46. Simmel, "Superordination and Subordination," p. 301.
47. Simmel, "Faithfulness and Gratitude," p. 392.
48. Simmel, "The Metropolis and Mental Life," Richard Sennett, ed., *Classic Essays on the Culture of Cities* (New York: Appleton-Century-Crofts, 1969), p. 49.
49. Ibid.
50. Ibid., p. 50.
51. See David Reisman et al., *The Lonely Crowd* (New Haven: Yale U. Press, 1950).
52. Simmel, "The Metropolis and Mental Life," p. 51.
53. Ibid.
54. Simmel, "The Web of Group Affiliations," Simmel, *Conflict and the Web of Group Affiliations*, p. 128. For an elaboration of the previous discussion of money's associative and dissociative effects, see Spykman, *The Social Theory of Georg Simmel*, pp. 219–231; see also Simmel, "A Chapter in the Philosophy of Value [Money]," *American Journal of Sociology*, 5 (March 1900), 577–603.
55. Simmel, "The Web of Group Affiliations," p. 130.
56. Ibid., pp. 142, 140–141.
57. Ibid., p. 163.
58. See ibid., p. 185; see also Simmel, "Superordination and Subordination," pp. 283–284.
59. Simmel, "On the Concept and Tragedy of Culture," *Georg Simmel: The Conflict in Modern Culture and Other Essays*, p. 44.
60. Ibid., p. 46.
61. Simmel, "The Metropolis and Mental Life," pp. 49–53.
62. Ibid., p. 51.
63. Ibid., p. 52.
64. Simmel, "Conflict," p. 20; see also Simmel, "The Metropolis and Mental Life," p. 53.
65. Simmel, "The Metropolis and Mental Life," p. 57.
66. Ibid., p. 59.
67. Simmel, "Secrecy," pp. 331–344.
68. Ibid., p. 340.
69. Ibid.
70. Ibid., p. 341.
71. Simmel, "The Isolated Individual and the Dyad," p. 119.
72. Ibid.
73. Simmel, "Knowledge, Truth, and Falsehood in Human Relations," p. 309.
74. Ibid., pp. 310–311.
75. Simmel, "Types of Social Relationships by Degrees of Reciprocal Knowledge of Their Participants," *The Sociology of Georg Simmel*, pp. 324–326.
76. Ibid.
77. Simmel, "The Quantitative Determination of Group Divisions and of Certain Groups," *The Sociology of Georg Simmel*, p. 112.
78. Simmel, "Knowledge, Truth, and Falsehood in Human Relations," p. 313.

79. Paul Honigsheim, "The Time and Thought of the Young Simmel," Kurt H. Wolff, ed., *Georg Simmel: 1858–1918* (Columbus: Ohio State U. Press, 1959), p. 170.
80. See "Superordination and Subordination and Degrees of Domination and Freedom," *The Sociology of Georg Simmel*, pp. 283–291; on worker self-managed organizational democracy generally, see G. David Garson and Michael P. Smith, eds., *Organizational Democracy: Participation and Self-Management* (Beverly Hills, Calif.: Sage, 1976).
81. Simmel, "On the Conflict and the Tragedy of Culture," p. 41.
82. Simmel, "The Secret Society," *The Sociology of Georg Simmel*, p. 357.
83. See the discussion of the vitalist dimension of Simmel's thought in Rudolph W. Weingartner, "Form and Content in Simmel's Philosophy of Life," Wolff, ed., *Georg Simmel: 1858–1918*, pp. 33–60, especially pp. 36–37.
84. Fritz Pappenheim, *The Alienation of Modern Man* (New York: Modern Reader Paperbacks, 1959), p. 32; see also pp. 20–24.
85. Simmel, "Conflict," p. 19.
86. Simmel, "Subordination Under a Plurality," *The Sociology of Georg Simmel*, pp. 236–237; see also the discussion by William Connolly of "Theoretical Self-Consciousness," William Connolly and Glen Gordon, eds., *Social Structure and Political Theory* (Lexington, Mass.: Heath, 1974), pp. 40–66.
87. Simmel, "Individual and Society in 18th and 19th Century Views of Life," p. 65.
88. Ibid., p. 66.
89. Ibid., p. 67.
90. Ibid., pp. 75–76.
91. See Simmel, "The Web of Group Affiliations," pp. 155–156.
92. Simmel, "Subordination Under an Individual," *The Sociology of Georg Simmel*, p. 209.
93. See the discussion of Simmel's views on this issue in Don Martindale, *Institutions, Organizations, and Mass Society*, p. 17f., and in Rosabeth Moss Kanter, *Commitment and Community* (Cambridge, Mass.: Harvard U. Press, 1972), p. 228.
94. Martindale, *Institutions, Organizations, and Mass Society*, pp. 88–89.
95. Simmel, "Super-Subordination without Degradation," *The Sociology of Georg Simmel*, p. 285.
96. Simmel, "Superordination and Subordination," p. 284.
97. Ibid., pp. 283–284.

Chapter 4
Roszak and Sennett: The Contemporary Urban Predicament

Radical decentralization, like politics, makes strange bedfellows. Theodore Roszak (b. 1933) and Richard Sennett (b. 1943) were born a decade apart in the city of Chicago. Roszak's writings made him a high priest of the youthful counterculture of the late 1960s. Sennett, particularly in his brilliant work *The Uses of Disorder*, rejects Roszak's call for a communitarian social order as repressive of mature personality development. Yet Sennett shares Roszak's penchant for decentralization, experimentation, and radical social change.

At one level, Roszak and Sennett share a common critique of contemporary American cities. Both see the American city as overbureaucratized, overmechanized, and inappropriately planned. Both identify negative consequences of rational-comprehensive planning. Yet the two social theorists disagree fundamentally about the root causes of urban alienation, the sort of personality they would like to see emerge if cities were planned differently, and the concrete steps each would take to reshape urban forms.

These two radical decentralists represent two contradictory strains in the anarchist tradition—communal vs. individualistic anarchism.[1] Accordingly, their ideas intersect at different junctures with the social theorists we have considered in earlier chapters. Both Roszak and Sennett reject Louis Wirth's mechanist model of rational-comprehensive urban planning. Yet unlike Sennett, Roszak is quite sympathetic to the human-ecological approach underlying Wirth's theory of city planning. Both Roszak and Wirth view the good city as a well-ordered social community. Where Wirth would impose a rationally based normative order on the city, to tame without destroying its underlying ecological base, Roszak would have us abandon technological rationality, rediscover the natural ecological order, and allow its spontaneous processes to regulate human behavior. Sennett, on the other hand, would radically reverse all processes, rational or ecological, that foster urban order.

Unlike Freud, Roszak does not fear our animal nature. He sees human nature as compatible with a naturally harmonious, transcendentally based spiritual order. Sennett is more at home with Freud, particularly with his view that conflict, aggressiveness, and contradiction are basic to human nature. Yet unlike Freud, Sennett regards the contradictions, divisions, and disorder in people and society as healthy harbingers of individual growth and social transformation. He believes that both inner and outer disorder ought to be cultivated rather than controlled.

Sennett carries his enthusiasm for conflict and disorder well beyond Simmel's thoughts about the negative psychic consequence of excessive stimulation—the overloaded personality. In Sennett's social theory, there are no inherent limits to stimulation; there is no point of diminishing returns where stimulating environmental differentiation and conflict become overstimulating vertigo. Sennett's ideal-typical personality is a being that thrives on conflict and disorder. Indeed, the very pain experienced when people encounter differentiated "otherness," which Roszak defines as the very essence of alienation, is for Sennett a necessary precondition of emotional growth.

For Sennett, this repression of conflict and disorder is as true of Roszak's ecological order as it is of Louis Wirth's rationally planned city. Where Roszak sees a hierarchically integrated personality, operating in harmony with a universal natural order, Sennett sees a re-creatable blank page, capable of developing in myriad ways, but requiring conflict in order to grow.

For Roszak, being a full personality requires social and spiritual community; for Sennett, it requires "being alone at the core." Thus where Roszak asks: *"What is to be done to create meaningful social and spiritual communities in our cities?"* Sennett's basic planning question may be posed as: *"What is to be done to rekindle the useful social conflict that current urban planning practice has done so much to repress?"* Both turn to radical decentralization of public authority to achieve their divergent goals. Where Roszak would decentralize political authority to small-scale consensual communities, Sennett would decentralize the situations where urban conflict takes place. In this way, no institutions, large or small, could shield people from experiencing, and haltingly learning to deal with, conflict for themselves. Let's consider first Roszak, and then Sennett, in greater detail.

ROSZAK'S THEORY OF HUMAN NEEDS

Romanticists like Theodore Roszak reflect the American folk cultural suspicion of big cities as breeding grounds of vice and corruption.[2]

But Roszak's social theory adds to this perception an important new dimension. The city, for Roszak, is a symbolic manifestation of a pervasive rationalism and a disorienting technical complexity that confuse the mind and deaden the spirit. A perceived rationalization and secularization of urban life is one of Roszak's central themes and the source of his most profoundly antiurban biases.

The break with the primitive rhythms of life, nature, communal intimacy, and a sense of the mysterious and sacred aspects of existence is the primary theme that gives coherence to Roszak's sometimes obscure and vituperative attack on urbanization and technological development. It is on this score that Roszak stands farthest from the values of Enlightenment thought reflected in Wirth, Simmel, and even Freud. Enlightenment thinkers tend to view both urbanization and modernization as reflective of the liberating aspects of science, education, and formal law. Indeed, for Enlightenment thinkers human progress is contingent upon the displacement of tradition, myth, and superstition by rational comprehension and control of the human environment.[3] Roszak rejects all these premises.

Roszak stresses the irrational side of people and seeks to liberate the primitive and spontaneous drives that Freud would repress. His view of primitive society puts him at loggerheads with Freudian thought, which perceived primitive life as nasty, brutish, and profoundly inegalitarian. Primitive people take their first steps toward civilized existence when they strive to assert mastery over foreboding nature. In place of this metaphorical image, Roszak substitutes a picture of primitive, egalitarian, democratic communities, free from domination and existing in harmony with a beneficent nature. For Roszak, unlike Freud and Simmel, domination and exploitation come into being only after the dictates of "civilization" destroy primitive tribal democratic forms.

Roszakian urban dwellers have lost awareness of these nonrepressive social forms. They have made the transition to a repressive mode of existence, dominated by an overly rationalistic world view that frustrates basic human needs. In Roszakian thought, contemporary urbanites acquire a sense of power and domination over nature and their social existence as they begin to view the world with detached objectivity. The "mastery" derived from the objective mode of consciousness that dominates urban existence is experienced psychologically as a sense of freedom from the constraining influence of superstitious community norms and subjective ties to others. When fully developed, this desire for mastery becomes a sense of unlimited freedom to manipulate and exploit the natural and the social world.

In Roszak's view, human alienation follows directly from these developments. By viewing the world "objectively," the urban dweller cannot help but experience the self as separated from both nature and the human community. By depersonalizing existence, the objective analyst loses a sense of continuity, kinship, and purpose. Feeling alone and alienated from the world is the psychic price to be paid for objective knowledge, scientific enlightenment, and technological mastery.

Furthermore, by ennobling this inherently alienating form of knowledge, modern urban culture degrades all alternative forms of awareness.[4] Those who strive to uphold the sacredness of self, others, and the natural environment in the context of a thoroughly secularized urban culture are deemed eccentric or obstructionist—troublesome "objects" standing in the way of rationally planned progress.

For Roszak, a series of concentric layers of motivation and need define human potential.[5] At the surface level are the needs for material survival, justice, and equality. In Roszak's view, these needs are so widely shared that they have become embodied in the dominant liberal and social democratic ideologies of the modern world. At a deeper level of human need resides the Freudian layer—our need to express sexuality and aggressiveness. Deeper still is our need to be "authentic" and to accept personal responsibility for our choices and our fate.

Beyond these individual-level needs reside our needs as social beings—the need for humanly scaled community and for direct participation in political life. At the very deepest level of Roszak's human needs theory is the need for spiritual fulfillment.

All these needs are viewed as both organically and hierarchically interrelated. Hence the human being cannot achieve fulfillment in a piecemeal fashion. For instance, if the needs for bread and social justice are satisfied paternalistically—without people's active participation in politics and decision making—resentment or demoralization are probable consequences. At another level, if participation in community and political life leaves no room for individual or spiritual fulfillment, festering discontent will emerge.[6]

Despite their interdependent natures, Roszak states that any one of the basic human needs may become enshrined as the ultimate purpose of a political ideology or movement. Once this occurs, the danger exists that some of the other basic needs may be repressed in the ensuing political struggle to realize the enshrined value. In this respect, Roszak believes that spiritual fulfillment is the most vulnerable of all human needs because it challenges the one assumption that all secular political and planning movements share in common—the belief that "all human needs can be fulfilled within the world of time and matter."[7]

Roszak distinguishes sharply between social and "cosmic" alienation.[8] In his view, the former may be remedied within the world of time and matter by socializing the means of production. But cosmic alienation, a condition of "spiritual disconnectedness," is unaffected by whatever political system or planning ideology organizes the production of social goods and the distribution of social opportunities and costs. Economic redistribution and social justice speak to other, and in Roszak's mind, "lesser" human needs.

The Roszakian person, the unfinished animal, is a transcendent religious being at the very core. This core need cannot be satisfied by politics. Political transformation may succeed in moving society a layer or so deeper into the hierarchy of human needs, but this he views as a segmental transformation, bound to leave cosmic alienation untouched. This is because all contemporary political movements and planning blueprints operate within the constraints of the "secular consensus" that all human needs can be satisfied by rational manipulation of the material and social environment. In Roszak's theory, rational-comprehensive planning, whatever its secular ends, does not cut deep enough to overcome spiritual alienation. And since spiritual fulfillment is for Roszak the most fundamental human need, no secular plan can grasp the roots of human discontent. Ultimately, "the way forward is the way inward."[9]

ROSZAK'S CRITIQUE OF URBAN LIFE AND TECHNOCRATIC PLANNING

The most direct critique of urbanism in Theodore Roszak's social theory is found in *The Making of a Counter Culture*, in his discussion of the visionary sociology of Paul Goodman.[10] Roszak's attraction to Paul Goodman stems from a shared aesthetic sensibility. He views Goodman's model of the city as a human community as similar to the model employed by novelists like Balzac, Joyce, and Dickens to portray urban life in Paris, Dublin, and London.

Roszak, like Goodman, is a quintessential Gestaltist, portraying the urban environment as intimately intertwined with the human personalities of the people who live there. Gestaltists postulate a primal organic unity that is spontaneously self-regulating.[11] Both Roszak and Goodman envision a purposive "give and take between every organism and its environment which has the same inexplicable spontaneity and self-regulation as the process of perception."[12] From this perspective, a continual natural dialogue, a sequence of "creative adjustments," is constantly taking place between the individual, the social community, and the natural habitat. People are by nature social creatures related to their physical and social surroundings. It is only when the seamless web of sociability is disrupted that they become isolated and segregated from the ecological whole. They become "a unit of defensive consciousness."[13]

For Gestaltists like Goodman and Roszak, the process of alienation occurs as people lose a sense of their organic ties to their environment and acquire in its place a consciousness of "external" reality, viewed as alien or even hostile.

When enough people lose faith in the ability of spontaneous mutual adjustment to integrate the human being into his physical and social milieu, they turn in frustration to external bureaucratic forms to regulate human conduct. In Goodman's terms, the free interplay of human faculties is displaced by a compulsive desire to manipulate deliberately the now negatively perceived environment. An aggressive urge to regiment "others" in the environment replaces informal mutual adjustments. Or as Roszak puts it: "We have lost touch with the self-regulation of a symbiotic system and have given over to a compulsive need to control, under pressure of which the organism freezes up and seems to be inutterably stupid."[14]

Roszak sees this loss of organic community as the first step in the direction of technocratic elitism. By losing confidence in spontaneous human emotion, one casts doubt upon human sociability. Once faith in sociability is lost, nothing positive can be expected to emerge from spontaneous mutual adjustment. If the members of the body politic are perceived as alien and hostile, people turn self-defensively to external authority to supervise conduct and insure social peace. In large-scale urban environments, this requires bureaucratic and social planning experts who understand the dynamics of controlling complex "aggregates" of egoistic units.

But how does the loss of confidence in one's fellow beings and the disintegration of organic community come about? Roszak traces the disintegration of community to a three-stage developmental process. First, the urban environment transcends the naturally decentralized human scale that allows free play and variety without regimentation. Next, "leviathian industrialism" reaches a point at which both high productivity and the norm that "More is better" are accepted as givens. Finally, planners and technical experts acquire a stake in the maintenance and expansion of their privileged social roles. At this point community ceases and technological society comes into being. The sections which follow examine these developmental stages.

The Denaturalized City

The "wasteland," which is the subject of Rozak's *Where the Wasteland Ends*, is the denaturalized city—an artificial environment engendered by urban industrialism and its technocratic political style.[15] In Roszak's view, urban society's headlong retreat from nature, human scale, and more primitive ways of life has established false measures of progress. Progress is taken to mean the ability to render the natural habitat increasingly predictable, controllable, and hence artificial. In seeking to master rather than simply to understand nature, the Roszak-ian urban personality loses sight of the seasonal rhythms and organic cycles which govern the natural environment.

In the modern city, "nature" becomes devitalized. Like the contemporary metropolis, the medieval city was a highly regulated human abode. Nonetheless, medieval urban dwellers were intimately aware of the untamed wilderness beyond the city's walls. Great medieval cities, Roszak tells us, could be brought to a literal halt by the plague-bearing rat. This ever-present fear—along with the primitive level of sanitation—were, for Roszak, "healthy" reminders of human dependence upon the forces of nature.[16] They gave the medieval urban community a humbling sense of limits. The inscrutability of nature provided a sense of connectedness with the sacred that is no longer present in the urban technopolis.

Megapolitan sprawl is taken by Roszak as a signal that contemporary metropolitan dwellers have completely severed their connections with the raw forces of nature. Unlike many urban analysts, who have seen in megapolitan sprawl a trend toward population deconcentration and dispersal to the suburbs, with a corresponding decline of the city,[17] Roszak interprets megapolitan development as an attempt by "the technocracy" to propagate the power of the supercity by drawing even the wilderness and backwater bayous into the supercity's technological metabolism. In his view, urbanization is no longer a strict derivative of industrialization. Although industry could be radically decentralized, it continues to engender supercities. Roszak is apparently oblivious to the very real decentralization of industrial production characterizing American economic development since the 1950s.[18] Instead of considering the implications of this trend, discussed in chapter six, he chooses to argue that urbanization continues apace because it has become a symbolic showcase of the urban-industrial way of life—a life style characterized by artificiality, insulation from natural phenomena, and an obsession with planning, production, and control.

In Roszak's denaturalized city, supercity technocratic elites propagate this style of life by technologizing agriculture, which displaces small farmers with agribusiness combines and forces the yeoman farmer from the country to the city; by pursuing development strategies that exploit natural resources, and thereby change rural ways of life; by shaping national consumption patterns through their concentrated control of transportation, communication, and product distribution networks; by pollution of the air, water, and earth; and by converting the wilderness into a weekend amusement park. More they do all this in the name of "progress," despite the environmental and human costs of their endeavors.

The Demystification of Life

By far the greatest cost of the advanced "urban-industrial" way of life is its impact on human consciousness. In *Wasteland,* Roszak coins the term *single vision* to designate the orthodox mode of consciousness fostered by urban industrialism. Single vision narrows the sensibilities. It is tantamount to the alienation of the knower from the "object" known. The artificial urban environment deeply penetrates the personality, thus altering the subconscious contents that shape, screen, and censor perception and cognition.

How does the social structure of urban industrialism alter human consciousness? It discounts vision and imagination when distributing social rewards; it conditions people to spend most of their waking life exercising orthodox consciousness; it structures incentives to sustain those who are "realistic" (i.e., who accept the status quo) and dismisses those who are idealistic as irrelevant utopians.

In the process of becoming realistic, people forget the "collective remembrances" that reside in the subconscious.[19] In so doing, the urbanite becomes a stranger to, indeed is alienated from, much of the residual experience of human beings.

The "dark mind" is wrapped in mysteries that perhaps only mystics can fully unravel; but this is only because urban-technological culture has denied the reality of the visionary world of the subconscious. In other, more primitive cultures, the very goals of pedagogy have been the exploration of dreams and the liberation of the imaginative contents of the collective unconsciousness.

The pressures of work life in the urban industrial order also encourage the repression of imagination. The demands of work, particularly among business people and politicans, drive them to prolong the waking state of orthodox consciousness well into the night, thereby arresting the development of imagination and visionary experiences.[20] Compulsive wakefulness is the bane of urban industrialism.

Urban culture and its supporting social structure do more than merely discount imagination and fantasy. By cluttering up our leisure time with passive spectator activities, they rob us of precious time that would otherwise be available for active participation in imaginative play. Passive spectator activities also provide insufficient opportunities for release of pent-up aggressive drives which often find release in such dangerous outlets as aggressive driving.[21]

Roszak argues further that single vision is closely tied to the separation of the religious impulse from life. The very act of objectifying the "external" environment reduces all realities to terms that objective consciousness can comprehend, predict, and control. For this reason all reality becomes *disenchanted*. To disenchant the world is to rob it of its mystery, complexity, autonomy, and sanctity. As an example, Roszak suggests that single vision "dis-integrates the landscape, reduces it to bits and pieces, discovers how it works, but not what it means."[22]

Modern urban culture discovers how the world works by specializing knowledge. But the price of this increased specialization is a breakdown in social communication. Complex differentiation and specialization of knowledge and work diminish the possibilities for enlightened communication among the generally educated. Conversation becomes a lost art, thereby diminishing the prospect of spiritual community.[23]

Moreover, the secularization of symbols and the specialization of language styles alter our expectations about the future. The heavenly city of Augustine and other utopian philosophers was once recognized by all as a source of inspiration and spiritual aspiration. In today's urban technological order, the heavenly city has become a real historical "project" to be dealt with by experts in science, planning, and policy making. The language of urban planning, in particular, is fraught with symbolism suggesting that ultimate well-being and happiness for all can be achieved in the earthly city through rational-comprehensive planning.

The planners' expropriation and cheapening of great symbols of flight, elevation, gravity, and buoyancy has cut these concepts from their root spiritual meaning and transcendent significance.[24] Transcendence thereby has lost its symbolic connection with experience. It has come to be viewed as beyond consciousness. Consciousness, as a repository of root spiritual meanings, has been transformed into a "liberated," and therefore alienated, "objective" mode of being in the world. The secularization of communication robs consciousness of its ability to experience and comprehend a rich wellspring of root symbolic meanings; objective consciousness thereby robs the urban dweller of the ability to experience transcendence in everyday life. Instead, that which is held to be "merely subjective" is defined as unreal.

The urban personality differentiates and dissects instead of looking for higher syntheses. What Georg Simmel viewed as the essential function of the mind—its ability to differentiate—is for Roszak a trait peculiar to the modern "urban-industrial" personality. For him, the cultivation of this trait weakens the mind's ability to integrate and synthesize, to see the natural interconnectedness in organic reality. Differentiation alienates the mind from a sensitive, intuitive awareness of organic unity and wholeness.

The Priesthood of Expertise

Expertise, for Roszak, is the "mystology" of advanced urban society. Its main function is to mystify the popular mind. Expertise conjures up illusions of omniscience and omnipotence that in earlier eras were invoked by a priesthood.[25] Under the guise of "demystifying" thought, planners and experts have created a new mythology—the myth of beneficent expertise. Urban planners, for instance, have their own preferred terminology, initiation rituals, badges of membership in the priestly strata, and methodological mysteries.

The chief methodological mystery is the planning technique known as "systems analysis." Roszak is especially critical of the extension of this technique, borrowed from the aerospace industry, to areas such as reforming educational institutions and redesigning cities. For him, this represents an extension of scientific technique into the essentially "spontaneous realm" of community development. Systems analysts mistakenly assume that urban alienation stems from the poor coordination of, rather than the intrinsic nature of, technological expertise. The growing depersonalization and denaturalization of the urban environment cannot be improved by impersonal, abstract, mechanistic methodologies. Systems analysis distracts people's attention from their real, concrete problems of existence.

In exchange for the abstract systematization of concrete human existence, urban dwellers are supposed to receive objective analysis of urban problems. But the "urban problems" industry offers only the trappings and not the reality of objective neutrality. Symbols and rituals of scientific objectivity become mistaken for the substance of ethically neutral analysis. In Roszak's words:

> The vocabulary and methodology mask the root ethical assumptions of policy or neatly transcribe them into a depersonalized rhetoric which provides a gloss of military or political necessity. To think and to talk in such terms becomes the sure sign of being a certified realist, a "hard research" man.[26]

Ironically, in the name of removing the metropolitan community from myth, religion, and ritual the urban technocracy merely substitutes a new set of quasireligious symbols and rituals for the old ones. These serve as masks, disguising the true meaning of existence. Thus, for instance, forcing blacks out of town becomes "urban renewal"; manipulating discontented workers becomes "personnel management"; token redistribution efforts become a "War on Poverty."[27]

Roszak carries this criticism a step further than most critics. Like the cultural anthropologist Lévi-Strauss, he believes that no society, not even the most secularized technocracy, can do without symbolism, magic, and ritual.[28] He regards the persistence of these concepts as proof of his view of human nature as inherently communal and spiritual. Mystery, symbolism, myth, and ritual are the very ties that bind all societies together. Every social order is held together by inarticulated common assumptions and collective motivations which require periodic public affirmation.

As Roszak correctly observes, some rituals truly reflect collective values, others are imposed from above. Some can liberate the imagination in the same way that inspirational poetry does. If rituals are the by-product of spontaneous mutual participation, they can become extensions of self-expression. They can celebrate as well as stultify spontaneity. Yet, as we shall see in chapter six, those rituals which only create the illusion of collective affirmation and "citizen participation" actually may bolster the discretionary authority of elites.

Given these assumptions, Roszak acknowledges that the continuities of inherited institutions, traditions, and ideological beliefs that preceded the rise of expertise may prevent the development of a technocratic utopia along the lines of Bacon's *New Atlantis* or Saint-Simon's administrative state.[29] Earlier bases for legitimizing the exercise of social power still stand in the way of the full institutionalization of a regime of experts. However, traditional ideals, symbols, and rhetoric tend to lose their force once the institutional power base upon which they rest is weakened and gradually displaced by the technological imperative. The technocracy may still be required to use the language and symbols of democratic political control, for instance, but actual control over policy directions increasingly rests with managers, technical experts, and planners found in both government and the corporate structure. The power of the technocracy stems from the dependence of the prosperity and survival of the urban-industrial order on the scientist and technician and their owners and managers.[30]

Moreover, the legitimization process itself is undergoing change. The freeways, airports, corporate headquarters, and other physical artifacts of urban-technological society are backdrops symbolizing the power to shape social change. These symbols of change, newness, and efficiency increasingly legitimate political control by the regime of social and corporate planning expertise. For instance, economic progress by means of planned urbanization becomes a justification for the exercise of power by even the most repressive of regimes in developing countries.[31]

By the "regime of expertise" Roszak does not mean full control by scientists, planners, and engineers. Rather, the experts themselves work within limits set by those who can pay the bill. Technically neutral planning experts put their services at the disposal of those who have the economic and social power to detemine what will be done with technology. Technocrats are the employees and legitimators of power; their owners are its possessors.

And who are these owners? They are the "owners and managers of the means of production."[32] At first glance, it seems incongruous that one of the chief social critics of the growing global power of "technocracy" would revert to this basically Marxian argument. Such an analysis appears to contradict a basic theme of most of his writings by stressing the role of capital ownership rather than technical knowledge as the dominant political resource. It also represents a type of objective analysis of social reality that his phenomenological epistemology rejects as unduly restrictive. Hence his argument bears more careful examination.

Roszak argues that in any political regime experts are forced to avoid public controversy. Dissensus among experts could undermine the very "scientific" basis of the legitimacy of the social power that experts now enjoy. Thus disagreements among experts generally do not extend to advocating major reallocations of social power.[33] They agree to work within the prevailing cultural context of politics, whatever that might be. In advanced capitalist political economies, this context includes alternative bases for legitimizing social power, such as ownership, as well as other cultural remnants like competition for office, interest representation, and the like.[34]

For Roszak, this constraining influence on technocratic elitism is not necessarily a permanent condition. Rather, some competing bases of legitimacy—particularly the political principles of representative democracy—are already being subverted by those who have both social legitimacy and objective foundations of social power: "those possessing money or guns, property or bureaucratic privilege."[35] For these corporate, governmental, and bureaucratic elites, the language of democratic politics becomes an instrument for deluding the population. It becomes symbolic eyewash that reassures people that the hands on the levers of power are those of elected politicans rather than those who control wealth, expertise, and the bureaucracy. The emerging oligarchy of planners and technocrats currently is held in check by those who possess wealth and bureaucratic power. At the present stage of historical development, it is wealth (owners) and bureaucratic power (managers) that employ the expert planners.

As Roszak puts it:

> The well-designed technocracy must have on tap experts who are eager and able to do *everything* technically feasible: but precisely what will at last be done is seldom of experts choosing—though their influence is far from negligible, their chance to do their thing much depends on their talent for being loyal employees.[36]

What Roszak has painted is a picture of planners and technical experts receiving a broad mandate from the owners and managers of the means of production. Experts can significantly influence the goals of the latter, provided they remain quiescent, avoiding basic systemic issues such as the fundamental reallocation of wealth and power. Roszak's sometimes omnipotent technical experts are depicted as influential "good soldiers." They are part of an army run by possessors of social power other than information and objective knowledge. In advanced capitalist political economies, possessors of wealth and corporate managerial prerogatives are still the generals.

The foregoing discussion of the role of owners and managers sets the stage for Roszak's discussion of the varieties of urban technocracy. Roszak envisages several forms of "bastardized technocracy" emerging on a worldwide scale "as urban-industrialism assimilates the ethnic continuities and economic conditions of different societies."[37] These technocracies are termed "bastardized" because none of them is likely, in Roszak's view, to put the scientist-technician and rational planner fully in charge. Rather, technology and planning expertise are used parasitically to expropriate a large measure of the benefits of urban industrialism for key vested interests.

The most visible of these forms is the *suave technocracy*. Found in Japan, Western Europe, and the United States, the suave technocracy is characterized by the close interdependence of corporate and public power. In these political systems, corporate power is "skillfully interwoven into the fabric of public life." The interweaving is so pervasive that alternatives to the present arrangement of social power can scarcely be imagined; the very fabric of national life has become permeated by the corporate way of life. Corporations are tied to politics and opinion formation at all levels of the polity and society. Suave corporate technocrats control jobs, professions, markets, and resources; by their domination of the major national channels of communication, they shape tastes, consumption patterns, and even self-images. Because they enjoy subliminal power, the suave technocrats do not have to resort very often to brutality or repression to maintain social control. They have substituted "the absorbency of the sponge" for raw coercive power.[38]

Other varieties of technocracy in Roszak's typology include: (1) the *vulgar* technocracies of the collectivist societies, whose bureaucratic elites, being caught up in a scientific orthodoxy, are more heavy-handed in exercising social control than are their advanced capitalist counterparts; (2) the *teratoid* technocracies of Brazil, South Africa, the Stalinist Soviet Union, and Nazi Germany, in which social planners bed down with fanatics, racists, or rabid nationalists; and (3) the *comic opera* technocracies of the underdeveloped world, whose political elites struggle to modernize rapidly through runaway urban-industrial expansion, destroying much that is culturally and socially valuable in the process.[39]

Although there are basic differences among each of these technocratic styles, Roszak argues that they have one overriding common feature—a movement in the direction of the suave technocracy. In Roszak's apocalyptic vision, as the major multinational enterprises of the developed societies work out advantageous alliances and spheres of influence, "the course of world affairs will flow toward a grand *urban industrial homogeneity*, spreading outward from five or six increasingly suave centers of technocratic power": the United States, the Common Market, the Soviet Union, Japan, and China.[40]

The Plight of the Citizen

Through technological development, the scale and complexity of urban economic, political, and cultural pursuits begin to transcend the competence of the amateurish citizen. For Roszak, "technocracy" is thus an inevitable by-product of "industrial urbanization." Confronted by bewildering complexity and organizational giantism, the individual citizen of urban-industrial society is psychologically compelled to turn to those who have more extensive information and specialized knowledge. To do otherwise would be foolhardy, at least from the standpoint of maintaining the economic structure of urban-industrial society.

According to Roszak, the roots of this technological imperative lie buried deep in the scientific world view of Western rationalism. The acceptance of scientific knowledge as the only form of reliable knowledge serves to buttress the social power of professional experts. Their expertise, in turn, serves to justify the policy-making elites who govern.

For Roszak, "technocracy" is a transpolitical phenomenon. In its advanced stages, it is a social structure that prevails over whatever political forms seek to contain and control it. It is "the working alliance of scientific expertise and social elitism."[41] Capitalist and developed collectivist societies both rely increasingly on the suave technocracy to provide industrial efficiency, social rationality, and objective knowledge. In both types of societies, technocrats assume the role of umpires in athletic contests—they set "the limits and goals of the competition and [judge] the contenders."[42] However, they are not yet powerful enough to make the rules.

Because advanced technological cultures are so deeply rooted in a scientific world view, the growing political power of the technocracy is not perceived as such. Its central role in policy making is simply assumed as a necessity, an issue beyond question and discussion. The methods of the suave technocracy in particular have become progressively more subtle and subliminal, thereby bolstering their preferred position in society:

The distinctive feature of the regime of experts lies in the fact that, while possessing ample power to coerce, it prefers to charm conformity from us by exploiting our deep seated commitment to the scientific world view and by manipulating the securities and creature comforts of the industrial affluence which science has given us.[43]

Technocratic power, then, derives from the ability of urban and social planners to persuade the average citizen that human needs can be reduced to technical problems, that solutions to these problems can be embodied in programs and material products, and that once this has been accomplished any residual human alienation must be the result of either inefficient administration or communication breakdowns. For if each indicator of human happiness has its own finely calibrated program, all of the prerequisites for human fulfillment are already either on the public agenda of policy planners or on the agenda of the corporate power structure. The task of planning elites with such an outlook, then, becomes to persuade those who have failed to see this "truth," rather than to respond to expressed grievances.

For Roszak, the ascendency of the suave technocracy is not the by-product of capitalism alone, but of "accelerating industrialism."[44] If profiteering and economic exploitation of the many by the few were eliminated, the technocracy would remain dominant, as it has in the collectivist societies. Indeed, without ownership, information and knowledge might become even more greatly concentrated in professional experts than they already are.

Whatever its political forms, this process of technological development diminishes the individual citizen's capacity for becoming fully human. By surrendering responsibility for moral choice, intellectual innovation, and popular control, the citizen's capacity to exercise moral and intellectual faculties gradually is weakened. Seduced by the mass media and other transmitters of advanced urban culture, the public is increasingly won over to a "total culture of adolescence based on nothing but fun and games."[45]

If domination were born solely from scarcity, the advent of affluence would mark the decline of domination. But for Roszak, domination continues in all urban industrial milieus; only its forms differ. The technocratic elites of urban-industrial orders have developed subtle strategies (e.g., the pseudochoices offered by the mass media and conventional ideological alternatives) for integrating "comfort, ease, permissiveness, and even rebellion into the logic of domination."[46]

Why do they do so? Roszak never directly tells us. But it is consistent with his underlying theory of knowledge that the elite itself is trapped in a scientific world view within which mastery and domination are key driving forces; in this mental framework, the existence of every creature is justified by its functionality. As an object of scientific inquiry rather than a sacrosanct subject, an individual is understood as nothing more than an agglomeration of functions.

This reduction of the human spirit to a collection of roles, behavior patterns, and functions dehumanizes cognition. In so doing, it makes it easier for elites to think in terms of "eliminating friction," "reordering functional priorities," and "resocializing roles," rather than in terms of destroying, discounting, or repressing human beings.

In this way scientists become desensitized to the human implications of their research, policy-planning elites to the actual consequences of their rhetoric and policies, and bureaucratic elites to the individual pain inflicted by their treatment of their clients. The scientific world view desanctifies both human beings and nature. It removes theory from the realm of experience, and thereby denies the concrete "factness" of those whose irreducible wholeness does not fit neatly into whatever happens to be the prevailing social theory.

Democracy suffers too. The lay citizen is baffled by the subtleties of contemporary science. This, in turn, engenders spiritual strain and, ultimately, self-loathing, for "One cannot go on indefinitely acknowledging that that which makes one's world go around and mediates all reliable knowledge is hopelessly beyond one's comprehension, and therefore one's control."[47] Because everyday life is nonparticipative for most of the population, modern urban society cannot sustain democratic contents to match its democratic forms.

Furthermore, Roszak sees little hope that countervailing expertise can prevent the development of technocratic elitism. Countervailing experts, for reasons already spelled out, do not challenge the appropriateness of the "urban-industrial" order of life; nor do they challenge the prevailing epistemology of objective science upon which that order rests.

Countervailing experts outside government or the corporate structure may win particular political battles, but ironically, their very success serves to undergird further the social power of technocracy. This is because the very terms of discourse are the language of technocracy. Such a language system cannot be used to demonstrate that urban industrialism is inherently technocratic, hence inherently undemocratic.[48] This outside expertise also serves to bolster the impression that pluralistic power centers can serve as an adequate substitute for effective mass political participation. In reality this too leaves politics an expert's game.

In summing up, Roszak holds that there is more to life than "the merchandise and marvels of scientific progress."[49] Expertise and rational planning rest on a diminished mode of consciousness. The symbolic and material rewards provided by the suave technocracy reassure citizens that they are completely free at the very point that they are most enslaved by a restrictive mode of thought. Citizens are seduced into a rampant materialism and alienated from each other by a scientistic epistemology. They are unfree to grasp creative vision, to embrace the sacredness that surrounds them in the world; unfree truly to experience love and communion.

WHAT IS TO BE DONE?—COOPERATIVE DECENTRALIZATION

Is psychic or social reality the prime mover of people's lives? The way we answer this question provides our view of human consciousness and the potentialities of human liberation. For Marx, the psyche is a reflection of the material mode of production. The socioeconomic structure distributes roles, rewards, sanctions, and the intellectual contents which shape human motivation and provide rationalizations for class interests. For Freud, social structure is the by-product of psychic contents, having been created and refined as sublimated expressions of basic drives.

How we answer this question determines whether we seek human liberation by social or by psychic change. Roszak accepts the psychiatric assumption that "alienation results from deep and secret acts of repression that will not yield to a mere reshuffling of our society's institutional structures."[50] He even suggests that, if understood in this way, "alienation" may be more heavily concentrated in the upper strata then the lower strata of advanced capitalist societies. This is because the upper classes are more likely to display a "monomaniacal acquisitiveness and ascetic self-discipline" that requires renunciation of the erotic instincts and channels psychic energy into "anal-sadistic aggressiveness."[51]

But Roszak's critique is an indictment of "technocratic society" per se, not solely of advanced capitalism. Capitalism's thoroughly irrational acquisitiveness, its "commodity fetishism," as well as the technocratic nature of the state socialist alternative, persuades Roszak that the only revolution that can free people from alienation must be therapeutic, cultural, and spiritual in character rather than institutional and social.

For Roszak, as for Marcuse, changed consciousness must precede social change. But unlike Marcuse, who seeks to reconcile Freudianism with Marxist humanism, Roszak assumes that both intellectual currents share a "scientistic" world view. For Roszak, Marxism is a mirror image of bourgeois industrialism. Both espouse technological solutions to human "problems." Neither is sensitive to the mystical dimension of human consciousness. Both posit reductionist images of human nature that rob people of their fantasies and dreams. Both demand a realism that Roszak terms "deadly practicality."[52] In orienting consciousness toward heightened rationality, both atrophy the human ability to wish, to dream, to experience the ecstatic vision of worlds that might be.

Expanding Limited Vision

What then is to be done to overcome the limited vision fostered by the technocratic approach to "urban industrialism"? Roszak concurs with Freud that every civilization expropriates a portion of the psyche for its own, requiring the adaptation of conscious thought and external behavior to a Reality Principle. But unlike Freud, who sought to relegate myth, religion, and fantasy to a subservient role, Roszak argues that the objective mode of consciousness upon which the reality principle and rational planning are based reduces to "mere fantasy" much in culture that is valuable and vital to creative growth. Freud's attempt to encourage people to "grow up" and "acquiesce in fate" is, in Roszak's view, derived from the particular urban-industrial culture within which Freud wrote. It cannot itself be subjected to scientific proof. It must be accepted on faith.

In Roszak's alternative view, the capacities of consciousness "may differ widely from age to age, culture to culture, person to person."[53] For him, different experiences lead to different postulated metaphysics, which define different phenomena as "real." In some cultures, for some ages, and for some people, artistic and spiritual phenomena are "real"; the objective material world is an illusion, to wit: Plato's allegory of the cave.[54]

For Roszak, the contemporary supercity is the symbol and ultimate manifestation of the psychological objectification of external reality—the bigger and more complex the city becomes, the more there is for the egoistic self to "work upon." In this context, the builder, planner, and "master" of the urban world displaces the artist, lover, and "seer" of the cosmos. The urban planner improves upon nature, but he does not feel at home in and reside within it.

True communal symbols must be "lived into" rather than improved upon.[55] Collective symbols are code words that call forth subconscious associations and deeper levels of personal meaning. For Roszak, the discovery and transmission of the universal symbols that reside in all great literature and art is an essential way to overcome the limited consciousness fostered by urban industrialism. Great symbols unravel unfathomable mysteries with a clarity and immediacy that has no parallel in strictly logical thought.

Nonetheless, the truth and reality that primordial symbols reveal is always partial, never complete. The mystery of great literature and art is that it creates an irreducible, universal meaning which can never be fully fathomed by the contemplator of the created object, but which yields in different degrees to each viewer some measure of the dark chambers of reality buried deep in the subconscious mind.

The way of knowledge recommended by Roszak constitutes a liberation of the spontaneous, subjective self rather than its rejection and policing, as required by both rational planning and objective science. For Roszak, the objectification of experience and the policing of the spontaneous are quintessentially acts of alienation—a denial of one's own faculty to discover interconnections through freely experienced intuition. If cultivated with discipline, sensitivity, and respect, Roszak believes that the human senses can make intuitive contact with the fluid inner rhythms of visionary consciousness.

To overcome single vision, Roszak holds that it is not necessary to abandon urbanization and technology, but only to put them in their proper place. For example, Roszak contends that in past historical eras technical progress of the most sweeping kind has taken place within visionary world views. Furthermore, technics, like art and ritual, has been a carrier of transcendent vision, its inventions unfolding from consciousness, "as so many material embodiments of transcendent symbols."[56]

Agriculture, hunting, weaving, brewing, and mining have all created tools which were more than utilitarian instruments. They were also cult objects, symbolizing the relationship of the vocation to society, nature, and the cosmic order. Roszak hopes that technology can once again become a way to deepen sacral consciousness. This would be possible, in his view, if technology would draw upon the root symbols of the organic universe, invent rituals to assign technics a diminished status in the world, and give meaning and purpose to existence by linking its symbols and rituals to the natural order.

But when urban technocrats lose touch with the natural order and with sentimental experience, they cannot discover the root symbolic meaning of the organic universe. Knowledge of root meanings deepens and personalizes what we know. When deeper levels of meaning are overlooked, ignored, or denied, consciousness moves on the surface of experience, knowing the world analytically, but without qualitative depth. Lacking the willingness and ability to use the intuitive faculty, urban technocrats fail to perceive the universal truths hidden deep in the vulgar particulars of everyday life. The union of opposites, made clear in "hunches, wordplay, metaphor, and rule-of-thumb,"[57] are lost to the more prosaic and "systematic" mind of the urban rationalist.

Restoring Concreteness and Ecological Planning

Unlike Freud, who posited the repression of sexuality as the chief consequence of civilized existence, Roszak posits the loss of intimate connection with all concrete physical reality as the chief price to pay for the "advancement" of urban culture. Lost, for Roszak, is our concrete connectedness with experience. Like Freud, Roszak holds that the assumption of an upright carriage has altered dramatically human sentient experience. Instead of linking the sense of smell to repressed sexuality, as does Freud, Roszak links the loss of smell to a loss of intimate connection with "the ground."[58] This is his metaphorical way of symbolizing the organic oneness of human and physical nature. In Roszakian theory, when the eye became the primary human sense, the individual became alienated from his surroundings in a way that was not possible when the eye shared power with the ear, the nose, and the sense of touch. It is through the eye that people first begin to perceive an "out there" that includes not only the environment but even one's own body. "In here" begins to reside somewhere between the ears and behind the eyes. "Out there" is experienced as an alien presence.

In primitive societies, argues Roszak, the auditory, olfactory, and sentient powers were far more intense. They intimately connected the human body to the organic universe. Urban industrialism represses this intimate connection of human beings with the natural universe by creating an entirely synthetic environment. It is the human being's organic destiny—the need to grow, mature, and ultimately, to die—which secular culture denies. It is Thanatos rather than Eros which urban industrialism represses. And for Roszak, Freud's Thanatos signifies "the body's need to live out its organic destiny, to ripen and die."[59]

For Roszak, the sex drive is still quite obviously alive. Otherwise we would not be so keenly aware of sexual repression when it occurs. Far more problematic for Roszak's urban rationalist are other sensory faculties that are so benumbed that their loss is no longer even experienced as a deprivation. Instead, removal of the "messiness" of organic reality—blood, sweat, and organic smells—is regarded as a blessing. Air conditioning, waste disposals, and other modern inventions insulate us from the concrete realities of life. They create a lifeless, synthetic world. In Roszak's view, the artificial urban milieu is "as lifeless and gleamingly sterile as the glass and aluminum, stainless steel and plastic of the high-rise architecture and its interiors that now fill the urban-industrial world."[60]

The preoccupation of primitive cultures with basic bodily functions is viewed by Roszak as a healthy childlike messiness. The modern urban rationalist destroys waste products rather than recycling them.

With a little care and a commitment to "ecological" planning, Roszak argues, urban-industrial societies can reclaim their own waste as cheap organic fertilizer. Communally based municipal compost heaps can replace ecologically dangerous chemical fertilizers. Such a step also would be of use symbolically, by calling attention to the life-giving continuities of all organic matter. By undertaking this symbolic act, we take a step in the direction of renewed consciousness. As the "head" of the urban personality becomes more tolerant of the organic realities of the environment, the chances are increased that it will become less sealed off from the organic body. The mind-body dichotomy can be resolved. This is essential, since the body, in the final analysis, is the concrete reality that participates in the organic process of growth, maturation, and death.

The fulfilled personality of Roszak's vision needs a living environment which is supportive of both richly symbolic dream life and concrete "sensuous participation in experience."[61] Deprived of such an environment, the urban rationalist stands alone. Cerebral faculties become the only resources that can be called upon to cope with life.

Pursuing his quest for an ecological approach to planning at the systemic level, Roszak turns to human and natural ecology as the scientific approaches most likely to overcome single vision. Although based firmly within objective consciousness, these sciences are the nearest approaches available for recapturing rhapsodic vision in a scientific cultural setting. The "holistic, receptive, trustful, largely non-tampering" approach of the ecologists represents for Roszak a search for wholes—natural and social harmonies—that are greater than the sum of their parts. Unlike other sciences, human and natural ecology are contemplative and judgmental in spirit. As Roszak puts it:

> The patterns the ecologists study include man in body, mind, and deed, and therefore they prescribe a standard of health. What violates the natural harmony must be condemned; what enhances it, be endorsed.[62]

The cultivation of this approach would surely slow the pace and scale of social research, possibly even ending altogether some lines of research and policy planning which prove too reductionist, insensitive, or ecologically risky.[63] By implication, the pace and scale of urban life would also slacken.

As ecological consciousness becomes an alternative paradigm for understanding the world and our place in it, Roszak expects it to function as a restorative psychology of cultural well-being. Insensitive, ecologically damaging, and humanly alienating planning projects will cease. Science will occupy a less dominant position in human culture; it will once again become a means to human fulfillment rather than an end in itself.

For Roszak, expertise must be put in its proper place. It must become subordinate to an "experiential science" that eschews abstract reduction of human beings to an agglomeration of roles, statuses, and functions. If this occurs, political democracy, social equality, and the human community will be given a new lease on life.

But the ecological approach will not bring about these results unless people are willing to heed the ecological lesson that spontaneous self-regulation is possible only in small-scale communities.

Radical Deurbanization and the Cooperative Commonwealth

Roszak's utopian image of the postindustrial future in an ecologically harmonious environment relegates both the city and industry to a strictly supportive role in human development. The city becomes an option and a storehouse of resources and skills rather than a dominant mode of existence. For Roszak, city life is properly the domain of intellectuals and merchants. The former relish the city as a breeding ground for new ideas and for fostering intensive conflict of values and tastes; the latter because the city is a marketplace for things as well as ideas. For these reasons, Roszak finds the city too large, heterogeneous, hectic, and wearying a milieu for most of humanity.

Like Georg Simmel, Roszak views the city as overstimulating. Unlike Simmel, he views the city as distracting the personality from its basic spiritual mission, rather than as providing a unique opportunity for achieving spiritual refinement. Unlike Simmel and Sennett (and even Wirth), Roszak regards the size, density, heterogeneity, anonymity, and mobility of the metropolis as unmitigated liabilities. Because of his particular theory of basic human needs, he views the city as an iron cage whose occupants remain caged from economic necessity rather than choice. Robbed of simplicity, natural immediacy, community, and spirituality, the Roszakian urban dweller has a latent need to deurbanize.

To bring this need to the surface, Roszak offers a "program" for planned radical deurbanization.[64] He would scale down and thin out cities, although he offers no specific incentives for achieving this objective. He would take unspecified steps to make rural and village life, and "autonomous" small towns, "live options" for urban dropouts. He would selectively reduce industrialism, replacing it with handicrafts, cottage industry, and less-energy-consuming technologies, until zero-growth is reached.

Roszak assumes that if alternative life styles and work options are made more widely available, the benefits of deurbanization will become obvious to all. Underlying this expectation is an implicit theory of alienated labor and its consequences for urban social organization.

Roszak holds that so long as bureaucratic and industrial work is performed to other people's specifications, rather than in response to the worker's own creative impulses, it will inevitably come to be experienced as alienating drudgery. As a consequence, there is still widespread popular support for labor-saving mechanization to eliminate the drudgery for workers. Urban social organization reflects this dynamic of mechanization.

But new social organization, or rather a return to older forms of social organization—handicrafts, cottage industries, and decentralized worker control of the work process and product—can alter the prevailing cultural perception of work as a monotonous chore. Once this is accomplished, current support for large-scale labor-saving technologies may well diminish. As Roszak cogently observes: "[W]here work becomes a personal project and is done in community, its character is wholly transformed. It can even become . . . a form of prayer. Work can be a chance to innovate, fraternize, and serve. . . . It can be a fulfilling expression of the personality."[65]

Within the interstices of the dominant urban-industrial culture there have developed a wide variety of communal groups, handicraft, organic food, community development and worker cooperatives, and voluntary social service clinics. Roszak is much encouraged by these developments, as they represent the basic ecological insight of the communal anarchist ideal—the intrinsic value of spontaneous self-regulation. Communal anarchism, for Roszak, is "the political style most hospitable to the visionary quest."[66]

Roszak locates his communal anarchist ideal of a "cooperative commonwealth" within the anarchist tradition of such thinkers as Tolstoy, Kropotkin, Gandhi, Paul Goodman, and the British economic decentralist E.F. Schumacher.[67] For all these theorists, the scale of organization is a central practical and philosophical problem. Communal anarchist thinking regards the large scale of any institution, public or private, as a potential threat to such humanistic values as personalism, sensitivity, fellowship, spontaneous self-development of human cooperation, and creative work. Both corporate capitalism and centralized state socialism, as in the Soviet model, are anathema to the communal anarchist because both divorce the ownership and management of economic organizations from the personal involvement of organizational members.

Roszak's commitment to the goals discussed above prompts him to offer a tentative laundry list of policy proposals that, taken together, comprise a blueprint for a new political economy. His preferred political economy is termed variously the "cooperative commonwealth," "anarchist socialism," and "decentralized socialism." It would be a confederated commonwealth of communities.

Within this confederated commonwealth, ecological planners would concern themselves with "discovering" people's natural needs by working directly with people themselves. Democratically controlled planning processes would strive to define the proper mix between handicrafts, intermediate technologies, and heavy industry; social services would be user-developed and user-controlled; big banks and insurance companies would be replaced by credit unions and mutual insurance; transportation and communication networks would be regionalized and controlled at the grass roots; the neighborhood would become the basic unit for delivering personalized welfare services; industries would be worker-controlled as a way to revitalize work as a nonexploitative activity; rural life would be encouraged through a policy of "organic homesteading"; producer's and consumer's cooperatives would abound.[68]

Despite his willingness to spell out the kind of world he would like to see emerge, Roszak is radically unwilling to devise a political strategy for achieving his communal anarchist ideal. Unlike other "urban anarchists" like Paul Goodman, Jane Jacobs, and E. F. Schumacher, Roszak rejects as "power politics" all strategies designed to fashion a more self-regulating urban environment.

The political power of Roszak's counterculture is the power of "living example." It is a redemptionist rather than a political movement. Redemptionist movements seek to change the world by inducing cultural change through "living example." They reject direct political action to bring about social change. As such, Roszak exhorts counterculturalists to form small-scale communities, and then to "disaffiliate, decentralize, cultivate non-violent relationships, look after their own needs."[69] Instead of building support or changing society, Roszak's visionary commonwealth is told to fight for its "privacy, freedom, peace of mind." By shutting out the urban-industrial society, Roszak refuses to engage in the messy world of urban political conflict. To preserve the inner harmony of small groups, he appears content to leave much of the rest of society radically alienated.

But in Roszak's theory, altered consciousness can bring about radical social change. For this reason, Roszak places unyielding confidence in the exemplary role model of the "authentically happy disaffiliate": "In changing one's own life one may not intend to change the world; but there is never any telling how far the power of imaginative example travels."[70]

The "One Best Way"

Roszak's antipolitical, redemptionist approach to urban alienation is most vividly evident in his most recent work, *Unfinished Animal*,[71] in which he explores the various "points of entry" to transcendence offered by a host of religious and quasireligious cults and movements. Roszak discerns several common elements in these diverse movements which he offers, ironically, as a kind of plan or technique for achieving "liberated sensibility." Each step in the "plan" is envisaged as a necessary but insufficient "path" toward the realization of transcendent being. Taken together, the eight steps that constitute Roszak's prescribed "way" are deemed the "one best way" to transcend the self-alienating dimensions of urban industrialism. Paradoxically, in this sense, the antitechnocrat Roszak adopts a major tenet of technological thought, its certainty that there is a one best way to achieve any given goal.

Roszak counsels us to view the individual as an unfolding, possibly infinite potentiality— a being in the process of continuous growth. The end point of human development, for Roszak, is religious transcendence. He fears that in pursuing human development we may settle "too cheaply" for lesser need fulfillments, thus never actualizing our full potential. To illustrate, he turns Freud upon his head: "Far from religion's being an 'aim-inhibited' manifestation of sex, it is sex that functions as a sublimated physical expression of transcendence, an early approximation in our lives of a higher goal—the experienced unity of metaphysical polarities."[72] For Roszak, actuality and potentiality, rather than ego and id, or form and content, is the basic metaphysical duality. He challenges the "unfinished animal" to become godlike.

Secondly, mirroring Wordsworth and the Romantics,[73] Roszak tells us that life should be experienced rather than explained. In his view, too many of us spend too much of our lives involved in abstract plans, calculations, and worries. This obsessive future-orientation robs life of its vivid immediacy. This is the chief reason he refuses to spell out a political strategy for achieving his preferred ideals of deurbanization and communal decentralization. Instead of rational policy planning, Roszak offers "structured rituals" and "proven techniques for awakening . . . visionary energy."[74] These may be found in Eastern religions, Western techniques of "participative learning," and meditative teachings.

Thirdly, Roszak would have us cultivate a new mode for communicating spiritual reality to others. We must acquire a new appreciation of the uses of myth, ritual, symbolism, dream, meditation, and trance as "indispensible means" for unfolding transcendental potentialities and to achieve "transpersonal subjectivity."

Next we are told to be open. Openness to the diverse particularities of various religious traditions can lead to a discovery of the "humanly common and constant" deeper symbolic meanings comprising the primordial religious impulse.

Once these steps have been achieved we are prepared to overcome self-division. For Roszak, all divisions of the self deny our essential wholeness and the natural "hierarchical" integration of the personality. Yet hierarchical integration may be imposed from an abstract blueprint rather than discovered naturally. Hence Roszak counsels us to explore the realms of experience. In his view, hierarchical integration can be achieved without repression only if it is dictated by "nature" rather than politics or planning.[75] For each of us, the integration of our needs and potentialities can be validated only by open experience.

Among the realms of experience are our own body, the profane world, and the community. At each of these levels Roszak counsels an enrichment of experience. First, the body must come to be experienced as an instrument of meditation and transcendence, rather than, as in urban capitalist societies, as a "grim, anal-aggressive machinery for the accumulation of profit and power vastly beyond anything . . . [one] could enjoy."[76] Secondly, we must learn to be perceptive, to discover the sacred in the profane. Following the way of Zen-Taoism, we must come to experience life "through the empowered presence of things."[77] By illuminating the commonplace, we can find enlightenment in the most profane aspects of everyday life.

Finally, we must be communal. We must seek out and form "sheltered and physically nourishing environments where work, friendship, family, and the transcendent impulse interpenetrate."[78] Small-scale, voluntary communities, religious groups, living and working associations, each can enhance the lives of its members. Each can also help to transform the rest of urban society indirectly.

The ultimate vision of Theodore Roszak's politics of transcendence is an act of mythmaking. As a source of inspiration to his supporters, Roszak offers the myth of "creative disintegration." Within the interstices of the urban-industrial order, participatory communities, capable of awakening the transcendent energies, arise. This represents "a healthy collective subtraction" from the dominant ethos of power, profit, and privilege.[79] The inspirational spirit of viable alternative environments erodes the very foundations of the urban-industrial order. The secular city gradually disintegrates and dies through "creative disintegration" rather than through power politics or planning. In its place stand healthy small-scale human communities built on the human remnants of dead institutions. Cultural revolution creates social change.

In the final analysis, Roszak invokes the spirit of Prince Peter Kropotkin,[80] who derived the value of spontaneous mutual aid from his observations of the primitive social structure of nomads and rural villagers. Roszak takes Kropotkin a step further. He holds that primitive tribal ritual, rite, and magic have intrinsic value. They unleash the creative spirit lying welled up beneath the surface. Through ritual, the shaman teaches that the world is a mysterious, sacred place. Participation of the community in the shaman's lore gives the members a healthy sense of humility and limits. Paradoxically, it also expands consciousness by showing the way to the poetic vision of organic unity. It is this expanded vision which establishes the real limits of human existence by commanding reverence for other presences, the community, nature, and the cosmos. Theodore Roszak is the shaman of contemporary "urban-industrial" culture, coaxing it toward the counterculture.

CITY LIFE AND PERSONAL IDENTITY: AN ALTERNATIVE VIEW

Richard Sennett, like Theodore Roszak, offers a powerful critique of urban planning. He, too, favors more active political participation in urban decision making, mistrusts centralized bureaucracies, would decentralize urban institutions, and calls himself an "urban anarchist." But beneath these surface similarities lies a profoundly different vision of human nature and a radically different set of social and political ideals.

Sennett's views on the nature of psychosocial development are derived from the theories of Erik Erikson. Erikson, a student of Freud, views psychological growth as occuring in sequential stages throughout life, each of which can be resolved only by experiencing and coping satisfactorily with crisislike inner and outer conflicts. Growth consists of the individual's working through of these conflicts. As neatly summarized by Sennett himself, Erikson holds that "the gaining of psychological strength derives from . . . experiences of conflict so that 'strength' implies both a power of mastery and a capacity for openness to internal disorder."[81]

Sigmund Freud and other instinctualists hold that all of our psychic processes are present at birth. Sennett and developmental theorists like Erikson hold that our psychic materials are generated by human action at critical junctures throughout the course of life. The "Developmental Personality" is a creator of its own psyche through the various ways it chooses to cope with environmental threats, crises, and disorder in everyday life.

Thus alienation, for Sennett, results from people's attempt to limit their potential for experiencing conflict in their lives. Because of the wish to detach the "self" from painful involvement in the apparently random chaos of external events, people often impose, prematurely, a rigidly fixed self-definition on situations they may encounter, prior to any actual experience. This provides a relatively clear-cut sense of personal identity in the face of the often bewildering events of concrete historical reality. The rigid self-image is a strong defense against the confusion of the outside world; however, it also alienates the individual from concrete participation in life, as well as from the developmental self. By defining the self in advance of experience, the personality becomes "a fixed object rather than an open person, liable to be touched by a social situation."[82]

Many such "purified identity" mechanisms emerge in late adolescence. Instead of being a period of wandering and exploration, late adolescence often becomes a troubling period, during which coping mechanisms are developed to enable avoidance of unknown and potentially painful experiences. For instance, the early selection of a career or an ideal mate, prior to exploring actual alternatives, is a commonplace occurrence at this stage of life. So, too, is the desire to acquire emotionless professional competence. This is done, in Sennett's view, to avoid feelings of powerlessness. To be "on top of things" is to control one's environment, so that nothing in it occurs outside one's power. This is an unrealizable adolescent wish for omnipotence.

Sennett contends that at times these desires to purify experience can become so pervasive in a social system that they become manifest as family and community phenomena. Like individuals, families—and even entire social communities—fearful of painful confusion and disorder, can build isolating social structures that shield them from disruptive influences, and in so doing rob their collective life of vitality, surprise, and growth.

"Purified communities" of this sort insulate themselves from conflict by creating a myth—the myth of sameness and communal solidarity.[83] Such a reassuring myth amounts to a denial of the individual uniqueness and human diversity that full exposure to the heterogeneous experiences of the city might reveal. The myth keeps people from having to interact with each other and provides a handy justification for repressing diversity and dissent within families and communities.

THE DECLINE OF URBAN HETEROGENEITY

Richard Sennett argues that contemporary American cities and their suburbs have lost the vitality, heterogeneity, diversity, and disorder of the great cities of the late nineteenth and early twentieth centuries. He attributes the vitality of earlier cities to the diverse human contacts facilitated by an urban social structure that has long since disappeared in most American metropolitan areas. The earlier cities were characterized by diverse patterns of land use. Homes, offices, shopping areas, bars, cafes and coffeehouses, political clubs, places of amusement, and industrial, religious, and cultural institutions spilled over into each other. Sennett holds that the interpenetration of this multiplicity of modes of labor and life fostered human contact and interaction among those who differed from each other ethnically, occupationally, by social class, and otherwise. In his view, this admixture was especially advantageous to the low income urban immigrant, who could not escape this diversity. The immigrants were surrounded by a multiplicity of "contact points" that added richness and diversity to their lives.

In Sennett's view, the Victorian bourgeoisie often was far less fortunate. The subject matter of Sennett's *Families Against the City*[84] is the plight of a middle-class Chicago neighborhood called Union Park, whose residents were able to shut themselves off from contact with the rest of the city. In this empirically based work, Sennett found that family life in Union Park served as a refuge for a group of white-collar fathers who remained stagnant in their work life. Because of their avoidance of urban conflict, these fathers were unable to prepare their children to cope with the rapidly changing urban society in which they must live. Life in Union Park was a defense against the conflicting demands of the urban environment. Family life was nuclear rather than extended, reflecting the reluctance of Union Park fathers to marry until their careers had reached a safe, if stagnant, plateau.

The life style of Union Park families foreshadows Sennett's critique of the "intense" suburban family of contemporary America in *The Uses of Disorder*. In both instances, little time, effort, or psychic energy is invested outside the self-sufficient nuclear family. Street life is nonexistent. Challenges of the outside world are avoided or ignored. The escapist defense mechanism of intense family life prevents members, especially children, from learning to cope with strangers and the strangeness of new situations. For Sennett, overprotective environments do not prepare their members to deal with a heterogeneous urban world.

The Union Park experience also foreshadows the current fragmentation of the metropolis into a congeries of latently warring, homogeneous residential enclaves. The modern metropolis in *The Uses of Disorder* has lost its capacity to foster human interaction among diverse subcultures. Social gathering spots have been destroyed by urban renewal. Rigid segregation of land uses, promoted by conventional city planning theory and practice, has robbed urban neighborhoods of their richness, vitality, and differentiation.[85] The capacity of affluent suburban residents to zone out class, ethnic, and functional diversity further contributes to a stultification of human experience. The contemporary metropolitan milieu becomes a series of stagnant fortresses rather than a vibrant place fostering intellectual stimulation, emotional diversity, and personal growth.

The contemporary American metropolis has undergone the development of elaborate techno-bureaucratic systems, on the one hand, and a simplification of social interaction and of the forums where social exchange can take place, on the other. How has this paradoxical combination of complexity and simplification come about? Older urban forms of complex human association, through multiple contact points, have been displaced by voluntary withdrawal from diversity and by the "renewal" policies of urban planners, who bulldoze vital social gathering places in pursuit of their own purified vision of the good city. To fill the void, the nuclear family has assumed many of the interaction functions once performed by other urban institutions—the bar, the coffeehouse, the political machine, the union, and the church.

In Sennett's view, material abundance also plays a role in the simplification of social life. In earlier historical periods, in many urban neighborhoods, people simply lacked the resources either to move out or to build a fortress around themselves. Such neighborhoods, as Jane Jacobs has shown, were more vibrant, diverse, and vital than today's homogeneous communities. Furthermore, growing abundance has meant that, except in poor areas, neighbors no longer need to share resources in order to survive. Sennett holds that the plight of the suburban family is fast becoming the plight of once vital working-class urban neighborhoods. As urban ethnic groups have become more upwardly mobile, they have withdrawn into the pattern of intensive family life of the affluent. Economically self-sufficient nuclear family life removes a major basis for social interaction beyond the family circle.

The general level of affluence also makes possible the physical separation of home life from all other aspects of life. In relatively affluent areas, land uses are rigidly segregated; housing is cut off from commercial, educational, and work activities, and from a lively street life. Dullness and sterility are the price people pay for the planned separation of land uses.

In this sort of environment, people run away from, rather than learn to deal with, conflict and disorder in their lives. Conflicts that do erupt in such circumstances tend to be more violent and damaging than they otherwise would be. In Sennett's view, this is because the absence of regular confrontation with "the stranger" impoverishes the public rituals once found to be useful for promoting civility amidst urban diversity.[86] Lacking settled political conventions for mediating conflict and achieving positive goals, people turn in frustration to bureaucratic authority to control disorder. When people will not learn to encounter and cope with conflict in their lives, the bureaucratic state is born.

Intense family members invest so much energy in the family because it is a relationship based on long-term trust. But in the larger social world such trust is rare. Sennett dislikes the intense family and the small-scale purified community not only because they repress diversity, but also because they maintain internal uniformity by repressing the aggressiveness that may well be necessary to deal with an unjust world. In place of the supportive, loving, and caring community, Sennett would foster the strong, impersonal, rugged individualist.

Sennett's penchant for impersonality, aloofness, and environmental mastery stems in part from his rejection of the "claustrophobia of intimate routine."[87] His dislike for close-knit families, neighborhoods, and communities also derives from his political beliefs that such groups are too weak to deal with the reality of concentrated political power. Participation in strong but impersonal, large-scale interest groups, such as national labor unions, is essential in his view although perhaps less appealing than local community ties. Such impersonal interest groups serve the vital function of combating other large-scale political and economic institutions (e.g., corporations) that have acquired increasing control over everyday urban life. "In politics," says Sennett, "intimate and warm human relations are a misplaced ideal; small may be beautiful, but it is also impotent."[88] Or as he says elsewhere of Roszak's counterculture: "Better tribal and intimate than impersonal and bureaucratic is a formula whose exercise is an admission of impotence to deal with and change bureaucratic structures of themselves."[89]

From Sennett's perspective, the Roszakian communitarian has the character of a refugee, fundamentally ambivalent about the assertion of aggression. Like Freud, Sennett views aggressiveness as a necessary ingredient of the mature personality. A totally open, trustful, warm, and sharing environment shields the personality from conflict and injustice. But politics rests on conflict and injustice, and their resolution. Those who never experience the frustration of injustice will neither be strong enough to deal with the everyday world nor to resist injustice aggressively when needed. Sennett's question to Roszak is: "Is it humane to form soft selves in a hard world?"[90]

The communitarian ideal of Roszak's counterculture is for Sennett a mirror image of the rigidly "purified" community life of Union Park and contemporary suburbia. All three reflect an adolescent refusal to deal with the pain, injustice, and complexity of the world. The counterculture becomes yet another variant of the urban planner's vision of the harmonious "city beautiful," where people live together in harmony and peace by denying the painful reality of their differences. For Sennett, Roszak's vision is akin to the ideal of Fyodor Dostoevsky's Grand Inquisitor, a community life that resembles "one unanimous and harmonious antheap."[91]

The Fallacy of Projective Planning

Just as adolescents, suburbanites, and counterculturalists seek to purify their identities, urban planners engage in projective techniques whose essential purpose is to explain reality in advance of experience. In Sennett's view, both the purification of identity and the techniques of planning serve to insulate their users from potentially disruptive and dislocating experiences. Orderliness, coherence, and consistency in planning, as in life, exclude from consciousness the messy concrete "factness" of real people struggling to shape their own everyday lives for themselves.

Thus, for example, the myth of communal solidarity is perpetuated by the planner's purification rituals of exclusionary zoning and formal "citizen participation" in planning that serve to deflect actual social conflict. Having become shut off from individual experiences of diversity, and having made "sameness" the basis of community relationships, members of purified communities treat heterogeneity, diversity, and change as threats to individual selfhood and collective dignity. They are encouraged in this view by planners' willingness to plan residential enclaves that are isolated from diverse social experience.

Furthermore, urban planners of housing, redevelopment, highways, and purified communities tend to treat "projective needs" that are abstractly deduced as fixed prescriptions. When real people, expressing themselves individually and through neighborhood groups, object to these abstract projections, their protests are treated as troublesome threats rather than as practical attempts to influence social reconstruction. In this way, planners can use their pencils to deny the inevitable surprise and conflict of historical development. Obsession with projective needs represents, for Sennett, the puritanical quest for a coherent self-image that screens out the threats, contradictions, and ambiguities of the concrete environment. The planner becomes immunized and immunizes others against social experience, thereby preserving an unambiguous image of the self and one's role in the world.

Three dimensions of rational-comprehensive planning are special targets of Sennett's scorn. First is the fallacy of projective needs, described above. By marshaling money and other resources in preparation for projected future states, in advance of actual historical experience, planners become locked into their plans. The "plan" is taken as more true than are the people affected by it. Second is what might be called the fallacy of linearity. Because plans project needs in a linear fashion, what seems future-oriented in planning is really past-oriented. Trends, observed to be clearly discernible from the past to the present, are projected onto the future in a linear fashion. In Sennett's view, the chief danger of this approach is that the lessons we draw from the past are themselves based upon selective perceptions. The information that planners "let through" is likely to be the more comfortable data upon which their sense of place, role, and identity is based. Uncomfortable experiences that may signal departures from familiar past trends often are filtered out. The upshot is that, like adolescents, "experience is being purified by having the dissonances interpreted as less real than the consonances with what is known."[92]

Thirdly, rational-comprehensive planning is both too mechanistic and too holistic. The metropolitan planners' attempt to coordinate the physical, social, and economic activities of entire urban regions represents, for Sennett, an ideology of "planning the parts from the nature of the whole."[93] For Sennett, the metropolitan area can be said to be a community only if the functioning parts of a machine can be called a community. Designing the "social parts" to fit a predetermined, projective urban whole can lead to inhumane results. For Sennett, as for Simmel, needs "reside in the human parts of the social whole, not in some social product apart from social experience."[94]

In place of the mechanistic desire to plan the metropolis as one would design an efficient, well-oiled, frictionless machine, Sennett would have urban planners return to the preindustrial craftsman's style of work. Rather than conceiving the product "as a whole" before production and mechanically fitting work materials to a preconceived image, the medieval craftsman felt free to alter his materials and forms throughout the process of creation. His was an act of creative exploration and experience, not a passive act of conformity to a preconceived blueprint.

For Sennett, the mechanistic approach to rational-comprehensive planning is yet another instance of the adolescent desire that nothing be out of control. The attempt to integrate aesthetic, economic, political, and humanistic values into coherent "wholes" is bound to reduce diverse human activities to their lowest common denominator. Ironically, this gross simplification of life is done in a fruitless attempt to establish a transcendent order of life that denies the variety, and thus the unavoidable conflict, in the world.

What is true of the Wirthian ideal of metropolitan planning is true as well of the Roszakian dream of organic wholeness. By seeking to impose order and harmony on diverse human activities, the inevitability of human conflict is, as Freud would say, wished away. Sennett concurs with Simmel that needs exist in individuals, not in abstractions called "society." They exist in the human parts of the social whole. Planning that downplays these needs, as they emerge from social experience, is bound to fail. Conflict-free communities are utopian—they can exist "no-where."

Moreover, the obsessive compulsion to avoid conflict is a self-defeating act of "disengagement." Both planners and counterculturalists, in their desire to create a frictionless order, leave the field of political conflict up to politicians and bureaucrats, preferring instead to keep their sights upon a purified "whole." In so doing, they abdicate political responsibility. Sticking to their ideal becomes an act of impotence. Making no provision for the uncertain and unexpected in their visions, they are bypassed by other historical forces. Thus, ironically, both the professional planners that Roszak so fears, and the cultural revolutionaries that dismay establishment planners, are, in the final analysis, Sennett's paper tigers.

WHAT IS TO BE DONE?—PLANNING FOR DISORDER

Richard Sennett poses a Hobson's choice between externally imposed bureaucratic order and the self-imposed boredom and slavery of life within the small, face-to-face community. Sennett's answer to the question "What is to be done?" is a call for "planned disorder" as a way out of this double bind. He urges Roszak's dropout to return to the city, debureaucratize its institutions, and in so doing, grow out of adolescence. For Sennett, full adulthood lies in openly accepting painful dislocation and disorder. Adulthood can only be achieved in a "dense, uncontrollable human settlement," such as a city.[95] A return to a preindustrial division of labor is neither possible nor desirable. The current level of technological development reflects basic technical and economic processes that cannot be reversed, but must be made humane. To humanize is to diversify social experience, not to simplify it.

If cities are to serve human needs, Sennett believes that a radically decentralized form of advocacy planning must replace rational-comprehensive urban planning. But Sennett's particular brand of "advocacy planning" resembles none of the existing models of planning that usually fall under this rubric.[96] Like most other advocacy models, Sennett's preferred scheme calls upon urban planners to work for rather than against the various conflicting class, ethnic, racial, and other interests that are directly affected by policy. Unlike most other models, that of Sennett does not want advocacy planners simply to express the wants of diverse community groups. Rather, it envisages advocacy planners who participate actively in creating the "social materials" that people need to grow out of adolescence.

And what are these materials? In their broadest sense, they are situations of social conflict in which people can grow to need the unknown, disorderly "otherness" that surrounds them. They are contexts within which humility, tolerance of ambiguity, and a penchant for self-criticism are fostered. They are triggering mechanisms that help people to overcome the passive "resignation in fate" that Freud viewed as so essential. They are places where childlike curiosity about the world is rekindled.

In Sennett's model of advocacy planning, the real task of urban planners is to enlarge the number of forums where people can directly experience the effects of their actions upon others. The essential task of the planner is to create stimulating and challenging social milieus, to help make society willingly chaotic. Sennett's advocacy planners must abandon the ideal of one harmonious community and replace it with the ideal of diverse "survival communities."[97]

In a survival community, people come to know each other through direct, face-to-face encounters, full of surprise, exploration, and disorder. But this can come about only if urban bureaucracies change their form and their functions. Power and conflict must be radically decentralized by stripping centralized order-maintaining bureaucracies of their social control functions. In addition, survival communities will not fully emerge unless urban land-use planning, as presently practiced, is abolished. In Sennett's view, "unzoning" the metropolis would serve two basic purposes. It would promote visual and functional disorder and would enable the character of a neighborhood to be established by the specifically evolving bonds, alliances, and common consents that emerge from community conflict. Neighborhoods would no longer be predetermined by a blueprint that guarantees a comfortable, but sterile, cultural homogeneity.

This sort of decentralized "community control" amounts to a "community" that is the conscious by-product of the halting and groping concrete acts of the "public" personality to work out a sort of "uneasy truce" among conflicting individuals and factions. Without zoning, police, and other bureaucratic social controls, Sennett believes that the people themselves would be forced to face disorder and to develop working arrangements for their community life. Yet Sennett never adequately deals with the problem of differential power within such "survival communities."

Why would mutual learning and creative accommodation rather than violence emerge from this arrangement? Sennett argues, somewhat obscurely, that each person's growing awareness of concrete and complex real people will reawaken a childlike curiosity about the puzzling "otherness" of adversaries. For this reason, rigidity, purification wishes, and stereotyped polarization can be avoided. Additionally, when disagreements have regular channels for expression and release, pent-up fears and self-repression can be overcome. Unlike Freud, Sennett holds that releasing aggression when it initially is triggered prevents its escalation to violence, when conflict can no longer be avoided. Finally, Sennett hopes that when people come to expect that they are inherently different, and hence in conflict with one another, they will no longer chase the illusion of harmonious community. Expecting less, Sennett's mature personality will settle for mutual survival rather than purified victory.

Herein lies Sennett's vision of the ideal "society." Adulthood requires coping with the challenges of the dense, heterogeneous, disorganized city. The chaos of the real world must be dealt with directly, by human beings alone, with no supports, no hiding place. And how would such a society be held together?

> The bonds of the adult society I envision would be difficult. Care between individuals would exist only to the extent that mutual curiosity and specific personal bonds developed. There would be no expectation of human love, no community of affection . . . laid down for the society as a whole. . . . Such an unstable and shifting community would have to be based on human beings who feel themselves limited, constantly changing, and unwilling to surrender their smallness to any grand vision, unwilling to make themselves whole.[98]

To nurture viable survival communities, cities require both individual and social differentiation. They require high population density and multiple contact points. They require the very conditions that Louis Wirth feared would make rational-comprehensive planning so difficult. The large, dense, and heterogeneous city, stripped of its formal social controls, becomes an environment too complex to control but too problematic to avoid. This is the basic goal underlying Sennett's desire to eliminate social control bureaucracies, preplanning, and restrictive zoning.

Ironically, Sennett holds that even if these three steps are taken, survival communities will not emerge spontaneously; they must be planned. His "plan" is entirely instrumental. It is designed to achieve his own ideal society, his own "purified" vision. To increase the visible contact points of urban areas, Sennett would redesign high-rise buildings, distributing their public places throughout each building, rather than entirely at the top or bottom; to facilitate interaction, he would build townhouses around common squares; to promote heterogeneity amidst density, he would take steps to achieve racial and socioeconomic integration of work, living, and recreation spaces; to foster community conflict short of violence, he would use public seed money to place an economic "floor" under urban conflict groups.[99]

If planned densification, diversification, and power redistribution are successful, Sennett expects important structural changes to occur. With the spread of alternative arenas for social interaction, family intensity is expected to weaken; with the expansion of concrete participation in political life, "image" candidacies would yield to new urban machines; with the diffusion of political experience, the pool of active urban political leaders would radically increase. Experience rather than formal training would form the basis of urban-planning expertise. For this reason, new patterns of political and planning consultation would emerge. The radical fragmentation of power would engender new urban institutions, like the old urban political machines, capable of holding together effective networks of power relationships, "getting things done," and responding effectively to concrete problems.

In the final analysis, Sennett would have urban planners become political brokers. The rise of new urban machines is Sennett's wish as well as his expectation. The political broker is Sennett's idealized rugged survivalist—tough, flexible, pragmatic, experiential, concrete. The political machine's clubhouse is Sennett's idealized social gathering place—outside the home where people can meet, interact, find help, experience conflict, and discover who they are. The machine's social function, in this context, becomes yet another purified ideal—a lost urban Eden where the working classes and the "little people" can express themselves and fight directly in a face-to-face way for power. In the end, Sennett, too, is a mythmaker. In place of Roszak's myth of creative disintegration is Richard Sennett's myth of personal strength and community survival through individual political struggle.

CONCLUSION

Richard Sennett's urban social theory is a useful antidote to Theodore Roszak's transcendent vision. By calling attention to some of the realities of power, the inevitability of conflict, and the potential claustrophobia of intimate warmth, he underlines the potentially escapist dimension of the counterculture. Sennett encourages us to face up to social injustice, even when so doing requires courage and causes pain. His theory also adds a psychological dimension to Roszak's epistemological criticism of rational planning. From him we learn the dangers of planning blueprints that serve the careerist and psychic needs of planners rather than serving clientele interests.

Despite these insights, and the brilliance of Sennett's intuitive style, several difficulties remain. At times, Sennett is himself guilty of the peculiar utopian blindness that he so effectively criticizes. For instance, by focusing on the diversity and vitality of the late-Victorian city, but ignoring its poverty and class divisions, by romanticizing the scarcity which made it impossible for low-income urban ethnics to escape social conflict, and by converting the harsh conditions of the urban proletariat into opportunities for psychic growth, Sennett reflects the very premise his book intends to refute—the belief that "since the past was better than the present, the future ought to restore the past."[100] The same difficulty holds true for Sennett's somewhat romanticized image of the old urban political machines. The machine for Sennett is first and foremost the clubhouse, a social gathering place where diverse people can meet, engage in conflict, and win for themselves some of the fruits of the machine's material resources. Lost in this analysis is the machine's well-documented role in pacifying the deprived urban proletariat, dampening class conflict, and impeding class consciousness by distributing its material rewards individually and ethnically rather than by social class.[101] In actuality, the old urban machine was an instrument for controlling potential disorder rather than for cultivating conflict, as Sennett supposes. The mutual exchange of votes for favors followed well-ordered political rituals, leaving little room for surprise or disorder. By providing clear-cut behavioral cues, the old machine simplified rather than diversified reality for its constituents. Indeed, the rising anger of today's "unmeltable urban ethnics," paralleling the decline of the favor-dispensing machine, is one indication of how well the old machines performed their basic function of urban pacification.[102]

Several current realities are also overlooked in *The Uses of Disorder*. As Edgar Z. Friedenberg has perceptively argued, the steps needed to create disorderly urban social spaces are the very steps that the social-psychological condition Sennett describes makes politically unfeasible.[103] Fearful, timid, defensive people, who find comfort behind fortresses, are bound to be radically unwilling to abolish bureaucratic social controls and unzone their defensive neighborhoods. The less equipped one feels to deal with conflict and disorder, the more one turns to those who promise stability, law, and order.

Crises, as Mark Fried has said, imply "giving up something from the past, relinquishing roles and relationships that may have proved very meaningful, and accepting some alteration in oneself as a social being."[104] What follows from the sorts of identity crises that Sennett would provoke is often a sense of threat, loss, and even grief that makes adaptations to new situations more difficult. Changes that are highly disruptive of past situations leave people with few experiences to draw upon to adapt to the new situation. Instead of triggering a dynamic of growth, perpetual public crises may precipitate maladaptive regression to the more familiar and reassuring past.

What Sennett appears to overlook is that some people have more *resources*—material, interpersonal, and cultural—to help them adapt to stressful crises than do others. In our highly stratified society, low-income people in particular are deprived of many vital supports in the face of environmental stress. Not only the poor but all of us are more willing and able to explore the unfamiliar, to abandon well-worn paths, when we feel we have reliable social supports, powerful incentives for personal commitment, and a sense of hope in the future. Sennett's image of lone individual struggle provides none of these cushions. Despite all of its shortcomings, Roszak's cooperative commonwealth does.

Notes

1. For a basic review of the history and theory of anarchism generally see George Woodcock, *Anarchism* (Cleveland, Ohio: Meridian Books, 1962). Classical representatives of the communitarian anarchist tradition include Peter A. Kropotkin, *Mutual Aid* (London: Heinemann, 1902) and *Fields, Factories and Workshops* (London: Nelson, 1912); *The Works of Leo Tolstoy* (London: Oxford, 1928–1937); and Paul and Percival Goodman, *Communitas* (New York: Vintage, 1960). See also Murray Bookchin's contemporary communal anarchist critique of industrial urbanism, *The Limits of the City* (New York: Harper Colophon, 1974). An anarchist position based on purely libertarian ideals may be found in the young Hegelian Max Stirner's *The Ego and His Own* (New York: Free Life Editions, 1976); see also Tibor R. Machan, ed., *The Libertarian Alternative* (Chicago: Nelson Hall, 1976).
2. See Morton and Lucia White, *The Intellectual versus the City* (Cambridge, Mass.: Harvard U. Press, 1962).
3. For a useful critique of Enlightenment rationalism and some of its public policy implications see Leonard Fine, *The Ecology of the Public Schools* (New York: Pegasus, 1972). An insightful discussion of the metaphors that have been associated with urban and rural life in world literature is provided by Raymond Williams, *The Country and the City* (London: Oxford U. Press, 1973).
4. Theodore Roszak, *Where the Wasteland Ends* (New York: Doubleday Anchor, 1973), p. 159.
5. The clearest statement of Roszak's personality theory may be found in Roszak, *Unfinished Animal* (New York: Harper & Row, 1975), pp. 226–230. Roszak's theory of human needs bears some resemblance to Abraham Maslow's theory of self-actualization. See Maslow, *Toward a Psychology of Being* (New York: Van Nostrand, 1968).
6. See Roszak, *Unfinished Animal*, p. 227.
7. Ibid.
8. Ibid., pp. 193, 197.
9. Ibid., p. 239.

10. Roszak, *The Making of a Counter Culture* (New York: Doubleday Anchor, 1969), chap. 6.
11. See, for example, Frederick Perls, Ralph Hefferline, and Paul Goodman, *Gestalt Therapy* (New York: Delta Books, 1951).
12. Roszak, *The Making of a Counter Culture*, p. 187.
13. Ibid.
14. Ibid., p. 188.
15. This section is based upon Roszak, *Where the Wasteland Ends*, chap. 1.
16. Ibid., p. 7.
17. See, for example, Brian J. L. Berry, "Aging Metropolis in Decline," *Society*, 13 (May/June 1976), 54–56; Matthew Edel, John Harris, and Jerome Rothenberg, "Urban Concentration and Deconcentration," Amos Hawley and Vincent Rock, eds., *Metropolitan America in Contemporary Perspective* (New York: Halsted Press, 1975), pp. 123–156.
18. See George Sternlieb and James W. Hughes, eds., *Post Industrial America: Metropolitan Decline and Inter-Regional Job Shifts* (New Brunswick, N.J.: Center for Urban Policy Research, 1975).
19. Roszak, *Where the Wasteland Ends*, p. 73.
20. Ibid., p. 77.
21. Roszak, *The Making of a Counter Culture*, p. 194.
22. Roszak, *Where the Wasteland Ends*, p. 273; see also pp. 228–232.
23. Ibid., p. 236. In this one respect at least, Roszak echoes one of the central themes of Richard Sennett's most recent work, *The Fall of Public Man* (New York: Knopf, 1977); see also Georg Simmel's discussion of the impact of specialization on perception and enlightened thought in chap. 3 above.
24. See Roszak, *Where the Wasteland Ends*, pp. 322–332.
25. The most direct and extensive discussion of the symbolic uses of expertise in Roszak's writings may be found in *Where the Wasteland Ends*, pp. 26–67, and *The Making of a Counter Culture*, pp. 142–150.
26. Roszak, *The Making of a Counter Culture*, p. 143.
27. Ibid., pp. 143–144. Numerous other vivid examples of the symbols and rituals peculiar to the field of urban planning may be found below in chap. 6, in my discussion of the ritual aspects of "citizen participation" in urban renewal. See also Robert Goodman, *After the Planners* (New York: Simon & Schuster, 1972).
28. See Claude Lévi-Strauss, *Structural Anthropology* (New York: Basic Books, 1963). For other critiques of the way in which myths, symbols, and rituals mask, distort, or otherwise shape the pursuit of objective material interests see Murray Edelman, *The Symbolic Uses of Politics* (Urbana: U. of Illinois Press, 1964); Edelman, *Political Language: Words That Succeed and Policies That Fail* (New York: Academic Press, 1977); and Michael P. Smith, "The Ritual Politics of Suburban Schools," Smith et al., *Politics in America: Studies in Policy Analysis* (New York: Random House, 1974), pp. 110–130.
29. See Francis Bacon, *The Advancement of Learning and New Atlantis* (London: Oxford U. Press, 1974); F. Markham, ed. and trans., *Henri de Saint-Simon:*

Social Organization, the Science of Man and Other Writings (New York: Harper Torchbooks, 1964). See Roszak's discussion of these and other "technocracies" in *Where the Wasteland Ends*, pp. 34–35.

30. For other critiques of "technocracy" and the government-corporate "technostructure" that have influenced Roszak's critique, see Jacques Ellul, *The Technological Society* (New York: Knopf, 1964); and John Kenneth Galbraith, *The New Industrial State* (Boston: Houghton Mifflin, 1967).

31. See Roszak, *Where the Wasteland Ends*, pp. 36–37.

32. Ibid., p. 38.

33. Ibid.

34. Ibid., p. 35. See Guy Benveniste, *The Politics of Expertise* (Berkeley, Calif.: Glendessary Press, 1972), who indicates that competing bases for legitimizing social and political power create the conditions for suspicion of as well as deference to expertise.

35. Ibid.

36. Ibid., p. 37.

37. Ibid., p. 38.

38. Ibid., pp. 39–41.

39. The latter three types are discussed in ibid., pp. 42–45.

40. Ibid., p. 45.

41. Ibid., p. 219.

42. Roszak, *The Making of a Counter Culture*, p. 8.

43. Ibid., p. 9.

44. Ibid., p. 19.

45. Ibid., p. 32.

46. Ibid., p. 112. For further development of this theme see Herbert Marcuse, *One Dimensional Man* (Boston: Beacon Press, 1964).

47. Roszak, *Where the Wasteland Ends*, p. 239.

48. Ibid., p. 50.

49. Ibid., p. 66.

50. Roszak, *The Making of a Counter Culture*, pp. 95–96.

51. Ibid., p. 96.

52. See ibid., pp. 100–101.

53. Ibid., p. 69.

54. See Plato, *Republic*, trans. Francis M. Cornford (New York: Oxford U. Press, 1970), pt. III, chap. 25, pp. 227–235.

55. Roszak, *Where the Wasteland Ends*, p. 129.

56. Ibid., p. 342. For his elaboration of these arguments see pp. 341–348.

57. Ibid., p. 353.

58. Ibid., p. 86.

59. Ibid., p. 87.

60. Ibid., p. 89.

61. Ibid., p. 91.

62. Ibid., p. 368.

63. Ibid., p. 374.

64. See ibid., pp. 381–408; especially pp. 383–388, 395–397.

65. Ibid., pp. 385–386; see also Harry Braverman's insightful discussion of

changes in the meaning of work in *Labor and Monopoly Capital* (New York: Monthly Review Press, 1974).

66. Ibid., p. 389; see also Roszak's defense of communal anarchism in his "Introduction" to E.F. Schumacher's modern classic, *Small Is Beautiful: Economics as if People Mattered* (New York: Harper & Row, 1973), pp. 1–9.

67. Roszak "Introduction," *Small Is Beautiful*, p. 9; see also n. 1 and 11 above.

68. Roszak, *Where the Wasteland Ends*, pp. 395–397.

69. Ibid., p. 391.

70. Ibid., p. 400.

71. See especially Roszak, *Unfinished Animal*, chaps. 1, 2, 7, 8, and 10.

72. Ibid., p. 241; see also pp. 185–188.

73. See, for example, the poetry of Wordsworth, Samuel Taylor Coleridge, and Percy Bysshe Shelley in William Frost, ed., *Romantic and Victorian Poetry* (Englewood Cliffs, N.J.: Prentice-Hall, 1961). See especially Wordsworth's selections from *The Prelude*; see also Owen Barfield, *Romanticism Comes of Age* (Middletown, Conn.: Wesleyan U. Press, 1966).

74. Roszak, *Unfinished Animal*, p. 243.

75. See ibid., p. 252.

76. Ibid., p. 254.

77. Ibid., p. 257.

78. Ibid., p. 259.

79. Ibid., p. 262.

80. See n. 1 above; see also Roszak, *The Making of a Counter Culture*, pp. 264–268.

81. Richard Sennett, "Stages in the Life Cycle," Richard Sennett, ed., *The Psychology of Society* (New York: Vintage, 1977), p. 203.

82. Sennett, *The Uses of Disorder: Personal Identity and City Life* (New York: Vintage, 1970), p. 6.

83. See ibid., chap. 2.

84. The following discussion is based on Sennett, *Families Against the City* (Cambridge: Harvard U. Press, 1970); see also Sennett, "Destructive Gemeinschaft," Sennett, ed., *The Psychology of Society*, pp. 192–200; and Edgar Z. Friedenberg, "In the Cage," *New York Review of Books*, September 3, 1970, pp. 13–17.

85. In Richard Sennett and Jonathan Cobb, *The Hidden Injuries of Class* (New York: Vintage, 1973), chap. 1, Sennett maintains, contradictorily, that it is *homogeneous* ethnic enclaves that have been destroyed because of urban renewal, as well as because of changing attitudes about the desirability of purified ethnic communities.

86. This is a basic theme of Sennett's most recent work, *The Fall of Public Man* (New York: Knopf, 1977). This work is not extensively discussed in this chapter, except insofar as it lends insight to the basic themes developed in *The Uses of Disorder*.

87. Sennett, "The Coldness of Private Warmth," *New York Times*, January 5, 1977, p. 23.

88. Ibid.

89. Sennett, *The Uses of Disorder*, p. xvi.

90. Sennett, "The Coldness of Private Warmth," p. 23.
91. Fyodor Dostoevsky, *Brothers Karamazov* (New York: Random House, 1933).
92. Sennett, *The Uses of Disorder*, p. 11.
93. Ibid., p. 92.
94. Ibid., pp. 96–97. See also Sennett, "An Urban Anarchist," *New York Review of Books*, January 1, 1970, pp. 22–24.
95. Ibid., p. xvii.
96. The most definitive definition of this role model is elaborated in Paul Davidoff, "Advocacy and Pluralism in Planning," *Journal of the American Institute of Planners*, 31 (November 1965), pp. 331–338; see also Frances Fox Piven's penetrating criticism of this approach, "Whom Does the Advocate Planner Serve?" (pts. 1 and 2), Richard A. Cloward and Frances Fox Piven, *The Politics of Turmoil: Essays on Poverty, Race and the Urban Crisis* (New York: Pantheon, 1974), pp. 43–72.
97. See Sennett, *The Uses of Disorder*, chap. 6.
98. Ibid., p. 135.
99. Ibid., p. 177. See also Sennett, "An Urban Anarchist," pp. 22–24, where Sennett advocates using public seed money to put a floor under small-scale handicraft industries and other competitive business in order to give greater "vitality" to the urban economy.
100. Ibid., pp. 50–51. For a less optimistic assessment of the plight of working-class communities in the late-Victorian city see David M. Gordon, "Capitalist Development and the History of American Cities," William K. Tabb and Larry Sawers, eds., *Marxism and the Metropolis* (New York: Oxford U. Press, 1978), pp. 25–63.
101. See, for example, Norman and Susan Fainstein, *Urban Political Movements* (Englewood Cliffs, N.J.: Prentice-Hall, 1974). On the urban political machine's conflict avoidance and pacification functions see Conrad Weiler, *Philadelphia: Neighborhood, Authority and the Urban Crisis* (New York: Praeger, 1974), p. 156 and Ira Katznelson, "The Crisis of the Capitalist City: Urban Politics and Social Control," Willis Hawley, Michael Lipsky et al., *Theoretical Perspectives on Urban Politics* (Englewood Cliffs, N.J.: Prentice-Hall, 1976), p. 224. Interestingly, Raymond Wolfinger's "pluralist" analysis of the functions of machine and ethnic politics concurs in key respects with the Fainsteins' and Katznelson's neo-Marxist critiques. See Raymond Wolfinger, "Machine Politics," Wolfinger, *The Politics of Progress* (Englewood Cliffs, N.J.: Prentice-Hall, 1974), pp. 74–129.
102. See Michael Novak, *The Rise of the Unmeltable Ethnics* (New York: Macmillan, 1972).
103. Friedenberg, "In the Cage," p. 14.
104. Mark Fried, "Effects of Social Change on Mental Health," *American Journal of Orthopsychiatry*, 39 (1964), 385; see also Peter Marris, *Loss and Change* (New York: Pantheon, 1974).

Chapter 5
Social Theory
And Social Reality:
A Critique

Class, status, and power are more than abstract categories for classifying human beings. They are objective positions in economy, society, and polity. One's position in the three structures is determined by the dynamic interaction among material conditions of existence, patterns of social intercourse, and the residual cultural heritage. These positions differentially shape the character and quality of people's everyday lives.[1]

The overall socioeconomic structure of any society distributes the social roles, the rewards and punishments, and the cultural forms that shape human motivation and behavior. Thus people's family structure, occupational role, immediate place of residence, and social class position are powerful determinants of personality development. These settings—the family, the workplace, the neighborhood—are partially overlapping "substructures of interaction"[2] linked by one's position in the overall class structure of society. Individual values are collectively organized through the learning that takes place within these socialization settings. Through primary social interaction, discernible structures of thought and behavior are organized and communicated.[3]

For these reasons, many different "ways of life" coexist in urban settings. These socially structured ways of life tend to persist unless they are acted upon by powerful environmental forces that cause adaptation and change. They tend toward stability, first of all, because patterns of socialization take place largely within a particular class setting that is part of a highly structured stratification system. As an example, Bennett Berger's research on working-class suburbs revealed that the move to suburbia was insufficiently disruptive to alter working-class attitudes and behavior patterns in significant ways. These attitudes and behaviors are primarily a function of social class and subcultural background, not of urban or suburban, or high or low density living. Thus, despite their moves, working-class family, kinship, and friendship networks did not fundamentally change. They have remained largely rooted within the same social strata in which they were found prior to migration.[4]

Patterned substructures of social interaction, and their resulting subcultures, also tend to persist because of the way the "opportunity structure" of society operates. The structure of opportunities in American society tends to produce relatively stable inequalities in access to social mobility.[5] Patterned inequalities tend to remain relatively stable, unless altered by economic crises or by the periodic mobilization of society's lower social strata (a difficult task in the best of circumstances). This vital link between the persistence of particular "class subcultures" and the opportunity structure of society has been captured nicely in Herbert Gans's definition of a subcultural way of life. In *The Urban Villagers*, Gans defines a subculture as

> an organized set of related responses that has developed out of people's efforts to cope with the opportunities, incentives, and rewards, as well as the deprivations, prohibitions, and pressures which the natural environment and society—that complex of co-existing and competing subcultures—offer to them.[6]

If the opportunity structure of a city or a society were equally open to all, absorption and eventual acculturation and assimilation into a single "metropolitan," "urban-industrial," or "post-industrial" way of life might be a conceivable possibility. Because the opportunity structure distributes rewards and access quite unequally, such uniform processes are unlikely to occur.

These realities of social class structure and of primary-group socialization bear directly upon my critique of the theorists we thus far have examined, particularly of Wirth, Freud, Simmel, and Roszak. In the sections which follow, I critique a series of myths that have emerged concerning the character and quality of social life in large cities as a result of the intellectual influences I have previously examined. My critique is grounded in the assumption that the overall class structure and political economy of a society, rather than its degree of urbanization, largely determines the patterned opportunities and constraints that affect both the persistence and change of people's everyday lives. In putting these prevailing myths to rest, I assess the role each theorist has played in provoking the development of my own perspective on the part that planners, political activists, and other "change agents" can play in using politics to alter the inequitable aspects of the American social structure and political economy. I then link my perspective to a critique of the contemporary "urban condition" in chapter six: "Advanced Capitalism, Social Theory, and Urban Political Conflict."

THE MYTH OF VANISHING PRIMARY GROUPS

A false dichotomy often is posited between Louis Wirth and such "neighborhood solidarity" theorists as Herbert Gans, Jane Jacobs, and Gerald Suttles.[7] Literature in this genre suggests that Wirth was ignorant of the high degree of social organization that existed in the "mosaic" of urban subcultures within the overall social structure. As my earlier exegesis of Wirth's social thought makes clear, however, such a criticism is overdrawn. On the basis of his research on the Jewish ghetto of Chicago, Wirth was well aware that relatively homogeneous urban subcultures existed in the urban milieu. In his 1928 study, *The Ghetto*, Wirth preceded any of the "neighborhood solidarity" theorists in illustrating the belief systems, social patterns, and personality types of the ghetto that provided a basis for communal solidarity.

It is true, nevertheless, that because of Wirth's preoccupation with unplanned change and "disorganization," he tended to focus attention on the many second-generation immigrants that left such ethnic neighborhood enclaves. As a result of increased social mobility, he both hoped and expected that the neighborhood would eventually decline in significance as an arena of social interaction and social organization, particularly insofar as neighborhoods reflected such traditional bases of community solidarity as kinship and ethnicity.

In any case, the main thrust of Wirth's critique of the social disorganization of the "community-as-a-whole" rests upon his explicit recognition of the "mosaic of social worlds" in the metropolis. He regards this mosaic of subcultures as a by-product of increased size, density, and heterogeneity, and as a cause of the fragmentation of the consensual moral order of the metropolis as a whole. There is little incompatibility between his perception of solidarity in limited social worlds and of the disorganization of the larger urban polity and society. In fact, given particularistic loyalties, socialization mechanisms, and competing ideologies, and the necessarily segmented social roles of the populace when participating in larger institutional settings, little else could be expected. Wirth viewed the very organization of the *local* community—whether geographically, ethnically, subculturally, or ideologically based—as a basic impediment to establishing a larger communal consensus—the desideratum of his social thought. This explains his hostility to the community organization movement, to social conflict among diverse subcultures, and to political interest groups. It is thus unfair to criticize Wirth for ignoring the reality of indigenous social organization in urban neighborhoods.

Nonetheless, it is fair to critique Wirth's expectation that heightened individual social mobility (a supposed by-product of increased size-density-heterogeneity) would weaken the impact of traditional loyalties of all kinds over time. Wirth anticipated an emerging metropolitan setting characterized by the decline in the social significance of the family; a weakening of kinship bonds; a more flexible class structure; the replacement of territorially based sociopolitical units with interest groups, and of primary with secondary forms of association; the assimilation of ethnic groups; and the eventual disappearance of the neighborhood as a significant social unit. Let us consider this line of argument in more detail.

Wirth's expectations, reflected in part also in the work of Simmel and Roszak, might be termed the thesis, "Urbanization leads to a decline of primary social networks." The literature on urbanization, migration, and urban social organization makes abundantly clear, however, that because primary-group social relations continue to perform important social, economic, and social-psychological functions, they cannot be expected to wither away, no matter how potentially disruptive are the forces of social mobility and rapid urbanization.[8] Families, as Sennett's and numerous other empirical studies have shown, play a central role in socializing people into the goals, attitudes, and behavior of particular cultures or subcultures. They provide motivation and economic and emotional support in achieving given goals. The primary social relationships found in kinship, in friendship, and in some neighborhood social networks also provide people with emotional support; a respite from the status striving so prevalent in economic and commercial relationships; and an outlet within which to relax, be open, and feel secure. Kinship attachments often help those of limited means to survive by facilitating the sharing of scarce resources. Ethnicity persists as a basis of interaction and social identification for a host of reasons. It provides a meaning, structure, and coherent sense of cultural "roots." It serves as an outlet for expressing frustration resulting from socioeconomic expectations and aspirations unsatisfied because of barriers existing in the larger social structure. In American society, it also persists because (in the absence of class-based political parties) it has served as a legitimate vehicle for organizing political demands in the face of discrimination and economic exploitation.[9]

A large body of empirical literature has insistently challenged the assumption made by theorists like Wirth, Simmel, and Roszak that urbanization inevitably engenders fundamental changes in the nature and quality of social relationships.[10] This literature has stressed the successful adaptation of rural social structures and cultural forms to urban settings. It has called attention to social areas that continue to resemble "urban villages" in their ways of life. It reveals kinship networks, mutual-aid associations (both formal and informal), and both neighborhood and nonresidential extended family relationships that have served as supportive mediating mechanisms to buffer the stresses of new cultural and structural demands of life in the metropolis.

The adaptation and survival of traditionally based social forms and human relationships in the face of large-scale demographic and ecological changes suggests that the past is never fully destroyed, but remains partially embodied in the present. As an example, close-knit kinship relationships persist alongside even the most impersonal marketplace relationships in advanced capitalist societies. Indeed, such relationships function for many as a necessary buffer that allows the dominant economic structure of society to continue to develop according to its own requirements. The more impersonal the economic system becomes, the greater is the need for personal ties outside the marketplace—friendship, kinship, neighborhood, and mutual-aid networks. More importantly, the more superfluous the unskilled marginal classes are to the advanced capitalist mode of production and distribution, the greater is their need for the extended family and kinship networks that provide them with mutual aid.

Mutual-aid networks have been found to be especially prevalent and necessary as a "mediating structure" for the poor and for unskilled rural migrants to Western capitalist cities. In their classic work *The Study of Urbanization*, Hauser and Schnore suggest that such networks facilitate "adjustment" to new conditions of existence by orienting newcomers into a set of social relationships and available unskilled work opportunities.[11] They also function to preserve links with traditional cultural values and to reduce the "urban-rural" gap by maintaining links to the original places from which people migrated. Such mutual-aid networks also have been characterized as vehicles for sharing scarce resources (e.g., money, appliances, information), as cultural "shock absorbers," and as a way to obtain the status satisfactions and sense of identity denied to the lower strata by the overall class structure.[12]

Viewed in this light, networks of mutual-aid need not necessarily be regarded as signs of social stagnation among the lower strata. Indeed, it may be more appropriate to perceive them as indicators of the creative adaptation of low-income migrants to the harsh conditions of economic scarcity. A mutual-aid network, provided it has enough economically viable members, may be regarded as a functioning cooperative community. It represents the survival of an older form of cooperative group life in the face of bureaucratic, social, and economic forces that threaten to make it extinct.

Consider a few concrete examples of the activities of mutual-aid networks. Basement stores and storefronts in black neighborhoods have served as cooperative daytime nurseries for families of recent migrants and as social gathering places for teenagers and adults. Shantytowns and squatter settlements in San Juan, Puerto Rico, have fostered extensive redistributive mutual-aid networks in which more economically stable members shared their refrigerators, utilities, tools, equipment, home repairs, and even their food with less advantaged members. American Samoan migrants to West Coast cities help new migrants find housing and jobs and render financial assistance as needed.[13] The frequently observed housing overcrowding in black urban neighborhoods is in large part obviously a result of poverty and discrimination, but it also is a form of mutual-aid.

These examples reveal a great deal of informal social organization in city slums that are frequently arbitrarily labeled "socially disorganized" by middle-class analysts operating in the Wirthian tradition. The examples mirror William F. Whyte's classic analysis of Boston's streetcorner society, which found that "problems" of slum life did not stem from any lack of social organization. Rather, the "slum" was perceived as problematic because of the "failure of its own social organization to mesh with the [middle class] structures of the society around it."[14]

Mutual-aid networks' performance of economic, in addition to expressive, functions is a reflection of the unequal distribution of opportunity for individual upward mobility in America. If the United States truly offered equal access to the means of success, there would be little need for mutual-aid networks to perform instrumental functions. The activities of such forms of social organization would then be limited to their socioemotional functions.

Disruptive Political and Economic Structures

Louis Wirth and many subsequent "urbanization" theorists offer a "linear development" model in positing the emergence of a new "urban way of life." According to this model, changes in individual attitudes, behavior, and culture are direct linear resultants of the increased population size, density, and heterogeneity of human settlements.[15] But the social structural model informing my analysis suggests that there is unlikely ever to be a single urban way of life. Rather, both community organization and diverse community subcultures are shaped by a complex web of patterned interaction and socialization that people experience. Social interaction takes place within families, kinship, friendship, and neighborhood networks. It also takes place in schools, workplaces, and informal social gathering places. People tend to experience regularized patterns of social interaction. The regularized patterns are powerfully shaped by the structured opportunities and constraints established by the prevailing class structure and the large-scale economic and political institutions of the overall society. These larger contextual influences determine a society's "opportunity structure." They determine who is likely to be socioeconomically mobile or immobile; who does managerial work, who is a day laborer; who can become financially independent, who must rely upon mutual-aid networks; who is rewarded for self-assertion, who is punished for it; who talks to whom, and who doesn't. Because primary patterns of social interaction tend to be exceptionally class based, social relationships tend toward stability unless the major contextual influences—the opportunities and constraints—change.

In chapter six I consider in detail the disruptive social impact of such major political-economic changes as government-sponsored urban-renewal and highway-building policies and the major interregional shift of industrial jobs away from large eastern and midwestern central cities. For the present, I wish to consider briefly some examples of the way that such larger contextual influences can disrupt organized mutual-aid networks among the disadvantaged social strata. The tragic irony of the examples that follow is that people who are struggling to keep their lives socially organized and economically bearable often find themselves unable to do so because of the mistaken theories of policy planners who start from the belief that lower-class subcommunities are, by definition, "disorganized." Such policy makers then rush in with policies designed to "reorganize" the social fabric in ways that destroy whatever indigenous coping mechanisms are available to people with limited life chances.

Consider first an example from Boston, whose "successful" urban renewal policies have "revitalized" an economically deprived (but socially viable) area known as the South End. In this area, urban renewal has meant the provision of conveniently located urban housing for many young upper-middle-class professionals. Many such "renovators" purchased their houses from stable, long-established black homeowners who had been part of a functioning mutual-aid network for less advantaged members of the black community. These working-class black homeowners helped to provide a stable cushion for recent low-income migrants to Boston. As described by one researcher: "Many of these Negro homeowners rented out their rooms to this mobile population. Through their personal interest and help, many of the newcomers, especially from the South, learned to adapt to urban living."[16] Needless to say, once the most economically viable links in the mutual-aid chain were broken, so, too, were the regularized patterns of interaction that helped poor black migrants survive in an economic system that has defined them as superfluous.

A second example is drawn from the previously mentioned shantytown of San Juan, Puerto Rico. Before this shantytown was destroyed by urban renewal and replaced by a low-income public housing project, it had been a squatter settlement on public land. It had developed spontaneously and had evolved over time into a heterogeneous settlement of oldtimers and newcomers. Oldtimers socialized newcomers into urban skills and coping mechanisms. Extensive mutual-aid networks existed in the shantytown. These networks contributed to a sense of community cohesion and solidarity. They prevented the development of sharp status distinctions by insuring that no one was destitute. They also increased interpersonal interdependence, which reinforced a strong "we feeling." Numerous local bars further solidified friendship ties. Neighbors often were brought into peoples' kin networks through the ritual tie of being "godparents." Informal social controls in the settlement were highly developed by the time the shantytown was leveled. Since everyone knew everyone else, "deviance" was socially disciplined within the various social circles.

What changes were brought by public housing? The projects became deadends for the poorest and least mobile members of the shantytown. Project residents were now denied vital socioemotional and economic links with their former friends and supporters. The harsh, formal regulatory social controls in the project served to "effectively curb strong incentives for upward mobility."[17] Administrators cultivated dependency and provided paternalistic care. For example, unlike the squatter settlements, no skills or coping mechanisms were transmitted informally. Management and police replaced informal social networks in maintaining social order. Additionally, planned design features contributed to the isolation of the project from the rest of the potentially supportive members of the community. The project was separated by a six-lane highway from its old working-class neighborhood. Many people lacked friends because they lacked adequate small-scale social gathering spots. The poorest community became stagnant and dependent on bureaucracy. In a nutshell, these changes may be characterized by one word—disorganization. Once again it was not poor people who were disorganized, but misguided public policies that disorganized their community instead of providing more sustenance for a functioning cooperative community.

Disruptive "Host" Cultures

Not only the political and economic structure of society but also its dominant cultural values can pose problems for low-income migrants struggling to adapt to new conditions. Each of the major "modern" approaches to economic organization and development—capitalist, socialist, and communist—creates particular structures of work and exchange and fosters an overall cultural milieu supportive of its dominant institutions. This cultural milieu may be termed the "host" culture. A host culture is a set of dominant values, norms, beliefs, and expected behavior patterns to which highly variable traditional migrant subcultures must respond, and within which they must function if they are to survive.

For some subcultures, the gap between their own core values and beliefs and the expectations of the host culture is not particularly great. Hence they find it relatively easy to "adapt." Janet Abu-Lughod's work on the adaptation of rural migrant Egyptians to the work and living requirements of urban life in Cairo is a pertinent case in point.[18]

Abu-Lughod's work emphasizes the importance of the variable cultural background that rural migrants bring with them to urban economic and social life. This accounts for different migrant adjustment patterns. In Egypt, for example, prior to migration, rural farmers raised products tied to international markets, were exposed to the mass media, traveled frequently to market towns, and sent their children to schools offering a national curriculum. For these migrants what might be termed the "adjustment gap" was not nearly as great as the formulations of Wirth and Simmel would suggest.

The previous cultural experience of migrants is also germane to developed capitalist societies such as the United States. In a comparative study of Samoan and American Indian migrant adjustment to city life in a large West Coast metropolitan center, Joan Ablon found that specific cultural experiences contributed to distinctively different patterns of adaptation.[19] Samoans, whose cultural values more closely approximated the structural and cultural demands of life in an advanced capitalist metropolis, were found to adjust more easily to city life than their Indian counterparts. In particular, Samoans are voluntary migrants from economically viable communities. They tend to migrate to gain further education, to obtain more material possessions than were available and affordable in Samoa, or to escape the "confines" of a traditional social structure. Samoans are an independent people who have selectively assimilated various Western values while maintaining traditional social structures. They maintain the Samoan language and customs, but their major operational values are basically middle class—hard work, the pursuit of good wages, and strong attachment to family, church, and job. The Samoan personality and value structure are compatible with the mainstream values of American capitalist culture. These include stress on rank and prestige, social conformity, conspicuous consumption, enjoyment of the dramatics of conspicuous display, and a precarious balancing of the need for order and security on the one hand with the potential for turbulence and violence on the other.

In contrast, the urbanization of most American Indians has been an involuntary result of a federal Indian policy of forced urbanization, euphemistically termed the "Voluntary Relocation Program," combined with lack of employment, educational, and health care opportunities on the reservations. Indians are given a relocation allowance and some vocational training, then left to fend for themselves in an aggressive and individually competitive capitalist culture that is alien to their own core values. As Ablon states:

> Many fundamental Indian values not only are incompatible with those of American culture, but work directly in opposition to the principles on which the modern competitive capitalistic order is based. It is the great value disparity that sets Indians apart from most other migrants now entering our cities.[20]

Products of a cooperative culture, Indians will avoid competitive and aggressive actions whenever possible. They regard the sharing of money and property as a sign of virtue. If others are in need, individual budgeting for the future instead of responding to this need is regarded as immoral. Their concrete orientation toward the immediate present contradicts the "future-oriented" striving required to function optimally in dominant capitalist institutions. Perhaps most significantly, they reject the alienation of the self from the natural world; their value system precludes the possibility of viewing persons as objects to be manipulated, as "malleable entities." Indeed, their lives are geared toward a stable, harmonious moral and natural order including the community, nature, and divine presence. Their culture is almost a prototype of Theodore Roszak's effort to create a visionary commonwealth. Needless to say, such a value system is incompatible with a capitalist cultural order that honors individual competitiveness, aggressiveness, and self-aggrandizement.

Added to these historical and cultural differences between Samoans and American Indians are differences in traditional forms of social organization. Like American society, Samoan society is vertically ranked and highly status conscious. Samoans relate very easily to hierarchical authority structures that demand deference and respect to hierarchical superiors. This pattern of deference is so pronounced that Samoans tend to reject out of hand all forms of political protest activity as inherently "disrespectful," even when they sympathize with the objectives of protesters.

In marked contrast, American Indian authority structures historically have been more democratic and consensual. They have espoused a concept of authority where family and community consensus, rather than elite will, determines collective action. This stems from a view of authority as "diffuse and ever-changing power, potentially and actually resting in many persons for differing occasions."[21] Since most American capitalist institutions more closely resemble hierarchical pyramids than consensual tribal democracies, Indians have greater difficulty adjusting to life in urban capitalist society than do deferential Samoans.

Significantly, the only major similarity between Indians and Samoans is that both groups tend to rely on mutual-aid networks to integrate new migrants into their new surroundings, help with finding housing and jobs, and render financial assistance as needed. But Indians are more likely to be in chronic financial straits than are their Samoan counterparts, owing to the different origins of their migration and their differential cultural-structural "adjustment gaps." Thus these networks are far more useful for the latter than the former. These is simply less collective surplus capital, services, and "useful" information concerning "artful social manipulation" to go around among American Indians than among Samoan migrants. Once again we find that people with a highly organized culture face a situation in which their culture is becoming disorganized not because of inner role conflict and personal maladjustment, but because of a deliberate public policy that forces them to live in an economic and cultural milieu incompatible with their cherished values.

THE MYTHOLOGICAL "COMMUNITY-AS-A-WHOLE" AND ITS CONSEQUENCES

Much public policy is justified on the ground that it serves large-scale population aggregates, sometimes referred to rhetorically as the "community-as-a-whole."

"Human ecologists" like Louis Wirth focus upon the population aggregate as the basic unit of analysis. Ecological analysis concentrates upon the various forms of social organization that emerge in response to technological, demographic, and environmental changes in the use of space.[22] The virtue of this mode of analysis is that it leads to the expectation that social organization is highly adaptable to various environmental conditions. Its chief weakness is that it often tends to treat as independent variables those environmental conditions that are by-products of the dominant mode of economic organization in any society. For example, population movements and spatial densities are induced by geographical patterns of job distribution determined by those who control the means of production; the pace, scope, and direction of technological changes are consequences of decisions made by the elites of dominant economic organizations. Standardization of the work process and products was the result of the factory system and mass marketing, not of the density or heterogeneity of the metropolis "as a whole."

Wirth's critique of the capitalist system of production—his commentary on the impersonality and exploitativeness of the "pecuniary nexus," the need for professional codes to check this predatory competition, the dangers of mass-media manipulation in the service of commercial values, the standardization of work processes and products, and the rise of large-scale corporate bureaucracy—is introduced within the context of his theory of spatial ecology. That is, rather than treating these developments as independent trends in the economic organization of society under advanced capitalism, Wirth treats them as emergent formal social controls that have sprung up as "functional" replacements for what he saw as lost informal ties, customs, and traditions that had been displaced by the changed spatial ecology (i.e., the growing size, density, and heterogeneity) of the "community-as-a-whole."

Ironically, then, despite Wirth's veiled critique of capitalism, the analytical perspective within which he introduces his social criticism blunts the thrust of his analysis. In fact, his perspective actually provides an implicit justification for the formal social controls of advanced capitalism. If, as Wirth fears, the center cannot hold, if people are becoming anomic, "communities-as-a-whole" are becoming "disorganized," traditional values are eroding, and consensual values have not yet emerged, then the formal social controls of corporate capitalism—hierarchy, bureaucratic routine, mass communication, professional and contractual arrangements to formally mediate the "cash nexus"—all can easily be interpreted as "functional" in maintaining the social order. Indeed, at one point, Wirth calls attention to certain "functional needs" that are fulfilled by these formal control mechanisms. To wit, bureaucratic work hierarchies and the corporate structure are viewed as essential for coordinating specializations, integrating roles, simplifying norms, providing predictable routines, and even for reducing friction stemming from competitive business practices.

Consider, as an example, Wirth's treatment of "professional codes." He argues that such codes may be viewed as a new form of social organization that has "evolved" to meet the new and more potentially abrasive conditions of urban spatial structure. This sort of conceptual approach puts a positive normative gloss on this "development" that is unwarranted. Such professional codes only act as a check on predatory competition *within* particular professions. In an economic system within which professions as a whole are left free to charge whatever fees the traffic will bear, professional codes that, for instance, forbid advertising and internal competition serve mainly to re-create exclusive producer guilds that often exploit consumers in the name of "quality control." More importantly, such codes are institutionalized as a result of deliberate political strategies by groups seeking to maintain social dominance. They are not mere by-products of spontaneous or evolutionary changes in the spatial structure of the "larger community."

The competitiveness that Wirth observed in American cities may well have been a result of the fact that the American political economy was, and continues to be, one of the least publicly regulated (as against publicly promoted) economic systems among advanced industrial countries. Yet Wirth treated this competitiveness as a by-product of general changes in spatial structure that created a peculiarly urban way of life, applying uniformly to all large, dense, and heterogeneous human settlements.

It is true that the pure operation of the "pecuniary nexus" does contribute to predatory and exploitative relationships. But this nexus itself is the result of the economic organization of a society, not its degree of urbanization. Furthermore, in various cultural contexts the pure operation of the cash nexus is already mediated informally by norms, customs, and rituals that seek to modify exploitation. These mediating mechanisms often become part of an overall culture or of a class subculture. Such cultural and subcultural rituals and norms can transcend metropolitan spatial boundaries, and thus do not depend upon the level of urbanization.

To illustrate, the high value placed on competitiveness in the overall American culture frequently is cited as one of the key reasons that people use home life and friendship and kinship networks as an escape from competition, as well as from hierarchical work requirements that entail domination or exploitation of others. One of the central themes of Richard Sennett's *Hidden Injuries of Class* is that white ethnics, raised in working-class enclaves, often are torn between a sensed lack of respect if they fail to take advantage of limited opportunities for upward mobility at work and "fear of success" if they do.[23] Successful bureaucratic upward mobility is seen as entailing a loss of intimacy and honesty with one's peers and requiring exploitation of subordinates. For these reasons, many choose to maintain their friendships with coworkers rather than climb the bureaucratic ladder.

Similar mediating cultural responses also help to explain why so many cling tenaciously to the "myth of communal solidarity" that Sennett views as so damaging to personality development. That is, neighborhoods, like friendship and kinship networks, often provide a retreat, however illusory, from exploitative economic and bureaucratic relationships. As long as they continue to perform this psychological function, a "sense of neighborhood" and other primary human ties are likely to persist, rather than to wither away, as Wirth expected.

Wirth did not offer an entirely one-sided interpretation of the uses of formal social controls in American and other bureaucratically organized advanced capitalist societies. Despite his fears of "anomie" and "social disorganization," Wirth did not uncritically favor all formal social controls that promised to provide a value structure for "society-at-large." His dislike for the prevailing commercial values of the industrial capitalist society of his day were plainly apparent throughout his writings. Thus, for example, Wirth offered a penetrating criticism of the dangers of commercial-elite control of the agencies of mass suggestion. He warned that the channels of mass communication were becoming reduced to instruments for manipulating symbolic language to create a pervasive commercial value structure. He hoped that rational planners might be able to convert these channels into instruments for public education and rational discourse on the meaning of the larger "public interest." Likewise, when Wirth referred to "planless" cities, he was referring only to the lack of effective governmental controls over private planning in the service of commercial values.[24] Here, too, he expected that rational planning by disinterested technical experts could offset the failure of the private planners to respond to widely held social values other than the profit motive.

In both these instances, Wirth's confidence that rational processes could displace the growing political influence of economic dominants was overly optimistic. Throughout his works Wirth displayed an almost naive faith in the ability of "objective science" and "rational policy analysis" to prevail against the social influence of economic elites and other contestants for political influence over the pace and direction of "urbanism" and social change.

Consider first Wirth's view that, for all their shortcomings, the modern mass media and commercial advertising were easier to control rationally than were earlier forms of symbolic manipulation by priests, tribal chieftains, and other nonsecular elites. Presumably, then, if Wirth were correct, both "commodity" and "mood" advertising (e.g., advertising designed to build a mood of confidence in a mythical "free enterprise" system) would be easier to control and less pernicious an influence than were more traditional forms of mythmaking because these technocratic processes were less shrouded in mystery. Yet as has been pointed out in my earlier discussion of Theodore Roszak and Richard Sennett, primitive symbolism in new guises is still quite capable of rendering people incapable of purposive social and political action on behalf of their own best interests. Many Americans appear quite willing to believe that "enterprise" is free, despite the growth of private corporate planning and oligopolist domination of major sectors of the economy; that "zoning" is apolitical, despite its political impact on society's opportunity structure; that smoking is "fun" despite its relationship to cancer; and that "war" is being waged on poverty, despite chronic inequalities in the distribution of resources and social benefits.

The rational "market research" that Wirth correctly feared is aimed almost entirely at structuring and restructuring people's consumer wants through manipulation of unconscious motivations. The products of market research are messages that use the most elemental symbolic forms to sell products and services by appealing to our most subconscious yearnings for power, prestige, pleasure, and transcendence of the mundane limits of everyday life. Short of a major restructuring of our political economy, such messages are unlikely to be offset by rational discourse alone, no matter what the weight of objective evidence, or how accessible the media become to "knowledge elites," such as technocratic planners.

The impact of the mass media as an agency for socializing people's attitudes and their behavior is complex. On the one hand, research suggests that mass-media communications tend to be mediated and interpreted by the primary groups to which individuals belong. For example, Katz and Lazarzfeld have shown that opinion leaders in small groups tend to be more concerned and informed about public issues than other members, and that these *subcultural* elites mediate the impact of mass-media communications on public opinion. Other studies underline a similar "short-run" mediating role played by subcultural elites in neighborhoods, extended families, and peer groups. Their opinions can ridicule, modify, and sometimes even reverse the intended impression of mass communications.[25]

This, in fact, is one reason why Wirth's belief that mass marketing would inexorably lead to standardization and a decline of primary group affiliations has not been borne out. Because market research reveals the tendency for audiences to screen out content with which their primary groups disagree, the "mass market" has become segmented into a congeries of submarkets. This tendency is sometimes termed the process of "market segmentation."[26] Such segmentation takes the form of subcultural movies; radio, magazine, and even television advertising geared to particular ethnic, racial, socioeconomic, and occupational submarkets; and even regional, occupational, and student editions of such supposedly "mass-market" magazines as *Time* and *Newsweek*.

The implication of this development for Wirthian theory is clear. Although Wirth was correct in assuming that the domination of the media by corporate elites encouraged a commercialization of life, this commercialization tends to reinforce subcultural diversity and even to create greater segmentation of points of view ("new markets"), rather than forming the basis for mass standardization. Furthermore, because messages, particularly political messages, are screened and interpreted by these primary-group contacts, and because much media communication is subliminal, there is little reason to assume that the use of the mass media by rational planners would be an efficacious way to build consensual support for rational policies that cut across people's group loyalties and serve the needs of the "community-as-a-whole."

Despite the short-run impact of mediating elites on the opinion of particular subpublics, commercial media advertising does seem to have been successful in raising the general level of consumption. The latent message of media advertising is that hedonistic consumption equals the good life. Such a definition—while doubtless beneficial for the economic institutions of advanced capitalism—is not especially beneficial to human development. The arousal of subliminal drives, which can be instantaneously fulfilled by assuming the basically passive role of consumer of new goods and services, entails a number of problematic consequences. Existing economic institutions are portrayed as benign. Their role in satisfying wants is emphasized; their failure to engender a sufficient number of opportunities for creative work ignored. This general message reinforces existing patterns of social control by encouraging a cult of leisure, reducing the normal anxiety that repressive work structures might otherwise generate, and legitimizing both the institutions capable of "responding to wants" and the life styles that they define as fulfilling.[27]

Just as Wirth overestimated the potential for freeing the mass media of these commercial biases, he also overestimated the apolitical rationality of urban planning. His belief that planning could and should remain apolitical stemmed from his failure to appreciate the positive functions of political conflict. His belief that rational planners could objectively assess the "functional needs" of the "community-as-a-whole" ignores the reality of contradictory interests that inhere in a diverse and class-stratified social system.

Louis Wirth's critique of interest-group and social-movement politics is colored by his view that the urban political system was becoming overloaded by all sorts of nonessential wants. In his view, these wants had been converted into political demands that overloaded, and thereby undermined, the ability of the polity to satisfy basic human needs. Wirth regarded certain human needs as basic: the need for economic security, social participation, creative work, and political power. Yet Wirth seemed unwilling or unable to acknowledge that some of the political groups and movements he denounced for "disorganizing" the polity pursued the very goals that he regarded as basic human needs. His condemnation of organized political groups and movements is blanket rather than selective. This is unfortunate because some political groups and social movements have always pressed for goals such as universal economic security, social equity, broadened political participation, and the transformation of alienating work. Furthermore, they have required organization in order to do so.

Wirth's treatment of social movements as inherently disorganized social processes is largely mistaken. Such movements often have been found to display some of the very conditions Wirth set forth as the sine qua non of social organization—order, continuity, regularity, and internal consensual purpose (e.g., the early Civil Rights movement in the United States).[28] Other social movements (e.g., the antiwar movement) more closely fit Wirth's definition of reorganization than of disorganization. They are rationally planned and deliberately pursued efforts to redefine a prevailing consensus. This too requires organization and some degree of internal consensus. The upshot of these misperceptions is clear. To condemn interest-group and political-movement politics as a whole because some social interests are exotic, confusing, or repress basic human needs is to throw out the baby with the bath water. It is also to deny subordinate structural interests the political "push factor" that is often needed to trigger the dialectics of social change.

Wirth was exceptionally concerned with maintaining social cohesion and integration through consensual mechanisms like rational planning. He envisaged an emerging role for planners in reducing the costs to the average citizen of acquiring vital information. Wirth's planners would inform the public of the social costs and benefits of particular policy choices and of the ends pursued by private power structures. They would proceed "objectively," "neutrally," and on the basis of the most systematically gathered social scientific data. This style of informing people does not envisage planners as "mobilizers" of the interests of the underprivileged social strata, whose needs are often ignored in the planning process. Wirth's planners are more at home issuing position papers, specifying the "fullest range of policy options," outlining mutually incompatible courses of action, spelling out alternative means to achieve given ends, and measuring the "quantifiable" costs of each option. Wirth's planners stop short at "public policy analysis," thereby avoiding commitment to particular social interests. They search for the "one best way" to discover and implement the "consensual common good." Thus Wirth the "social scientist" feared intellectuals who became advocates of the points of view of particular social interests. Interestingly, however, at various times in his life, Louis Wirth was a social activist as well as a sociological and planning theorist. His concrete activities on behalf of causes that he cherished (such as family planning and improved race relations) support the position advanced in chapter six that there is a legitimate role for planners as advocates of structurally deprived class interests.

Curiously, although Wirth recognized that ideologies serve to sanctify formal actions and institutions of social control (and thereby undermine the prospects for effective citizen control of policy directions), he failed to turn this same insight in upon the planning profession itself. Planners often use the consensual rhetoric of "rational comprehensive" planning to mystify the essentially political process of dealing with adversary interests. The ideology of rational comprehensiveness protects some conflicting interests at the expense of others by legitimizing the pursuit of private profit under the cloak of "objective science."

To illustrate briefly, Wirth justifies federal government subsidies that are directly beneficial to the corporate power structure, such as highway construction that helps the highway lobby; housing production subsidies that aid homebuilders and lending institutions; and other infrastructure investments that benefit specific economic interests. Wirth justifies these subsidies on the ground that the federal government should "assume the risks of economic development." This goal, in turn, is justified on the ground that "economic development" necessarily furthers individual mobility, freedom, and opportunities for individual self-development. Whatever the merits of this chain of reasoning, its chief function is to divert attention from the actual social costs of subsidizing corporate "risk," such as job dislocation, suburban sprawl, the flight of industry from the central cities, and the chronic pockets of unemployment and underemployment that disproportionately burden the lower social strata of our core cities. In effect, Wirth's own efforts at "objective analysis" lead directly to the socialization of the costs of economic development with no guarantee that the benefits of this development will extend beyond private profit, corporate growth, and increased opportunities for speculative investment.

OVER- OR UNDERSTIMULATING CITIES?

Georg Simmel's reflections on the overstimulating aspects of metropolitan life were formulated prior to the widespread emergence of the automobile. His "Metropolis and Mental Life" also failed to anticipate the functional separation of land uses, the increased social class segregation, and the suburbanization movement that make up key components of Richard Sennett's image of metropolitan life as harmfully understimulating. Considerable evidence suggests the need to revise the Simmelian theory of overstimulation to take into account the changes in exposure to external stimuli that the emergence of an automobile society has brought about.

That we live in a society dominated by the automobile is certainly clear enough. By the end of the 1960s nearly 15 million Americans worked in jobs that directly or indirectly were connected with support for the automobile. This was nearly one-fifth of all wage earners. One-sixth of all American businesses are automobile related, as are 50 percent of the twenty-two largest manufacturing concerns. Government support for the automobile-related sector has taken the forms of massive "infrastructure development" expenses for suburbanization, financed out of general tax revenues, and highway building, funded by the sheltered Highway Trust Fund. Public subsidies "buy rights of way, construct roadways, build overpasses, push back the sidewalks, . . . subsidize parking expansion."[29] They also subsidize suburban home ownership, sewer construction, and other public works that foster population dispersion to suburbia and increase reliance on automobiles.

But what is the impact of these developments on the amount and diversity of stimuli to which automobile users are exposed when they drive, and to which pedestrians are exposed when they walk? Automobiles are both overstimulating and understimulating. On the one hand, automobiles open seemingly infinite possibilities of mobility and choice. But by vastly increasing the sense of choice, they also open up the possibility of "overchoice." The perception that one has too many choices, but lacks firm value criteria for choosing among them, can lead to a feeling of being overloaded in the Simmelian sense. This can lead to attendant frustration and uncertainty about choices made. On the other hand, the actual act of traveling in an automobile tends to isolate drivers and passengers from physical and social experiences of duration and intensity. Furthermore, expressway driving has been found to be monotonous and understimulating when engaged in for extensive periods.[30] Within cities, automobile travel alienates the driver, in particular, from surroundings that must be screened out and simplified in order to avoid disorientation and possible accidents.

Recent psychological research suggests that too little mental stimulation may be as problematic (if not more so) as too much. Too little stimulation can lead to chronic boredom. Many aspects of the external environment of contemporary American metropolitan life offer people relatively monotonous surroundings. In addition to superhighways, the monotony of factory work, suburban residential enclaves, home life for suburban housewives, and even standardized shopping malls have been associated with chronic boredom.[31]

Other research lends support to Sennett's general picture of metropolitan life in contemporary America. For instance, the "simplicity, economy, and efficiency" that is the hallmark of modern urban architecture is consistent with the functional needs of major economic institutions; but the redundancy of such architecture tends to understimulate aesthetic sensibilities. As Duane Elgin states: "The apparent 'diversity' of our structures seems primarily a diversity of quantity, specialization, and differentiation of economic functions rather than a substantial qualitative diversity."[32]

Perceptual diversity is further reduced by the decline in patterns of mixed land use and of the ethnically and socially more heterogeneous residential areas discussed by Sennett. This reduction in diverse stimuli is an immediate consequence of several factors, including the increased "functional rationality" of major American cities in the postwar period; the out-migration of the more mobile members of urban ethnic groups to suburban enclaves; the attendant decline in the social class heterogeneity of urban residential areas (except, in part, among blacks, where class heterogeneity is maintained by housing discrimination); and the destruction of numerous small-scale shopping outlets and social gathering spots by publicly and privately induced urban redevelopment.

Why Understimulation?

To a considerable extent, the mixed patterns of land use that once fostered multiple contact points among socially diverse urban dwellers are less noticeable than they were in the Victorian city. To this extent Richard Sennett is correct. But why such arenas of contact and communication are no longer with us is the important question, and it is a question that Sennett's analysis obscures. Sennett places a great deal of blame on technical planners who rigidly pursue abstract theories of segregated land uses that ignore concrete human needs. He also faults the suburban middle class that seeks escape from potential social conflict in homogeneous residential enclaves. Yet nowhere does he explore the role played by economic dominants in rewarding planners for designing highway and land-use patterns that serve the comfort, convenience, and profitability of major corporate, manufacturing, and financial interests. Nor does he examine the role of advanced capitalist institutions in determining the basic shape of the publicly subsidized urban renewal projects that have destroyed viable social gathering places. Lost in his analysis is any glimmer of the role of real estate and shopping-center investment capital, of government tax incentives and housing-subsidy policies, and of the auto-industrial complex in inducing the suburbanization of America of which he is so critical. Sennett's preferred explanation for suburban isolation and sprawl is almost entirely psychological rather than economic. Perhaps this explains why his perferred solution—"unzoning," introducing physical changes in land-use patterns to encourage heterogeneous contact points and social conflict, and devolving public authority to the "people themselves"—tends to ignore the cumulative inequalities in economic and social power that exist in our distributively unequal society. These inequalities, as Simmel has shown, would be as oppressive, if not more so, in a completely libertarian environment (the laissez-faire state) as they are in a society where economic dominants have captured large segments of public authority for their own purposes. To cite one specific example, given the relative ease with which political and economic influentials can obtain zoning variances, it is doubtful that "unzoning" would lead to very much more visual and functional diversity than the metropolitan environment already contains.[33] Thus, for instance, the unzoned city of Houston rather closely resembles most other major capitalist cities that do have formal zoning provisions.

In similar fashion, Sennett's explanation of the growth of formal bureaucratic social controls relies exclusively upon psychological factors. He assumes that psychologically immature individuals have turned to police and other social control bureaucracies to deal with the overstimulating conflicts that they are unable to face by themselves. This sort of analysis ignores the support for the growth of these bureaucracies by major corporate interests who benefit from a stable legal and social order buttressing advanced capitalist institutions. It further ignores the social control bureaucracies' own vested interest in survival and expansion. Bureaucracies, once established, tend to develop self-protective and growth strategies. Consequently, we cannot expect that a shift in popular demand for bureaucratic social controls would lead to debureaucratization and heterogeneity, as Sennett seems to hope. To make people feel less defensive in their personal and public lives may be a desirable goal in its own right, or because of particular consequences that might be expected to flow from it (e.g., increased openness and trust in society). But planning steps to achieve this goal is unlikely to diminish the pervasiveness of bureaucratic social controls, so long as they continue to serve the needs of the dominant interests of the capitalist political economy. Furthermore, bureaucratic minions are unlikely to stop performing their functions voluntarily simply because there is less sociopsychological support for these functions. Thus, in this respect at least, Sennett's plan for debureaucratization is an unworkable strategy.

Despite these shortcomings, Sennett's critique of both the "metropolitanwide" vision and the "projective needs" techniques of urban planners has considerable merit. This is not so much because planners exercise autonomous social power, but because they often disguise the exercise of power by dominant economic and political interests. Actual experience with metropolitan planning suggests that when the "needs" of the "organic metropolitan whole" are given precedence over the needs of concrete human beings, these larger "needs" tend to reflect the policy priorities and economic infrastructure requirements of major economic and political dominants—for example, the "need" for superhighway access ramps that destroy neighborhoods, for regional industrial parks that relocate jobs out of central cities, for mass-transit arrangements that serve affluent commuter needs more than the needs of carless inner-city residents.[34]

Ironically, even if we were to wish away these harsh political and economic realities, the accelerated pace of change in many parts of the globe render the sort of projective planning critiqued by Sennett increasingly problematic as a planning tool. A prime case in point is the Nigerian city of Lagos, which has grown in population by such leaps and bounds that its transportation, public works, and housing plans based on linear arithmetic projections become obsolete even before they are implemented. Attempts to implement such plans have tended to ignite social tensions, disrupt communities, and create numerous unanticipated side effects.[35] Paradoxically, these are the very outcomes that Richard Sennett expects that projective planning will avoid. In the end he fails to recognize that truly repressive "projective needs" are capable of triggering the dialectics of conflict and resistance.

THE MYTH OF PATHOLOGICAL DENSITY AND CROWDING

Among the "projective needs" pursued by urban planners has been the assumed desirability of urban residential deconcentration. Low-density neighborhoods often are assumed to alleviate psychic stress accompanying dense and crowded living conditions. However, much recent research refutes urban theorists like Louis Wirth and Georg Simmel, who believed that population density and interpersonal crowding would lead directly to psychic frustration and social friction.[36] Jonathan Freedman's recent work, *Crowding and Behavior*, is especially illuminating in this regard. Freedman provides extensive experimental evidence and reviews a large body of demographic and survey research demonstrating that crowding and population density do not produce stress or any other social pathology, unless accompanied by other stress-producing conditions.[37]

Crowding does not appear to be what behavioral psychologists term a "simple stressor." That is, crowding tends to intensify or accentuate feelings that already are present in particular situations, rather than causing such feelings. For instance, when the feelings called forth by a situation are unpleasant, as in the case of being in jail or living in poverty, crowded conditions can make matters worse, psychologically. A prison situation is itself highly stress producing; when accompanied by room crowding or high internal population density, stressful feelings can become accentuated. It is thus not surprising to find that suicides result from overcrowded conditions in an inherently demeaning prison setting.[38] Similarly, the room overcrowding and high population densities that exist in central cities are greatest in those areas where housing discrimination and lack of income are most pronounced. It is these latter factors that produce stress, by minimizing the personal choice of urban ghetto residents, rather than overcrowding or density per se.

Conversely, crowding may actually enhance the positive reactions that people have to experiences that tend to be pleasant, such as a friendly social gathering or a theater crowd. Crowding does increase the importance of other people, and often makes some form of interaction with them more likely than in uncrowded situations. But if the people are pleasant, or of they expect the situation to be pleasant, their presence can add to the stimulation and excitement of the moment.

Even potentially unpleasant situations can be made quite tolerable by the way in which human beings informally manage the use of space. For instance, crowding on public buses often leads to the symbolic manipulation of limited space to allow strangers to maintain social distance, privacy, and personal dignity. Queuing up in line is another indicator of people's adaptive capacity in the face of potentially unpleasant or stressful situations. Unlike animal populations, human beings have social organization, culture, and technology. This enables humans to create liveable habitats amidst high population density, scarce space, and crowded situations (provided they have the economic means to do so).[39]

For all of these reasons, it is mistaken to assume, as planners and urban social theorists often have done, that people who live under crowded conditions automatically suffer from being crowded; or that high population density necessarily entails social pathology. The policy and planning implications of these mistaken assumptions are clear. As Freedman himself put it: "If the world cannot conveniently blame its problems on overcrowding, it will be forced to look elsewhere for the causes."[40] Because the "stress-producing situations" in which residential crowding occurs are usually associated with lack of income and lack of social choice, it is to these factors that we must look if we are to alleviate human misery, rather than to the pursuit of purely demographic strategies designed to decrease urban densities.

A clear distinction must be made between population density and room crowding. Population densities are measured in persons per acre; room crowding, in persons per room. Room crowding has been shown to correlate with level of poverty, segregation, and inequality, although not necessarily with population density.[41] For instance, the

Watts area of Los Angeles combines low density with overcrowded housing among its poor residents; conversely, high density high-rises in affluent areas of central cities often are accompanied by spacious, commodious, and insulated living space.[42] Crowding among the former is a problem because the lack of social choice, the unpleasant feeling of being trapped, and other stresses (proximity to air and noise pollution, inadequate public services, poverty itself) are intensified by crowding. High density among the latter is no problem at all, both because high incomes guarantee high levels of social choice and the ability to avoid room overcrowding and because high population density per se shows little relationship to social pathology.

The upshot of these findings is that planned strategies to "depopulate" cities may have no effect at all on unpleasant room crowding. Moreover, such a quest actually overlooks the positive consequences that have been associated with high population densities in various studies.[43] These include livelier neighborhoods, a more vital street life, safer streets resulting from the presence of many potential witnesses and informal agents of social control, the presence of mutual-aid networks within close geographic proximity, and even the "critical mass" of population size needed to sustain small businesses and major cultural facilities.

There are other policy implications of the myth that crowding and population density are inherently undesirable. One is the already emergent tendency for affluent suburbanites to use the rhetoric of "overcrowding," "loss of open space," and "ecological preservation" to keep the poor out of their privileged residential enclaves. Such rhetoric enables the affluent to believe the reassuring myth that their resistance to low-income public housing is based upon ecological grounds, rather than to recognize its basis in race and class discrimination and in the desire to protect upper-middle-class property values.[44]

Some defenders of suburban sprawl likewise have claimed that this pattern of low-density living contributes to peoples' mental health by eliminating the social pathologies incorrectly assumed to follow directly from population density. Although the public policies that contribute to suburban sprawl appear to fit well with the rustic antiurban cultural tastes of middle-Americans, suburban sprawl actually destroys open space, consumes inordinate amounts of scarce energy resources, and increases pollution from automobiles and visual blight. Yet such policies continue to find advocates among suburban planners who hold that suburban life helps people to escape the nonexistent threat of high population density. The actual economic and political interests served by this mistaken planning myth are detailed in chapter six. Suffice it to say now that such myths are likely to die hard as long as they continue to provide a cloak of legitimacy for the economic interests of the highway lobby; suburban real estate speculators; subdivision and shopping center developers; and financial institutions; along with the manufacturing corporations that save money on land, taxes, and transportation costs as a result of suburban sprawl.

Finally, the myth of pathological density and overcrowding makes it difficult to convince public policy makers and the public that high density land uses have some distinct policy advantages. High densities enable cost savings for mass-transit systems that operate best moving people from one high density area to another; high densities in housing can yield savings in utilities expenses, because detached single-family dwellings are costly to heat; they provide more opportunities for walking to work, recreation, and shopping. Finally, as Sennett points out, high densities are likely to increase the variety and richness of experiences available to people in their everyday lives.

THE MYTH OF "TECHNOCRACY" AND THE CULT OF NATURE

Like Richard Sennett, Theodore Roszak offers a penetrating discussion of the symbolic potency of "expertise" in advanced technological cultures. He calls attention to the willingness of planners to use this "mystology" to advance their own social influence. He lucidly illustrates that not even the most secularized culture can function without myths, rituals, and symbolism designed to legitimize the social and political power of dominant social interests. Nonetheless, Roszak is far less persuasive when arguing that scientific, technological, and "knowledge" elites are about to displace the institutional power base of the economic, political, and bureaucratic elites who are now their masters. Those who can "pay the bill" are still very much in charge of the key planning questions: "What should be planned, for whom, and at whose expense?" Roszak offers no convincing evidence that either American corporate and governmental elites or, for that matter, Soviet party bureaucrats are about to surrender their decision-making prerogatives to "knowledge elites." Nor does the literature in general support this view.[45] Instead it supports a portrait of planners and other scientific experts as changing increasingly from intellectuals into technicians who lack political skills and defer to the authority of others in fields outside their own increasingly narrow field of vision. In this context, wealth and bureaucratic power can still buy and sell "expertise," no matter how cherished a symbol that commodity has become. Experts remain on tap rather than on top. Technocratic planners may increasingly shape the vocabulary of politics, but the very language of technocracy often serves to mask the realities of who has power, whose interests are being served, and who suffers from planning decisions.

In the final chapter of this book I attempt to demonstrate the validity of the preceding argument and to illustrate its applicabililty to the field of urban planning. I examine the various ways by which the language, symbols, and accoutrements of technology are used to mask the actual elite and class interests served by urban-renewal planning in Americn cities. For the present I wish to take issue with Roszak's rather cavalier attitude toward social justice, and toward concrete plans to alleviate the material deprivations of the lower social strata.

Distributive social justice is a basic issue for planners and political activists, but it is one which Roszak's "politics of transcendence" tends to treat as unimportant, particularly in his most recent work. Roszak may well be correct in asserting that general material well-being, social justice, and equality have become embodied in the dominant liberal and social democratic ideologies of the developed world. But acceptance of these values at the symbolic level does not necessarily entail their actualization in the policies of any given society, particularly in advanced capitalist societies such as the United States, where they must compete with both entrenched structural interests and other ideological values stressing competition, egoistic individualism, and private property. Hence to dismiss these material needs as either no longer salient issues, or as "hierarchically subordinate" to the quest for spiritual transcendence, is to ill serve the dispossessed.

This dismissal of important distributive and redistributive issues is akin to Roszak's critique of socialism for its failure to overcome "cosmic alienation" and "spiritual disconnectedness." The just organization of social machinery and the equitable distribution of social costs and benefits are not easy tasks. Labeling the pursuit of these tasks trivial or "purely material" does not make the achievement of just outcomes any easier. In fact, by sharply separating the "social" from the "cosmic" level, Roszak invites people to withdraw from the struggle for social justice in order to save their souls. This is not only an act of political irresponsibility; it also contradicts the common belief that "saving the soul" is directly related to the ethical conduct of life at the "social level."

According to Kenneth Kenniston, the personalistic, transcendental style of the counterculture impedes the possibility of creating a political movement committed to mounting an effective national program for altering oppressive social structures and achieving more equitable social outcomes.[46] To be politically effective requires a willingness to view the world in instrumental terms, a willingness to make plans for alternative futures, and a willingness to organize a concerted effort. Roszak's answer to this argument appears to be that organizational impotence is an acceptable price to pay for heightened "cosmic consciousness." In his view, only by cultivating nonmanipulative human relationships will any society ever make the great leap into nonintellective modes of consciousness.

The very language used by Roszak is what might be termed the "language of communion." It is a highly expressive language, fraught with vague condensation symbols of transcendence and shared ecstasy. Such symbols are purposely designed to carry the mind away from daily concerns, to remove individuals from social contexts so that they may personally experience communion with divinity.[47] In transporting the mind in this way, one escapes from having to deal with real sources of injustice in the world of time and matter. This, it seems to me, is the double bind of the counterculture. Social justice defined in conventional redistributional terms means opening up access to the goods and opportunities of material well-being (and by implication, to materialistic, middle-class life styles) to those who heretofore have been excluded from participation in the benefits of the technical and economic system. From the Roszakian perspective, social justice, defined in these terms, becomes technological integration, impedes the quest for transcendent experiences, and thus ought to be resisted.

In my view, the Roszak of *Unfinished Animal,* who calls upon people to "look after their own needs" in a purely cosmic realm, has forgotten some of the important political insights of the earlier Roszak of *Where the Wasteland Ends.* The early Roszak realized that bureaucratic and political elites are willing to tolerate any number of "prescientific atavisms" so long as they do not become the basis for organizing people into politics.[48] The later Roszak advocates involvement in any of a wide variety of quasimystical cults as the "one best way" to achieve transcendence. In so doing, he forgets his own earlier view that the diverse encounter groups, erotic circles, and "therapeutic communities" made possible by abundant leisure time, not only fail to disturb the social power of dominant elites, but actually help to reinforce it. Such "cults" help to divert psychic energy from politics to therapeutic self-indulgence. They help people "cope with" frustration that might otherwise be channeled into politics as concrete grievances. Most importantly, they create the impression that dominant elites are highly tolerant of subcultural diversity, when in fact the degree of tolerance extends only to groups that do not threaten to undermine the stability of dominant interests. This illusion of benevolent tolerance serves as a depoliticizing weapon, thereby leaving the political marketplace an arena dominated by owners, public and private managers, and their supportive experts in shaping the future.

In the final analysis, Roszak's call for counterculturalists to drop out, to seek freedom, small-scale community, and peace of mind, and to "look after their own needs" becomes a typical American response to the prospect of social conflict. It resembles the quest for the purified homogeneous community so extensively criticized by Richard Sennett. This is not to say there is nothing to be gained from Roszak's social thought. One of the chief benefits of the counterculture has been the spread into the larger society of an emerging ecological ethic geared toward achieving the simplification and durability of the world of objects surrounding the self. This shift, as yet only dimly perceptible, is from a life style aimed at increasing income to one based on simplifying needs. It is a shift that Georg Simmel would have found most congenial. Yet the successful realization of this goal is dependent upon a structural and technological simplification of environmental conditions that is impeded by corporate bureaucracies—whose profit and growth rates depend upon new product research, development, and diffusion—and by government policy planners—who are not soon likely to concede that decision-making processes need to be demystified. Thus the quest for simplification, too, becomes a political question. It is a problem that cannot be resolved satisfactorily simply by cultivating one's own garden.

Despite the inspirational value of Theodore Roszak's critique of "single vision," his overall world view poses a number of other difficulties. He excessively romanticizes "nature," causing him to denigrate or ignore major improvements in the human condition that have resulted from scientific development. In similar fashion, his trenchant criticism of advanced capitalism is partially obscured by his nearly obsessive reiteration of the theme that it is not the economic organization of society but rather "technocracy" that threatens human development. His call for a "back to the land" movement to escape this mythical "technocracy" leaves those who lack resources and mobility out in the cold. Finally, his systematic refusal to address questions of political strategy makes it probable that future generations will inherit a world dominated by the value structure of the economic, political, and bureaucratic elites that continue to control technological development.

Let us consider these issues in greater detail. Roszak's depiction of natural ecological processes stresses nature's order, harmony, and hierarchical integration. His critique of the rational planning of human society is based largely upon the expectation that if left alone, unfettered by reason, science, technology, or industrialism, the "natural" individual will achieve cooperative working and living arrangements. But Roszak's view of nature tends to overlook the insights that underlie Wirth's and Simmel's views. Roszak forgets that dynamic ecological processes include competition as well as cooperation, domination as well as integration, conflict as well as harmony, change as well as stable order. The primitive rhythms of life are not all peaceful and harmonious.

Roszak infuses all of nature, including those aspects that contribute to human misery, with "eternal presences." In so doing, he uncritically accepts anything natural, regardless of its human consequences. Consider an example previously mentioned, the poetic license that allows him to interpret the primitive sanitation and plague-bearing rodents of the medieval city as humbling symbols of human limits. By using such examples to show that contemporary city life has become "denaturalized," Roszak implicitly denigrates major advances in public health planning that have eliminated much death, disease, and human suffering from urban life in both the developed and undeveloped worlds.[49] Indeed, Roszak explicitly argues that such strides rob people of their intimate sense of connection with the inevitability of death. This sort of rhetorical overkill does an injustice to his otherwise persuasive critique of the "single vision" of the technocrat by substituting for it an equally restrictive cult of nature.

Roszak's faith in spontaneous mutual adjustment is akin to Louis Wirth's faith in the possibility that democratic consensus can be achieved by rational discourse alone. Both ignore the realities of contradictory interests that are part of the class structure and political economy of American society. Without major structural changes aimed at equalizing economic and political resources, it is doubtful that leaving conflict resolution either to nature or to reason can produce democratic outcomes.

Relatedly, Roszak's powerful critique of the Freudian ideal of "calculative egoism" is partially blunted by the alternative mode of consciousness that he upholds. Leaving oneself entirely open to communion with all of humanity and the cosmos, as Roszak advocates, entails the suspension of critical faculties. It is possible to reject calculative egoism and still recognize the real adversary interests that exist in a class-stratified society dominated by economic and bureaucratic elites. To shut our eyes to the seamy side of our social system in order to commune with nature and the cosmos is to blur real adversary interests in a fruitless hope of achieving universal human communion.

Roszak's unyielding insistence that city life is "unnatural" and "dehumanizing" in comparison with rural life provides ideological support for a set of urban development priorities that depart quite sharply from his ideal of "anarchist socialism." His critique of "denaturalized cities" provides urban planners with a handy excuse for ignoring real inequities in economic distribution and social service delivery on the ground that the "real" problem of "alienation from nature" requires more public parks, planned low-density suburban enclaves, and rural recreation communities. His view of the city as an "iron cage," robbed of simplicity, natural beauty, and community, is the very perspective that provides continued justification for suburban deconcentration. Dominant structural interests are more likely to hire planners to pursue this vision of the future than they are to encourage the development of producers' and consumers' cooperatives. Suburban deconcentration, after all, has been a most profitable development for powerful economic interests. Roszak's theme also provides an unintended rationalization for the class interests of the builders, investors, and users of affluent low-density residential and recreation "communities," at the expense of the nonaffluent who are left behind in our financially starved urban centers.

Conventional planners are not the only ones to have gained ideological support from Roszak's social theory. There has been a growing interest among some more radical planners in developing new styles of planning that factor the "subjective" or "personal" knowledge of those directly affected into the urban planning process. This is a major concern underlying John Friedmann's efforts to institutionalize "transactive planning." By "transactive planning" Friedmann means a process designed to close the "communication gap" between planners and clients through a "continuing series of personal and primary verbal transactions."[50] The desideratum of this process is a fusion of technical knowledge, personal knowledge, and social action. Going beyond Friedmann, two more radical "subjectivists," Gabrow and Haskin, recently have advocated an "ecological ethic" patterned directly on Roszak's theory of knowledge. Mirroring Roszak, Gabrow and Haskin call for "the merging of the development of the individual with the unity of the world."[51] They ask planners to substitute cosmic insight for objective policy analysis. They espouse a style of planning in which the planner rejects the goal of mastering the world and instead becomes "at one with the world," as an equal participant with all others in the spontaneous flow of history. Their goal is a nonrepressive society where reason, passion, planning, and spontaneity are one.

Approaches such as these may well have inspirational value, encouraging planners and people in general to be more spontaneous, creative, insightful, and open to others. They may, as Roszak hopes, inspire great leaps of imagination and make planners more sensitive to the human costs of the plans they espouse. Nevertheless, these more radically utopian approaches ignore the realities of power and domination in the world. Like Roszak himself, the call by utopian planners for an "I–Thou" approach to the whole outer world requires the suspension of the critical awareness that injustice abounds, and that it should be resisted rather than ignored. Unjust people, structures, and processes should be opposed and changed rather than loved and sympathetically accepted as parts of the great chain of being.

Dealing with Diversity and Injustice

Having earlier pointed out several shortcomings in Richard Sennett's analysis, what can be said in his defense? First, and foremost, Sennett's critique of the Roszakian countercultural response to social and political alienation in American society has considerable merit. The thrust of this criticism goes beyond his occasional Marxian rhetoric about the "idiocy of rural life." The heart of his critique is that (1) love and innocence are not enough to rid the world of social injustice; (2) some elements in the external environment are threatening and deserve hostility rather than "sympathetic cooperation"; and (3) aggressive self-assertion is sometimes necessary to gain a clear sense of personal identity.

In these respects Sennett's analysis closely resembles psychologist Rollo May's recent, penetrating criticism of the widespread refusal of many people to deal with the reality of power and injustice in the world—preferring instead to remain seemingly blissfully innocent. In *Power and Innocence,* May defines "innocence" as a failure to acknowledge the reality of power in the world.[52] According to May, people who seek psychiatric help often do so because they have expressed too little hostility toward the constraints and injustices of their environment. Feelings of resentment against appropriate sources of resentment, when they remain unexpressed, become internalized as a sense of powerlessness, sometimes assuming symptomatic forms. May, like Sennett, disputes Freud's contention that existence can be reduced to a struggle between eros and death. The need for social power is seen by both as an equally basic need that must find expression in some concrete realm of self-assertion and self-affirmation. When channels for self-assertion are blocked by the socioeconomic environment, this need is frustrated. A sense of powerlessness festers. In periods of stress, the frustrated need for power over the environment may surface in violent behavior.

Like Sennett, May points to the realities of power and injustice in the world as a useful counterpoint to Roszak's counterculturalists who posit the pursuit of a basic state of harmony and innocence as the best approach to life. The pervasiveness of injustice, of real adversaries, of social barriers to self-expression and self-mastery, and of misused power in the world renders the quest for harmony and innocence mere wish-fulfillments. Sennett's chief virtue is that he recognizes that it is not power but innocence and impotence, or the inability to express adversary interests, that often leads to violence. There are thus good reasons to agree with Richard Sennett that social injustice should be resisted aggressively when encountered.

Still, a lingering difficulty remains. People cannot learn the ethical values that lead to social justice simply by becoming the "hard" personalities that Sennett prefers. Courage is needed in order to act; but the courage to act stems as much from an awareness of and sensitivity to the reality of human suffering and degradation as it does from a sense of rugged individual strength. In the long run, a deliberate posture of "individual" strength may lead only to a sense of frustration and impotence in the face of the persistent, large-scale bureaucratic injustices that Sennett wishes to remedy.

Unless linked to a strategy of collective political action, the aggressive self-assertion of the lone individual is unlikely to get very far. Sennett's own preferred political strategy of working through some large-scale bureaucracies such as established unions to countervail the growth of corporate power may make sense under some historical conditions. But it seems less useful under current political-economic circumstances, where major national union elites have become symbiotically tied to the growth and development strategies of the corporate structure.[53] This does not invalidate the notion that some forms of collective action may be a more effective way to fulfill the need for self-assertion than is lone individual struggle. It merely suggests that we must look outside the universe of well-entrenched institutions to find such organized expressions of social discontent.

Because of its penchant for innocence and avoidance of conflict, we must also look beyond Roszak's counterculture. Richard Sennett's critique of the potential tyranny of small groups and of the "intimate warmth" of the counterculture is germane in this regard. The other side of communal cohesiveness, friendliness, and consensual social control is often oppressive intolerance and the repression of deviance. Intimate community in small-scale settings sometimes entails a trade-off in exchange for the social support and sense of belonging that reduce anxiety and give order and meaning to life. A sense of solidarity is often derived from the enforced sharing of values, tastes, and common life styles. The price of this conformity to common understandings is the sometimes subtle, occasionally direct suppression of deviant behavior and the denial of inevitable social conflict, insightfully discussed by Richard Sennett. Sennett's call for the diversification of social experience thus represents an important dimension of the growing recognition by scholars and social critics alike that urban density and heterogeneity can have liberating social consequences.

Despite this recognition, the goal of re-creating a primitive "communal solidarity" continues to be among the most potent themes in the literature of both social theory and urban planning. This is especially unfortunate because the pursuit of "planned community" often has distracted the attention of planners and social critics alike from focusing on real inequities in the society's overall system for allocating resources and opportunities. It is unfortunate as well both because it ignores some of the costs of intimate warmth, recognized by Sennett, and because "planned communities" have often displaced the actual social networks of mutual aid and support found among low-income urban dwellers. Finally, the pursuit of "planned community" has absorbed large quantities of human energy in pursuit of an unachievable harmonious folk society myth.

THE MYTH OF PRIMITIVE COMMUNAL SOLIDARITY

The myth of "primitive communal solidarity" is a major misleading assumption that underlies much urban social theory. Wirth's and Simmel's critiques of urban social relationships as fragmented, exploitative, and impersonal begin from a contrast model of a "rural way of life" assumed to be cooperative, fraternal, and relatively conflict free. This implicit view of the rural community closely parallels Robert Redfield's classical formulation of "The Folk Society"—a highly integrated, culturally homogeneous, and spontaneously self-regulating social system, free from social class divisions, and exhibiting a strong sense of in-group solidarity.[54] It is this same sort of primitive, consensual social order that Theodore Roszak wishes to "recapture" in the counterculture. Although Freud self-consciously rejects the idealization of earlier social forms, he too nonetheless occasionally lapses into descriptions of a primitive existence that is relatively more erotic, and hence more tightly integrated, than the civilized modern world. Even Richard Sennett views the homogeneous solidaristic community as a retrogression to earlier actual forms of social control, currently manifest in affluent suburbs and rural communes.

In my view, this myth of "primitive communal solidarity" creates a special problem for urban planning. Both utopian and physical planners have consistently sought to create spatial and social environments offering the illusory hope of escape from social conflict into an idyllic past that never was, and never can be. The perpetuation of "good old days" myths serves to legitimize the social role of those who seek to re-create semblances of a rustic past. But it also serves to delegitimize social conflict situations *a priori*, without carefully examining the bases of particular historical conflicts or their justifications.

Thus it may be a useful antidote to consider briefly some of the more revealing findings of researchers who have attempted to study the quality of social relationships in rural/folk societies. These studies reveal that, in a variety of different cultural settings, rural and village life is more differentiated, more conflictual, and more class stratified than the myth of "Gemeinschaft" would suggest.

For instance, Mann's research calls attention to observable patterns of residential segregation in rural village life.[55] These patterns are less noticeable than comparable patterns in urban settings because the sheer numbers of people within each subgroup are not large enough for distinct "social areas" to become visible to the outside observer. Although less noticeable, they are nonetheless quite real. They often serve to reduce overt conflict stemming from class antagonism and other social contradictions that exist in even relatively simple social systems.

Research reveals other details of the reality of "folk societies." Oscar Lewis's critique of Robert Redfield's work (and by implication the work of Wirth, Simmel, and Roszak) shows that interpersonal relationships in small Latin American peasant societies often are characterized more by "distrust, suspicion, envy, violence, reserve, and withdrawal" than by openness and spontaneity.[56] More importantly, both Lewis's work and research by Pitt-Rivers[57] and Tilly[58] reveal that class stratification, status rivalry, and intense social conflict following from these structural conditions all are capable of developing in preurban, rural-peasant environments.

Pitt-Rivers's study of a small rural community in France is especially noteworthy. The peasant village that he studied was moving from a relatively high degree of isolation and a simple social structure to an occupational structure more closely attuned to national patterns of economic development. While the initial social structure was simple, it also was polarized, exhibiting a high degree of antagonism and conflict between farmers and villagers. Ironically, therefore, the changes in language, life style, and occupational structure that have occurred as a result of economic "modernization" cannot be said to have destroyed a cohesive and solidaristic social community. To the contrary, Pitt-Rivers found that the changes which brought new life styles and greater complexity of social structure to the village also created latent opportunities for new patterns of cooperation, as well as new conflicts. By complicating a relatively simple, but bifactional, class structure, with new cross-cutting cleavages, the bitter and acrimonious single cleavage actually was somewhat reduced.

These studies indicate that even in a relatively small and isolated social setting there may be social class or other structural barriers to intimacy, openness, and fraternity. Since this is so, it suggests the futility of efforts to create communal solidarity and consensual order simply by reducing the size or increasing the rusticity of human settlements, without altering the class stratification system in basic ways. The myth of "communal solidarity" is a moral ideal, not a historical reality. As an ideal, it can only be approximated by pursuing egalitarian social policies designed to reduce the conditions that create social conflict—class stratification, economic maldistribution, and status envy—not by striving to recapture a past that never existed.

THE MYTH OF PRIMITIVE AGGRESSION AND ACQUISITIVENESS

A key defect of Sigmund Freud's social theory stems from the lack of empirical support for his basic proposition that aggression is a primordial instinct rather than a culturally induced pattern of behavior. Vivid evidence contradicts the Freudian view. In *The Gentle Tasady*, John Nance carefully describes a primitive, isolated Philippine tribe whose people are almost entirely nonaggressive.[59] Their social relationships are wholly peaceful and cooperative. Their language even lacks words for war, kill, and bad. This does not mean that all primitive societies are inherently peaceful and communal. In discussing the "myth of communal solidarity" I have just shown that the degree of conflict or cooperativeness depends upon such variables as the degree of class division and the type of culture and social organization characterizing particular "folk societies." Because this is so, grand theories that posit any universal instinct, whether for aggression, acquisitiveness, or natural harmony, ignore the formative impact of historically variable social structures and cultures in inducing conflict or cooperation.

Recent experimental research suggests, for example, that in the American context, males but not females are made slightly more aggressive by stress situations, because aggressiveness is a learned norm.[60] It is a legitimated coping mechanism assigned to the male sex role within the American social system. These studies call into question the notion that aggression is a universal biological instinct, rather than a culturally learned and structurally induced response to particular situations.

Even within the modern psychoanalytic view, aggression is believed to be a more modifiable phenomenon than Freud assumed. Some contemporary psychoanalytic thinkers, like Gregory Rochlin, author of *Man's Aggression*, suggest that aggression is not a primary instinct, but rather a derivative of a more basic desire for self-esteem.[61] In this view, aggression emerges to defend social esteem, which is distributed unequally in most societies. In similar fashion, Karen Horney rejects Freud's unwillingness to acknowledge the crucial impact of particular culture contexts on personality development.[62] In place of Freud's essential pessimism, Horney substitutes an ongoing struggle for self-realization, a basic urge to develop one's best native potentialities. From this perspective, the need for support and for security from one's environment replace the sexual and aggressive drives as basic human needs. Environments that are unsupportive engender anxiety, which, in turn, can lead to neurotic or compulsive behavior, such as aggression.

Much of what Freud regarded as biologically fixed in the instinctual drives is now perceived as a mere barrier to growth that can be lifted by making appropriate changes in the social structure. This is because the forms that particular neuroses take depend upon the prevailing myths and self-images of one's culture and social structure. For instance, in a social structure such as our own, that cultivates extraverted and assertive male behavior patterns, the neurotically frustrated male may try to act out an idealized self-image by excessively aggressive behavior. This pattern of adaptation to an "unloving" environment creates a tension between the spontaneous self and the idealized self-image. Such a person seeks approval and reassurance by becoming a kind of caricature of a culturally valued and structurally rewarded trait. Spontaneous inclinations that do not match up with this idealized self are repressed, those which do are cultivated. In this way, people become less than they are capable of becoming. Their personalities are structured by environmental conditions, rather than allowed to develop freely.

To illustrate concretely, Horney, who practiced psychiatry in both Chicago and New York, found her American patients to be very different from those of her German practice. Reflecting upon these differences, she became convinced that her departures from Freud were eminently sensible. She clearly demonstrated that many of Freud's theoretical formulations were both time and culture bound. Her clinical experiences revealed that the American success ethic was an especially severe source of neurotic behavior, on a scale unprecedented either in her own past European experience or in the case of Freud's earlier middle-class, central-European clinical patients. The American emphasis on life as a competitive game—with clear-cut winners and losers—produced both tormented losers and insecure winners. The latter failed to experience security and satisfaction because the resentment of their success by others denied them the environmental reassurance so necessary to mature personality development.

For Horney, the basic contradictions in American culture and social structure engender ambivalence and frustration. Americans are taught to value both success and altruism; love and competitiveness. But the overriding structural incentives reward competition, achievement, and success. Frustration is further engendered by mass-media stimulation of wants which people find impossible to satisfy by legitimate means. The final contradiction of our cultural and social system is between the ideal of individualism and autonomy and the reality of pervasive formal and informal social controls. This can produce an unstable personality structure alternating between delusions of omnipotence and feelings of utter helplessness.

In a highly competitive setting that fosters insecurity, these contradictions are especially problematic. Instead of moving easily in and out of patterns of interaction as the situation requires, the neurotic personality becomes compulsively locked into a repetition of the chosen self-image, even in inappropriate situations. Reminiscent of Richard Sennett's "purified" personality type, Horney's neurotic American is especially troubled by unrealistic, culturally induced expectations of immunity from such unavoidable urban constraints as crowds, delays, and other external sources of frustration. These are based on fantasies of perfection which are often fueled by the pervasive success ethic.

The foregoing recalls the frustrations that Georg Simmel posited as "inherent" in the urban conditon, as well as his theory that acquisitiveness must be counted among the "basic" drives. Simmel defined acquisitiveness and the protection of possessions as "natural instincts," rather than as structurally induced and culturally reinforced dispositions. Yet he offered no evidence to support this proposition, except for describing several behaviors and social relationships that seemed motivated by these two ends. Since Simmel, like Freud, wrote during a period when entrepreneurial capitalism was still quite strong (1890–1918), it is perhaps not surprising that he might take the pervasiveness of possessive individualism as an indicator of a "basic" drive, nor that he felt no need to support this assumption. Now that we have the benefit of anthropological and sociological research which challenges this assumption by calling attention to numerous nonacquisitive cultures, the proposition that acquisitiveness is a basic instinct no longer seems so self-evident.[63] Indeed, now that our own society has experienced widespread disillusionment with the pursuit of acquisitiveness and possessive individualism (e.g., Roszak's countercultural grand refusal, the more recent "born again" phenomenon), the Simmelian assumption of natural acquisitiveness seems as lacking in firm support as is Freud's concept of "basic" aggression. Moreover, like the Freudian view, it reflects a common nineteenth-century view of "natural man." In this view the human personality is naturally aggressive, competitive, and acquisitive. "Natural man" becomes social only because of the instrumental need to satisfy more basic instinctual drives, not because of any primary need for sociability or community.[64] In the final analysis, such a Darwinian perception of "society" becomes an apology for the dominant form of social organization—laissez-faire capitalism—that characterized the urban societies of Freud's and Simmel's day. In this way, prominent social critics become unwitting apologists for the systems they find repressive. The bourgeois city, for all its faults, is construed as less repressive than traditional cultures that placed taboos on competitiveness and possessive individualism. In this respect, both Freud and Simmel reflect the nineteenth-century faith that unfettered "individual reason" must be left unregulated. For Freud it is the reason of the scientist and the "calculative egoist," for Simmel the reason of the free creative spirit that should be liberated by "modernity." In this belief, both theorists reflect the liberal desire of their day to free the bourgeoisie from the constraints of feudalism and traditional social order.

THE CULT OF CALCULATIVE EGOISM

As in the case of Freud's theory of aggression, so also in his model of individual mental health and self-actualization, he failed to rise above the image of human development prevalent within the contemporary capitalist societies of his day. The Freudian ideal of self-actualization stressed individual extraction of pleasure from the environment, the conversion of all aspects of the external world into potential objects of individual pleasure, and the pursuit of "calculating prudence" by a strong but isolated ego. The goal of existence is to obtain pleasure while avoiding pain, risk, and possible destruction. When applied to the economic sphere, these are the same ideals that legitimized the predatory behavior of the nineteenth-century laissez-faire capitalist—an extraction of the maximum amount of surplus profit from economic exchange; the use of a calculating ego to accumulate capital and to avoid the risk of being driven out of business by other aggressive competitors.

Karl Marx defined classical economic theory quite succinctly as "the science of renunciation, of privation, and of saving."[65] For the sake of capital accumulation, the nineteenth-century capitalist practiced industry, asceticism, and savings. He "stored up" his money in order to maximize economic returns with minimal loss. In this same way, Freud's emotionally mature individual is a calculating egoist, who "saves up" or hoards his psychic energy. He is cautious and prudential. He develops no social relationships that might bring pain (e.g., love and friendship). Instead, he "invests" psychic energy prudentially in those erotic "objects" from which can be "extracted" the maximum of individual pleasure. Freud's ego-dominated "calculative individual" rises above his socialized conscience (superego); he nonetheless exercises willful "discipline" over spontaneous instinctual drives that threaten to "squander" scarce psychic capital. The Freudian ideal of individual mental health thus is almost identical to Marx's model of social alienation under capitalism. To wit:

> Society, as it appears to the [classical] economist, is civil society, in which each individual is a totality of needs and only exists for another person, as the other exists for him, in so far as each becomes a means for the other.[66]

As with the classical economist, Freud's model of psychodynamics rests heavily upon the basic assumption of scarcity. In each analytical framework, "There is a limited amount of money, or of psychic energy to be distributed; it can be redistributed and obstacles to its maximum or optimum distribution can be removed, but it cannot be enhanced or enriched."[67] This sort of theory amounts to the adaptation of a theoretical system prevalent within a historically rooted economic system to explain the operation of a supposedly ahistorical, universal psyche.[68]

Freud's obsession with "possession" and his fear of the loss of "possession" in the sexual realm thus represents a common concern of the middle classes of his day in their economic activities. In this sort of framework, feelings are something people "have." Love can be "lost." Hence people "withhold" commitment to others. They cautiously "calculate" the costs and benefits of social relationships in order to avoid the unpleasure of "loss." They establish the limited goal of "rational conquest" of passion, rather than the positive enjoyment of being with others, as a life goal. Libido can be "spent." It is a fixed quantity of energy that can be "used up." Hence, Freud reasons, people have no right to carelessly "throw away" their love.[69]

Love and all other forms of human fellowship engaged in openly without calculative egoism as a guiding compass, are equated with an "infantile" oceanic feeling of oneness with nature. Freud's view of the mature self thus becomes the model of human development that Theodore Roszak sets up as his contrast model of alienated consciousness— the self as an atomized unit of "calculative egoism." Love, sex, and all other forms of human experience are thereby reduced to sources of stimulation and release. They are never sanctioned as acts of mutual unity and surrender, as acts of communion.

Another time- and culture-bound aspect of Freud's social theory is his Victorian attitude toward woman's liberation. Apparently reacting against the late nineteenth- and early twentieth-century laissez-faire capitalist economic system, Freud viewed the release of women from the domestic role quite dimly. He viewed the absorption of women into occupational roles as tantamount to relegating them to the status of "competitors" in the "struggle for existence." Instead, Freud implores women "to withdraw from [this] strife into the calm, noncompetitive activity of [the] . . . home."[70] In turn, he views the home as a retreat from social conflict, a prudential escape to be used in much the same way the middle-class families in Richard Sennett's *Families Against the City* used their homes as fortresses against turmoil.

Freud's theory is time- and culture-bound in still a third sense. Freud wrote at a time when entrepreneurial business elites were becoming dominant political and social elites. Freud's theoretical reflections on the best way to order the psychic functions tend both to reflect this emergent pattern of social domination and to provide an implicit justification for it. Recall that for Freud the psychologically healthy personality is typified by rational calculation. For the "rational-calculative" personality, the ego is the organizing center of the psychic functions. The ego is highly developed and relentlessly strives for autonomy over the guilt feelings of the superego and the intense but directionless drives of the id. Alternative orderings are possible. "Social man" is a personality dominated by the superego. Such a personality type tends to be a guilt-ridden social conformist. A third alternative is "natural man," a personality type dominated by repressed drives that have come to the surface and dominate both the social norms that reside in the superego and the willful calculation of the ego. For Freud, those who order their psychic functions so that calculative rationality dominates the other two basic psychic functions tend to become (and in his view should become) history's dominant reality builders. In the context of late nineteenth- and early twentieth-century political and economic realities, this sort of ideal-typical speculation tends to provide a gloss of legitimacy, and indeed, even of historical necessity, for the exploitative behavior of the entrepreneurial capitalists who were the dominant "reality builders" of the epoch.

The period-bound nature of Freudian thought is further underlined by the fact that the actual historical trend in capitalist political economies has been in the direction of Freud's prototypical "social man" in the realm of production and "natural man" in the sphere of consumption. That is, the large-scale corporate structures that emerged from once competitive entrepreneurial firms now tend to perpetuate themselves and expand their power and domain by demanding conformity of workers to behavioral conditioning (which Freud might term an externalized superego) on the job. Conversely, the consumer is conditioned by the "id arousal" that is part of mass-media advertising and subliminal socialization.[71] In these ways, Freud's ego-dominant personality, like Simmel's market calculator, is replaced as a prevalent middle-class personality type by the manipulated social conformist partially anticipated by Louis Wirth.

For all these reasons—the conceptual similarity between Freudian theory and classical economic theory, Freud's desire to protect women from the "competitive struggle" of occupational life, his tendency to view the calculative entrepreneur as best equipped to shape social reality, and the replacement of this entrepreneurial pattern of accommodation to reality by a corporate bureaucratic world that rewards conformity over ego-strength—it can be concluded that the type of urban environment Freud was experiencing, and the economic and theoretical system from which it emerged, basically shaped Freud's social thought. The corollary of this conclusion is that a particular form of socioeconomic organization—laissez-faire capitalism—produces the calculative egoist as much as, if not more than, the calculative egoist creates social reality.

THE MYSTIFICATION OF HUMAN SUFFERING

Another problematic aspect of Freud's therapeutic model of problem solving is its tendency to mystify the experience of human suffering. Freudian thought locates the source of human misery primarily within the realm of intrapsychic dynamics. Just as Louis Wirth's conceptualization and terminology tend to mystify land-use planning, so the jargon and analytical perspective of Freudian psychology mystify the realm of "social problem" solving. They divert attention away from the historical context within which people's troubles occur and from the socioeconomic and political arrangements that often account for psychological stress. Overemphasis on unconscious drives and on the inner dynamics of ego, id, and superego locates human suffering outside of the world that provides the context, roles, and social structural opportunities and constraints that channel behavior.[72]

In light of this narrow focus, it is ironic that one of Freud's basic goals was the potentially revolutionary objective of bringing the "self" to the surface of consciousness by the use of individual reason, skill, and strength. To accomplish this, Freud proposed that people firmly ground their perceptions of their environment in reality, freeing themselves from comforting myths, childish illusions, and dogmatic superstitions. Yet in pursuing this goal, Freud ignored or misinterpreted many of the realities of social structure that we have considered in this chapter. Let us consider a few of the historical and structural origins of human suffering by way of illustration.

First, consider Freud's use of the concept "weak ego strength" to explain both the lower capacity for self-denial and the greater capacity for communal solidarity (for Freud a character defect) thought to characterize the lower social strata.[73] Such an emphasis on "deficient" character development glosses over numerous possible social causes of "weak ego strength." For example, the continuous economic stresses that are part of the everyday life of the poor, combined with the abuse and low status accorded to their social role, may well lead to despair, and from there to "weak egos." But to treat this consequence as a cause is to do injustice to the poor. Such "psychologization" of structural defects in the economic and the status system often leads to the use of psychotherapy to compensate for the inadequacy of economic remedies for poverty. This sort of psychotherapeutic approach to social issues is the preferred model of "problem solving" in social work, personnel management, and even in education in general. It teaches people to "cope with" existing socioeconomic and political arrangements rather than questioning them. As Ryan has ably pointed out, this approach often is tantamount to "blaming the victim."[74] Professional therapy provides people with a handy excuse (lack of expertise) for doing nothing to deal with social and political problems. The mystology of Freudian terminology lends further credibility to the sensed lack of expertise and to the feeling that the victim is to blame for his or her own plight. This, in effect, undermines one of Freud's central goals, the desire to equip people to assume personal responsibility for their own fate. That "blaming the self" is a by-product of the psychotherapeutic approach to social problems is indeed ironic since Freud himself felt that too much self-blame was likely to produce overdeveloped superegos and too many guilt-ridden people. Although ironic, this development is hardly surprising. The very creation of a technically expert psychoanalytic movement with its own mystical beliefs, rituals, and definitions of reality, all seemingly rooted in the "objective science" of the unconscious, highlights the inability of the users of therapy to comprehend their actions or to determine how they can act responsibly.

To illustrate further how the therapeutic approach can undermine self-confidence, consider the following example. One of the basic Freudian coping mechanisms is "resignation in fate." The Freudians assume that because human existence is essentially tragic, acquiescence in fate is the most sober response to perceived personal and social problems. Freud himself ultimately rejected all comprehensive political, social, religious, or planning programs for building a future social structure that was permanently nonrepressive. As Erich Fromm puts it, Freud's ultimate message is that "the full understanding of man's mind could show the irrationality of all these answers and could lead man . . . to a sober, skeptical rational appraisal of his past and his present, and to the *acceptance* of the fundamentally tragic nature of his existence."[75]

Depending on particular historical and structural circumstances, such a posture of resignation can be quite harmful to the individual as well as to society. For example, as Alvin Pouissant has shown in the context of black racial oppression, the acceptance of one's lot and fatalistic acquiescence in the face of clear oppression and injustice amount to a compromise of one's integrity as a human being.[76] This equivocation, in turn, can lead to self-loathing. One begins to hate not only the source of oppression, but also one's self. Acquiescence in injustice may also lead to a trained incapacity to be self-assertive and to painfully suppressed rage. These conditions carry a potential for explosiveness, even when triggered by seemingly trivial external events. Yet these conditions are primarily structural and historical. They result from patterned inequalities in social opportunities, institutionalized discrimination, and structured powerlessness, not from underdeveloped egos. They are made worse, rather than relieved, by therapeutic advice of passive resignation. They improve when channeled creatively into political and social movements dedicated to resisting injustice, rather than when politics is avoided.

This brings us to a second major instance of conceptual mystification that characterizes Freudian thought—his analysis of "group psychology." Once again, Freud reduces human motivation for joining and participating in groups to terms that fit his basic theory of the unconscious. Recall that Freud treated group life primarily as a coping mechanism used by isolated units of consciousness seeking to find tame outlets for sexuality or to escape responsibility for their fate. Yet it is almost too obvious to point out that people enter into groups for economic, political, and social reasons, as well as psychological ones. Group formation and the behavior of people in groups is no mere by-product of the individual quest for substitutive satisfactions or for escape from responsibility, as Freud assumed. Freud's ahistorical approach to groups overlooks the numerous socioeconomic and political functions of groups discussed elsewhere in this book. It also ignores the fact that group life, as in the previous example, can become a source of self-mastery, self-actualization, and heightened self-consciousness, as well as a barrier to these objectives. Participation in political groups and movements, in fact, may be the most effective way to act responsibly in particular historical contexts (e.g., the antiwar movement), rather than an escape from freedom and responsibility. Whether participation in collective action is either liberation or escape once again depends upon particular historical situations, rather than on the dynamics of intrapsychic conflict. Like his individual psychology, Freud's group psychology creates more illusion than it strips away. His reduction of group life to intrapsychic struggles trivializes the real historical struggles of people to achieve a better existence through political action.

A key implication of this weakness of Freud's social thought has been nicely captured by Keith Brooks. Brooks argues that for Freud:

History is the mere backdrop for the drama of intra-psychic conflicts. Ego against id, reality against pleasure principles . . . and ultimately Eros against Thanatos—the social world is no more than the playing out of these internal dynamics. The world and other people are merely instrumental means to the end of instinctual gratifications.[77]

In this way, the structure, content, and even the terminology of Freud's social theory leads him and his adherents to mystify still a third component of urban political reality—the close relationship between community organization and community conflict. Freud explains social conflict and collective violence by reference to the struggle between Eros and Thanatos, and the compelling strength of a primary aggressive instinct. Yet close students of social conflict and collective action have shown that social conflict generally emerges as a result of structured relationships among unequally situated groups, classes, and interests within given social systems. Conflict arises as goal-oriented, objectively based conflicts of interest between or among privileged and unprivileged strata. The unequal distribution of power, wealth, status, and other resources has always been a fundamental aspect of urban social organization.[78]

Urban political and social conflict emerges out of these structured patterns of inequality. When such conflict takes the form of collective violence, there is no need to posit a universal aggressive instinct to account for aggressive acts. Indeed, on the part of both resisters and authority figures, the resort to violence generally has been part of a goal-oriented, deliberately pursued struggle for political or social power. Irreconcilable conflicts of value and interests are rooted in historically specific conditions of life. These account for a large measure of both collective action and political violence. It is thus unnecessary to search the unknown depths of the unconscious mind, when historical realities provide a direct, adequate, and demonstrable explanation.

Thus, for instance, the highly stressful environment of the urban poor, when combined with the particular historical situation of the 1960s—structural unemployment, high rents, consumer exploitation, unresponsive if not custodial government service and regulatory bureaucracies, and the like—prompted a black urban rebellion that was characterized by a highly selective choice of targets for collective violence. For example, according to the Kerner Report, in nine central cities where major black rebellions occurred, those white-owned businesses that were viewed by the black community as disrespectful or unfair to blacks were the targets of serious vandalism, while nearby residences and public buildings were left untouched.[79] Where public authority became a target of ghetto rebellions, it tended to be focused upon the two basic instruments of formal social control in the ghetto—the police and the school systems. These examples illustrate the organized, instrumental use of selective violence or the threat of violence as a political weapon. They suggest that good jobs, more dignified treatment, and more social justice can do a great deal more to stabilize urban social life than policies that demand greater "personal discipline," but deny people the opportunities needed to achieve and consign them to an environment within which victims are blamed for their own plight.

In the final analysis, Freud paid insufficient attention to structured inequalities in the distribution of resources in industrial capitalist societies. Like many liberal advocates of "partisan mutual adjustment," he valued the ability of people to mutually adjust their sociopolitical relationships. Like many rationalistic thinkers, he "believed that if man understood intellectually the causes for his misery, this intellectual knowledge would give him the power to change the circumstances which caused his suffering."[80] This point of view tends to ignore the implications of structured inequalities in political resources for the outcomes of partisan mutual adjustment (i.e., those who have resources are likely to have their interests factored into the structure of sociopolitical relationships). Those who have few resources have little choice but to "adjust" or be repressed by the formal agencies of social control that enforce the political mandates resulting from social and economic inequality.

To be sure, Freud did call for modest redistribution of economic resources to the working class and a loosening of the high degree of sexual repression common among the middle-class strata of his day. Yet his aim in doing this was to avoid a more fundamental social transformation that might fully redistribute the resources needed to enter into the process of "mutual adjustment" as an equal. Instead, he held that full political and social equality was a fruitless ideal because some degree of repression would be necessary in any social system.

Like all incremental liberal social reformers, Freud tries to "mitigate man's burden within the very framework of a traditional picture of man."[81] This was the prototype of self-actualization during the period of economic history when Freud wrote, the "calculative egoist." Such a role model is itself repressive of the possibilities for human development. Freud's basic theoretical assumptions led him to fear the breakdown of social control that might emerge if all members of society were fully liberated sexually, socially, and politically. This fear tended to override his liberal reformist enthusiasm for more challenging work routines, more just economic distribution, and fewer repressive social controls. Even if such reforms were to eliminate "surplus" privation, he believed in the end that the id drives must be held in check by a combination of formal controls and the inspirational qualities of charismatic elites who had the strength, knowledge, and power to set an example for the intemperate lower social strata. His advocacy of an elitist political structure entails an unwillingness on Freud's part to sanction the development of political equality to a point where relatively equal and participatory political structures could convert the ideal of partisan mutual adjustment from a remote wish to a possible reality. For, without a healthy measure of political, social, and economic equality, "mutual adjustment" cannot be truly mutual. To the extent that adjustment lacks mutuality it is by definition asymmetrical, entailing relationships of domination and subordination that are predicated upon existing social inequalities. In this setting, politics becomes a mere recorder of outcomes already inherent in the structured inequality of society, rather than a means for mutual adjustment and creative social change.

THE CULT OF CREATIVE INDIVIDUALISM AND THE REALITIES OF SOCIAL STRUCTURE

Georg Simmel's theoretical reflections on the development of segmental interest groups, on changes in the meaning of work, and on the social impact of monetary exchange tend to overestimate the fluidity of the class structure of urban industrial capitalism. Simmel expected that the capitalist money economy would foster a high degree of geographic and social mobility, thereby creating the potential for a high degree of individuality in personality development. This it has done. But it has done so selectively and with somewhat different consequences than Simmel anticipated. Simmel expected a gradual secular decline in primary-group ties, an increase in individual "rootlessness," the rise of "segmental" friendships to replace comprehensive ones, and of transitory interests to replace enduring ones.

Simmel held that various types of interpersonal relationships were likely to encompass or exclude a reciprocal knowledge of the full personalities of their members by different degrees. For him the rise of special-interest groups represented a paradigm case of the growing rationalization of modern culture "whose phenomena consist more and more of impersonal elements and less and less absorb the subjective totality of the individual."[82] He assumed that the transition from social organization based on tradition to organization based on rational interests would make possible the fullest development of human personality according to the dynamic of individual needs and drives. Diverse interest groups, he felt, provided a variety of alternative routes whereby discrete individuals might develop the full potential of the many facets of their personalities. Interest-group memberships could provide some social supports while at the same time fostering a high degree of personality individuation among people who were social products of a unique constellation of group interests. This was a pattern of personality development that Simmel highly valued. In this sense he was an eloquent exponent of the nineteenth-century individualist ideal that each individual "should realize what is unique in himself and thereby distinguish himself from all others."[83]

Whatever its merit or shortcomings as a normative ideal, Simmel's expectations about the growing potential for individuality under urban capitalism needs considerable qualification. First, the power of social custom to regulate behavior did not tend to break down in large cities to the extent that Simmel expected. Most people, particularly the less economically mobile, remained tied to a reinforcing set of primary and secondary groups that together made up their basic socialization agencies. These informal controls coexisted along side the less extensive and more impersonal regulatory mechanism of the state and corporate bureaucracies. The "sphere of freedom," mobility, and individuation outside the realm of formal social controls that Simmel (and Wirth) treated as universally applicable to the "urban dweller" has in fact proven to be quite variable, depending on one's position in the social class structure.

Secondly, research on membership in voluntary organizations suggests that such secondary group memberships tend to reflect people's positions in the class structure. People do not seem especially inclined to join a large number of widely diverse groups to give free reign to the diverse and contradictory facets of their personalities. The pattern of group memberships in secondary associations indicates that these claims more often tend to reinforce rather than to contradict each other.[84] For instance Catholic church members tend to join antiabortion groups; businessmen tend toward probusiness groups, and so forth. Because group claims tend to reinforce each other, people reinforce distinctive subcultural patterns of interaction more often than they cultivate individual uniqueness by joining groups. This not only suggests that Simmel overestimated the fluidity of the class structure and the scope of individuality under urban capitalism, but also that there is a less widespread danger that group cross pressures in large cities will lead to individual role conflict, inner turmoil, and mental breakdown than Simmel and Wirth feared.

Another problem with the Simmel–Wirth "overlapping membership" concept is that it ignores the fact that entire societies vary in the degree of conformity and receptivity to "innovative" personalities that are dominant social norms. Accordingly, "In a society that is highly conventional, group affiliations may be so rigorously prescribed that one may belong to a large number of groups without perceptibly increasing one's differences from others."[85] Even in less traditional societies which engender diverse subcultures, such as the United States, if subcultural values are clearly defined and homogeneously reinforced, they provide their members with a clear sense of identity. So long as these subcultures satisfactorily anchor and integrate the personality, there is no reason to expect widespread individual uniqueness, innovative behavior, or mental breakdown resulting from group cross pressures.

Georg Simmel tended to discount the empirical reality of the primary groups, kinship, and extensive friendship networks of his day. He focused instead on such purely formal properties of groups as their size and number. Only individual human beings were concretely real for Simmel. The "meaning" of social organization was found in the formal properties of individual acts rather than in a reflection of the concrete historical circumstances that give rise to or sustain particular group or class relationships.

Such an approach has the virtue of calling attention to recurrent and constraining social rituals and forms of interaction in a wide variety of seemingly unconnected circumstances. Its chief weakness, however, is that when we compare relationships sharing formal properties in common, although occurring in substantively different social contexts (e.g., comparing the ritual sociability of a cocktail party with the ritual aspects of life in a penal colony), the meaning of these contexts is often lost sight of. Real normative differences often are obscured in the process. A cocktail party is not qualitatively the same as slavery or class oppression, no matter how enslaved to ritual forms the partygoer appears to the detached observer. Likewise, competition in sports is not qualitatively the same as economic competition for survival, even though both activate psychic energy and reduce the persons with whom one is competing to the status of "competitor."

Additionally, the development of mutually beneficial or antagonistic social relationships requires a preliminary process of interaction and communication. Simmel pays insufficient attention to the social process whereby people learn about their shared or contradictory "interests." Social learning requires a common language and a universe of discourse as well as regular opportunities for interaction. These structural and cultural requirements, in turn, suggest that there are some structured limits to individual, rational choice prior to the developed "consciousness" that one is engaged in particular forms of being for, with, or against others.

Simmel argues that social and organizational forms were originally created so that people might cope with the concrete demands of practical existence, but that over time they have lost their entanglement with practical life. This position contradicts his belief that organizations based on rational interests were becoming the dominant form of social organization. Furthermore, if "practical life" is taken to mean the concrete historical conditions in which people find themselves situated, it may be argued that these conditions of existence—material and social—powerfully affect how people perceive problems, possibilities, and their very selves. For instance, the material conditions of existence—one's work, the location of one's house, the available means for economic and social development—combined with the social conditions of existence—one's position in the class structure—tend to predetermine the range of social roles in which people's lives are cast. The "individual" is a social product. The individual's opportunity for free, creative individuality has always been limited by the social and material conditions of existence and by the cultural patterns of interaction that are differentially available to people.

These realities of social structure have a number of important implications for Simmelian theory. First, consider Simmel's belief that calculative-instrumental rationality is a by-product of urban existence. Presumably Simmel intends this condition to apply to all urban dwellers, who are expected to be equally exposed to the rhythm and tempo of the urban money economy. Yet exposure to the basically business practices, which Simmel confused with "urban" practices, depends upon where people are concretely situated in the class structure. The bourgeois businessperson, given the requirements of job and relatively mobile position in the class structure, is more likely to become obsessed with a calculative-instrumental rationality than is, say, the low-income urban migrant, who is both more economically dependent upon and has a greater frequency of interaction with the same circle of kin, friends, and fellow sufferers.

This tendency toward overgeneralization that ignores the reality of social structure is a common problem in grand theoretical analysis and one well exemplified in the theories we have chosen to examine. Oddly, except for Freud's concept of "surplus privation," the class structure of society plays only a peripheral role in the various critiques of urbanization. Wirth's ecological variables, Simmel's calculativeness, reserve, and overstimulation, and Roszak's "single vision" presumably affect all urban dwellers equally, regardless of their position in the class structure. Richard Sennett is more aware of the continuing importance of social class and primary group socialization experiences. The middle-class suburbanite is the chief example of Sennett's psychological condition of "purified identity." Yet even with Sennett there is nothing peculiar to the experience of members of that social class that predisposes them to maintaining self-images more rigidly than members of other classes. Indeed, Sennett believes that planned and unplanned physical changes in the urban environment deny all metropolitan residents the heterogeneous contact needed to experience conflict and emotional growth.

It is now well established that people do not acquire their basic values, beliefs, and perceptions from their encounter with the "city-as-a-whole." Rather, as the literature reviewed above amply demonstrates, it is within families, neighborhoods, and class-stratified primary social networks that people are socialized. Socialization is a class, not a mass, phenomenon. Different class situations provide people with different material and cultural resources for coping with, adapting to, avoiding, or resisting psychic overstimulation, ecological change, the scientistic culture of "single vision," or the absence of heterogeneous contact.

People are social and cultural beings who seek to act out the norms and values of their particular subcultures. In part this is because of a second reality that Simmel tends to downplay. The mind is a synthesizing as well as a differentiating organism. It gives order and meaning to the diverse contents of the external world, as well as making distinctions. The particular order and meaning attributed to the external world by the individual receive confirmation or rejection as a result of social interaction with other members of the primary and secondary groups to which the individual belongs. This is what we mean by culture. Particular subcultures within the metropolis screen, sift, and interpret the diverse stimuli that individual human beings experience. As Roszak (and even Wirth) recognized, subcultures are key mediating mechanisms between mind and society. They are capable of reducing the stimuli that can potentially penetrate into consciousness to manageable proportions, thereby protecting the organism against the destabilizing psychic overstimulation that Simmel expected.

Culture is more than a rigid social form. It often functions as a dynamic mediating mechanism—helping its adherents adapt to rapid social and environmental change. Culture is not inherently restrictive, as Simmel held. It can function to nurture the personality and facilitate its development by providing the individual with a sense of continuity and purpose. This function of culture is especially necessary for the vast number of individuals who lack the will to take the "leap of creativity" Simmel thought necessary to reject and transcend old social forms.

Yet, having said this, it is important to note that psychic overstimulation and mental overload may become a serious emotional problem for some urban dwellers, depending, once again, on their particular life situations. For example, overstimulation may be a problem for social isolates who lack supportive subcultural reference points that give order and meaning to their lives. It may be problematic for a worker who is engaged in numerous daily interpersonal transactions, but who lacks adequate screening mechanisms and resources to deal with each transaction effectively and must assume a posture of "reserve" (e.g., a low-level clerk in a welfare office). It appears to have been a problem as well for Richard Sennett's isolated middle-class nuclear families in *Families Against the City* who dealt with diverse stimuli by shutting them out indiscriminately.

Like overstimulation, Simmel's concern about the growing spirit of objectivity and impersonality (foreshadowing Roszak's critique of "single vision") also is based in reality but applied too generally. If the money economy of urban capitalism rewards intellectual over emotional development, it does so in particular "substructures of interaction" within the overall social class structure, rather than universally. Professors, corporate executives, and public administrators, for instance, are far more likely to interact in work situations that reward rationality over emotionalism and intuition than is the case for taxi drivers, football players, or craftsmen. If work life consistently requires impersonality, calculability, or abstract thinking, these traits may well have an impact upon after-work interests and relationships. If not, no such pattern of personality development need be expected.

Simmel's critique of work alienation under industrial capitalism is another facet of his general theory of growing individualization. Recall that Simmel held that because less consciousness was "used up" in routinized work, individual workers became free to cultivate a wide diversity of outside interests that transcended the world of work. They were free to become multidimensional in their avocational interests, thereby enriching their personalities. Contradictorily, Simmel, like Marx, also criticized the excessive demands of work specialization. For him, narrow and repetitive work specialization was a key regulatory mechanism that discouraged individual creativity and human development. It established rigid standards of role and job performance that stifled depth of thought and spontaneous self-expression. Simmel implicitly resolved this contradiction by his view that just as the "urbanite" became "blasé" about alienating aspects of city life, so too could the worker become "indifferent" about work, thereby "storing up" psychic energy for cultivating a richly diverse leisure life.

This resolution of the contradiction of alienated labor is a common one in social analysis. It is a response that forms the basis of major works on the "indifferent" pattern of adaptation to unchallenging blue-collar work life.[86] But as I have argued elsewhere in critiquing one such organizational theorist, the arbitrary separation of work from the rest of life ignores the fact that people's personalities are "wholes" as well as facets. Hence what happens in any one facet often influences the development of the whole. The "indifferent" in particular draws a sharp distinction between his work and his life. He reveals his "real" self only to family and intimate friends. Is not his superficial cordiality at work likely to develop into a habit which may affect the genuineness of his afterwork relationships?[87]

In short, if a third of each day is spent on the job, work life is bound to have some impact on the way a person deals with the rest of life. Research on the social-psychological functions of work indicate that people's work is intimately bound up with their sense of identity and self-esteem. When work challenges vital faculties, it can enhance a person's sense of personal efficacy, bolster his or her sense of mastery over the environment, and confirm that one is performing a socially useful role.[88] Because this is so, unchallenging, uncreative, and non-autonomous work—the work of the "indifferent"—can be expected to carry over into the rest of life, weakening self-confidence and self-esteem rather than bolstering individuality, as Simmel argued. Or in Albert Camus's nice counterpoint to Simmel: "Without work all life goes rotten, but when work is soulless, life stifles and dies."[89]

Given the centrality of work to personality development (a fact clearly recognized by Freud, Sennett, and Roszak), Simmel's advocacy of worker controlled organizational democracy takes on added significance. Indeed, it is precisely the structural separation of work from the rest of life that has driven many people inward in search of the meaning, unity, and integration that a fragmented social structure no longer adequately provides. To this extent Simmel's thought was quite perceptive. But, ironically, given the structure of work life, this inward voyage of the Simmelian "lone individual" has led to increased personal dependency, rather than to autonomy and individuation. The diminished quality and meaning of much of industrial and bureaucratic work life seems to have generated a market for the wares of Sigmund Freud's psychoanalytic movement, as many of those who gained free time for close introspection found the experience of integrating the personality that their social world had fragmented too painful to "manage" alone. Ironically, also, the fragmentation of social meaning has generated new needs for trust and intimacy and a sense of identity.[90] Because work life no longer occupies a central role in satisfactorily defining personal identity for a large part of the work force, these needs for a social identity structure are often satisfied in more intimate primary group relationships such as Sennett's "intense" nuclear family and Roszak's counterculture.

In a highly developed society, where it is difficult to return en masse to precapitalist economic formations to overcome the fragmentation of social life, it may nonetheless be possible to increase the degree of control over the form, pace, scale, and content of work life by experimenting with forms of worker self-management that seek to restore some of the power over creative work that once characterized the medieval craftsman. This is a goal that Simmel himself would highly value, for as he said in describing the work life of the creative artisan:

> In the happiness of the creator with his work . . . we find, beyond a discharge of inner tensions, the proof of his subjective power, his satisfaction over a fulfilled challenge, a sense of contentment that the work is completed, that the universe of valuable items is now enriched by this individual piece.[91]

Additionally, Simmel's analysis of worker self-management, discussed earlier, suggests that organizational democracy might be an effective way to overcome the oppressive aspects of hierarchical domination in bureaucratic societies. The democratic values of equality and fraternity are closely linked through the role the former plays in enhancing the self-concept of the individual. Friendship is greatest where status differentials are lowest and self-concepts are high. This makes possible the development of truly mutual relationships, based on openness, reciprocity, and trust. Participation in equalized authority structures likewise increases the frequency of social interaction, which, in turn, can be expected to reduce prejudice, foster cooperative arrangements, and thereby free creative energy and promote organizational productivity.[92] These goals are especially important for the development of the social nature of human beings, who are much more than isolated units of individual consciousness.

A third basic facet of Simmel's social theory (and normative ideal) of growing individuality under urban-industrial capitalism was his belief that social relationships based upon monetary exchange were less binding, and hence more potentially liberating, than were more traditional loyalties. Ties based purely upon economic exchange clearly are transitory and "noncommital." However, the increased individual autonomy that Simmel expected to follow from the replacement of personal and feudal loyalties by the less extensive dependencies of the "money economy" did not evolve as he had anticipated. During the early period of *commercial* capitalism, following the breakup of the feudal social order, an image of increasingly autonomous, self-sufficient individuals may have approximated the changes that were actually taking place in the social structure of Western Europe. But by the turn of the nineteenth century and early twentieth century, when Simmel wrote, *industrial* capitalism had already rooted factory workers in place and made them extensively economically dependent upon a single employer. Furthermore, oligopolistic and monopolistic tendencies were already beginning to convert "individualistic" middle-class entrepreneurs into a paid professional "salariat," somewhat more geographically and socially mobile, but only slightly more personally autonomous on the job than were proletarian workers. This, in fact, was the other side of the coin in Simmel's portrait of urban-industrial capitalism—the apparent price of the growing world of objects of mass production that Simmel bemoaned.

If the middle classes that Simmel implicitly depicted in "The Metropolis and Mental Life" were actually obsessed with calculation and computation, perhaps it was because they had not yet had time to adjust to the transformation of their role of entrepreneurial producer to that of bureaucratized employee and mass consumer. Perhaps they had not yet learned the passive traits of excessive hedonism, consumption, and self-indulgence that were called for by the emerging *advanced* capitalist consumer society. Perhaps they had not yet fully developed the habit of credit purchasing that has made calculative exactness for consumers exceedingly problematic—by disguising interest payments, delaying the computation of actual costs, and creating the illusion of costless, instantaneous gratification.

The industrial capitalist city did grossly increase the total world of objects confronting people, as Simmel held. But these objects were, and remain, primarily objects of consumption. The sheer volume of things in the world has not produced a generalized attempt to shut out those things from consciousness in order to preserve creativity and the inner core of individual personality. Rather, the explosion of consumer goods has been accompanied by institutional developments (such as the spread of undemanding and nonautonomous jobs, the commercialization of mass media) that foster an overall capitalist culture that defines human fulfillment more in terms of having and consuming than in terms of being, doing, or creating. Yet, once stimulated, desires to have and to consume are inherently limitless. They are bound to outstrip the personality's ability to assimilate possessions. In point of fact, it was Simmel himself who poignantly expressed what might be termed the tragedy of *passive stimulation*—that is, the stimulation to have, to view, to "own," with no corresponding stimulation to act creatively.[93] Since Simmel recognized the potential stultifying effects of this tragedy, it is surprising that he placed such confidence in the ability of the isolated, socially unsupported, apolitical, individual creative spirit to "transcend" a condition of objectively declining opportunities for individual creative expression.

In the advanced capitalist economic structure, this condition of passive stimulation is even more problematic than it was in the pre–World War I era when Simmel wrote. Consumer no longer directly confronts producer as an "intellectually calculating economic egoism." Some producer exchanges with other producers may continue to transform social interactions into a quantitative arithmetic problem; but the real economic and social "costs" to consumers of the advanced capitalist economy are increasingly shrouded in mystery. When inner-subjective "sovereign traits" do come to the surface of consciousness in this sort of society, it is more likely to be because they "irrationally" surface by means of the rampant manipulation of consumer wants than because of the increased "rationality" of consumer-producer exchange. As "producers," the professional salariat of the corporate world may still be rewarded for impersonal, specialized, abstract thinking. But in the world of consumption they, along with the other strata of society, are subject to different cues. They are encouraged to suspend rational judgment, calculative exactness, and critical intellectual faculties.

Paradoxically, the numbered, computerized, automated, credit-card economy has brought quantitative calculability for the corporate managerial strata to a high point, while creating the illusion of personalism (in the form of the name-embossed credit card) and of unlimited purchasing power (requiring no calculability) for consumers. The upshot of this sort of economic structure is to drive up gross annual purchases and consumption, while removing rationality and calculability from the consumer side of the market exchange.

In the final analysis, Simmel's ultimate ideal of "individuality" represents a confinement of the individual as much as a release. Simmel's concept of spiritual transcendence entails a devotion to the objective values of beauty, knowledge, and significance that transcend all connections to other social beings.[94] Confinement and release appear to be dialectically linked. To release the free, creative spirit from the constraints of social convention requires that the individual "reside" in a purely psychological realm, divorced from both other social beings and from the "overstimulating" dynamics of modern society. Simmel's creative individual is a social isolate.

Simmel defined freedom as a purely inner-psychic rather than a behavioral act. This leaves him open to the criticism that his self-actualized personality can discover the "true self," and thus achieve perfection and fulfillment in any political or economic system, no matter how exploitative or oppressive. Furthermore, when this inner-psychic being does reach out beyond the self to become social, he or she often doe so "segmentally." When individuals assume a posture of "reserve" and only reveal fragments of themselves, calling forth specific capacities but concealing others that might disrupt social relationships, this also can serve to perpetuate existing social institutions. The "individual" avoids social conflict and personal stress by selectively concealing those facets of personality, values, and interests that would be deemed "inappropriate" to particular situations. Consequently, "segmental friendships" enhance the ability of existing relationships to dominate behavior. It is only by acting "inappropriately" that the socially repressive settings identified by Simmel and our other theorists can be challenged and forced to change. But people who lead inauthentic lives, using "reserve" and "segmental" revelation to cope with social existence (while concealing their actual inner life), often develop socioemotional problems that render them incapable of becoming agents of creative social change. Seeman, for instance, describes this form of social alienation as "role inversion," a term signifying that when spontaneous impulses are converted into "coolness," the result is a damming up of genuine self-expression and emotional release.[95] This condition is likely to prevent such people from actively resisting repressive social conditions.

To be fair to Simmel, it must be recalled that he was a dialectical thinker. For Simmel, human existence contains polar potentialities for future historical development. Through creative synthesis, he expected that the human personality could reconcile such contradictory aspects of social life as harmony and conflict, compliance and resistance, stability and change, social forms and creative impulses. He criticized all linear thinkers who sought causal explanations for historical developments. For him, life was an inherently dialectical ebbing and flowing of contradictory tendencies—"an infinite rhythm where we cannot stop at any stage we have calculated but where we must always derive that stage from an earlier, opposite one."[96] Viewing the world in this way— as a process of constant change—he felt free to criticize both the planning of "lifeless" harmonious communities and the laissez-faire doctrine that left the strong free to exploit the weak. He expected that each phenomenon contained within itself the seeds of its own transformation. In the hands of neoconservative thinkers, Simmel's dialectical awareness of the impossibility of ever achieving complete unity and harmony through a priori planning can easily become an excuse for doing nothing to influence the process of becoming. This is an implication that Simmel would probably reject. Indeed, his very view of history as an unfolding of humanity's creative spirit, replacing old forms with new creative tendencies, would seem to require that, to achieve fulfillment, people must struggle to shape the process of becoming rather than passively resigning themselves (à la Freud) to the dominant social forms of the present. For Simmel, all conventional social forms, including outmoded organizational forms, threaten to repress creative life. They must and they would be transformed through the dialectics of submission and resistance.

The chief difficulty with Simmel's approach to creative social change is its excessive reliance on lone individual struggle. Perhaps individual struggle can produce new art forms, but it is unlikely to transform the structural inequities of an unjust political or economic system. By definition, creative changes in political and economic organization require collective action rather than individual struggle. Collective action is needed to mobilize interest in rectifying social and economic injustice, to create a political "push factor," and to build support for the exercise of political control over such inequities as bureaucratic domination of subordinates, the negative externalities of advanced capitalism, and the unequal distribution of access to society's opportunity structure. Such major changes cannot be achieved by isolated individuals, no matter how much their own consciousness of injustice is raised. Political (as against purely individual) resistance must be a collective struggle if it is to succeed in overcoming systemic injustice. Individual resistance may be able to transform particular relations of domination-subordination (e.g., in a specific marriage or work relationship). But more than this is required to create structurally nonrepressive organizational forms, social structures, and political-economic systems.

In the final analysis, Georg Simmel's underlying dialectical theory of history may be a more important contribution to planning theory and practice than were either his explicit critique of purposive decision making and a priori planning or his abiding confidence in individual creative struggle. The basic implication of dialectical thinking for planning has been nicely captured by Karl Mannheim. The dialectician assumes that "we cannot calculate a priori what a thing should be like and what it will be like. We can influence only the general trend of the process of becoming."[97] Dialectical thinking implicitly sanctions a dynamic political process for shaping the future. It suggests that any "planning" that is to have an effective influence upon the historical process of becoming must be explicitly political, bringing to the surface underlying social contradictions. It suggests further that political "push factors," both within and outside the planning profession, can constructively influence the process of becoming by converting these social contradictions into political conflicts of value and interest that must be dealt with by a creative political synthesis.

To be sure, this notion of "dialectical planning" is one that I have implicitly derived from Simmelian thought. Simmel's explicit rejection of "planning" is based upon his assumption that planning invariably must entail the arbitrary imposition of an a priori blueprint leading to enforced social harmony that denies the basic human need for variety and contrast. In part, Simmel probably based this assumption upon his "detached" understanding of the utopian socialist movements of his day. In part, his mistrust of "planning" also stems from his confusion of "planning" with the activities of centralized bureaucratic states. Simmel mistakenly accepted the classical economic myth that the basic institutions of industrial capitalist culture were by-products of the hidden hand guiding uncomprehending individual market choices. In fact, even during the stage of industrial capitalism when Simmel wrote (1890–1918), the economic and social structure of the capitalist metropolis were being powerfully shaped by the *private* plans of possessors of concentrated economic wealth. Today the reality of private planning is even more evident. The advanced capitalist city and its surrounding suburbs are by and large the result of private planning—the private planning of industrial corporations; the highway planning of the auto-industrial complex and its government allies; the "investment planning" (also known as "redlining") of savings institutions; the "development planning" of local, regional, national, and multinational possessors of investment capital. The central question for the social theory of planning thus becomes a different one from the planning versus individual spontaneity dichotomy posed by Simmel. The question is not planning or no planning but planning by whom, how, and at whose expense.

I agree with Simmel that conflict and contradiction can become driving forces behind more creative modes of human existence. I disagree with his belief that planning must necessarily undermine conflict and contradiction. If social planning is linked to the political pursuit of the heretofore unexpressed class interests of the lower social strata, it can become a dialectical process. It can become a vehicle for revealing rather than concealing repressed class interests. Richard Sennett suggests that it may be possible to "plan" for social conflict and diversity as well as for consensus and homogeneity. This can be done by deliberately designing political structures that will factor contradictory social interests into *politics* rather than by the present tendency to use physical and social segregation of land uses and formal social controls as instruments to avoid, conceal, or suppress these underlying conflicts.

CONCLUSION

The changes that have taken place in the economic organization of advanced capitalist societies since the early twentieth century suggest that the problems addressed in this chapter may be part of a more general problem—the hedonistic self-indulgence that the dominant institutions of advanced capitalism need to grow and stimulate in order to reproduce themselves. Middle-class social mores have shifted since about the 1920s, from an obsession with savings to a life style predicated upon consumption and immediate gratification. This shift has been rationalized in part by psychoanalysis. But its root cause lies elsewhere. Structural changes in the economic organization of corporate capitalism have made possible the development of a mass consumer society on a scale unprecedented in the nineteenth century. The price of being a mass consumer is passive social conformity on the job; the reward, pervasive private consumption and self-gratification for those who contribute to the reproduction of advanced capitalist institutions; the social costs, a denigration of social consumption, the perpetuation of repressive hierarchies of employment, and a repressive permissiveness that creates the illusion of enhanced individuality, while diverting the struggle for social justice into socially acceptable channels.

As social critic Christopher Lasch has said:

> The culture of hedonistic self-indulgence . . . is . . . the inner logic of advanced capitalism, a social and economic system that is based not on "functional rationality" . . . but on the promise of individual enrichment and the satisfactions of an empty leisure, by means of which the masses are expected to compensate themselves for political impotence, the trivialization of work, the impoverishment of public life, and the general meaninglessness of the social order itself.[98]

This kind of social system does not provide the external goals that give meaning and purpose to life. Nor does it provide an inspirational vision of what nonalienating social forms and relations might look like. Human meaning cannot be found in the sphere of consumption. Georg Simmel once said, "Every property is an extension of personality; property is that which obeys our wills; that in which our egos express, and externally realize, themselves."[99] If this view is correct, it may help to explain the pervasiveness of hedonistic self-indulgence in our culture. In a society in which power in other forms is badly maldistributed, a tendency will be engendered for much of the populace to cling desperately to the objects of consumption that give vent to their need to express their will. When alternative channels for self-expression in the political and social world are largely closed, when political and social power are reserved for elites, much of the populace finds it difficult to turn away from the one role, that of "consumer," where they can gain a sense of autonomy, however illusory.

What can be done to provide a vision, a set of external goals that give human meaning to life? What can be done to influence the process of becoming, without prescribing a rigid endpoint? Since social structures vitally shape personality, social relationships can be made less alienating by altering social structures and social organizations in the direction of equality rather than hierarchy; by moving from a culture based on domination, competition, and exchange value to one based on reciprocity, mutual aid, and use value; by encouraging personalities that are active rather than passive; by fostering social relationships that move from temporary and shallow to those which are enduring and deep. If this can be done, people will have purpose outside themselves and life will not require a larger purpose outside itself.

Notes

1. Robert A. Gorman, "Phenomenology, Social Science, and Radicalism: The View from Existence," *Politics and Society*, 6, no. 4 (1976), 488–502.
2. For a theoretical discussion of the relationship between social substructures of interaction and subcultural beliefs and perceptions see "The Social Structural Paradigm," Michael P. Smith and Edward T. Jennings, Jr., *Distribution, Utilization and Innovation in Health Care* (Washington, D.C.: American Political Science Association, 1977), chap. 3, pp. 66–87.
3. See Ralph E. Turner, "The Industrial City and Cultural Change," Allen M. Wakstein, ed., *The Urbanization of America* (Boston: Houghton Mifflin, 1970), pp. 223–232.
4. Bennett Berger, *Working Class Suburb* (Berkeley: U. of California Press, 1960).
5. See Peter Blau and Otis Dudley Duncan, *The American Occupational Structure* (New York: John Wiley, 1967), p. 56; Christopher Jencks et al., *Inequality* (New York: Basic Books, 1972); John A. Brittain, *The Inheritance of Economic Status* (Washington, D. C.: Brookings Institution, 1977).
6. Herbert Gans, *The Urban Villagers* (New York: Free Press, 1962), p. 249.
7. See ibid.; Jane Jacobs, *The Death and Life of Great American Cities* (New York: Vintage, 1961); Gerald Suttles, *The Social Order of the Slum* (Chicago: U. of Chicago Press, 1968); for interesting parallels see Louis Wirth, *The Ghetto* (Chicago: U. of Chicago Press, 1928).
8. See, for example, Richard Dewey, "The Rural-Urban Continuum: Real but Relatively Unimportant," *American Journal of Sociology* 166 (July 1960), 60–66; Janet Abu-Lughod, "Migrant Adjustment to City Life: The Egyptian Case," *American Journal of Sociology* 67 (July 1961), 22–32; the literature reviewed by R. N. Morris, *Urban Sociology* (New York: Praeger, 1968); and the literature cited in notes 6, 7, 9, 11, 12, and 13 of this chapter.
9. See Wendell Bell and Marion Boat, "Urban Neighborhoods and Informal Social Relations," *American Journal of Sociology*, 63 (January 1957), 391–398; Morris Axelrod, "Urban Structure and Social Participation," *American Sociological Review*, 21 (February 1956), 13–18; John Kasarda and Morris Janowitz, "Community Attachment in Mass Society," *American Sociological Review*, 39 (June 1974), 328–339; and Djuro J. Vrga, "Differential Associational Involvement of Successive Ethnic Immigrations," *Social Forces*, 50 (December 1971), 239–248, on the socioeconomic and socioemotional functions of family, friendship, kinship, and ethnicity. The political functions of ethnicity are fostered by the prevailing American political structure. That is, political elites who have organized politics along ethnic lines develop stakes in perpetuating the ethnic identifications that keep them in

their jobs. Thus they engage in political symbolism designed to heighten ethnic consciousness. This further impedes the development of class-based political organization and fosters ethnicity as a continuing basis of social organization.

10. In addition to the sources noted above in notes 4, 6, 8, and 9 see also notes 11, 12, and 13 below.

11. Philip M. Hauser and Leo F. Schnore, *The Study of Urbanization* (New York: John Wiley, 1965), pp. 494–495.

12. See Oscar Lewis, "Further Observations on the Folk-Urban Continuum and Urbanization with Special Reference to Mexico City," John Walton and Donald Carns, eds., *Cities in Change* (Boston: Allyn and Bacon, 1977), pp. 59–66. See also Rudolph Gomez's insightful discussion of the creative aspects of Mexican-American mutual-aid networks in "Mexican Americans: From Internal Colonialism to the Chicano Movement," Rudolph Gomez et al., *The Social Reality of Ethnic America* (Lexington, Mass.: Heath, 1974), pp. 317–333.

13. See Anselm Strauss, "Strategies for Discovering Urban Theory," Leo F. Schnore and Henry Fagin, eds., *Urban Research and Policy Planning* (Beverly Hills: Sage, 1967), p. 93; Helen Safa, "Puerto Rican Adaptations to the Urban Milieu," Peter Orleans and William Ellis, eds., *Race, Change, and Urban Society* (Beverly Hills: Sage, 1971), pp. 153–190; Joan Ablon, "Retention of Cultural Values and Differential Urban Adaptation: Samoans and American Indians in a West Coast City," *Social Forces* (March 1971), pp. 385–393; see also Herbert H. Hyman, "Organizational Response to Urban Renewal" (Ph.D. diss., Brandeis University, 1967), p. 230; and Lyle W. Shannon and Magdaline Shannon, "The Assimilation of Migrants to Cities," Schnore and Fagin, *Urban Research and Policy Planning*, pp. 49–75.

14. William F. Whyte, *The Street Corner Society* (Chicago: U. of Chicago Press, 1955), p. 273.

15. This concept and its contrast to the social structure approach is developed in Kasarda and Janowitz, "Community Attachment in Mass Society," pp. 328–339.

16. Hyman, *Organizational Response to Urban Renewal*, p. 230.

17. Safa, "Puerto Rican Adaptations to the Urban Milieu," p. 156.

18. Abu-Lughod, "Migrant Adjustment to City Life: The Egyptian Case," pp. 22–32.

19. The following discussion is based on Ablon, "Retention of Cultural Values and Differential Urban Adaptation," pp. 385–393.

20. Ibid., p. 387.

21. Ibid., p. 389.

22. Otis Dudley Duncan and Leo F. Schnore, "Cultural, Behavioral and Ecological Perspectives in the Study of Social Organization," *American Journal of Sociology*, 65 (September 1959), 144.

23. Richard Sennett and Jonathan Cobb, *The Hidden Injuries of Class* (New York: Vintage, 1972), pp. 15–22; see also Robert Presthus, *The Organizational Society* (New York: St. Martin's Press, 1978), chap. 7.

24. Gerald Suttles, *The Social Construction of Communities* (Chicago: U. of Chicago Press, 1972), p. 10.
25. See Morris, *Urban Sociology*, pp. 76–77, 165; Elihu Katz and Paul Lazarsfeld, *Personal Influence* (New York: Free Press, 1956).
26. For a discussion of some sociocultural implications of market segmentation see Alvin Toffler, *Future Shock* (New York: Bantam Books, 1971), pp. 276–278.
27. On this last argument generally see Edward S. Greenberg, *Serving the Few: Corporate Capitalism and the Bias of Government Policy* (New York: John Wiley, 1974), chap. 2.
28. See Anthony Oberschall, *Social Conflict and Social Movements* (Englewood Cliffs, N.J.: Prentice-Hall, 1973).
29. Kenneth Schneider, *Autokind vs. Mankind* (New York: Norton, 1971).
30. See Lewis Mumford, *The Highway and the City* (New York: Harvest Books, 1963), for an interesting discussion of the isolative aspects of automobile use; on the understimulation of expressway driving see *New Orleans Times-Picayune*, February 16, 1975, p. 14.
31. See A. E. Parr, "City and Psyche," *Yale Review*, Autumn, 1965, pp. 71–74; *New Orleans Times-Picayune*, February 16, 1975, p. 14.
32. Duane Elgin, "Social Consequences of Increasing City Size," *City Size and the Quality of Life* (Washington, D.C.: U.S. Government Printing Office, 1974), p. 51.
33. See Alan Altshuler, *The City Planning Process* (Ithaca: Cornell U. Press, 1965); see also an excellent analysis of the uses of zoning by affluent suburban elites in Michael Danielson, *The Politics of Exclusion* (New York: Columbia U. Press, 1976).
34. See, for example, Alan Lupo, Frank Colcord, and Edmund P. Fowler, *Rites of Way: The Politics of Transportation in Boston and the U.S. City* (Boston: Little, Brown, 1971).
35. See *New York Times*, June 22, 1975, p. 3.
36. See, for example, Thomas R. Dye, "Population Density and Social Pathology," *Urban Affairs Quarterly* (December 1975), pp. 265–275; George W. Carey, "Density, Crowding, Stress, and the Ghetto," *American Behavioral Scientist* (March/April 1972), pp. 495–509; Douglas Carnahan et al., "Urbanization, Population Density, and Overcrowding: Trends in the Quality of Life in Urban America," *Social Forces* (September 1974), pp. 62–71.
37. Jonathan Freedman, *Crowding and Behavior* (New York: Viking Press, 1975).
38. *New York Times*, October 15, 1972, p. 66.
39. See Freedman, *Crowding and Behavior*, chap. 6; Strauss, "Strategies for Discovering Urban Theory," p. 92; Carey, "Density, Crowding, and Stress in the Ghetto," pp. 49–50; and David Karp, Gregory Stone, and William Yoels, *Being Urban* (Lexington, Mass.: Heath, 1977), chap. 4.
40. Freedman, *Crowding and Behavior*, p. 1.
41. Dye, "Population Density and Social Pathology," pp. 265–275.
42. Carey, "Density, Crowding, and Stress in the Ghetto," p. 498.
43. See Jacobs, *Death and Life of Great American Cities*; Richard Sennett, *The*

Uses of Disorder: Personal Identity and City Life (New York: Vintage, 1970); and the literature summarized in Freedman, *Crowding and Behavior*, pp. 62–67 and chap. 9, pp. 106–118.

44. As an example of this use of ecological rhetoric to mask class interests see *New York Times,* January 21, 1973, p. 22.

45. See, for example, Guy Benveniste, *The Politics of Expertise* (Berkeley, Calif.: Glendessary Press, 1972); Morris Janowitz, "Review Essay on Daniel Bell," *American Journal of Sociology,* 80, no. 1, (July 1974), 234–235; Jeffrey D. Straussman, *The Limits of Technocratic Politics* (Edison, N. J.: Transaction Books, 1977).

46. See Kenneth Kenniston, *The Uncommitted: Alienated Youth in American Society* (New York: Dell, 1965).

47. See Herbert Schneider, "Community, Communication, and Communion," Carl J. Friedrich, ed., *Community* (New York: Liberal Arts Press, 1959), pp. 216–224.

48. See Theodore Roszak, *Where the Wasteland Ends* (New York: Doubleday Anchor, 1973), p. 50.

49. For a precise discussion of the varieties of human misery resulting from primitive sanitation in parts of the Middle East see Ailon Shiloh, "Rapid Urbanization and Its Health Concomitants in the Middle East," *Urban Affairs Quarterly* (December 1969), pp. 207–214.

50. John Friedmann, *Retracking America: A Theory of Transactive Planning* (New York: Doubleday Anchor, 1973), p. 177.

51. Stephen Gabrow and Allan Haskin, "Foundations for a Radical Concept of Planning," *Journal of the American Institute of Planners,* 39 (March 1973), 106–114.

52. Rollo May, *Power and Innocence: A Search for the Sources of Violence* (New York: Norton, 1972).

53. See, for example, John Kenneth Galbraith, *Economics and the Public Purpose* (Boston: Houghton Mifflin, 1973).

54. Robert Redfield, "The Folk Society," *American Journal of Sociology,* 153 (January 1947), 293–308.

55. See Peter H. Mann, *An Approach to Urban Sociology* (London: Routledge & Kegan Paul, 1965).

56. Lewis, "Further Observation on the Folk-Urban Continuum and Urbanization with Special Reference to Mexico City," pp. 60–61.

57. Julian Pitt-Rivers, "Social Class in a French Village," *Anthropological Quarterly,* 33 (1960), 1–13.

58. See Charles Tilly, "Introduction," chap. 3, "Communities," Tilly, ed., *An Urban World* (Boston: Little, Brown, 1974), pp. 179–190.

59. John Nance, *The Gentle Tasady* (New York: Harcourt Brace Jovanovich, 1975).

60. See Freedman, *Crowding and Behavior,* chap. 7.

61. Gregory Rochlin, *Man's Aggression* (Boston: Gambit, 1973); see also Roger N. Johnson's review of a large body of research in experimental psychology questioning the Freudian thesis concerning aggression in Johnson, *Aggression in Man and Animals* (Philadelphia: Saunders, 1972).

62. Rona Cherry and Laurence Cherry, "The Horney Heresy," *New York Times Magazine*, August 26, 1973, 6, pp. 12, 75–80, 84; see also Karen Horney, *Our Inner Conflicts: A Constructive Theory of Neurosis* (New York: Norton, 1945).

63. See, for example, Nance, *The Gentle Tasady*; Margaret Mead, *Sex and Temperament in Three Primitive Societies* (New York: William Morrow, 1935); Joan Ablon, "Retention of Cultural Values and Differential Urban Adaptation," pp. 385–393; E. S. Kahn, ed., *Our Brother's Keeper: The Indian in White America* (New York: World, 1969).

64. See the excellent discussion of this nineteenth-century image of natural personality as well as of nineteenth-century liberal ideological aspects of Freud's thought in Erich Fromm, *Sigmund Freud's Mission* (New York: Harper Colophon, 1972), pp. 2, 98.

65. Karl Marx, "Needs, Production, and Division of Labor," *Karl Marx: Early Writings*, ed. T. B. Bottomore (New York: McGraw-Hill, 1963), p. 171.

66. Ibid., p. 181.

67. Helen M. Lynd, *On Shame and the Search for Identity* (New York: Harcourt, Brace and World, 1958), p. 84.

68. See the excellent discussion of this point in Keith Brooks, "Freudianism Is Not a Basis for a Marxist Psychology," Phil Brown, ed., *Radical Psychology* (New York: Harper Colophon, 1973), p. 335.

69. See Fromm, *Sigmund Freud's Mission*, pp. 36–37, for further development of this aspect of Freud's thought. See also Marshall Berman, *The Politics of Authenticity* (New York: Atheneum, 1972), pp. 314–315.

70. Quoted in Fromm, *Sigmund Freud's Mission*, p. 21.

71. See Ralph Hummel, *The Bureaucratic Experience* (New York: St. Martin's, 1977), chap. 3, for an interesting discussion of some of the implications of the displacement of ego-dominant personality types in contemporary bureaucratic work settings.

72. Brooks, "Freudianism Is Not a Basis for a Marxist Psychology," pp. 340, 316; see also Howard B. Waitzkin and Barbara Waterman, *The Exploitation of Illness in Capitalist Society* (Indianapolis: Bobbs-Merrill, 1974).

73. See chap. 2 of this book; see also Fromm, *Sigmund Freud's Mission*, p. 37.

74. See William Ryan, *Blaming the Victim* (New York: Pantheon, 1971); see also Michael Lewis, *Urban America: Institutions and Experience* (New York: John Wiley, 1973), for additional illustrations of this problem.

75. Fromm, *Sigmund Freud's Mission*, p. 81.

76. Alvin F. Poussaint, "Minority Group Psychology: Implications for Social Action," Gomez et al., *Social Reality of Ethnic America*, p. 53.

77. Brooks, "Freudianism Is Not a Basis for a Marxist Psychology," p. 36.

78. See Joe R. Feagin, "Community Disorganization: Some Critical Notes," *Sociological Inquiry*, 43 (1973), 124; Oberschall, *Social Conflict and Social Movements*; Tilly, "The Chaos of the Living City," *An Urban World*, pp. 86–108.

79. National Advisory Commission on Civil Disorders, *Report* (New York: Bantam Books, 1968).

80. Fromm, *Sigmund Freud's Mission*, p. 7.

81. Ibid., p. 100.
82. Georg Simmel, *The Sociology of Georg Simmel*, ed. and trans. Kurt Wolff (New York: Free Press, 1969), p. 318.
83. Donald N. Levine, "The Structure of Simmel's Social Thought," Kurt H. Wolff, ed., *Georg Simmel, 1858–1918* (Columbus: Ohio State U. Press, 1959), pp. 17–18.
84. See Michael P. Smith, "Pluralism Revisited," Smith et al., *Politics in America: Studies in Policy Analysis* (New York: Random House, 1974), pp. 3–32.
85. Matthew Lipman, "Some Aspects of Simmel's Conception of the Individual," Wolff, *Georg Simmel, 1858–1918*, p. 126.
86. See Presthus, *The Organizational Society*, chap. 7.
87. Michael P. Smith, "Self-Fulfillment in a Bureaucratic Society: A Commentary on the Thought of Gabriel Marcel," *Public Administration Review* (January/February 1969), p. 30.
88. Special Task Force, Department of Health, Education and Welfare, *Work in America* (Cambridge, Mass.: M.I.T. Press, 1973), chap. 1, pp. 3–10.
89. Quoted in ibid., p. xx.
90. See, for instance, Eli Zaretsky, *Capitalism, the Family, and Personal Life* (New York: Harper Colophon, 1976), p. 66.
91. Georg Simmel, "On the Concept and the Tragedy of Culture," *Georg Simmel: The Conflict in Modern Culture and Other Essays*, ed. and trans. K. Peter Etzkorn (New York: Teachers College Press, 1968), p. 32.
92. See G. David Garson, "Toward a Political Theory of Decentralized Socialism," (unpublished manuscript, n.d.), p. 16; see also G. David Garson and Michael P. Smith, eds., *Organizational Democracy: Participation and Self-Management* (Beverly Hills: Sage, 1976).
93. Georg Simmel, "On the Concept and the Tragedy of Culture," pp. 32–46.
94. Georg Simmel, "Conflict," Simmel, *Conflict and the Web of Group Affiliations*, trans. Kurt Wolff and Reinhard Bendix (New York: Free Press, 1955), p. 25; see Zaretsky, *Capitalism, the Family, and Personal Life*, pp. 59–61, for an excellent discussion of the socially isolative consequences of the Romantic tradition of the "lone individual."
95. Melvin Seeman, "Status and Identity: The Problem of Inauthenticity," *Pacific Sociological Review* (Fall 1966), pp. 353–367.
96. Georg Simmel, "Conflict," p. 108.
97. Karl Mannheim, *Ideology and Utopia* (New York: Harcourt, Brace and World, 1936), p. 126.
98. Christopher Lasch, "Take Me to Your Leader," *New York Review of Books*, October 18, 1973, p. 66; see also Zaretsky, *Capitalism, the Family and Personal Life*, p. 68; Turner, "The Industrial City and Cultural Change," pp. 226–227; Fromm, *Sigmund Freud's Mission*, p. 116; and Lasch, "The Narcissist Society," *New York Review of Books*, September 30, 1976, pp. 5, 8, 10–13.
99. Georg Simmel, "Secrecy," *The Sociology of Georg Simmel*, p. 344.

Chapter 6
Advanced Capitalism, Social Theory, And Urban Political Conflict

In the writings we have considered, as well as in the literature on urban society generally, urbanization is often confused with capitalism. The effects of capitalist economic development often are mistaken for effects of urbanization. Urbanization, or the concentration of population in relatively compact human settlements, has been blamed for displacing tradition and custom, creating an industrial proletariat, exploiting nature, and disrupting local communities.[1] But tracing these consequences to urbanization clearly puts the cart before the horse. The concentration of the working population in large cities is itself a consequence of the economic necessities of Western capitalism at a particular point in its historical development.

History records numerous examples of urban settlements that were centers of religious custom and tradition (e.g., the cities of Mayan civilization); that segmented and cultivated local communities (e.g., caste-based Indian cities); that had no industrial proletariat (the medieval occidental city of merchants and artisan guilds); and that gave nature its due (the classical Greek polity). Louis Wirth's analysis does not provide a universally valid set of variables for understanding "urbanization" and "urban" culture.[2] His model typifies the modern, Western, capitalist mode of city life at one period in history—the period of corporate consolidation and industrial concentration that prevailed in the United States prior to the transportation and communication revolutions of the late 1950s and early 1960s. The Western capitalist city, in its slightly earlier and more entrepreneurial European variant, formed the basis of Simmel's critique of the money economy and provided grist for Freud's speculations on the "surplus privation" of the proletariat and the social mastery of the ego-dominated calculative personality.

THE ROLE OF ADVANCED CAPITALISM IN
SHAPING URBAN FORM

This confusion of urbanization and urban culture (civilization) with Western capitalism is not really surprising. Western industrial cities emerged as a direct consequence of the growth of industrial capitalism as a dominant mode of economic organization. In the United States, when laissez-faire capitalism flourished in its most unfettered form, in the latter half of the nineteenth century, the basic structures, functions, and form of American cities were determined. Economy shaped both polity and society. As Jane R. Lowe has observed in *Cities in a Race with Time:* "Municipalities handed over their land and resources to private profit and exploitation, and our cities became the abused by-product of national industrial development."[3]

Since then, the transition has been from an "embedded" economy to an autonomous economic structure that powerfully shapes the society and culture in which it once was embedded. In the first half of the twentieth century, prior to the construction of the interstate highway system and the electronic communications revolution, industrial capitalism required a concentrated labor force and centralized productive facilities. This led to the concentration of the population in our larger urban centers. In agriculture, the capitalist form of economic organization called for the use of advanced technology, expensive equipment, and modern management skills. These required large capital investment, which many small farmers neither possessed nor could borrow. The result was additional urban concentration as small farmers and sharecroppers were driven off the land.

More recent developments in the economic organization of advanced capitalism have radically altered the need for concentrated labor and production facilities. Technological advances in transportation and communication have significantly shrunk physical distances. For corporate capitalism, these changes have reduced the costs and time of transmitting goods, services, and information over vast geographic distances. Corporations no longer require concentrated labor and production in order to maintain coordination and control over economic functions.[4] They still benefit from relatively concentrated consumer markets, but these can be reached by metropolitanwide media and distribution networks, thereby rendering dispensable the previous need for central city growth.

The tendency of capital is to concentrate and then to move globally to the least expensive points of production. The trend of corporate capital concentration is clear enough, as are its implications. In 1941, for example, 1,000 manufacturing firms controlled approximately two-thirds of all manufacturing assets. Today the 200 largest firms do so.[5] This concentration of capital provides key corporate elites with the resource base needed to coordinate, command, and control critical trade, communication, manufacturing, and distribution networks, without the need for close geographic proximity.[6] In production, major corporate location and relocation decisions are made by a small circle of individuals, independent of loyalty to particular nation states, let alone to local communities. Decisions are taken on the basis of criteria internal to the microeconomic planning of corporate profitability, growth, and convenience. Thus, for example, the decentralization of manufacturing to suburbia and to the South and rural areas enables corporate planners to take advantage of cheaper southern and rural labor, to escape the countervailing power of a well-organized labor force, to save money on land costs, and to exploit state and local tax incentives. The resulting out-migration of industrial jobs from central cities, particularly in the Northeast and Central states, is only partially offset by more poorly paid jobs in the lower reaches of the hotel, entertainment, and tourist sectors of those cities that have been "renewed" with federal urban aid.

As a result of these largely corporate land-use and investment priorities, the demographic map of the United States has changed significantly in the past fifteen years. During the decade of the 1960s, in the nation's ten largest cities, 70 percent of the increase in employment and 95 percent of the increase in manufacturing occurred in the suburban rings surrounding these cities.[7] In that same period, American suburbs as a whole accounted for three-quarters of all new manufacturing and retail jobs.[8] This pattern of job shift to suburbia is nationwide, as Table 1 indicates.

Overlaid upon this pattern, and exceeding it in significance since 1970, has been a major interregional shift in employment opportunities, particularly in manufacturing. The older industrial cities of the Northeast and the Midwest have suffered substantial decline in industrial jobs. The South, the Sunbelt, and the Rocky Mountain states have been the chief beneficiaries of changes in the organization of production in the current decade. The scale of this shift is unprecedented. For instance, between 1970 and 1973 the nine northeastern metropolises with populations larger than 750,000 experienced job declines in manufacturing that equaled their aggregate losses in the previous twenty-year period.[9] The Department of Commerce's Bureau of Economic Analysis projects a continuing and pronounced shift of income away from the Northeast and North Central states and toward the southern and western regions over the next two decades.[10]

As a result of corporate location and relocation policies, often subsidized by government contracting practices, the Southern Atlantic

Table 1

HOW JOBS HAVE SHIFTED TO THE SUBURBS
(in the 15 largest metropolitan areas)

Metropolitan Area	Year	REPORTED MET AREA WORKERS	THOSE WHO WORK IN THE CITY	THOSE WHO WORK IN THE SUBURBS	THOSE WHO LIVE AND WORK IN THE SUBURBS		CITY'S SHARE OF METRO AREA JOBS
		figures in thousands of workers			number	percent	percent
New York	1970	4,943	3,172	1,771	1,593	77.7	64.1
	1960	4,929	3,511	1,418	1,267	74.9	71.2
Los Angeles–	1970	2,483	1,133	1,350	1,053	78.6	45.7
Long Beach	1960	2,432	1,270	1,162	947	68.8	52.2
Chicago–Gary–	1970	2,737	1,438	1,299	1,065	73.2	52.5
Hammond	1960	2,460	1,670	790	674	65.4	67.8
Philadelphia	1970	1,597	772	825	744	77.8	48.2
	1960	1,381	870	511	459	69.8	63.0
Detroit	1970	1,393	537	856	695	76.3	38.6
	1960	1,223	693	530	433	65.1	56.7
San Francisco–	1970	1,113	557	556	500	70.4	50.0
Oakland	1960	1,008	555	453	448	73.8	55.1
Washington D.C.	1970	1,089	492	597	544	66.7	45.1
	1960	757	483	274	238	52.8	63.8
Boston	1970	988	374	614	564	74.2	37.8
	1960	920	409	511	467	70.8	44.5
Pittsburgh	1970	786	286	500	465	76.2	36.3
	1960	762	274	488	465	83.0	36.0
St. Louis	1970	809	340	469	426	70.0	42.0
	1960	661	401	260	239	59.9	60.7
Baltimore	1970	723	368	355	282	67.3	50.1
	1960	591	390	201	164	61.4	65.9
Cleveland	1970	726	392	334	273	56.9	54.0
	1960	646	463	183	159	47.7	71.7
Houston	1970	714	537	177	135	76.2	75.6
	1960	427	360	67	53	54.1	84.3
Minneapolis–	1970	694	409	285	227	56.7	58.9
St. Paul	1960	534	408	126	125	51.7	76.4
Dallas	1970	587	417	170	133	50.1	71.0
	1960	401	303	98	89	63.1	75.6
TOTAL	1970	21,382	11,224	10,158	8,699	72.3	52.4
	1960	19,132	12,060	7,072	6,227	67.8	63.0

SOURCE: New York Times analysis of Census Tract Reports, *New York Times* (October 15, 1972), p. 58.

states grew in total employment between 1967 and 1972 at a rate five times faster than did the Middle Atlantic states. Hardest hit have been major cities like New York, which suffered a net loss of 380,000 jobs between 1970 and 1975.[11] Since 1970, the growth of white-collar jobs in the Northeast, which had previously partially offset manufacturing losses, practically ceased.

Mirroring this shift in jobs has been an interregional shift in population. Since 1970, the Standard Metropolitan Statistical Areas of both the Northeast and North Central regions have manifested no growth. The moderate suburban growth in these areas has been offset by sharp declines in central city populations. For example, the Midwest cities of St. Louis, Cleveland, Minneapolis, Detroit, and Pittsburgh lost between 11.8 and 15.6 percent of their population between 1970 and 1975. Eastern cities also experienced substantial out-migration. The net out-migration of whites from the Northeast in the 1970–1975 period nearly equaled the out-migration experienced in the previous thirty years. In contrast, the South and West continued to gain population during this period, particularly the South, whose net gain tripled in the five-year period to 1.8 million. Five of the top ten American cities are now located in the Southwest Sunbelt.[12]

Furthermore, the plight of the cities that are deemed no longer economically profitable locations by the corporate structure is exacerbated by other major private investment decisions, aided and abetted by federal taxation, transportation, and housing policies that conspire to produce suburban sprawl. Sprawl is a direct consequence of employer-created job patterns, combined with uncontrolled land speculation supported by the self-interest of highway engineers, developers, builders, and construction unions and often subsidized by government at all levels.

The adage that people can vote with their feet if they are unhappy with their environment tends to distort reality. The single most important determinant of "why people move" has been shown to be "where the jobs are."[13] This means that corporate-elite decisions about where work will be available contribute significantly to the pattern of population movement to suburbia, to rural areas, to the South, and to the Sunbelt. Neither random citizen choice nor public planning has determined the basic pattern of population distribution; rather, employers pursuing criteria of profit, economic efficiency, and internal convenience have set that pattern.

Within this basic context of employer-created job patterns much room remains for the economic forces of land speculation. In the suburbs, investment in shopping centers has had a major impact on the sprawl pattern of population movement. In the central cities affected by loss of manufacturing jobs, population, and tax base, the chief governmental response has been to subsidize speculation in office and luxury apartment buildings through "urban renewal." Both speculative ventures have contributed to the spread of people throughout the metropolis—the former intentionally, the latter inadvertently, by converting central cities from places to live to places to do office work and be entertained.

Let us briefly consider these two forces in turn. Decisions to build shopping centers in rural regions are now made increasingly at the national level by "temporary organizations"—coalitions of real-estate entrepreneurs, banks, and large corporate investors, including national insurance companies and even large corporate and union pension funds. The nationalization of the investment process in shopping centers is nicely illustrated by a New Jersey-based development group which had developed eighty shopping centers in thirty states and was in the process of building thirty-six additional centers as of 1974.[14]

These kinds of large-scale investments no longer follow population flows but shape the pattern of population movement, so as to yield further profitable mobility.[15] This pattern of *mobility-inducing* investment is aided by favorable federal taxation policies on rapid depreciation and investment tax credits. It also has had the willing support of state and national highway planners, whose own bureaucratic growth needs are served by encouraging mobility, and thereby the demand for more and better highways. Needless to say, the auto-highway-rubber-oil-asphalt industrial complex remains supportive of suburban sprawl and the speculative investments that contribute to it.

But it is people like Frank Angelli, a seventy-one-year-old small-restaurant owner in the Hyde Park neighborhood of Boston, who pay many of the social costs of suburban sprawl. For Mr. Angelli, the large-scale land-use decisions of advanced capitalism have meant declining business and changes in his neighborhood's character and social life. In his own words:

> Back in the 40's you couldn't walk on the sidewalk because there were that many people walking around—shopping and visiting. Now you can practically have the sidewalk to yourself. We didn't have shopping centers in the 40's; Hyde Park was real busy then.[16]

The plight of Frank Angelli is a typical one among small business people located in urban renewal areas, as well as merchants in urban neighborhoods that have experienced residential out-migration because of suburban and interregional job shifts. Many of these small business people were dependent upon particular personal relationships with their clientele that could not be replicated in other locations.[17]

Nor is the small shopkeeper the only loser. As a result of decentralization of industry to the suburbs and the general decline in blue-collar jobs of all kinds in central cities, urban blacks do not have access to the same employment opportunity structure that earlier generations of white urban migrants enjoyed.

Attempts to "revitalize" declining central centers through urban renewal have only worsened the situation in several distinct ways. First, these efforts have subsidized large-scale capital investment with few strings attached. This has consumed public revenues that otherwise might be devoted to social programs of direct benefit to the poor. Secondly, renewal has converted many downtown business districts from retail, light manufacturing, and residential uses into large-scale "office parks" for technologically advanced corporate firms. This conversion of central business districts into professional-managerial "transactional" centers renders the central city increasingly incapable of absorbing the unskilled into the economy. This incapacity reflects an inherent contradiction of advanced capitalist technological development. By engendering changes in production, distribution, and demand, this development unavoidably "threatens to 'marginalize' new categories of working persons in all strata."[18]

Third, renewal has destroyed much existing low- and moderate-income urban housing, thereby initially worsening the market position of renters. Redevelopers, motivated by profit incentives, nearly always chose areas in or adjacent to central business districts, both because such areas already contained some elements of vitality and because they harbored good investment potential for large-scale luxury housing, office buildings, and shopping and entertainment facilities. Because Central Business District (CBD) rebuilding thus became the typical form of publicly subsidized redevelopment, the structures cleared to make way for renewal usually were the homes of low-income residents who typically lived in the less expensive, older portions of central cities adjacent to downtown. As a result of these publicly subsidized and sanctioned "market choices," approximately 70 percent of the people displaced by renewal by the late 1960s were low-income blacks. By 1965, although 85 percent of cleared land was previously primarily residential, four dwelling units had been destroyed by renewal for every one built.[19] This initially drove up rents by rapidly increasing the demand for the low- and moderate-income housing that remained.

By the mid-1970s, however, the impact of employer-related job patterns and centrifugal investment decisions had stimulated enough population movement to modify this urban housing situation. Many older central cities today have experienced so much out-migration that their problem is not too few houses, but too many dilapidated older houses, with people too poor to maintain them.[20] Maintenance subsidies in such older cities thus might be more fruitful than construction subsidies that help builders, developers, banks, and investors more than they do urban neighborhood residents.

A fourth shortcoming of urban renewal has been its general failure to stem the tide of housing deterioration in urban neighborhoods. Given the very structure of the renewal program, this defect was unavoidable. Local renewal administrators could build nothing but public facilities on cleared land. Thus if there was to be any redevelopment at all, it must be as a result of the willing cooperation of participants in the private real-estate market. This meant that, in practice, renewal sites were selected through prenegotiation or knowledgeable estimates of the likely benefit to private developers, rather than on the basis of criteria of maximum direct community benefit. In Newark, for example, renewal officials were faced with a dearth of takers for a renewal project that had cleared land on the basis of educated guesses of profit potential. Thereafter, in the words of one renewal official, "we let the redevelopers *tell* us where they want to build."[21] In such cities as Boston, Chicago, and San Francisco the potential market value of some renewal projects was such that they were chosen for renewal even though most structures in the area were sound and other more dilapidated areas were bypassed. Despite their physical soundness, because of their desirability to developers and investors, the areas were labeled "blighted" by renewal authorities to justify massive clearance and redevelopment.[22]

Finally, both urban renewal and the corporate desire for regional headquarters cities have undermined the urban diversity that has been one of the hallmarks of American cultural pluralism. To the extent that San Francisco, Atlanta, Houston, Boston, Phoenix, and Minneapolis all begin to resemble each other in function and form, social choice diminishes, as does the richness of our culture. When one city becomes the functional equivalent of the next—a standardized office-park for the managerial-professionals of the corporate structure—economy begins to transform the culture which was once its home.

Some corporate and government researchers have gone so far as to openly celebrate the growing trend toward "office park" cities, while ignoring the class oppression and standardization that are social costs of this pattern of urban development. For example, Louis Bolan, a vice-president of the Real Estate Research Corporation, recently conducted a 1,400-page study of twenty-five American downtowns for the Department of Housing and Urban Development (HUD). (Interestingly, the survey was conducted for HUD under a contract agreement with the International Downtown Executives Association.) The study found that, while downtown retail stores and residential population in and around central business districts continued to decline, office space, office employment, and total capital investment had increased significantly in the past decade. The report's tone is optimistic about the fact that downtown areas are becoming more like suburban office complexes than like traditionally heterogeneous downtowns. Indeed, the report suggests that the viability of future downtowns may increasingly rest with the people who work in these office parks rather than with the people who live in the cities' neighborhoods.[23] While the report makes no explicit policy prescriptions, its impact upon city planners may be to encourage them to continue supporting office park patterns of development rather than concentrating on improving the quality of urban living space.

The geographer Jean Gottmann has described this pattern of advanced capitalist urban development as the emerging "transactional society." In this sort of society, the dominant mode of work life (for the upper strata) consists of abstract transactions among people. Information is processed, distributed, and interpreted in these transactions. The performance of transactional tasks requires specialized technical training and advanced educational credentials. In Gottmann's view, the chief social consequence of this trend is the transformation of modes of work. The "Manhattanization" of San Francisco, Atlanta, Houston, Phoenix, and other major urban centers represents a proliferation of the prototypical transactional hub to a broad spectrum of regional command and control centers. It also represents a redistribution of the opportunity structure geographically, but its concentration vertically. That is, as transactional jobs grow in urban centers in all geographical areas, jobs in the more traditional manufacturing sector continue to shrink. This creates "surplus labor that is difficult to reconvert rapidly for . . . [transactional] usefulness."[24]

Yet because the average level of prosperity rises, the illusion is created that many of our central cities (particularly in the South and Sunbelt) have once again become centers of economic opportunity. This, in turn, prevents people from seeing the very real class inequities that the "transactional" pattern of urban development entails for the unskilled, the untrained, and the unwanted. It also conceals the continuing average economic decline in those other cities that, for one reason or another, have been bypassed as corporate transactional centers or as beneficiaries of urban renewal, defense installations, aerospace research and development facilities, and other government-subsidized capital investments.

Indeed, the very same study that took heart in the rise of office park cities also noted that the much heralded "back to the city" movement has been more symbolic than real. This is because the overall shift of manufacturing, commerce, and employment continues to be centrifugal, accompanied by a gross shift in income away from central cities.

Where the affluent middle-class "back to the cities" movement has had some appreciable impact, as in such central-city neighborhoods as the Irish Channel of New Orleans, the Adams-Morgan section of Washington, D.C., and Boston's South End, the net impact of this in-migration has been harmful to the lower and working classes. It has driven up rents and property tax assessments; caused many evictions and much displacement and dislocation among low- and moderate-income residents; and reduced the social heterogeneity of these neighborhoods by driving out the nonaffluent. The dislocation caused by individual moves is compounded by developers who purchase entire blocks, evict low-income tenants, and convert their former homes into high-rent apartments and townhouses. They then cash in on the emerging upper-middle-class demand for proximity to urban work, entertainment, and cultural facilities. Furthermore, because many of the new migrants are young, childless couples, support for urban public education has declined. The upshot of the "back to the cities" rehabilitation movement is nicely captured by a rhetorical question posed by a low-income neighborhood leader at a recent meeting of the National Association of Neighborhoods: He asked: "Who are we rehabilitating neighborhoods for? For the people who are there, or for the middle class moving back in?"[25] The answer is painfully obvious.

Aside from white-collar "transactional" jobs, the principal job markets in central cities have become government services and low-paying jobs in restaurants, hotels, entertainment centers, clerical work, and other fields of personal service. Central-city locations still offer corporate headquarters the face-to-face access needed for financial, managerial, and sales transactions and a concentrated supply of clerical personnel needed for typing, data processing, and other office support services. These latter personnel tend to be women who are paid on a separate and less costly wage structure.[26] Thus, although there has been some recent outward movement of corporate office headquarters to the suburbs, this pattern has not been as pronounced as the flight of manufacturing from the city.[27]

Aside from the corporate office sector, the city remains the home of the secondary and tertiary sectors of the capitalist economy—the unorganized, undercapitalized, technologically underdeveloped small business, small manufacturing, maintenance, and personal service sectors. These sectors provide wage earners with incomes ranging from moderate to "working poor." They also provide too few jobs to employ the large numbers of unskilled migrants who came to the cities initially seeking increased economic opportunity. This contributes to a rise in persons eligible for public assistance and thus indirectly to increased white-collar employment in social service bureaucracies.

Consequently, major alterations in the opportunity structure of advanced capitalism since the end of World War II have radically altered both the form and the economic functions of major central cities. They have made the city at once an office park for the advanced transactional sector and a dumping ground for the working poor, the unskilled, the technologically obsolescent, and the unemployed—and for the public bureaucracies that regulate them. Neither changes in the work ethic nor overgenerous public policies have created the "urban welfare crisis."[28] Its root cause has been the uneven pattern of capitalist economic development I have been describing. The central cities merely experienced the consequences of national economic decisions, technological changes, growth and obsolescence patterns, and attendant migration patterns initiated elsewhere. These trends have been compounded by government policies that underwrote the infrastructure development of both interregional job shifts and suburban sprawl. It is to these policies that I now turn.

The Supportive Role of Public Policy Planning

An array of government policies, some deliberately, some inadvertently, have combined to subsidize, accelerate, legitimize, or otherwise support this process of privately planned office park cities, industrial relocation, and suburban sprawl. The most deliberate government effort to support advanced capitalist land-use priorities has been urban renewal. Instead of seeking to control the social costs of corporate development, urban renewal sought to subsidize the corporate structure's ability to redefine the form and the functions of our cities at minimal private cost.

Under urban renewal, from 1949 until 1974, three principal types of subsidies were used to attract private investors and developers. These included (1) subsidized land costs; (2) an interrelated package of federal tax benefits and mortgage insurance subsidies; and (3) local real-estate tax abatements. The sale price on cleared land packages that local renewal agencies assembled was generally "written down," that is, set at a rate considerably less than its cost to the governments involved. The federal government assumed two-thirds of the total net governmental cost of site acquisition and preparation, land clearance, legal fees, and other expenses related to assembling a redevelopment area. City governments were expected to assume the other one-third either through issuing general obligation bonds or in the form of federal "credits" allowed to the cities in exchange for other projects like street improvements and school construction deemed related to the renewal projects. This latter approach was often used by local governments to circumvent the need to directly confront the voters with approval of potentially controversial local bond issues for urban renewal. The upshot of this land cost subsidy to private developers was a substantial direct benefit, amounting to as high as $600,000 to $1 million per acre in New York City.[29]

Federal mortgage insurance subsidies were offered as an additional incentive to attract private developers. This made it possible for developers to participate in implementing the program by risking a mere fraction of total development costs. By agreeing to a nominally limited rate of return on investment, some large-scale United States developers actually managed to "mortgage out" of any financial obligation to the development project. Actual profits earned in this way were usually far greater than the stipulated low-yield return, because tax and other housing law provisions allowed additional financial returns resulting from rapid depreciation, management and packaging fees, and construction profits.[30]

Aside from these forms of federal largesse, many urban areas seeking long-term revitalization were willing to forego short-term income by offering local real-estate tax abatements to redevelopers and low-assessed evaluation on redeveloped property to business investors willing to establish facilities in project areas. These latter local incentives were deemed necessary because, even with the federal "write down" subsidy, the cost of large packages of land is generally high in and around high-density downtown urban centers. Additionally, the high cost of renewed property—which must be sold at market values—amounted to a disincentive for businesses to relocate in urban renewal areas; accordingly, selling project sites in many renewed areas proved difficult.[31] To compensate for these difficulties, local tax abatements to redevelopers and low tax assessments to business users were offered by many city governments, thereby undercutting hopes for renewal as an answer to urban fiscal problems.

Other government policies have supported the out-migration of industry to the suburbs, reinforced the nation's heavy reliance on the private automobile, and thus added to the high-energy costs and urban fiscal woes that these patterns of development entail. During the 1950s and 1960s, Federal Housing Administration (FHA) mortgage policies insured one of every four suburban housing starts.[32] The FHA's terms for insuring the purchase of older homes in the central cities were far less generous. This meant that even those moderate- to middle-income people who might have wished to remain in the central cities found that a move to the suburbs was the least expensive means to solve their particular housing needs. The ensuing publicly subsidized population and tax base loss for central cities was, of course, a major economic gain for large developers of new housing subdivisions.

The National Defense Highways Act of 1957 provided funds to absorb 90 percent of interstate highway construction cost. The act created a separate Highway Trust Fund that earmarked federal gasoline taxes for the specific purpose of road building. This insured that highway construction would not be subject to the normal vagaries of the political process for appropriating public expenditures. It also meant that the economic interests of automobile manufacturers and the highway construction, petroleum, and rubber industries would have a guaranteed market for future profitability.

Since the act provided no aid for mass transit, state governments naturally chose to link cities and growing suburbs by means of highways.[33] As more highways were constructed, the flight of industry to the suburbs became more convenient and thus accelerated. More people began to relocate to suburban areas in response to the combination of employer-created job patterns and federal highway planning and mortgage insurance policies. Massive shopping centers sprang up to stimulate land investment and tract development in surrounding areas. Urban renewal continued to help create office park central cities for affluent white-collar workers.

All these developments necessitated increased reliance on the private automobile. Affluent professionals and managers continued to commute into central-city office headquarters. Many blue-collar workers, who lacked the means to relocate to the suburbs where the factories had moved, were required to "reverse commute." Those who could move to the suburbs often were required by the opportunities available to them to live in one community, shop in another, and work in still another. The ensuing pattern of commuting, reverse commuting, and intersuburban commuting meant more highway travel, more gasoline consumption, more taxes for the Highway Trust Fund, and more money to build still more highways. This meant still more opportunities for investors and developers to profit by developing cheaply acquired vacant land into still more housing tract developments, shopping centers, industrial parks, entertainment districts, and the like. The cycle of suburban sprawl became an endless extension of advanced capitalist culture and social structure, supported by vital public policies that socialized the costs of the infrastructure developments (i.e., roads, water and sewer grants, urban renewal) that made this pattern of privately profitable land speculation possible. These policies did very little to socialize equitably the benefits of uneven economic development, save for providing regressive tax deductions for home ownership that further accelerate suburban sprawl.

Federal investment decisions also have aided the process of interregional job shift from heartland to rimland. For example, the three largest Sunbelt states—California, Texas, and Florida—received twice the defense contracts and payrolls, nearly twice the Highway Trust Fund expenditures, and nineteen times more agricultural subsidies during 1974 than did the three largest "Snowbelt" states—New York, Pennsylvania, and New Jersey—in the previous year. Similarly, the high technology industries located in the rimland states rely far more heavily upon federally subsidized research and development costs than do comparable industries in the North Central and Middle Atlantic regions.[34]

The Sunbelt's economic growth has been spurred by the ability of states in this vast southern rimland to extract a disproportionate share of federal tax revenues in comparison with the contributions of their taxpayers to the federal treasury. Major federal subsidies to the economic development of this region have included the Tennessee Valley Authority; huge military and aerospace installations such as the Marshall Space Flight Center, and over 140 other major installations; almost one-half of all Pentagon research contracts, and large subsidies for energy exploration and development. In states such as Louisiana, Georgia, and New Mexico the defense industry is the largest single employer. In 1974 alone, the Sunbelt states received $15 billion more in federal subsidies than they paid into the treasury.[35]

Houston is a paradigm of the urban development that results from corporate land use and investment planning subsidized by federal tax revenues. In Houston, over 150 corporations have located headquarters or major branches in the metropolitan area since 1970. This shift has led to a pattern of population growth of over 1,000 people a week. To keep pace with this pattern of growth, Houston annexes increasing suburban territory, thereby perpetuating a suburban sprawl pattern of development. Houston's economic boom is largely a function of its reputation among corporate elites as a metropolis that harbors an "excellent business climate." Yet Houston's apparent prosperity has not trickled down to the city's lower social strata. The state of Texas has neither corporate nor personal income taxes. It is characterized by low government spending, minimal indebtedness, and weak unions. Texas ranks dead last in expenditures for the retarded and pays low workman's compensation. Because of its unwillingness to support social welfare programs, Texas actually ended the 1975 fiscal year with a $1.5 billion budget surplus. This laissez-faire climate has contributed directly to the tragedy of desperate poverty amidst opulence.[36]

Despite much criticism of all the privately planned but publicly subsidized economic and land-use changes described above, federal government policy planners have been unwilling or unable to break out of the apparently endless cycle. Two prominent attempts to do so are especially noteworthy because they illustrate the mental blinders and systemic constraints that prevent federal policy planners from moving to transform the economic structure that is the root cause of urban social problems, job dislocation, and suburban sprawl.

The Final Report of the President's Task Force on Suburban Problems. This seven-volume report strongly criticizes suburban sprawl for contributing to blight, social homogeneity, cultural dehydration, scattered public services, and a decline in the sense of community.[37] Paradoxically, the *Final Report* recommends that suburbia be opened to blacks, other minorities, and people of moderate incomes who currently are sealed off from this less than satisfying living environment. Instead of seeking to reverse the trend toward sprawl by making urban neighborhoods more livable, the Task Force recommends more public and private capital investment in outlying areas, additional housing aids to veterans and the elderly to locate there, minority out-migration from central city neighborhoods, and subsidies to build still additional "new communities." But if past patterns of capital investment, land speculation, government mortgage subsidy policy, and highway building have taught any lesson, it is that further geographic dispersal of the population can only compound the key problems underlined in the *Final Report,* in addition to consuming energy needlessly and adding to environmental pollution. The chief beneficiaries of these socially absorbed costs would be the usual private planners of rapid geographic mobility—developers, land investors, the highway lobby, insurers, realtors, home and highway builders, the transportation industry, banks and other credit institutions, and those who supply this complex of interests with goods and services.

Yet the *Final Report*'s authors continue to rely on the same old "urban renewal" strategy whereby the public treasury pays for the infrastructure costs of private development (e.g., water and sewerage, land acquisition, site improvements), disguised as "public planning." The only difference is that the *Final Report* recommends that renewal be made a state rather than a local activity, thus increasing its scope and impact. This approach amounts to what social critic Paul Goodman would term a "compulsion neurosis." Government planners seem destined to ward off panic by repeating their past failures on an even larger scale. That the policy planners who prepared this document were only partially aware of their neurosis is suggested by the following revealing passages from the report:

> Out of regard for private property rights, the power of the community to achieve development toward social goals which expresses its social values is strictly limited to either exhortatory devices (such as advisory comprehensive plans without enforcement provisions) or regulatory devices such as zoning, whose provisions are basically proscriptive and negative.
>
> Similarly, development decisions made in the market place are multitudinous and uncoordinated—dictated by the values of the market place, which are not necessarily consistent with the social values of the community. At the same time, a nation founded on principles of freedom and individual-

ism must remain vigilant against unwarranted encroachments by government on property rights and the free functioning of an economic system on which the nation's productivity and prosperity basically depends.[38]

Contradictorily, the federal government

must get its own house in order, coordinate its own activities and stop dealing with problems relating to the suburbs in such a piecemeal fashion that it not only undermines their effectiveness, but discourages local and state authorities from taking more comprehensive and coordinated approaches. It is a notorious fact that instances are to be found throughout the United States where the actions of one federal program have undercut or interfered with those of another—where decisions of the Bureau of Public Roads have interfered with urban renewal projects financed by the Department of Housing and Urban Development; where federal sewer and water grants have encouraged urban sprawl by private developers rather than guiding that same development in accordance with locally established master plans.[39]

The answer to this contradiction? The policy planners recommend more of the same—more suburban development, more public subsidies of private profit, more infrastructure support services—in a word, more of what some social critics have termed "socialism for the capitalists." To wit:

Land is the suburban frontier's major resource. To a great extent achievement of the Nation's housing and recreational goals will depend in large measure on suburban sites. Suburbia is where the land is: it is where the home building industry concentrates; it is where land is still available at prices lower than in the city and often in vast quantities; and it is where cost can still be kept down. . . .

[We] are using larger tracts of land for urban growth activities. New airports need thousands, not hundreds, of acres. Factory "spreads" often need one parking space per employee and great tracts for future growth. Nobody with good sense buys land just for today's needs—he buys for the future.

Today, planning and zoning have had only a limited effect on the quality of the development that has occurred because they at most can only serve to preclude certain types of development. But there is no iron law of nature that says our land development must repeat the mistakes of the past—and that haphazard, destructive use of land must continue.

The experience of such programs as urban renewal, multiple use of water resources and highway right-of-ways has established precedents for a stronger role for government in the process of urban and suburban development.

The cutting edge of these programs is a combination of three elements, namely: (1) the power of eminent domain for site assembly; (2) the authority to dispose of land to private and public developers for development in accordance with governmentally-prepared plans; and (3) the power to spend public monies to provide facilities required to achieve desired development.

The Task Force recommends a greater direct public participation in the land development process to facilitate more orderly growth in the private market and to permit public sharing in the new wealth created by the process of metropolitan growth.

The Task Force recommends, therefore, a federal demonstration program of grants, and long-term, moderate interest loans to assist the creation of State Land Development Corporations.

Such a corporation would have the authority under state enabling statutes to acquire land and assemble sites; prepare development plans within local metropolitan and state plans; hold, lease, sell or otherwise dispose of land to private developers or public bodies; construct site improvements; borrow against pledges of future revenue; and contract for federal loans and grants.[40]

The *Final Report* on suburban problems goes on to recommend the creation of an Urban Development Bank (URBANK) to grant loans and technical assistance to suburban developments. It terms this proposed policy "creative collaboration between government and private capital," in the grand spirit of the Federal Housing Authority (FHA). The basic purpose of the URBANK would be to underwrite the capital projects which make up the infrastructure of suburban growth. No radical analyst of the American political economy could have been more candid in specifying the basic function of the state under advanced capitalism.

Lest any doubt remain about what this function is, the *Final Report*'s authors conclude their work by outlining "A Philosophy for the Suburban Future":

In our kind of society, to speak of better planned growth is not to speak of the imposition of arbitrary federal, state or local authority upon the form and function of our communities. It is rather, to speak of finding a reasonable balance . . . between the claims and rights of private property on the one hand and the interest and needs of the community on the other.[41]

The problem with this concept of "balance" is that economic growth usually is defined as a key "community" need. The cards thus are stacked in advance in favor of a "reasonable balance" that corporations, developers, and investors will find to their liking. And so it goes.

The Carter Administration Urban Policy Review. After eight months in office and in the face of heavy criticism from black leaders for inaction, President Carter ordered a critical review of federal urban policy. A cabinet-level study and planning group was called upon to create a comprehensive urban policy. A major facet of that plan now has emerged. Prepared by a Task Force on Urban Development in the Treasury Department, this public plan calls for a variety of special government financing arrangements, tax incentives, and grants aimed at luring business back to the cities. In effect, the proposal is a warmed-over and expanded version of the Urban Development Bank recommended by the earlier Suburban Task Force *Final Report,* but concentrated upon central cities.

Abandoning the direct-aid programs to low-income people favored by his most recent Democratic predecessor, President Carter's policy planners have apparently chosen instead to "stimulate the private sector to locate, remain, and expand in depressed urban areas."[42] Under the proposed Urban Development Bank this would not be done by introducing national public controls on locational and investment decisions. Instead, the plan would provide for tax-exempt industrial revenue bonds and other federal guarantees against financial risk to induce manufacturers and service industries to return to economically depressed urban areas. As with urban renewal, local development agencies could also issue local bonds to pay for specific projects of plant construction. The proposed "plan" also would provide a billion dollars in outright grants to help land development concerns obtain large tracts of land for development.

This sort of "public plan" is neither public nor an act of planning. It relies instead on government subsidies to stimulate private market mechanisms. It provides no protection for areas of the country that might suffer economic dislocation if plants and service industries left their areas to take advantage of federal subsidies. It relies on a non-comprehensive "project approach." Like urban renewal, this approach forces local areas to compete with each other for grants, federally guaranteed bonds, and other stimuli to private investment. Most importantly, it continues the basic supportive role the federal government has played to advanced capitalist development since the earliest days of federal urban policy. President Carter's long-awaited urban development scheme promises only more of the same—more transfer payments of public monies upward in the economic structure in hopes that these subsidies will eventually trickle down to the poor, the dislocated, and the jobless and underemployed, who are the principal victims of the uneven pattern of capitalist economic development. The compulsion to repeat is apparent once again.

Since neither the corporate structure nor the state can be counted upon to reverse the trends we have been discussing, some have placed hope in the creative potential of the planning profession itself. But if past experience is any guide, such hopes are not well founded. City planners in capitalist settings have more often aided rather than challenged the major thrusts of private corporate planning. Let us now consider the role that planners have played in the urban development process.

CITY PLANNING AND ADVANCED CAPITALISM

Daniel Burnham, a turn-of-the-century Chicago architect, introduced his Master Plan for Chicago with the exhortation: "Make no little plans," for they lack the "magic to stir men's blood." This statement, along with the self-justifying rhetoric of the planning profession about the need for "strong statements," "rational-comprehensive land-use controls," and "objective planning" by centralized urban designers, has helped perpetuate a mythical image of urban planning. This image permeates the critique of urban planning offered by Richard Sennett and to a lesser extent Theodore Roszak. It is the image of rational-comprehensive planning advanced by Louis Wirth as an ideal model, but taken by many critics as an actual picture of the way urban planners function in the real world.

According to this model, the planner is the scientifically objective, value-neutral architect of "orderly development." The planning processes envisaged in this model are a centralized process of urban design and execution by technical experts philosophically committed to their vision of the general public interest. In calculating public costs and benefits, such central planners employ the most advanced rational methods of data gathering and analysis, simulation models, and systematic evaluation of all possible ends and means. This methodology of calculative-instrumental rationality is essential to Wirth's system-level and to Freud's individual-level ideal for society, but is most troubling to social critics like Roszak, Sennett, and Simmel.

Ironically, it is Richard Sennett, a chief critic of rigidified modes of thought, who furthers a stereotype of planners as autonomous technocrats pursuing apolitical goals. Like sociologist Daniel Bell, his analysis furthers the illusion that "knowledge elites" are converting their expertise into an autonomous power base.[43] The realities of planning practice in urban design do not support this view.

Planning is a value-laden activity. Value choices affect what planners define as "problems," the type of data they gather, the standards they use for interpreting their data, and the very aims of their research and analysis. In capitalist societies, urban planners have tended to serve the values and interests of corporate capitalist city builders and suburban developers, rather than making key land-use decisions themselves. Theodore Roszak acknowledges (but treats as a temporary condition) the fact that planners work within limits set by those who can pay their bills. Their chief political function is to cloak the major private beneficiaries of the land-use and investment decisions that have shaped contemporary American society, justifying profit seeking behavior as beneficial to the larger public interest.

The American planning profession grew out of turn-of-the-century urban movements for housing and recreational improvement for workers, "settlement houses," and educational reform. Subsequently, public land-use controls through zoning regulations became a focus and rallying cry of professional planning work, architects and engineers its major practitioners. The thrust of the early movements was middle-class, conservative reformism.[44] Their aims were to pacify and integrate the urban worker, to depoliticize public service delivery and make it more "businesslike," and to build "model tenements" to achieve social control over the immigrant slum dweller. They planned for such relatively limited goals as civic beautification, public parks, housing-code enforcement, and municipal zoning.

In practice, urban land-use planners have lacked the political skill and social power to fully realize even these limited goals. Historically, American city planning has stressed civic beautification and public investment in monuments, parks, and, later, subsidized highways and urban renewal, rather than public controls of private investment and development decisions. In thus defining their mission narrowly, land-use planners have accepted as a "given" the basic economic structure of American capitalism. Working within these boundaries, both early and more recent urban planners have defined problems in ways that contributed to the system's smooth functioning. They have assumed that economic growth was an unmitigated benefit to the "community-as-a-whole." They have worked to reduce the unpleasant visual blight that might be interpreted as a negative consequence of the economic organization of advanced capitalism. They have planned parks, at times, explicitly to "tranquilize" the factory laborer out for a day in the open air, so that he might gain "the recuperation of force" needed to perform his job efficiently.[45] They have resisted the "politicization" of decision-making processes that built "office park" cities and sprawl-inducing highways and suburban shopping centers.

Zoning, the major effort at "public" controls by traditional urban planners, has amounted to an instrument for enhancing private property values. It has won an upper-middle-class base of support for a very limited conception of "planning" that excludes facilities from upper- and upper-middle-class residential enclaves that might have provided employment and housing opportunities for the working and lower classes.[46] In addition to exclusionary zoning, other goals pursued by suburban planners—low-density zoning, efficient service delivery, and better highways—also serve the class interests of middle-class commuters, while implicitly denying housing, a taxation base, and mass transit benefits to those left behind in central cities.

Sharing the professional-managerial values of their masters, land-use planners have acted in ways that deny the complex cultural pluralism of our society. Before the planning profession was rudely awakened by the neighborhood and poor people's protest movements of the late 1960s, they remained insensitive to the values and interests of nondominant classes and subcultures. They supported the corporate economy's interrelated goals of growth, development, and "higher land uses," regardless of their social and economic costs to disadvantaged groups. As Warner Bloomberg has put it:

> Planners have thought in terms of industrial parks, not loft industry; of people who wanted backyards, not those who enjoyed streetlife. They have neither designed neighborhoods for poor people nor called for the economic programs which would minimize need for such designs.[47]

Wirthian urban sociology, upon which much urban land-use planning is based, implies a general theory of society, namely, that spatial forms engender social relationships and that the physical environment determines the cultural patterns of human communities. This sort of theory can become a powerful depoliticizing weapon in the hands of policy makers and planning elites. As Manuel Castells has pointed out: "Such a 'theory' is extremely useful to ruling political elites inasmuch as it conceptualizes social organization as depending less on social data, in particular class relations, than on natural, spatial, technical, and biological data."[48]

In the American context, many "antiurban" planners operating from this perspective have sought to use environmental engineering to alter spatial forms in ways that could avoid the risk of systemic crisis and class antagonism, without changing the prevailing class structure in any basic way. This they did by building urban parks, enforcing residential zoning, and cooperating with the economic and political decisions that dispersed the once dense and heterogeneous urban population into separate residential enclaves throughout the metropolitan region. These measures offered those who were dispersed the illusory hope of escape from industrial life into an idyllic past. Yet no such measures can erase the very real social divisions inherent in a class-stratified society.

Thus, to further the illusion that social contradictions are amenable to spatial engineering, the specialized language of physical planning is invoked to mystify thought. As this language becomes further and further enmeshed in the technical vocabulary of the organization of space, social-conflict groups are gradually disarmed. Technocratic planning defuses political struggle. What is more, the pursuit of profits is justified by reference to the spatial model. Often viable social communities are labeled "dense" and "crowded" slums. These areas are bulldozed, their land uses altered, and the class exploitation of displaced residents is disguised as a form of "help."

In part because of such mental blinders, in part because of the structure of the privately induced public policies within which they worked, in part also because of professional self-interest, urban land-use planners in the 1950s and 1960s often became willing tools in the hands of economic and political dominants. They "managed" the ritual of "citizen participation" in public planning to symbolize accountability and popular control of policy, while in fact shunting aside the residents of areas that were bulldozed to build highways, high rises, luxury apartments, office parks, and sports arenas. This role of city planners as supporters and legitimizers of private investment decisions is nowhere clearer than in the case of urban renewal policy making. Accordingly, it is to this facet of urban land-use planning that I now turn to illustrate the foregoing argument in some detail.

Urban Renewal, Legitimation, and Class Interests

The official goals of urban renewal planners were closely related to their need to accommodate to the needs of major economic interests, without whose support their program would yield minimal results. Planning conceptions supported by private redevelopment interests and accepted by relevant federal and state agencies needed to be "sold" and implemented by city governments and local renewal agencies. This made it difficult to incorporate major objections of neighborhood protest groups into urban renewal plans. In addition, over a period of time, renewal planning officials came to share the perspective of the interests they served. The resulting shared commitment to maximize "higher and better land uses" combined with the normal administrative desire to "get on with the business at hand." These major imperatives prompted a search by renewal planners for effective ways to cope with the pressures of local protest groups that they tended to view as obstructionist.

In the early years of urban renewal implementation, renewal planning elites often reacted to citizen group demands by *symbolic deflection*. As Murray Edelman has shown, the use of symbolic language and gestures detracts attention from tangible issues of resource allocation. Symbols evoke and reinforce abstract values, attitudes, and beliefs. In most cultures, symbols of governmental action are enmeshed in deep-seated popular attachments to authority and protectiveness, thereby making challenges to public authority problematic. Symbolic language oversimplifies political reality in ways that evoke support for a speaker or his proposals or cast doubts upon those labeled as dissidents. These oversimplifications and distortions are designed to induce political quiescence or political arousal.[49]

In urban renewal planning, the symbolic use of public settings and presentations often successfully deflected citizen demands. At formal public sessions, as well as in media campaigns which preceded such events, renewal planning officials argued that federal renewal subsidies were crucial to the continued growth and survival of the community because limited resources were available locally. This argument was often readily accepted by most reference groups, because most citizens realized the general financial difficulties facing central cities. Statistics about budgets and municipal debts were quoted to support the general argument, but citizens lacked the technical competence to review specific claims. Renewal officials argued that because of the fiscal plight of the city, they were constrained by prior agreements between themselves and higher levels of government. Therefore, any major modifications in proposals might upset the delicate balance and shut off badly needed renewal subsidies. These higher governmental levels often appeared remote and inaccessible to the average citizen. When the imagery of "the Feds" is invoked, the situation may seem inevitable, local control impossible, and protest a waste of time. By thus focusing attention on higher political units, the crucial role played by private developers in shaping the prenegotiated redevelopment project often was overlooked or downplayed.

Also overlooked was the rather limited control that agencies within the Department of Housing and Urban Development (HUD) often actually exercised over local renewal planning once private developers and other major corporate interests had lined up in support of redevelopment. Pressed by national political forces to show "results," the Urban Renewal Administration frequently "winked at" Workable Program violations and accommodated itself to interests whose support was crucial to achieving visible results. Final federal approval came once a redevelopment package had been prenegotiated with private real-estate interests and a local elite consensus had been built. The federal agency's effective choice often was "between this project and no project."[50] Additionally, the ideology and limited staff capacity of regional and national HUD officials weakened its effective control over the renewal process. Large city redevelopment agencies often had more sizable and technically competent staffs than federal regional offices that nominally supervised renewal activities. The staff personnel it did have working in this area generally were sympathetic to large-scale Central Business District (CBD) redevelopment and thus were disinclined to monitor closely projects which promised comprehensive results. Yet, whatever the reality of particular intergovernmental relationships, the belief that matters were beyond local control served to induce fatalism and quiescence.

In local public discussions about urban renewal programs, the strategy of symbolic deflection was continued by various rhetorical appeals to the interests of the "community-as-a-whole." General public support was courted by planners emphasizing new commercial facilities, economic growth, better housing, employment, tax relief, a "city beautiful," and "clean industries" such as tourism and recreation. Renewal elites stressed that, in order to improve physical, social, and economic conditions in the long run, a troublesome short-term process must be accepted. This amounted to a kind of medical metaphor: "Every surgery is painful, so also is urban renewal."

To bolster their image of general responsiveness without actually having to respond to particular objections, renewal planning elites frequently employed language emphasizing their past accomplishments. For example, to preclude the mobilization of protest centered around lack of citizen participation, literature disseminated by the Boston Redevelopment Authority pointed with pride to the fact that its representatives "attended 155 meetings to inform numerous organizations in the South End about its planning concept."[51] At the same time, renewal planners justified unresponsiveness to particular objections by pointing to concessions already made and prior sacrifices of "good design concepts" to accommodate opposition. Statements issued by city governments, renewal agencies, and other local planning bodies extensively enumerated the major past achievements and future hopes of urban renewal. Boston's Master Plan took credit for reshaping a declining city into a "City of Ideas."[52] This served to justify its previous major projects that were beneficial to medical, scientific, and educational institutions and upper-middle-income housing development, and to justify the deprivations to low-status groups which such patterns of development entail.

Often the use of public settings was combined with the ritualistic display of technical resources. Prior to public meetings, colored maps and specifications of proposed plans were sent out to those likely to attend. At public meetings, blackboards, city maps, zoning plans, photographs, and models of future reconstruction were used as symbolic props. Often a staff of planning experts was introduced to explain different technicalities. Various specialists served to reinforce each other's public arguments; prior to public sessions, advanced staff meetings were held to iron out possible technical contradictions and to agree on a common position.[53] This was done so that neighborhood groups would be unable to detect and use contradictions among experts as a viable argument at public sessions. Expertise thus was consolidated to bolster public confidence in official plans.

Outside consultants were used to shore up support and reinforce the "aura of objectivity" created by the consolidation of expertise. Consultants were used to conduct preliminary planning studies and economic feasibility studies which served to legitimize massive land clearance. Well-known consulting firms whose work could be expected to be supportive of official agency goals were especially likely to be hired. Despite all this technical showmanship, in actuality the lack of careful demand and economic feasibility studies in many U.S. cities meant that land acquisition and clearance moved considerably faster than project disposition and ultimate completion.[54] In the long run, this gap between projection and realization served to undermine public confidence in renewal planning elites. Thus urban renewal planners eventually were forced to take into account the realities of adversary political interests. This they did by seeking to contain antagonism and conflict within the constraints of conventional political rituals that could be expected to defuse more abrasive forms of social conflict.

Ritual Conflict and Participation

As a close student of ritualized social forms, Georg Simmel was keenly aware of the fact that conflict, when it took the form of ritualized antagonism, could become a mode and a stabilizer of social order. This perceptive truth—that conflict behavior could become an ordered and routinized pattern of interaction—was missed by both Freud and Wirth, who assumed conflict to be a spontaneous and potentially disintegrative form of interaction. It also was missed by Richard Sennett, who welcomed conflict for these same reasons.

The formal planning practices of "citizen participation" and "pluralistic advocacy planning" are two such forms of routinized antagonism. The former provides a formal structure that symbolizes "openness" and "accessibility" to a congeries of diverse and potentially conflicting community interest groups, while masking the realities of concentrated power and social domination by key economic and political dominants. The latter carries this illusion a step further by providing subordinate interests with technical assistance and organizational expertise. This serves to disguise cumulative social structural weaknesses that require more than mere technical expertise to redress.

When attention is thus diverted from the content to the form of a political controversy, outcomes are likely to be altered. This has been true in the case of urban renewal—the formal responsiveness of renewal planners often has overshadowed lack of substantive responsiveness to grievances of low-status protest groups. By stressing the supposedly democratic character of such consultative processes as "citizen participation" and "pluralistic advocacy planning," various reference groups have been placated sufficiently to induce them to accept consequences of public policy that were incompatible with their material interests. Formal citizen participation in planning reassured outside audiences of the democratic character of political decision making. Those offered formal participatory status often were placated by their involvement in what was no more than ritual activity, granting participation without yielding bargaining power. When ritual participation in decision making thus induces cooperation and quiescence, the urban renewal program can basically proceed without resistance.

Ritual participation in decision making takes several forms. Formal public settings have been used to provide mass audiences with "pseudochoices" which heighten the illusion of choice and citizen power. In this situation, renewal planners have provided citizen groups with a variety of different "alternative plans," all of which basically were acceptable to the renewal agency and to its redeveloper, but which created the illusion of choice as well as of responsiveness. The alternatives introduced by the agency served as the basis for subsequent public discussion.[55] When citizen groups expressed choices among the available alternatives, the agency was in a position to accept costless pseudoconcessions, dramatize their actions, and take public credit for making concessions without actually having given up anything.

Citizen survey research is another type of formal "participatory" activity sometimes used as a substitute for citizen influence. To create a "sense of involvement," members of neighborhood groups have been invited to serve as unpaid interviewers in planning surveys. Using sometimes doubtful "one-shot" questionnaires and closed-ended interview techniques, renewal planners tried to determine "officially" the interests, needs, and priorities of residents. While data were being obtained, citizen groups were placated by assurances that the situation was under study. Once hard data were obtained, whatever the shortcomings, the interpretation of survey results was discussed with citizen representatives, both to heighten their feeling of involvement in policy making and to guide them toward interpretations favorable to agency priorities. If such gestures failed to placate a neighborhood group, the planning agency was still in a position to discredit the group by skillful use of survey data to challenge the group's representation of citizen attitudes.

Michael Lipsky has observed that defusing a political issue by using survey research initially serves a procrastination function.[56] Once a citizen survey is completed, it also can function as a potent symbolic weapon, insulating planners from outside pressures inconsistent with survey results and enabling them to lend legitimacy to the priorities of their corporate clients that coincide with broadly defined goals (e.g., growth, prosperity) supported in citizen surveys.

In addition to formalizing opportunities for participation in planning to gratify citizen demands, renewal planners also have symbolized responsiveness to popular pressures by verbal reassurances, piecemeal actions, and various other public gestures of sensitivity to the interests and concerns of protest groups. Assurances commonly are given that all urban renewal plans are tentative. As an example, in New York City a community representative objecting to various aspects of a large-scale Lower East Side redevelopment project underwritten by the federal Economic Development Administration was told reassuringly: "Don't get upset with anything you read in the proposal; we had to write it to get funds."[57] Controversial plans have been sent back to planning staffs with injunctions to consider citizens' objections. The impression thereby is created that renewal planners consider the objections to be serious and that original plans will be reconsidered. Yet, because citizen groups lack the opportunity and/or resources to monitor the review process, newly considered plans often simply are old wine in new bottles. Without close monitoring, verbal concessions seldom find their way into final plans.

To induce political quiescence, tangible rewards are sometimes offered in addition to symbolic gratifications. Tangible rewards may be collective or individual. In urban renewal policy making, collective tangible rewards have taken the form of granting or threatening to withhold low-income housing units, relocation payments, technical assistance to citizen organizations, and the material concessions which accompany piecemeal symbolic gratifications (e.g., relocation of stop signs). Individual tangible rewards have included the assignment of community leaders to paid positions within the city administration or redevelopment agency and offering cooperative citizen leaders future agency contracts or paid consulting work.

In the Western Addition, Mission Hill, and Hunters Point renewal areas of San Francisco and in the Shaw area of Washington, D.C., for instance, federally funded community organizations were designated as formal community representatives and were paid to "oversee" housing activities of the local Redevelopment Agency.[58] This close involvement with the agency's housing functions induced a cooperative posture with respect to its demolition functions. A more militant posture might have jeopardized citizen representatives' interdependent customer-supplier relationship with the agency. The promise of housing was used as a tangible inducement to promote cooperation and quiescence.

Under the rubric "planning with people," renewal agencies have granted technical assistance and "design concessions" to citizen groups willing to work closely with them. Such tangible concessions as the relocation of public facilities, stop signs, and minor design changes were exchanged for the support and legitimacy accorded to the land-clearance and displacement activities of the agency by means of a plan's endorsement by neighborhood groups. In the main, it has been others who have benefited from this process at the expense of stable working-class renters and the poorer residents who are the victims of displacement. For example, in the South End of Boston, an area regarded by some as a shining example of the success of "planning with people," thousands of low-income people have been displaced. The "consensual" goal of upgrading the area's housing stock that emerged as a result of the technical assistance granted to neighborhood groups by the Boston Redevelopment Agency has mainly benefited interests seeking a new hospital complex, as well as many upper-middle-class people seeking housing convenient to Boston's newer Back Bay office developments. The influx of new migrants has driven up rents, causing many long-standing moderate-income residents to leave.[59] Some low-income families were compensated by additional units of public-housing-level subsidized rental units, but not nearly in proportion to the number displaced.

Because the activities of citizen protest groups are often in the hands of a small number of vocal leaders, individual material inducements may succeed in producing cooperation and quiescence. The viability of the group is dependent on their voluntary time and their availability. If individual inducements such as jobs and promises of future contracts can be used to co-opt these leaders, future citizen protest activities can be hindered or permanently undermined. In San Francisco, for instance, in several renewal areas "the most vocal community leaders tend to be co-opted by the [Renewal] Agency, which places them on its staff in well-paying jobs connected with the Project Area Committees."[60] In other cities, grants of housing rehabilitation contracts have been used to elicit the support of community-based organizations by awarding the grants to development corporations founded by organizational leaders.

Co-optation is defined as "The process of absorbing new elements into the policy-determining structure of an organization as a means of averting threats to its stability or existence."[61] Where the community leaders so absorbed into urban renewal planning remained active in their groups, they sometimes became a moderating force. Alternatively, where co-optation of protest leaders failed to induce the support of their following, the planning agency often still gained by selectively dispensing material inducements. Such rewards were used to recruit citizen leaders to permanent administrative positions, contractual or consulting activities. Protest groups thereby were denied some of their most vocal and talented leaders. Lacking such leadership, the groups often experienced internal dissensus and recruitment problems, leading gradually to organizational decline and ineffectiveness. The upshot of both these developments has been an emergent role for urban planners as practitioners of a ritualized process of "citizen participation" in planning. The chief function of this ritual has been to stabilize and legitimize the prevailing political and economic order.

Other Roles for Planners

Not all planners operating on the urban scene today can be classified as witting or unwitting servants of centralized economic and political dominants. Some advocate planners work outside the established reward system, serving as volunteer advocates and technical advisors for neighborhood groups that are adversely affected by urban economic development planning. Others function as planners within particular urban social service agencies. These practice what has come to be known as "client-centered" planning. Their image of planning practice stresses planned public expenditures for social and economic services rather than land-use changes. They often believe it is their responsibility to introduce competing plans into the "marketplace of ideas." They, like neighborhood advocate planners, seek to become a countervailing political force on behalf of the poor and other disadvantaged groups.

In theory, this approach seems to represent an improvement of the situation I have been describing. "Client-centered" social and advocacy planners no longer assume, in straightforward Wirthian fashion, that physical structure determines social structure. They appear to be aware that both physical and social structure are powerfully shaped by the economic and political structure of society. At times this has led to political struggles between centralized physical planners serving economic dominants and advocacy-oriented social planners serving as spokesmen for either the clients of social agencies or the neighborhoods impacted by downtown redevelopment, highway expansion, or other "civic beautification" projects that entail land clearance and displacement.

Yet, in practice, we have seen that urban politics is not a simple marketplace of ideas where truth is bound to prevail in the long run. The very cultural context within which political debate takes place is itself powerfully influenced by the economic institutions that shape mass tastes and social expectations.

The economic structure of society influences the social structure by channeling opportunities to some and not to others; by creating life-style images that induce particular patterns of consumption and not others; by furthering patterns of land use and investment that segment workers occupationally and residentially, thereby reducing their opportunities for social interaction and the formation of class-conscious public opinion. Some analysts have termed the situation just described the "non-decision-making" process.[62] This process shapes both elite and mass perceptions of the kinds of ideas that are deemed "feasible" and "realistic" policy alternatives. The sorts of redistributive and public regulatory policies that might truly benefit the lower and working classes now occupying the secondary labor markets of our central cities currently fall outside the prevailing structure of power and opinion.

The implications of this non-decision-making process for the "pluralistic" politics of advocacy planning have been nicely captured by Donald Mazziotti:

> Social demands made by a group outside of the prevailing structure are predetermined by the capitalistic structure. For the urban and regional planner this linkage should be immediately apparent: the private automobile becomes a social necessity; urban space is organized in terms of private transportation; public transportation becomes a secondary infrastructure consideration; land use decisions are made in conformance with industrial demands and development markets; the social costs generated by industry . . . are absorbed by consumers . . . [63]

Aside from the self-reinforcing institutions and ideology that perpetuate commitment to a capitalist culture, pluralist advocacy planners are plagued by other constraints. When they function as supports for insurgent groups, they must rely on volunteer efforts, outside seed money, and a limited staff capacity. This reduces their ability to engage in effective special pleading. Furthermore, since there are no binding courts to which advocate planners can take their "case," they have been forced to rely on the public hearing as their main vehicle for gaining a fair hearing.[64] As we have just seen, the symbolic setting of public hearings systematically disadvantages insurgents representing particular segments of the city or the class structure. It systematically benefits those in positions of official power who can lay symbolic claim to broad constituencies such as the "community-as-a-whole." When such officials are themselves mere recorders of major economic decisions made outside their borders, the outcome of political conflict is anything but a rational weighing of social costs and benefits.

Furthermore, because low-income and working-class urban communities seldom contain indigenous institutions that can carry on permanent planning activities, they frequently become dependent on outside help to pursue their political struggles. If such communities do devote scarce resources to developing "alternative plans," this activity drains valuable time and energy that might otherwise be devoted to political organization and to the raising of levels of awareness about the political-economic structures and processes that shape the urban environment. Lacking organizational resources and political consciousness, such groups are frequently unable to create the level of conflict and resistance needed to reduce the social and class costs of urban development.

In the face of these sorts of political and economic constraints on their freedom of action, some planners have preferred to escape into the realm of abstract utopian visions. Following in the footsteps of the Italian architect Paolo Soleri, utopian planners dream of "mile-high cities," self-contained, encapsulated geodesic cities, or even space colonies.[65] In my view, this choice amounts to a kind of Freudian wish fulfillment. Unable to bear the harsh realities of poverty, blight, and class exploitation found in the decaying cities of advanced capitalism, such planners have chosen to escape into their own more malleable abstract images, rather than addressing the concrete contradictions that exist in the historical environment.

WHAT IS TO BE DONE?—THE POLITICS OF CONFLICT

Several recent developments in planning practice contain key elements of an alternative planning framework that recognizes the realities of ritual politics, the social costs of economic development, and the class interests that have stakes in urban planning decisions. A brief consideration of these new forms should serve to convey concretely a sense of an emerging alternative planning model.

The first sign of change has been a shift in emphasis within the mainstream of the planning profession itself toward the neighborhood as the appropriate urban planning unit. This shift has been accompanied by a growing skepticism about the value of master planning and the impact of unbridled economic growth. One indicator of this emerging doctrinal change occurred internationally at the United Nations Conference on Human Settlements, an urban planning meeting held in 1976. The conference, known popularly as "Habitat," issued guidelines for planning practice that contained a host of ideas once viewed as radical by establishment planners. These included public participation in community planning; large-scale land clearance as a planning tool only as a last resort, should revitalization of existing neighborhoods prove "unfeasible"; and the avoidance of "costly, wasteful, and ecologically destructive" urban sprawl. The conference guidelines were critical of the commitment of developers to economic growth at any cost. They also urged that planning priorities be based on local rather than national or international concerns and interests. A film shown at Habitat even went so far as to ridicule the once highly regarded, but clearly grandiose, design plans of French architect Le Corbusier. The theme of the film was that such sweeping plans bring blight.

Despite these signs, the conference report is very much a compromise document. Fleshed out following extensive debate, the report fails to specify conditions under which neighborhood renewal might be deemed "unfeasible." It thus implicitly continues to sanction major land clearance projects. The report contains other contradictions. While endorsing the neighborhood as the basic planning unit, it continues to call for comprehensive regional planning on the essentially Wirthian basis that there remains an urgent need to modify the boundaries within metropolitan areas "to correspond to functional and natural limits."[66] Nowhere does the report point out that, given political realities, such a shift would serve to dilute whatever leverage neighborhood groups currently can exercise in urban politics, nor that the shift would be likely to benefit those groups that can organize politically at this level, particularly private corporate interests. This lack of an explicit political consciousness is one of the chief weaknesses of the Habitat report.

To be sure, the Habitat planners espouse "social planning" as preferable to purely physical planning. But their report fails to acknowledge planners' actual historical role as political actors on behalf of specifiable class interests. In advanced capitalist cities, as we have seen, planners have tended to serve the interests of corporate city builders, using the rhetoric of the "community-as-a-whole" to mask both their own supportive role in the private development process and to cloak the actual beneficiaries of key land-use decisions in the symbols of larger public purpose.

As Frances Fox Piven has perceptively observed, this sort of critique of the "tunnel vision" of physical planning in favor of social planning, as well as the planners' advocacy of increased "citizen participation," serve a number of key political functions for the planning profession. Most obviously they provide the ideological justification for expanding the professional domain of planners. They also obscure the fact that the planners' involvement in past land-use decisions has led directly and unavoidably to various forms of race and class exploitation, such as forced relocation, decreased housing, and increased rents. By implying that poor communication (rectifiable by more direct citizen contact) and narrow vision have caused planners to overlook the poor, key elements of the social structuring of political conflict are obscured or denied. In particular, the vulnerability of people who occupy subordinate roles in the socioeconomic structure and the planners' own structural role as paid employees of dominant economic and political interests are obscured by the new rhetoric.[67]

Planning and Class Interests

A more promising sign of self-criticism has emerged in the city of Cleveland. The staff of the Cleveland City Planning Commission, headed by a conflict-oriented planner named Norman Krumholz, has openly abandoned any pretense that planners can function politically as aloof technicians, capable of designing some long-term "city beautiful" by the use of "objectivity" and abstract mathematical modeling. Cleveland's planners have come to recognize that if they fail to assume the role of politically committed activists serving the interests of the urban poor and working class, these groups will continue to be exploited by the economic development and land-use decisions of major economic and political interests.

They have apparently learned the lesson that the once unquestioned gospel of growth, development, and "higher land uses" entails heavy social and economic costs for those at the lower reaches of the social structure. The key question Cleveland's planners have begun to ask is "Who pays, and who benefits?" Krumholz has said that every planning proposal that has any impact at all upon the future may adversely affect the lives of the remaining residents of urban neighborhoods, while obviously benefiting developers, business users, builders, and construction unions. His words and actions have been aimed at reversing this cost-benefit ratio.

The commitment of the Cleveland Planning Staff is in some ways remarkable. It has produced a document, "The Cleveland Policy Planning Report," which spells out its basic philosophy, describes the Planning Commission's day-to-day operations, and advocates specific public policies to improve the income, housing, and public transportation facilities of city residents.[68] In general terms, the operating philosophy of the agency is to combine activism, class advocacy, and policy planning on behalf of the city's poor and its existing neighborhoods. For each proposed "redevelopment" project, Krumholz and his staff ask whether it can be clearly shown to provide more jobs at livable wages for city residents; what will be its impact on the level and quality of public services; and whether it will support neighborhood vitality or contribute to neighborhood deterioration. Projects which fail to meet these distributive criteria are opposed vigorously by the commission. As examples, Krumholz, thus far successfully, has opposed a new west side highway for Cleveland on the grounds that it would destroy too much existing housing and take too much money off the city's tax rolls. He also has successfully demanded reduced transit fares, expanded bus services, and assured a new "dial-a-ride" service for the elderly as the price for his approval of the transfer of the Cleveland Transit System to a regional transit authority. The Cleveland activist planners' basic approach is to choose immediate local issues, join forces with indigenous neighborhood organizations, and provide them with the research and other support services necessary to make their voices effectively heard.

Of course, not all of the Cleveland class advocate planners' battles have been won. Their unsuccessful struggles underline the chief limitation of the class advocacy approach—its tendency to trigger a backlash by economic and political dominants. For instance, responding to pressure from developers, the Cleveland City Council overrode Krumholz's objection to costly bridge and road improvements, paid for by the taxes of low- and moderate-income neighborhood residents but serving a proposed massive downtown office and apartment building project termed Tower City.

Yet a number of signs of change remain. The Cleveland planners have departed from the traditional planning concern with urban design and zoning in favor of direct action designed to cope with people's real personal problems, such as unemployment, neighborhood deterioration, and inequities in the accessibility of jobs, public services, and mass transportation. Moreover, they have targeted their efforts correctly. They seek to alter the shape of the commercial and financial decisions that have created urban social problems—redlining by banks, suburban relocation by business and industry, socially costly downtown redevelopment, and the like. Their single most important goal is to promote a wider range of social choices for those who have heretofore had few choices open to them. This is a distinct change in emphasis. The Cleveland planners also seem aware that people's choices are structured for them by the opportunities and constraints they encounter in their everyday life. This is why they advocate an "income strategy" that alters customs and institutional practices as well as redistributing resources.

But these structural changes cannot be achieved unless America's overall national opportunity structure is altered in basic ways. Thus a purely local approach, however encouraging, is not enough. The very context within which politics takes place must be transformed if neighborhood planning and class advocacy are to achieve any significant long-term expansion of social equity.

Still, it is a healthy sign when professional planners can support income redistribution and can declare, in very un-Wirthian fashion:

> No public action distributes costs and benefits equally among all members of society. Government decisions frequently raise questions of balancing the interests of suburbs against those of the central city, downtown business against neighborhood residents, rich against poor. . . . The Commission does not seek consensus. . . . When proposals appear to offer more benefits than costs to City residents—particularly the poor—the Commission endorses them. Those that do not are questioned and often publicly opposed.[69]

In this way, the traditional Wirthian image of consensus planning in the service of a rational public interest has been rejected in favor of conflictual planning on behalf of the powerless and the poor. Like Simmel and Sennett, the commission recognizes the useful functions served by social conflict—raising new issues to the political agenda; calling attention to heretofore invisible social costs; and most importantly, increasing the political costs of pursuing repressive policies disguised as rationally planned allocational, locational, and investment choices. The commission practices what it terms "protracted participation" and "vocal intervention." It wages a kind of guerrilla warfare inside the bureaucracy—channeling information, analysis, and policy recommendations where they will do the most good. It also takes an active role in "going public" with issues, if necessary. Confronting a fragmented public decision-making process, it tries to intervene in all the small decisions that lead up to ultimate policy choices having major public impact.

An example of how the commission's shift in perspective can redefine issues serves to illustrate how conflict, activism, and class advocacy on behalf of heretofore unarticulated class interests casts an entirely new light on the key planning question: What is to be done? Traditionally, urban transportation "problems" have been defined in terms of highway access, avoidance of congestion, and providing adequate parking needs. But these very ways of defining the problem beg the critical question of whose interests are being served at whose expense. Starting from the question: Who benefits from highway expansion, the commission has come to realize that, in addition to major auto-industrial and real-estate investment interests, the chief beneficiaries of highway expansion have been middle- and upper-middle-class automobile drivers, whose overall mobility has been enhanced by conventional problem definitions. Furthermore, those who do not own cars (over 40 percent of Cleveland's residents) have been forced to pay more for inadequate public transit facilities. The cost of these facilities has steadily increased, both because increased automobile ridership has reduced the use of buses and trolleys and because the widespread reliance on automobiles has contributed to low-density scattered development, making mass-transit facilities to these pockets of development economically unfeasible. The upshot is accessibility to fewer places, at higher fares, with longer waiting periods for the lower and working classes. The automobile society is inherently regressive in the pattern of social costs and benefits that it entails. Recognizing this unarticulated class interest, the Cleveland policy planners have taken their stand on the side of increased mobility for the "transit dependent" population in the form of fare reductions, more bus service, neighborhood-oriented transportation arteries, and avoidance of capital-intensive rail service that benefits the upper end of the class structure most. Their political victory described above is a victory for the poor, the elderly, and the "carless." It illustrates that even under our present social structure, conflict-oriented planning can bring the class contradictions of advanced capitalism to the surface and redefine the terms of political discourse.

A similar class-conscious approach has prompted the Cleveland Planning Commission to promote rehabilitation of the existing low-rent housing stock and direct subsidies for the poor through housing allowances, rather than subsidizing costly new housing developments that mainly benefit the class interests of developers, builders, bankers, and investors. The Cleveland planners also have refused to sanction any public subsidies of private development unless public benefits can be conclusively demonstrated before the fact; they have advocated federal income maintenance and public service employment policies and have called public attention to the fact that "The availability of employment opportunities and their distribution in the Cleveland area are largely a product of national economic conditions and Federal economic policies."

Most promising of all is the Cleveland planners' frank recognition of their actual past political role and of the possibilities of future political action. As Krumholz and his associates cogently state:

> Attempts to implement policies spell politics. This does not introduce politics into planning; it has always been there. The critical question is: whose politics, whose values will planners seek to implement?[70]

Class Interests and Class Consciousness

As the foregoing analysis should make clear, I subscribe to Ira Katznelson's basically Simmelian view that analysis of the urban condition must begin "not with value systems that hold the social order together, but with objective patterns of dominance that are essentially exploitative and that present those who dominate with problems of social control."[71] This is what Simmel's dialectic of resistance is all about. Simmel holds that every form of external repression contains within itself the seeds of its own destruction. This is done by putting people in touch with the core of their personality that is threatened by domination. If Simmel is correct, it becomes incumbent upon those who benefit from current patterns of social power to disguise their objective domination in order to defuse potential resistance. This they do by employing a variety of institutional buffers and symbolic myths that blur clear-cut lines of responsibility for social decision and deaden critical awareness of basic social contradictions. This in turn decreases people's capacity to act on behalf of their interests.

In *The Sociological Imagination*, C. Wright Mills calls attention to the growing gap between the apparent functional rationality of our social forms and the growing incomprehensibility of the social structure to the average person. As society becomes more bureaucratized, complex, and fragmented into specialized functional routines of work and life, individuals lose the capacity to understand the interconnections among the various parts of their social structure. Only from a few lofty vantage points in the social system can these structural forces easily be seen and understood. Most people are rooted in the limited milieu of everyday life. They cannot trace the connections between the structures and processes of society and their everyday cares and troubles. Events in the world often seem the result of inexplicable outside forces.

Those who control major socioeconomic and political institutions do little to fix clear lines of responsibility for decisions and actions. Thus those who experience unsettling troubles and wish to convert these into political issues often "cannot get clear targets for thought and action; they cannot determine what it is that imperils the values they vaguely discern as theirs."[72] Individuals cope with this lack of substantive awareness as best as they can. But each new "adjustment" to uncertainty slowly diminishes the will and ability to reason about their situation and to compare that situation to freely posited ends of a more satisfactory human existence.

Empirical research suggests that those farthest removed from the lofty vantage points described by Mills are especially likely to find themselves depoliticized by a sense of incomprehensibility and lack of control.[73] As a result of the realities described by Mills and Katznelson, working- and lower-class citizens generally are unaccustomed to abstract language styles and abstract thinking. Their lives are, of necessity, very concretely oriented toward immediate problems which they do not relate to a larger social context. Thus discussions about abstract ends, means, priorities, long-term planning conceptions, and long-term social and economic goals are difficult to follow, let alone to influence. As Claus Mueller has shown, the political import of the primarily descriptive, concrete, and particularistic language style of many working- and lower-class people impedes the instrumental use of language in politics. The shared limitation of this linguistic code is that the very categories used to comprehend and express reality are deeply grounded in the "here and now" aspects of everyday existence. Hence the available tools for cognition and expression do not easily allow for an abstract analysis or transcendence of one's current social situation. Mueller concludes that:

> Seen politically, this language reinforces the cohesion of a group which shares a specific code, but it can prevent the group from relating to the society at large and to its political institutions. The individual experiences his deprivation subjectively; cognitively speaking, however, he lacks the

reference points necessary to perceive the objective reasons for his condition and to relate it to the structure of the society in which he is living.[74]

In a word, what is missing is what Karl Mannheim and Louis Wirth would term "substantive rationality"—insight into the relationship between personal goals and the structure and processes of society and the polity which impinge on the probable realization of those goals. Such sociopolitical consciousness is generally a function of education and political experience, both in short supply in lower- and working-class urban neighborhoods.

This class-culture barrier to political cognition and action has several implications. It means that lower- and working-class people may have greater difficulty than middle-class citizens in perceiving and publicly articulating their political interests. Further, they lack substantial opportunity to develop greater political awareness through frequent political participation.

Finally, to the extent that political and economic elites choose to mute the symbols of external threat to class interests by eliciting the formal participation of lower social strata in urban planning, political mobilization is made immeasurably more difficult. This is because formal participation blurs previously clear-cut adversary role perceptions; creates new time-consuming maintenance tasks (e.g., attending planning meetings); creates ambivalence concerning group norms; and insures the defection of more militant and hence more activist group members. All these forces conspire to weaken a group's cohesion and undermine one of its major power resources—its potential for disruptive action.

What can be done to overcome these obstacles to class consciousness? It is my view that in order to insure the activation of heretofore repressed social strata, problems of everyday life must be linked to political structures that are neighborhood based, independent of the formal political and planning processes, and able to link small-scale neighborhood issues to the larger concern for basic changes in the pattern of class inequity and the maldistribution of wealth, status, and power. Why neighborhood based? Why independent? How can neighborhood consciousness be tied to class consciousness? Let us now turn to these basic questions.

The Basic Local Planning Unit: Metropolis or Neighborhood?

Why do I reject the Wirthian ideal of metropolitan planning in favor of the neighborhood as the basic local political unit? In part because metropolitanizing the polity would create serious obstacles to the possibility for organizing working- and lower-class interests into politics.

Commercial elites, banks, the mass media, utility companies, and corporate executives have consistently been among the chief backers of various plans for the creation of regional planning and metropolitan government. This is not at all surprising. These interests are well equipped to influence government decision making at that level.

Business elites in particular, while strongly resisting central economic planning by the federal government, enthusiastically support metropolitanwide physical planning. In addition to being well organized to influence metropolitan reformers, business elites tend to equate the public good of the metropolitan region with a "dynamic business climate." They remain confident that regional planners and decision makers share this point of view. Furthermore, they are aware that the diverse segments of the regional population are unlikely to become politically activated if the metropolitan region becomes the basic unit of planning.

This stems from the fact that the issues with which metropolitan planning units deal often seem remote from the immediate problems of the average inner-city resident. As one commentator has put it, if you were an inner-city working-class black, whose chief problems were housing, crime, and teenage drug abuse, why would you go to a distant public hearing to discuss regional land-use plans?[75] Furthermore, if a connection actually is made between personal problems and abstract issues, such as regional land-use planning, the size and remoteness of the planning unit can be expected to further the inner-city dweller's sense of ineffectualness.

A number of political costs would be entailed if class advocates, neighborhood leaders, and community organizers were forced to channel their efforts into "citizen participation" in metropolitan planning. At present, regional planning meetings are held in places far removed from their localities, making protest demonstrations at public meetings and hearings more difficult to organize. If large numbers of other neighborhoods have to become active at the higher level, each neighborhood's proportionate political influence is bound to be diluted. To the extent that regional planning and decision making require the acquisition of formal planning language and technical skills, creative energies are diverted from the goals of mobilization and community organizing. At decision-making levels as far removed from people's everyday experiences as the metropolitan region, the chances that elites will downplay concrete human concerns is even greater than when the "city-as-a-whole" is the basic arena of political conflict.

In contrast to these liabilities, decision making at the neighborhood level offers some distinct advantages to disadvantaged groups. It offers the probability that more diverse values will be factored into politics and planning. We have seen that our complex social structure has engendered a wide variety of subcultural value systems. Neighbor-hood-level planning and decision making make it easier to get beyond an outmoded "grand theoretical" approach to planning that focuses upon the urban dweller, while ignoring the different situations that structure the lives of a socially diverse and class-stratified metropoli-tan population. Because of this structured diversity, there is a need for urban politics and planning to specify precisely the social costs likely to be paid by each impacted segment of society when proposing so-cial, land-use, and other policies. Neighborhood decision making can provide a vital barometer of diverse subcultural values and prefer-ences. This in turn can make the measurement of social costs more reliable.[76]

If neighborhood planning is taken a step further and becomes gen-eral-purpose neighborhood control, other dividends may occur. Effec-tive neighborhood government may reduce the degree of political alien-ation that deprived urban residents now experience from remote and distant political structures that vest decision making in a complex web of professionalized urban social service agencies, intergovernmental re-lationships, and public-private organizational networks that blur lines of responsibility and deny people clear targets for voicing discontent.

Research suggests that both overcentralization and too much com-plexity contribute to political alienation.[77] The scale of government and corporate decision making contributes to a sense of powerless-ness; the complexity of the political economy to a sense of incompre-hensibility. Both powerlessness and incomprehensibility reduce people's sense of efficacy, thereby discouraging active political partici-pation. To illustrate, low- or moderate-income urban renters experi-ence meaninglessness when they neither see nor are offered good reason for an urban development decision that requires them to relo-cate their families; they experience powerlessness when they have no focal point toward which to direct protest against the decision. The web of public-private bureaucracy appears complex and impenetrable. This makes accountability difficult to pin down, thereby adding fur-ther to political alienation.

If neighborhood government is to reduce alienation, it must be gen-eral purpose rather than fragmented by policy area. This is because the addition of new governing bodies for each existing or emergent issue area would be unduly expensive and would only add further complexity to the governmental structure. Too much complexity is a major source rather than a solution to the problem of passivity and nonparticipation. If the targets for voicing discontent are clearly fixed, have comprehensive decision-making authority, and are sufficiently proximate to actual urban subcultures, these subcultures will be more likely to express political demands.

Local political life is more likely to stimulate widespread interest if the stakes are high—if, for example, key aspects of local community life such as work, housing, health care, and other services are placed within the potential control of localized communities. If decisions about housing, jobs, and public services are left in the hands of neighborhood political units that have decision-making authority, local political participation would in all likelihood increase, provided that national-level planning decisions insure localities of a stable economic base and adequate local revenues to meet basic needs. Apathy and alienation are born as much by the perception that local political life can do little to control powerful and distant bureaucracies as they are by anything else. If resources were reallocated to insure that the local stakes were high and that neighborhood involvement could make a difference, local political life would be likely to generate a good deal more interest and participation than presently is the case. It must be recognized that, with this increased level of interest and concern, both the coalescence of common interests and intense conflict among dissimilar interests would characterize neighborhood politics from issue to issue, and time to time. This, after all, is what politics is all about.

The Need for a "Push Factor"

Howard Hallman's studies of neighborhood development corporations financed under the poverty program of the 1960s suggest that some changes in human response can be expected if neighborhood governing bodies are constructed in an altered, more supportive, political-economic environment. Even under the conditions of the late 1960s, where Community Development Corporation (CDC) boards lacked the support of centralized political and economic elites, Hallman found that neighborhood residents came to view the corporations (CDCs) as "theirs," in contrast to their view of more distant public and private bodies as alien and impersonal bureaucracies.[78]

Yet resident satisfaction is not enough. People may be mistaken in their perceptions of the functions performed by neighborhood planning boards. We have already seen how easily the symbols of accessibility and responsiveness can be manipulated by political elites to induce citizen satisfaction and quiescence. For this reason, participation and resistance must become part of a single political strategy for the alienated neighborhoods. If formal political structures are to be made to work to fulfill the needs of neighborhood residents, both the political structure of neighborhoods and the consciousness of their people must become attuned to the Simmelian dialectics of political form and content, deliberation and direct action, participation and resistance.

Paradoxically, participation in formal channels and resistance to those very channels are dialectically linked. Without conflict, controversy, and resistance, as Sennett and Simmel have shown, there can be no creative social change. In the words of the late community organizer Saul Alinsky: "Controversy has always been the seed of creation."[79] Yet without control over formal channels, the basic victories of political struggle can never be recorded, refined, and implemented. Or as Robert Aleshire has succinctly put it: "Participation should precede action, but action is necessary to secure the interest of citizens and thus support their participation."[80]

Futurist planners, including many supporters of the basic arguments presented here, too often project and even magnify current trends and circumstances into the future while ignoring the dynamics of political conflict and social change. They uncritically embrace the abstract concept of "neighborhood planning," because it currently has growing support and seems to be responsive to both local desires and current federal policy priorities. What such people fail to realize, however, is that concrete historical reality moves sometimes by ebbs and flows, sometimes by sudden shifts, but seldom in predictable and linear fashion. Today's support for formal neighborhood planning may become tomorrow's opposition, particularly if basic neighborhood interests in urban areas (e.g., race and class interests) are forcefully pursued.

The crucial question thus becomes not so much what can be done to alter the formal governmental structure to make "rulers" more accessible, but what can be done to modify the overall political and social structure, to insure that, unless and until a truly participatory society can be constructed, people's basic rights and interests can be protected. The paradoxical dilemma faced by consensualists like Wirth and communitarian followers of Roszak's participatory commonwealth is that conflict behavior inherently is required to produce the momentum necessary to create a participatory democratic society, the basic goal of which is a new personality structure based on cooperation, group consensus, and social integration.

Perhaps the best that those who wish to build a cooperative commonwealth can hope for, for the present, is an approximation of cooperative behavior within the political and social organizations that provide the "push factor" for constructing the commonwealth. Conflict among groups and classes in a society that is both socially heterogeneous and class stratified cannot be wished away, as Simmel and Marx, and even reluctantly, Wirth, well knew. Instead of wishing away conflict groups, it is time to begin viewing them historically, in terms of their functional contribution to the dialectics of social change. Instead of bemoaning the fact that social subgroups exist and undermine consensual order, it is time to begin asking such questions as What ends do conflict groups serve; whose interests do they satisfy; what functions do they perform in promoting either social integration or change?

As a concrete example of the way that participation and resistance are dialectically intertwined, consider the following. In a comprehensive study of the actual political impact of Community Action Agencies (CAA) in twenty American cities, David Austin found that only in approximately one-third of the agencies where neighborhood participation was adversary was there a relationship between resident action and changes in any heretofore unresponsive urban institutions. The changes that did occur were a result of direct action by local community organizations and coalitions of associations in the CAA target areas.

An additional benefit of the adversary pattern of participation over more consensual patterns was the strengthening of internal organizational solidarity on the part of poor people's movements. The political struggle of neighborhood groups with the established local CAA Board provided the impetus for further political organization. In the adversary-oriented neighborhoods, local political and social movements were motivated by particular political struggles. The partial gains obtained by direct action provided the incentive to move forward independently on other important political and social issues.

Austin concluded his analysis of conflictual vs. consensual community participation by underlining the fact that "adversary participation" (i.e., conflict and resistance) provided neighborhood groups with vital training and experience in the fusion of staff work and adversary social-movement politics.[81] In our normally placid political culture, this represents no small gain. It represents a small-scale, but thus far permanent, modification of the basic sociopolitical structure of urban politics.

The importance of what Austin calls "adversary participation," and what I am terming resistance, is underlined by the inability of groups that have chosen to remain "insiders" rather than "adversaries" to modify basic institutional and structural patterns that systematically disadvantage them, politically and socioeconomically. Gaining inside "access" to policy makers is fraught with subtle implications. "Citizen participation" in planning is, on the one hand, a direct and formal "access point" to government officials; on the other hand, because it drains time and energy and raises the possibility of co-optation, it has proven to be a generally ineffective method of political participation for insurgent protest groups. Influence over policy outcomes can be gained without formal access in other ways. Government agencies may anticipate and partially accommodate group demands because protesters previously have gained access to the cognitive processes of governmental elites either through fear, sympathy, or the successful mobilization of publics to which elites normally are attentive.[82] Under these circumstances, protest group leaders also may gain informal "consultative" access to elites.

Paradoxically, the symbolic impact of this sort of "consultative" status actually also may serve to inhibit protest leaders' long-term ability to mobilize affected constituencies, maintain internal cooperation, and build political support from other reference groups. As Scott Greer has observed: "When two or more widely differing aims are allocated to the same social organization, particularly if the basic logic of these aims is not congruent, that organization appears opportunistic and lacking in integrity."[83] This perceptual phenomenon may work against protest leaders who have accepted informal access to policy makers. Protest leaders, whose perceived role is "agitation," may lose members when they blur this clear-cut adversary role by assuming other functions such as "planning" or negotiating "behind closed doors." This is especially true in the case of lower- and working-class neighborhood protest leaders, whose actual and potential followers lack identification with professional planners, and understandably tend to be chronically suspicious and cynical concerning the probable outcomes of "back room deals."

Supportive reference groups and the wider general public are also likely to view the acceptance of regularized consultative access with some ambivalence. The act of acquiring such access communicates to some supporters that all is well and that their sympathy and support is no longer crucial; to others it conveys the suggestion that an open and public process has once again become an insider's game. In either case, gaining informal access entails risks; it can undermine the protest leader's long-term opportunities to mobilize directly aggrieved people or to build political support from general and specific reference groups. To accept informal "consultative" access is to run the risk of being perceived as opportunistic and lacking in integrity.

Similarly, local protest groups seldom benefit from formal citizen participation structures, unless their formal participation is backed by their ability to maintain a credible threat of disruption and instability if their interests are overlooked. Even with such potential for open resistance, groups that have remained "outside" protestors generally have fared as well in achieving self-determined goals as those who have chosen to become "inside" planners. The American experience with pluralist advocacy planning is once again illustrative. In New York City, the availability of technical resources and formal "insider" status have been shown insufficient conditions for winning major planning concessions. According to Piven and Cloward, ten years of involvement by advocacy planners and neighborhood representatives preparing and negotiating an "Alternate Plan" for the Cooper Square neighborhood of New York yielded no more than delay in the original large-scale clearance plan and formal approval of a small portion of the Alternate Plan. The principal advocacy planner for the project concluded in frustration that the major accomplishment of warding off the threat to the neighborhood could have been accomplished by protest without planning.[84] Plans without power yield few tangible results. What they do is to channel neighborhood protest leaders into narrowly defined political roles which may drain their available time and energy, learning new roles for which they initially are ill-equipped.

The successful acquisition of formal decision-making responsibility by neighborhood protest groups may actually obstruct rather than facilitate the realization of group or class interests. This is because the very formality of the access granted to previously dissident groups blurs adversary relationships in the eyes of potentially supportive reference publics. Instead, formal access symbolizes the "fairness" and goodwill of elites, and the "openness" of the citizen participation process. Attention thereby is focused on the form rather than the content of political life. Public opinion which might focus on the substantive demands of protesters is reassured by the very existence of a formal channel which suggests that the grievances of the powerless are being considered in policy making. As Murray Edelman so perceptively cautions, the danger is that

> by focusing upon popular participation, by clouding recognition of adversary interests, by presenting authorities as helping and rehabilitative, . . . [formal participation] symbolizes the construction of elite power within narrow limits. Public attention then focuses upon procedures rather than upon their outcomes, so that the power to coerce, degrade, and confuse dissidents is greater.[85]

Conversely, power without formal responsibility offers some distinct advantages. Informal adversary protest activities often inform wider publics, thereby serving both support building and political mobilization functions. This politicization facilitates a wider dissemination of relevant political information. Without such heightened political consciousness, protesters become vulnerable to distorting symbolism that blurs their own class interests and the real influence enjoyed by those who do have the resources to shape policy outcomes.

In an interesting paper entitled "The Role of Alternative Groups in Creating Democratic, Community Controlled Local Government," Joan Rothschild has identified a number of important potential political functions that one particular type of resistance-oriented group, the "alternative group," can perform in a future urban politics.[86] "Alternative groups" are groups that are committed to member participation and control of internal decision making as an alternative to the traditional organizational pattern of hierarchical domination. The specific types of groups Rothschild examines closely resemble the prototypical countercultural organizations of Theodore Roszak's visionary commonwealth—co-ops, Community Development Corporations, worker-control experiments, community controlled day-care centers, alternative social-service institutions, collectives, and the like.

Unlike Roszak, who disavows political strategy, Rothschild sees such groups as capable of far more than serving as redemptionist models of democratic practice. Alternative organizations can become another component of the push factor I have been talking about. Member control of local social and economic institutions can become a needed first step toward more comprehensive political democratization and social change. Such groups can generate internal resources, organize communities, and engage in consciousness raising designed to demystify the cult of expertise. Additionally, their very existence serves to foster a spirit of experimentation with structures and processes that may make other institutional changes appear more feasible and desirable.

A function not suggested by Rothschild, but central to the dialectical perspective being developed here, is the role that such groups can play in "keeping honest" institutions that are formally responsible for controlling public policy. This informal function is especially important because of the patent deficiencies of existing formal "watchdogs." We have seen the ease with which "citizen participation" can become little more than a legitimizing ideology, uncritically cloaking the decisive influence of economic and political dominants with the aura of "grass-roots democracy." We have seen that moderate forms of pluralistic advocacy planning may serve similar symbolic functions by furthering the illusion that poor people can effectively compete with the corporate power structure if only they are provided with technical planning expertise.

Much the same can be said for that other popular formal watchdog, the "urban ombudsman." Research on the actual operation of ombudsmen reveals that such institutions tend to assume a passive role. Ombudsmen generally "wait for cases" rather than actively seeking to uncover injustice. In practice, ombudsmen tend more often to view themselves as impartial mediators between complainants and government rather than as citizen advocates.[87] The manifest function of ombudsmen is to channel complaints by individuals into the system, thereby serving to defuse protest by groups and classes against the system. The "ombudsman" constitutes a symbol of formal responsiveness to citizens "as a whole," while in fact operating only on a case-by-case basis. The ombudsman is a relatively inexpensive way for systems to gain public credit for equitability, while avoiding the need to address questions of systemic injustice.

Given these related shortcomings of formal accountability mechanisms, neighborhood groups, social movement protest organizations, class advocates, and alternative groups are well advised to remain "outsiders," using whatever pressure they can muster to prod the institutions that now control their lives. When engaging in direct action, such groups must avoid the pitfall of myopia. They must be continually conscious of the national economic forces that shape the opportunity structure. They must select their targets wisely, remaining cognizant of the need to alter the ongoing system for allocating resources among the various elements in the political economy.

In our society, the need for a resistance-oriented "push factor" is especially clear for yet another reason. Unlike Europe, we lack a self-conscious and well-organized parliamentarian political Left. There, new programs of participatory control of socioeconomic institutions have been formulated and in some cases even implemented by European socialist parties. Lacking such political structures, advocates of social change in America have been forced to engage in direct action to further their goals. Direct action is nothing more than the application of direct pressure by "outsiders" to obtain favorable actions and decisions without sharing in the official responsibility for them. In our current social structure, this option often has been a critical push factor. It has proven to be a necessary informal accountability mechanism because of the existing inadequacies of formal counter-controls already discussed.

Direct action likewise may be needed to secure the basic right to vest political control in neighborhood jurisdictions. This will be no easy struggle, for, as Reidel notes: "No one gives up power to others unless he no longer needs it, can no longer sustain it for personal reasons, or is forced to do so."[88]

The basic position argued here, however, suggests that even if at some future stage of political development neighborhood governments replace neighborhood planning boards, direct action will in all likelihood still be needed. Barring a major transformation in social structure or political consciousness, direct action by neighborhood protest groups and poor people's movements will still be required to prod neighborhood political elites, who themselves may become unresponsive to demands for political equity and social justice.

Social Structure, National Planning, and Localized Conflict

Heartening signs of political ferment at the local level are not without their ironic elements. Just at the time when some segments of the planning profession are beginning to redefine their professional role and are beginning to work on behalf of the values of the city's lower and working classes, and some neighborhood groups are showing signs of political vitality, key investment, location, and land-use decisions that can benefit these interests are increasingly being made at the national level. Once again Cleveland offers a good example. At the very time that Cleveland's planners were engaged in "protracted participation" and "vocal intervention" to uplift that city's neighborhoods, Cleveland's public schools were facing an early shutdown only a month after opening because of lack of operating funds.

This urban fiscal crisis is a direct outgrowth of the flight of corporate capital investment from Cleveland. As discussed above, older northern industrial cities like Cleveland have become the largest casualties of the flight of industry to the countryside, where land and operating costs are cheaper, and to the South and Sunbelt, where the level of unionization and labor's political and class consciousness are lower. In Cleveland, the out-migration of jobs, people, and wealth has shrunk the tax base by $200 million in the past decade. Since most of this decline was industrial, Cleveland's remaining taxpayers have had to pay higher amounts of regressive property taxes. Because of inflation, these increases have purchased proportionately fewer services. In many other northern cities faced with Cleveland's plight, taxpayer revolts have followed upon the increasing fiscal pinch.[89] Yet despite the obvious long-term "cause" of these cities' fiscal condition, commentators and politicians alike continue to blame such easy symbolic targets as "poor management" and "primitive borrowing practices," as if either management shakeups or higher debt ceilings were an adequate solution to the larger problem—the unchecked ability of corporate capitalist institutions to move to those spots on the globe where profits can be most easily maximized.

In the context of the ideas I have been discussing, I thus foresee a need to pursue two forms of national political-economic planning. Both would be designed to equalize the context within which localized conflict and decision making would take place. The first dimension is public control over major economic development decisions.

National-level public controls are needed to insure that the locational decisions of major productive enterprises and the investment decisions of major financial institutions be taken to maximize social need rather than private profit. Among the major social needs that public control mechanisms would seek to guarantee would be (1) balanced regional economic development; (2) ecological protection which insures that if the costs of environmental protection are socialized, the benefits also are socialized, rather than allowed to accrue to private corporate hands in the form of tax "incentives," higher prices, or both; (3) publicly directed investment in economically disadvantaged neighborhoods within metropolitan areas, to insure even economic development by social class; and (4) the provision of sufficient revenues to insure that each locality has enough resources to supply or insure basic material needs—employment, food, health, housing, education, public transportation, and energy. To guarantee these social needs would require the use of the federal tax structure as an explicitly redistributive mechanism. Once these steps were taken to allocate an adequate amount of stable resources to local political systems, the establishment of policy priorities could then be placed at the most decentralized level possible.

A second dimension of national planning for decentralized priorities would entail a cumulative series of steps to subsidize those forms of local social and political organization that could be expected to further the replacement of hierarchical by egalitarian social relationships. Political life is shaped by work life and by home life in particular neighborhood contexts. The interactions that take place at this level either encourage or frustrate use of people's active and creative faculties. Where work life is a hierarchically structured system of domination and subordination, where neighborhoods are powerless to affect their own development, passivity and fatalism, rather than social activism and politican participation, are encouraged. National public policies to encourage experiments in worker-controlled work settings and the devolution of real political power to neighborhoods can do much to alter this pattern. The goal of such subsidies would be to redistribute political experience. This goal would be achieved by (1) gradually introducing major changes in the very structure of social interaction (hierarchy) that heretofore has characterized work life; and (2) devolving policy-making controls down to a level that local social networks can have a real chance to influence.

Why is it important to link the strategies of decentralized neighborhood and workplace democracy and national controls over the negative "externalities" of corporate capitalist development? The answer to this question is complex. In contrast to the incorrect image of cities as composed of socially disorganized and rootless individuals, the research we have reviewed in chapter five reveals that cities in fact comprise a complex web of subcommunities, "variously organized according to the bonds of ethnicity, nationality, occupation, social class, life styles, and subcultural values."[90] Further, subcommunities are organized by the requirements of political and economic dominants, whose decisions vitally affect patterns of land use, the availability of employment, the opportunity structure of society, and the distribution of positions and roles in the social class structure. All these forces collectively comprise the overall social structure.

Socially structured opportunities and constraints vitally shape the life experiences of people by organizing their lives around regularized patterns of social interaction and communication that are relatively stable over time. One's position in the social structure thus largely determines one's life chances, expectations, and even one's sense of identity. People's lives thus tend to be socially structured (organized), rather than chaotic, atomistic, or disorganized.[91]

Because this is so, the basic units of the political organization of society and the design of those units become important. As Edward Soja has said: "The political organization of space . . . functions . . . primarily as a means of structuring interaction between its component units (individuals and groups)."[92] Public bureaucracies, neighborhoods, and workplaces already are arenas for interaction, for acculturation, and for politics—for example, for the informal conflict and cooperation that are part of everyday life. If people's everyday cares and troubles, their interests and concerns, are to find effective expression, accompanied by the political power to alter environmental conditions, units of political decision making must be decentralized to the neighborhood, the point of social service delivery, and the workplace.

If decentralized units of political organization are to foster a sense of community based on principles of reciprocity and social justice, steps must be taken to encourage the redesign of localized institutions in a more egalitarian direction. Experiments in workplace democracy and community control of public bureaucracies are two prominent efforts to realize this redesign. If we are to undo the damage wrought by institutions, like ghetto schools and hierarchical workplaces, that currently prepare people to accept their inferior social status, we need to provide people with more egalitarian socialization experiences. This will require the construction of alternative institutions, such as worker-controlled enterprises, tenant-managed housing complexes, community-controlled schools, and neighborhood governments, that guarantee the right to participate in decision making and insure the power to do so effectively. Such democratically structured alternative institutions can serve to prepare people psychologically to become active in shaping the future direction of their lives.

Yet such efforts at social reconstruction are, by definition, long-run projects. To achieve the sort of Roszakian cooperative commonwealth envisaged by proponents of economic democracy and community control requires people to undergo long-term personal transformation. First, their opportunities for egalitarian, nonhierarchical interaction must change. Then, they must interact and communicate. Through this process they gradually can acquire a new sense of selfhood based on self-confidence, mutual respect, and what some analysts have termed a "democratic character."[93]

As pointed out earlier, the paradox of this futuristic vision is that until such a stage of social cooperation is achieved, patterns of domination, hierarchical socialization, and social inequality will still remain. I thus agree with Richard Sennett that, for the present, the arena where social and political conflict takes place should be decentralized. This will give people and groups who are presently struggling to further the cause of social equality at the grass-roots level an opportunity to have their voices heard and factored into both public and private decision-making centers that impact upon local community life.

Some analysts have charged that such a radical decentralization of decision making will forestall the long-run goal of social equality by channeling creative political energy into the "dead end" of "trivial" local conflicts that prevent people from grasping their real class interests.[94] But this need not be the case. Many of the localized groups now struggling to protect their neighborhoods, even some apparently socially conservative groups, have begun to realize that they must organize against the real economic sources of their current condition. For example, one hopeful sign that neighborhood groups are in fact beginning to identify their interests in a more class-conscious way is the spread of the strategy of "greenlining" against the banking practice of "redlining."

Greenlining is simply a tactic whereby coalitions of urban neighborhood groups threaten to withdraw their members' individual savings deposits en masse from banks that use their savings to finance suburban developments, high rises, and out-of-state projects, while deeming their own neighborhoods poor credit risks. If actual withdrawals become necessary, the monies withdrawn are then used as a "carrot" to attract savings institutions willing to earmark specific portions of their deposits to remain in their neighborhoods.

Actual experience with greenlining has been mildly encouraging. For example, in Chicago a coalition of one hundred community organizations operating within an umbrella organization known as Citizens Action Program recently obtained a signed contract from the Republic Federal Savings and Loan Association, agreeing to grant nearly $3 million in mortgages to the section of Chicago in which the bank was located. This action followed upon a successful campaign by the umbrella group to raise people's consciousness about the threat of redlining. By mid-1975 the campaign had obtained pledges of potential withdrawals totaling $105 million as a result of their research, organizing, and protest activities.[95]

This example suggests that it is not necessary to homogenize workers into similarly situated wage-slaves in order to get them to perceive their material interests. Broad class-conscious coalitions have been built in the past when specific historical situations revealed basic class contradictions (e.g., the 1930s), and they can be built again. Recent protests against redlining, car-oriented transportation policies in Cleveland, and power rates in Arkansas and Louisiana are embryonic examples of such class-based coalitions. They suggest that class consciousness need not be incompatible with sociocultural pluralism.

While such signs are encouraging, they clearly are not enough. Ours is a culturally diverse society with institutional structures that enhance group differentiation and segmentation. Our "social problems," however, are national in scope. Most of these problems stem from unbridled capitalist economic development. Poverty and underemployment, pollution and environmental degradation, the emerging bankruptcy of large northeastern and midwestern cities, suburban sprawl, and work alienation are all by-products of the uneven pattern of capitalist economic development since World War II. This situation calls for the design of mechanisms that will publicly control this socially irresponsible pattern of economic development nationally, without robbing diverse local subcultures of their capacity for self-expression and political development in the process.

Since concentrated economic power centers transcend the boundaries of all local communities, neighborhood decentralization must be accompanied by changes in the national political economy. If there is no national planning to control the negative consequences of corporate capitalist development, those who control neighborhood jurisdictions will find themselves powerless to effectuate their environment. The power to control locational, development, land-use, and environmental impact decisions must be socialized. Public controls over critical areas of production and distribution must be established. Determining the form, pace, and content of these political controls is the critical planning task of the coming decade.

If we begin to view the entire environment as a public good, we will be required to modify our current legal, institutional, and symbolic supports for the system of private ownership that now legitimizes the corporate form. If we are unwilling to take this critical step, we can expect that urban settlement patterns will continue to be shaped in crucial ways by the current socially irrational criteria of private gain. The "urbanscape" will continue to emerge as a consequence of a haphazard combination of profit-oriented investment planning by banks, insurance companies, and other large investors; affluent consumer tastes; autonomous locational choices made by industrial corporations and major retail outlets—all woven together by publicly subsidized highway, transportation, land clearance, and other "infrastructure" policies, also undertaken to service major economic users.[96]

Some states are beginning to recognize that unplanned economic development produces many negative consequences. However, the movement for state-level land-use management in Colorado, California, Maine, and Vermont has been aimed mainly at pollution and amenities controls.[97] They have lacked critical consciousness of the need to control uneven capitalist economic development nationally, to restrict the freedom of private investors to ignore social needs, or to modify the structured inequalities that are by-products of capitalism per se.

A more fruitful first step toward a publicly controlled national economy, combined with a decentralized political and planning structure, has been suggested by Gar Alperovitz and Jeffery Faux. Alperovitz and Faux call for federally guaranteed public jobs in such fields as housing, environmental protection, health, and transportation as a first step toward building the cooperative commonwealth. The chief advantage of such a step, in the context I have been discussing here, is that the public job guarantee would stabilize unsettled economic conditions in cities whose residents have suffered greatly from corporate flight. This would lessen the degree of forced migration. By lessening the sense of economic insecurity facing the unemployed and underemployed, one of the major factors accounting for working-class resistance to social change also might well be lessened.[98] Conditions would then be ripe for the introduction of more participatory work, neighborhood, and social service structures. What now appears to be a remote ideal might then become an emergent reality.

CONCLUSION

A final cautionary note must be added to the ideas expressed in this book. It is my view that anyone working to achieve major structural change in advanced capitalist societies must begin from dialectical rather than linear logic. The dialectician may be disappointed but is never surprised by unexpected and unpredictable events. This is often the way that people's history unfolds. A true dialectician must maintain what some have termed a "dedication to tenuousness."[99] This sort of posture toward the world entails a willingness to revise both theoretical formulations and the plans and political strategies that flow from these formulations, in the face of what some have termed praxis and others social action, but which I prefer to call historical experience.

It is in this spirit of the irreducibility of concrete historical experience that I have sought to develop the components of a theory of social action based on a dialectic of neighborhood participation and resistance. Both active participation in political institutions and resistance to those institutions are part of the single process of working to alter the contexts that discourage people from experiencing their own history and learning to take an active part in shaping their own destiny.

There is a danger that clarifying the structural and systemic barriers to achieving social justice may discourage all but the most hearty spirits from engaging in political struggle. But it is people who make history, though the conditions under which they do so are not always those they might have wished. To spell out the realities of social structure provides an awareness of opportunities, as well as revealing constraints. It roots the central question "What is to be done?" to a set of clear targets for social action and to a tentative strategy for institutional reconstruction. It locates a strategic response to the "urban crisis" in contexts such as the economic system and the workplace that may appear at first blush to be far removed from the realm of urban political and social issues.

To reveal systemic injustice is not to condone inaction. As Michael Harmon has said, what we see as the real world is "a world which is created and changeable by us and hence is a world for which we bear responsibility."[100] It is through creative action, through struggle to change those aspects of "objective reality" that can be shown to be inequitable, that we act responsibly. Creative action is a way to transcend the apparent dualism between participation and resistance. Both participation and resistance are forms of social action. Both can become part of a single process of reconstructing unjust social realities, rather than learning to live with them.

Simmel and Marx, for all their differences, ultimately shared the proposition that change is the only constant in the flow of history. If this is so, the central concerns of politics and planning become joined. Both require us to face three basic questions: Whose values, interests, and social actions will determine the purpose, pace, and direction of historical change? Can the costs and benefits of historical change be distributed fairly? Can the changes that do occur further the cause of social justice?

Given our current social structure, planning is bound to engender social conflict. Intense conflict often is a precondition of creative social change. Through the interaction of planning, participation, and resistance the dialectical process of historical change is set in motion. To expect this process to be rational or cosmic is to expect too much. "Dialectical planning" is a material struggle for social justice, not a cultural quest for social order or a spiritual struggle for salvation.[101] The material political struggle can produce both inner and outer change. This is no small consequence. But we must look elsewhere to build moral order or to save our souls.

NOTES

1. These themes are found in the works of Wirth, Simmel, and Roszak and are common in intellectual discourse upon city life. See, for example, Raymond Williams, *The Country and the City* (London: Oxford U. Press, 1973), pp. 292–294.
2. See Gino Germani, "Urbanization, Social Change, and the Great Transformation," Germani, ed., *Modernization, Urbanization, and the Urban Crisis* (Boston: Little, Brown, 1973), p. 4.
3. Jane R. Lowe, *Cities in a Race with Time* (New York: Random House, 1967), p. 10.
4. See Germani, "Urbanization, Social Change, and the Great Transformation," p. 29.
5. Jay S. Goodman, *The Dynamics of Urban Government and Politics* (New York: Macmillan, 1975), pp. 19–20; see also David Gordon, "Digging Up the Roots: The Economic Determinants of Social Problems," Gordon, ed., *Problems in Political Economy: An Urban Perspective* (Lexington, Mass.: Heath, 1977), p. 18.
6. For an interesting discussion of the key resource of electronic data processing in fostering centralized control over economic decision making while dispensing with the need for close geographic proximity between control, production, and consumption locations see Roderick Bell and Orion F. White, Jr., "Toward a Realistic Utopian Psychology" (paper delivered at Annual Meeting of the American Political Science Association, 1971), pp. 16–17.
7. Ralph C. Deans, "Mobility in American Life," *Editorial Research Reports on the Future of the City* (Washington, D.C.: Congressional Quarterly, 1974), p. 100.
8. *New York Times,* October 15, 1972, p. 58.
9. George Sternlieb and James Hughes, "Introduction," Sternlieb and Hughes, eds., *Post-Industrial America: Metropolitan Decline and Inter-Regional Job Shifts* (New Brunswick, N. J.: Center for Urban Policy Research, 1975), p. 31.
10. Sternlieb and Hughes, "Prologue," Sternlieb and Hughes, eds., *Post-Industrial America,* p. 10.
11. Sternlieb and Hughes, "Introduction," Sternlieb and Hughes, eds., *Post-Industrial America,* p. 32.
12. *New Orleans Times-Picayune,* April 14, 1977, p. 4; Sternlieb and Hughes, "Prologue," Sternlieb and Hughes, eds., *Post-Industrial America,* p. 9.
13. "Overview of City Size and the Quality of Life," *City Size and the Quality of Life* (Washington, D.C.: U.S. Government Printing Office, 1974), pp. 17–18; see also James Sundquist, "Where Shall They Live?" *Public Interest,* Winter 1970, p. 90; Williams, *The Country and the City,* pp. 293–294.
14. *Boston Globe,* February 28, 1974, p. 40.
15. See Mark Gottdiener, *Planned Sprawl: Private and Public Interests in Suburbia* (Beverly Hills: Sage, 1977); see also ibid.; and Goodman, *Dynamics of Urban Government and Politics,* pp. 6–33.

16. *Boston Globe*, August 18, 1971, p. 37.
17. Oliver P. Williams, "Technology, Location, and Access Strategies," Stephen Gale and Eric Moore, eds., *The Manipulated City* (Chicago: Maaroufa Press, 1975), p. 22.
18. Gino Germani, "Urbanization, Social Change, and the Great Transformation," p. 4; see also Manuel Castells, "Immigrant Workers and Class Struggles in Advanced Capitalism: The Western European Experience," *Politics and Society*, 5, no. 1 (1975), 33–66.
19. Scott Greer, *Urban Renewal and American Cities* (Indianapolis: Bobbs-Merrill, 1965), p. 56.
20. Norton Long, "Another View of Responsible Planning," *Journal of the American Institute of Planners*, September 1975, p. 312.
21. Quoted in Harold Kaplan, *Urban Renewal Politics: Slum Clearance in Newark* (New York: Columbia U. Press, 1963), p. 24.
22. See Chester Hartman et al., *Yerba Buena: Land Grab and Community Resistance in San Francisco* (San Francisco: Glide, 1974), p. 41; Mike Royko, *Boss* (New York: Dutton, 1971), p. 144; and Greer, *Urban Renewal and American Cities*, p. 77.
23. Wayne King, "Optimistic Researchers See Different Kind of Downtown," *New York Times*, September 21, 1977, p. 14.
24. Jean Gottmann, "When in Milwaukee, Do as Bostonians Do," *New York Times*, June 2, 1975, p. 25. On the surplus labor or technological unemployment produced by monopoly sector growth see James O'Connor, *The Fiscal Crisis of the State* (New York: St. Martin's Press, 1973), pp. 25–29.
25. *New York Times*, June 5, 1977, p. 58. See also Shirley Laska and Daphne Spain, "Impact on New Orleans of 'Back to the City' Movement" (paper delivered at Annual Meeting of Southern Sociological Society, New Orleans, 1978), for a consideration of the implications of these sorts of developments for urban social conflict.
26. See Ira Katznelson, "The Crisis of the Capitalist City: Urban Politics and Social Control," Willis Hawley, Michael Lipsky et al., *Theoretical Perspectives on Urban Politics* (Englewood Cliffs, N.J.: Prentice-Hall, 1976), pp. 214–229, for an interesting neo-Marxist analysis of the implications of these developments for maintaining social control in advanced capitalist cities.
27. Although not yet a clear trend, it is, nonetheless, true that corporate headquarters are beginning to be established or relocated in suburban areas. National and regional headquarters of major corporations once found in New York, St. Louis, and Detroit are now found in such places as Greenwich, Conn., Clayton, Mo., and Southfield, Mich. The national headquarters of several of the top one hundred American corporations, including I.B.M., Coca-Cola, General Electric, and Allied Chemical, have left New York for suburban environments. One upshot of these corporate decisions is a redistribution of public goods and services upwards in the class structure. For instance, because of its corporate headquarters' impact upon local taxes, the affluent community of Clayton, Mo., has had no local property tax increases since 1954. See *New York Times*, April 28, 1971, pp. 1, 78; *New York Times*, June 17, 1973, p. 6; see also Wolfgang Quante, "Flight of Corporate Headquarters," *Society*, May/June 1976, pp. 36–41.

28. See Leonard Goodwin, *Do the Poor Want to Work?* (Washington, D.C.: Brookings Institution, 1972), a well-documented social psychological study of work orientations that punctures the myth that welfare recipients prefer welfare to stable employment; see also Katznelson, "The Crisis of the Capitalist City," pp. 214–229. Katznelson points out that, in any given year for the past decade, no more than six in ten persons eligible for welfare assistance actually have received support.

29. Robert Goodman, *After the Planners* (New York: Simon and Schuster, 1971), p. 64.

30. Ibid., p. 65; see also Robert Levine, "San Jose, the Urban Crisis and the Feds" (paper prepared for presentation before Legislative Action Committee, U.S. Conference of Mayors, San Jose, Calif., May 15, 1972), p. 6. Levine indicates that the rapid depreciation provisions of the federal tax code also have contributed to the further deterioration of central city slums by making it possible for entrepreneurs to buy up buildings, take advantage of quick tax gains, and then turn the property over to someone else. Maximum profit is achieved by getting in and out with minimal maintenance, thus furthering deterioration.

31. Suzanne Farkas, *Urban Lobbying: Mayors in the Federal Arena* (New York: New York U. Press, 1971), p. 244.

32. See Alan Shank and Ralph Conant, *Urban Perspectives: Politics and Policies* (Boston: Holbrook Press, 1975), pp. 340–365, for a good discussion of the impact of FHA policies on suburbanization and racial segregation.

33. See John Lindsay, *The City* (New York: Norton, 1970), p. 211.

34. Susan and Norman Fainstein, "The Federally Inspired Fiscal Crisis," *Society*, May/June 1976, p. 28.

35. Wayne King, "Federal Funds Pour into Sunbelt States," *New York Times*, February 9, 1976, p. 24. The overall pattern I have been describing in this section amounts to a fusion of the power of the corporate structure and the state. See C. G. Pickvance, "Housing: Reproduction of Capital and Reproduction of Labor Power," John Walton and Louis Massotti, eds., *The City in Comparative Perspective* (New York: Halsted Press, 1976), pp. 271–289.

36. James Sterba, "Houston, as Energy Capital, Sets Pace in Sunbelt Boom," *New York Times*, February 8, 1976, pp. 1, 24.

37. "President's Task Force on Suburban Problems, Final Report," vol. 1 (Washington, D.C.: Department of Housing and Urban Development, 1968), 57 pp., typescript.

38. Ibid., p. 35.

39. Ibid., p. 38.

40. Ibid., pp. 39–42, emphasis in original.

41. Ibid., p. 55.

42. Judith Miller, "White House Orders Urban Policy Review," *New York Times*, August 31, 1977, pp. 1, 14.

43. Daniel Bell, *The Coming of Post Industrial Society* (New York: Basic Books, 1973).

44. Warner Bloomberg, "The Goals," Symposium on Governing Megacentropolis, *Public Administration Review*, September/October 1970, pp. 514–515. On the value-laden aspects of planning see also Thomas Reiner, "The

Planner as Value Technician," H. Wentworth Eldredge, ed., *Taming Megalopolis: Volume 1* (New York: Doubleday Anchor, 1967), pp. 232–248.

45. Christopher Tunnard, *The Modern American City* (Princeton, N.J.: Van Nostrand, 1968), p. 32.

46. See ibid., p. 76; see also David Gordon, "Capitalism and the Roots of Urban Crisis," Alcaly and Mermelstein, eds., *The Fiscal Crisis of American Cities* (New York: Random House, 1977); and Edward Soja, "The Political Organization of Space in Metropolitan Areas," Gale and Moore, eds., *The Manipulated City*, pp. 33–34.

47. Bloomberg, "The Goals," p. 515; see also Frances Fox Piven, "Planning and Class Interests," *Journal of the American Institute of Planners*, September 1975, pp. 308–310.

48. Manuel Castells, "Urban Sociology and Urban Politics: From a Critique to New Trends of Research," *Comparative Urban Research*, 3, no. 1 (1975), 8; see also Castells, *The Urban Question* (Cambridge: M.I.T. Press, 1977), and Ruth Glass, "The Alarming but Tired Cliches about Urban Doom," *Times* (London), August 4, 1976, p. 5, for good discussions of the use of environmental engineering and technical jargon to depoliticize planning and zoning decisions.

49. See Murray Edelman's seminal writings on political symbolism: *The Symbolic Uses of Politics* (Urbana: U. of Illinois Press, 1964); *Politics as Symbolic Action: Mass Arousal and Quiescence* (Chicago: Markham, 1974); *Political Language: Words That Succeed and Policies That Fail* (New York: Academic Press, 1977).

50. Greer, *Urban Renewal and American Cities*, pp. 119, 98.

51. Herbert H. Hyman, "Organizational Response to Urban Renewal" (Ph.D. diss., Brandeis University, 1967), p. 199; on the limited staff capacity of federal renewal officials discussed above see Hartman et al., *Yerba Buena*, pp. 81–82.

52. Hyman, "Organizational Response," p. 74.

53. Ibid., pp. 142, 103.

54. Greer, *Urban Renewal and American Cities*, p. 157; on the co-optation of consulting firms see Hartman et al., *Yerba Buena*, pp. 75, 80; and John M. Mollenkopf, "The Post-War Politics of Urban Development," *Politics and Society*, 5, no. 3 (1975), 290.

55. Hyman, "Organizational Response," p. 92; on ritual participation in political decision making generally see Michael P. Smith, "The Ritual Politics of Suburban Schools," Smith et al., *Politics in America: Studies in Policy Analysis* (New York: Random House, 1974), pp. 110–130; Michael P. Smith and Hermann Borghorst, "Toward a Theory of Citizen Participation in Urban Renewal in Two Federal Systems" (paper delivered at the Tenth World Congress, International Political Science Association, Edinburgh, Scotland, 1976), and Sherry R. Arnstein, "A Ladder of Citizen Participation," *Journal of the American Institute of Planners*, 35 (July 1969), 216–224. On ritual inducements to accept authority see Erving Goffman, *Asylums* (Chicago: Aldine, 1961).

56. See Michael Lipsky, "Protest as a Political Resource," *American Political Science Review*, 62 (December 1968), 1146.

57. *New York Times,* November 29, 1971, p. 51.

58. Hartman et al., *Yerba Buena,* p. 113; *Washington Post,* February 23, 1972, pp. C1, C4.

59. Compare *Boston Sunday Globe,* May 12, 1974, p. A57, and Hyman, "Organizational Response," pp. 69, 86, 185–186. On this problem more generally see Mollenkopf, "Post-War Politics," p. 284.

60. Hartman et al., *Yerba Buena,* p. 113; see also Kaplan's discussion of the uses of jobs, favors, and other patronage by Newark party machine leaders to buy off neighborhood opponents of renewal projects, Kaplan, *Urban Renewal Politics,* pp. 138–139.

61. James D. Thompson and William McEwen, "Organizational Goals and Environment," Amitai Etzioni, ed., *Complex Organizations* (New York: Holt, Rinehart and Winston, 1964), p. 184.

62. See Peter Bachrach and Morton Baratz, "Two Faces of Power," *American Political Science Review,* December 1962, pp. 947–952; Frederick W. Frey, "On Issues and Nonissues in the Study of Power," *American Political Science Review,* December 1971, pp. 1081–1101.

63. Donald T. Mazziotti, "The Underlying Assumptions of Advocacy Planning: Pluralism and Reform," *Journal of the American Institute of Planners,* January 1974, p. 40.

64. See John Dyckman, "New Normative Styles in Urban Studies," *Public Administration Review,* May/June 1971, pp. 330–331, for a good critique of this and other handicaps facing pluralist advocacy planners; see also Goodman, *After the Planners,* pp. 11–31.

65. See Paolo Soleri, *Archology: The City in the Image of Man* (Cambridge, Mass.: M.I.T. Press, 1969); R. Buckminster Fuller, *Utopia or Oblivion: The Prospects for Humanity* (New York: Bantam Books, 1969).

66. Quoted in *New York Times,* June 13, 1976, p. 21.

67. Frances Fox Piven, "Planning and Class Interests," p. 309; see also Piven, "The Social Structuring of Political Protest," *Politics and Society,* 6, no. 3 (1976), 297–326.

68. The following discussion of the Cleveland adversary approach to planning is based upon Norman Krumholz, Janice Cogger, and John Linner, "The Cleveland Policy Planning Report," *Journal of the American Institute of Planners,* September 1975, pp. 298–304; and Neal R. Pierce, "Cleveland Planner on Wave of Future," *New Orleans Times-Picayune,* April 25, 1977, p. 9.

69. Krumholz, Cogger, and Linner, "The Cleveland Policy Planning Report," p. 299.

70. Both quotations ibid., p. 303. For an interesting class-conscious analysis of environmental policies see Richard England and Barry Bluestone, "Ecology and Class Conflict," *Review of Radical Political Economics,* 3, no. 4 (1971), 31–55.

71. Katznelson, "The Crisis of the Capitalist City: Urban Politics and Social Control," p. 220.

72. C. Wright Mills, *The Sociological Imagination* (New York: Oxford U. Press, 1959).

73. See the literature reviewed in Walter Gove and Herbert Costner, "Organizing the Poor: An Evaluation of a Strategy," *Social Science Quarterly,*

December 1969, pp. 643–656, and their discussion of the implication of these findings for politically mobilizing poor people.

74. Claus Mueller, *The Politics of Communication* (New York: Oxford U. Press, 1973), p. 55; see also Jewel Bellush and Murray Hausknecht, "Planning, Participation, and Urban Renewal," Bellush and Hausknecht, eds., *Urban Renewal: People, Politics, and Planning* (New York: Doubleday Anchor, 1967), pp. 283–284.

75. Clifford W. Graves, "Citizen Participation in Metropolitan Planning," *Public Administration Review*, May/June 1972, p. 198.

76. See Bloomberg, "The Goals," p. 513–520.

77. See Robert S. Gilmour and Robert B. Lamb, *Political Alienation in Contemporary America* (New York: St. Martin's Press, 1975); see also Melvin Seeman, "On the Meaning of Alienation," *American Sociological Review*, December 1959, pp. 783–791.

78. Howard W. Hallman, *Community Corporations and Neighborhood Control* (Washington, D.C.: Center for Governmental Studies, 1970), pp. 7–9; but see also Joseph F. Zimmerman, "Neighborhoods and Citizen Involvement," *Public Administration Review*, May/June 1972, pp. 202–203.

79. Saul Alinsky, "Citizen Participation and Community Organization in Planning and Urban Renewal" (1962, mimeo.), p. 7.

80. Robert A. Aleshire, "Power to the People: An Assessment of the Community Action and Model Cities Experience," *Public Administration Review*, September 1972, p. 435.

81. David Austin, "Residential Participation: Political Mobilization or Organizational Co-optation?" *Public Administration Review*, September 1972, pp. 409–420.

82. For a good discussion of this latter mobilization strategy see Lipsky, "Protest as a Political Resource," p. 1146.

83. Greer, *Urban Renewal and American Cities*, p. 119. Urban renewal agencies constitute the social organization that forms the basis of Greer's discussion, but his general point is applicable to protest leaders and their environment.

84. Richard Cloward and Frances Fox Piven, *The Politics of Turmoil* (New York: Pantheon, 1974), p. 47. Another good example of the problems facing outsiders who became insiders is the plight of civil rights workers who subjected themselves to the constraints of federal funding and guidelines when they became government employees or contractors; see Piven and Cloward, *Regulating the Poor* (New York: Vintage, 1971), p. 276. More recently, numerous consumer advocates joined the Carter administration only to learn that they were required to enforce consumer protection laws that lacked strong enforcement penalties. Yet their very presence inside the system lent symbolic legitimacy to these inadequate laws. See *New York Times*, November 14, 1977, pp. 1, 28.

85. Edelman, *Political Language*, p. 134.

86. Joan Rothschild, "The Role of Alternative Groups in Creating Democratic, Community Controlled Local Government" (paper prepared for delivery at the Annual Meeting of the American Political Science Association, 1974).

87. See, for example, Larry Hill, "The Citizen Participation–Representation Roles of American Classical and Quasi-Ombudsmen" (paper prepared for

delivery at the Annual Meeting of the American Political Science Association, 1977).

88. James A. Reidel, "Citizen Participation: Myths and Realities," *Public Administration Review*, May/June 1972, p. 219.

89. *New York Times*, November 25, 1977, p. 18; see also *New York Times*, October 17, 1977, pp. 1, 24.

90. John Walton, "Toward a Synthesis of Studies on the Urban Condition," John Walton and Donald Carns, eds., *Cities in Change* (Boston: Allyn and Bacon, 1977), p. 583.

91. Ibid.; see also my discussion of socially structured interactions and urban social organization in chap. 5, as well as chap. 3, "The Social Structural Paradigm," Michael P. Smith and Edward T. Jennings, Jr., *Distribution Utilization and Innovation in Health Care* (Washington, D.C.: American Political Science Association, 1977).

92. Edward W. Soja, "The Political Organization of Space in Metropolitan Areas," Gale and Moore, eds., *The Manipulated City*, p. 30.

93. G. D. H. Cole, *Guild Socialism Restated* (London: Leonard Parsons, 1920); see also Carole Pateman, *Participation and Democratic Theory* (London: Cambridge U. Press, 1970).

94. See, for example, David Harvey's discussion of possible conflicts between "parochialist forms of community action" and "class struggle" in "Labor, Capital, and Class Struggle Around the Built Environment in Advanced Capitalist Societies," *Politics and Society*, 6, no. 3 (1976), 290–293.

95. William E. Farrell, "Small Homeowners Press Chicago Banks," *New York Times*, May 3, 1975, p. 42.

96. Bloomberg, "The Goals," p. 517.

97. See the discussion of Colorado's refusal to underwrite the 1976 winter Olympics and environmentally oriented land-use controls in Maine, Vermont, and California in John Hamer, "Restrictions on Urban Growth," *Editorial Research Reports on the Future of the City*, pp. 46, 60; see also *New York Times*, June 1, 1977, p. 11.

98. See Gar Alperovitz and Jeffery Faux, "The Economy: What Kind of Planning?" *Working Papers*, Fall 1975, pp. 67–73; Alperovitz and Faux, "Building a Democratic Economy," *Progressive*, July 1977, pp. 15–19.

99. Stephen Gabrow and Allan Haskin, "Foundations for a Radical Concept of Planning," *Journal of the American Institute of Planners*, March 1973, p. 113.

100. Michael Harmon, "Social Equity and Organizational Man: Motivation and Organizational Democracy," *Public Administration Review*, January/February 1974, p. 14.

101. I here have in mind criteria of distributive social justice similar to those proposed by David Harvey in *Social Justice and the City* (Baltimore: Johns Hopkins U. Press, 1973), namely, material need, followed by contribution to the common good, and only once these are satisfied, merit. See also Harvey, "Social Justice and Spatial Systems," *Antipode Monographs in Social Geography*, no. 1 (1972), pp. 87–106, for a succinct application of these criteria to a geographical theory of "territorial" distributive justice.

Epilogue

Because people are highly adaptable creatures, they can adjust to the requirements of a wide variety of social structures and stressful environmental conditions. But these adaptations exact a price. It is therefore necessary to distinguish the merely tolerable forms of human existence to which human beings can adapt from alternative, and more desirable, modes of human existence that enhance personality development, encourage substantive rationality, foster friendship, and increase the outer limits of human creativity. The research on the persistence of older forms of social organization and the vitality of people's adaptive capacity reviewed in chapter five merely show us the tenacity of the human spirit in the face of rapid economic and technological change. It does not provide us with adequate alternative models of social structure and cultural development capable of inspiring human consciousness and action.

All the social theorists we have examined were concerned about the need to redirect the "diversion" of human energies from the pursuit of "wants"—which were viewed as in some sense inauthentic, artificial, or false—to the pursuit of "basic needs"—viewed as natural, universal, or true. Louis Wirth defined these basic needs in terms of economic security, social participation, and political power which serve to enhance individual freedom and self-realization in the context of a consensual moral order. For Freud, these basic needs were biologically rooted and could be reduced socially to the need for legitimate outlets for erotic and aggressive energy. The self-actualized Simmelian personality was a free, spiritually refined wellspring of creative expression who vitally directed the forces of life against outmoded forms. Roszakian self-actualization combined the mundane with the sublime. Through immediate communion with physical nature and with concrete personalities in small, communal work and play groups, the Roszakian personality could learn to experience spiritual ecstasy and self-transcendence. Richard Sennett's viewpoint was quite different, stressing the need for the developing personality to escape the constraints of homogeneous communities, to experience inner and outer conflict, in order to grow.

Each of these theorists had a vision of what a more authentic human existence might resemble if a variety of social forms, deemed to be repressive, were altered in basic ways. In this respect, although the content of their theoretical vision differed dramatically, the form that their social theory assumed was quite similar. This is a form which many social theorists having a reformist bent have chosen to develop. The motif stresses a natural state of human existence which existed ostensibly either in some earlier historical epoch or in an "essential" state of human perfection that could be deduced by observing spontaneous human functioning, unfettered by artificial convention. Thus, for example, Aristotle deduced the premise that human beings are naturally political and rational animals because of their natural capacity for speech and communication combined with their unique ability to evaluate their actions, and therefore to act reflectively. In the Aristotelian era of small-scale human settlement, most social philosophers felt it was possible for the natural personality to fulfill an essential human nature in and through the political community.[1]

But as social systems grew in size and complexity, and economic functions began to occupy more and more of people's daily round of life, this optimism diminished. Like Georg Simmel, but much earlier, the political philosopher Jean Jacques Rousseau warned that in the eighteenth-century cosmopolis, the natural personality was becoming caught up in a self-destructive, overstimulating "whirlpool of social life."[2] He felt, as did his later counterparts Roszak and Wirth, that only through active involvement in political life, in a relatively stable human setting, could the personality regain a lost sense of purpose, regularity, and self-control. He wished to create social forms that could foster the use by each person of all his or her faculties for life. In his words, "Life is not breath, but action; to live is to make use of our organs, our senses, our faculties, every part of ourselves which gives us the feeling of our own existence."[3] To achieve this objective, Rousseau recommended a participatory democratic political order. He thought that such an order, by calling forth each person's creative potential, would overcome the division of the person into thinking and feeling activities that was at the heart of human alienation. He wished to overcome this inner division, which he viewed as a byproduct of a materialistic and class-stratified culture and social structure that created false wants.

The creation of artificial wants and their conversion into "felt needs" is a recurring theme in social philosophy. Hegel and Marx, for instance, approached this theme from distinct vantage points.[4] Despite their differences in perspective, both theorists perceived the need for human beings to rise above the automatic level of existence to achieve their destiny as free moral agents, responsible for their own lives. Hegel's view of history envisaged a progressive movement toward increased freedom and rationality as people acquired self-consciousness by becoming aware of the gap between their essential nature as free moral agents and existing cultural forms. The latter, once freely created, now stood over against them, limiting their moral autonomy. To overcome the barriers which these cultural productions created required a willful act of transcendence to a higher level of cultural development. Hegel viewed this process as a never-ending struggle between old and new ideas of perfection through which history progressively unfolded. His influence upon both Wirth and Simmel should now be apparent.

Marx too was concerned about the barriers to the fulfillment of the genuine human need for moral autonomy. Marx held that the dynamic that drove the capitalist mode of production was capitalism's tendency to generate new desires, and thus new "markets" to supplement existing ones. In his view, this creation of false needs, which he termed "commodity fetishism," served to undermine the sense of human relatedness which was capable of motivating social actions toward social justice, communal fellowship, and creative work. Instead, the stimulation of false needs structured behavior in ways that converted social, political, and work life into mere instruments for individual acquisitiveness and aggrandizement.

In this way, the "wants" generated by capitalist culture came to be seen as "needs." Once released from subordination to more basic needs—fellowship, creativity, social justice—these newer "felt needs" tended to expand more rapidly than did society's productive powers. This gap between expectation and performance produced a high level of general dissatisfaction with life. As long as we refused to exercise rational control over these false wants, we would remain entrapped at the automatic or animal level of our nature. We were doomed to an alienated existence on a frustrating treadmill.

Even French sociologist Emile Durkheim, who in other respects differed sharply from Marx, was deeply troubled by the tendency of capitalism to stimulate insatiable appetites for new "needs," while distributing the means to achieve these in such a way that most would find their means inadequate. Durkheim linked the frustration he believed would accompany this situation to a variety of social pathologies, including individual aimlessness, social instability, and suicide. His answer to this situation was to restructure individual life in social systems to impose limits on the acquisitive instinct: "Man can live only if his needs are in harmony with his means; which implies a limitation on the latter."[5]

Thus we can see that although all these theorists differ greatly from each other in most respects, they are united in their opposition to the Freudian ideal of optimal satisfaction of the basic id instinct, limited only by calculative egoism. Each would pose some more general limits on this id instinct to achieve goals as diverse as moral purpose, creative cultural development, social justice, or personal integration.

In my view, these theorists (along with Wirth, Simmel, and Roszak, for all their shortcomings) have provided a comprehensive argument against a mode of economic organization based on the continuous creation of false consumer wants to maintain its dynamic vitality. This pattern of economic organization is particularly problematic in American society because we have a grossly underdeveloped social redistribution sector, compared even with other advanced capitalist countries. Additionally, our cultural stress on individual acquisitiveness and success is bound to produce frustration in the face of grossly unequal social structural opportunities to acquire and to "succeed."

In the face of this situation, many social critics argue that the goal of "social justice" ought to be limited to an equalization of opportunity to "acquire" and to "succeed." My point of view is different. I think that even perfectly equal access to the fruits of consumer society will not entirely alter the level of alienation in American society. This is because the type of alienation I have in mind stems from the inability of material consumption per se to satisfy our need to construct a life that has purpose, wholeness, and a will to set limits on instinctual gratification for the sake of social equity, rather than in response to the Freudian ideal of prudential calculation.

Some theorists have suggested that the way out of the bind of excessive consumerism is to substitute an ecological perspective or an ethic of "human development" for economic growth as a basic planning goal.[6] In practice, this would entail the creation of a new political economy—one bent upon enabling all persons to exercise moral choice by putting a floor under their income sufficient to enable them to act out of choice, rather than necessity; but permitting no individuals, groups, classes, or corporate entities to have an income so great that they are able to ignore social and ecological needs when making economic choices. It would further require the "decommercialization" of the mass media to weaken the manipulative influence corporate elites now have to stimulate desires for ever more goods, services, and consumption levels. Finally, it would require the creation of alternative political, planning, and work structures capable of engaging people's thinking and feeling abilities in a context where their active involvement can make a difference in their living environment. Since these goals are bound to be viewed as unachievable for the present, the best we can expect in the short run are inroads on corporate hegemony made through the dialectics of participation and resistance. What can be done in the long run, however, is an open question.

NOTES

1. For an interesting discussion of these aspects of Aristotelian thought see Dante L. Germino, "The Crisis in Community: Challenge to Political Theory," Carl J. Friedrich, ed., *Community* (New York: Liberal Arts Press, 1959), pp. 83–86.
2. Jean Jacques Rousseau, *Emile*, 4, 217, quoted in Marshall Berman, *The Politics of Authenticity* (New York: Atheneum, 1972), p. 167.
3. Ibid., 1, 9–10, 171.
4. See, for example, Marx's critique of Hegel in Karl Marx, *Contribution to the Critique of Hegel's Philosophy of Right*, and "Critique of Hegel's Dialectic and General Philosophy," *Karl Marx: Early Writings*, trans. and ed. T. B. Bottomore (New York: McGraw-Hill, 1964), pp. 41–59, 195–219.
5. Emile Durkheim, *Suicide*, trans. George Simpson (New York: Free Press, 1951), p. 403.
6. See the literature discussed in chaps. four and five, in my discussion of Theodore Roszak.

Index